Lifelong Learning

A brave and proper vision

Selected writings of Naomi Sargant

Edited by Andrew McIntosh, Derek Jones,
Alan Tuckett and Alan Woodley

niace
promoting adult learning

This collection ©2009 National Institute of Adult Continuing Education
(England and Wales)
21 De Montfort Street
Leicester
LE1 7GE

Reproduced chapters © their publishers

Company registration no. 2603322
Charity registration no. 1002775

NIACE has a broad remit to promote lifelong learning opportunities for adults.
NIACE works to develop increased participation in education and training, particularly for those who do not have easy access because of class, gender, age, race,
language and culture, learning difficulties or disabilities, or insufficient financial
resources.

You can find NIACE online at **www.niace.org.uk**
Cataloguing in Publication Data
A CIP record of this title is available from the British Library

Designed and typeset by Book Production Services, London
Printed and bound in the UK by Page Bros, Norwich

ISBN: 978 1 86201 378 0

Contents

Research, evaluation and public policy

A consumer voice

Lifelong learning

Introduction

For several years, I had been urging Naomi to enrol for an Open University DPhil by publication: not so much for the doctorate itself as for the opportunity to bring together her many writings over more than thirty years on distance learning, educational broadcasting, and lifelong learning, which were dispersed in speeches, journal articles, internal OU, Channel 4 and NIACE papers, chapters in books and books themselves. She got to the stage of identifying supervisors, but the sheer volume of work in sorting her papers, amid 150 box-files of surrounding material, to identify those which would make a coherent volume, with lasting value, would have been immense: and she had never stopped working on new projects.

When, in early July 2006, we knew that her cancer was incurable, I promised her that I would bring together her life's work in a book. She smiled, but did not respond. Then, two days before she died, she was visited by Alan Tuckett and Tessa Blackstone. She told them about the book, and told them that it was her idea. So I have had no choice but to obey.

Andrew McIntosh

Naomi Sargant had an extraordinary ability to see the implications of changes in technology, and the uses of mass media, and the evolving possibilities of distance learning for adult learners. Her skills as a market researcher and educational policy analyst were applied over thirty years to map the beneficiaries and for her most importantly, those excluded by the changing policy landscape, and to identify what was to be done about it. Above all Naomi was a democrat – passionate in her own advocacy, and determined to create opportunities for those at risk of marginalisation and exclusion.

This volume of her writing raises themes as relevant and challenging today as when she first wrote them. The rights of women to educational opportunity and recognition; the challenges posed by the digital divide; the importance of recognising what learners have in common, and what separate needs must be addressed if they are to benefit from opportunities to learn – on each she locates her argument in a specific time and policy context, but the principles she articulates are universal.

As her *Times* obituary noted (see Appendix), Naomi spent much of her life battering at traditional barriers to education for adults. Naomi, who was born in 1933, began her life as an advocate while a student at Bedford College, active in national student politics. After 12 years in market and social research, she taught at Enfield College of Technology before joining the Open University at its inception.

As the first woman pro-vice chancellor in the country she brought the disciplines of marketing to education before anyone else did. At the Open University she was the voice of the students, fronting the on-air Open Forum, and developing a programme of research on their needs, patterns of participation and achievement which is reflected in the selection of her work made by her close collaborator Alan Woodley.

It would be exciting enough to be at the inception of one major educational initiative in a working lifetime. But, following her time at the Open University, Naomi moved to be the first (and only) Senior Commissioning Editor for Education at Channel 4 from 1981 to 1989. Her major impact there, apart from commissioning a rich vein of programmes, was to unlock the educative potential of programming of all sorts across the Channel's output. The selection here of her writing on broadcasting and the media has been made by Derek Jones, who worked with Naomi throughout the Channel 4 years.

Her skills as an advocate were to the fore in many of the positions she held in public life outwith education, ranging from chairing the Children's Committee on Haringey Council, to the chair of the National Gas Consumers' Council and of Great Ormond Street Hospital for Sick Children. Even the long list in her obituary from *The Times*, reprinted in the Appendix at the end of this volume, is probably not complete. Her writings on the democratic rights of consumers, and on issues of research and evaluation in education and in wider areas of public policy, have been selected and edited here by Andrew McIntosh her husband, collaborator in much of that work, and co-editor of this collection.

Naomi's first major impact outside the Open University, in the wider field of lifelong learning, came through her membership of the Advisory Council on Adult and Continuing Education, where she chaired the committee charged with identifying strategies for future development. Her report, 'Continuing Education: from Policies to Practice (1982)' was seminal – and whilst government failed to act on the full range of recommendations, its major themes helped shape the work of a generation's adult educators. I was lucky enough to work with her for almost twenty years, as she shaped the quantitative research agenda of the National Institute of Adult Continuing Education, and contributed to the work of successive national initiatives in lifelong, distance and open learning. The section of the book I have drawn together comes from her writing on lifelong learning. Working with Naomi was not always easy, but it was always rewarding, since her rigour and intellectual curiosity led to challenge, robust dialogue and re-framing the task. I miss her hugely.

The great majority of the work to create the book was, of course, done by Naomi herself. The editors have been ably supported by Alec McAulay and Lucia Quintero-Re at NIACE. Generous support from the Robert Gavron Charitable Trust made the publication possible and we have been encouraged by Channel 4, which hosted the debate at the book's launch, and by the Open University.

There is an on-line archive of the full range of Naomi's writing available through **www.niace.org.uk**, again supported by the Robert Gavron Foundation, and by the work of Lucia Quintero-Re.

I hope the readers of this will be tempted there to encounter more of Naomi's rich and distinctive arguments for a democracy where everyone has the opportunity and encouragement to become informed, educated and active citizens.

Alan Tuckett

A note on names and citation of sources

Writings before December 1982 were in the name of Naomi McIntosh. However, when I entered the House of Lords she was determined not to be tainted, and reverted to her maiden name of Naomi Sargant. We have retained the names she used at the time.

Andrew McIntosh

First, an amuse bouche: *her contribution to the weekly 'Don's Diary'
column in the* Times Higher Education Supplement *in July 1987, when
she was working for Channel 4. A taster for the wide range of interests and opinions which fill this book.*

Don's diary

Friday

Having been in Zurich all week for the annual Working Party of European
educational broadcasters, I decide to stay an extra night to visit a Swiss 'au
pair' girl who looked after our children fifteen years ago. She and her
husband, both teachers, live with their two children with a view of the Eiger
and the Jungfrau, when it is not raining – which it is every day this week. I
get my first view of Superchannel which is delivered to their home along with
18 other channels, for a cost of under £20 a month. She watches the 10.00
p.m. ITN News on Superchannel to keep up her English. David Suchet's
enunciation is specially slow and clear to assist this, or so it seems to me.
Nice to think of Richard (Hooper ex OU, BBC) and Carol (Haslam ex OU,
BBC and C4) doing such a good job!

Saturday

The children are up early: school on Saturday is 7.30 a.m. – 11.30 a.m. By
the time we have finished our leisurely breakfast they are back, and we
engage in happy non-verbal communication since their spoken language is
Switzerdeutch. They start learning written German in primary school but do
not use *spoken* German. Italian, their father's subject, is likely to be learnt
next, then French. So different from us. Each of the 26 cantons controls its
own education and does not even yet start the school year at the same
season. Was private education an issue? I asked. Certainly not, the teachers
in private schools got paid less and were poorer quality! Back to Zurich on
the efficient Swiss train and thence to London.

Sunday

Sunday lunch is the last remaining family institution where three generations
meet. Today is particularly poignant as our middle son says goodbye to us
and his grandparents before he sets off to travel 'round the world' after six

years of paint spraying. The afternoon is spent in cleaning out his flat so it can be let while he is away.

Monday

Get to work late having to wait for the bank to open to subsidise departing son. Then a total gear switch, watching the rough cut of three one hour films which follow three mentally handicapped adults move from a hostel to living in a flat in the community. They show, movingly, what is involved in the policy of 'care in the community' and the high quality of the support that the local social services department needs to and does provide. With CCETSW, we are planning support materials to go with the programmes.

A producer from Scotland has arrived on spec to try to talk about alternative energy, but there is no time before a working lunch with colleagues from the Royal Society of Medicine to discuss a series for parents and health workers about children's health: we have named it 'When to Worry'. It would fit in to a planned 'Family Fortnight' with Health Education Authority backing in 1988. Check on immediate crises before joining a major meeting with Open College colleagues to review progress on programming for their September start. We have jointly identified the two companies which will make the weekly live programmes for learners on Monday and trainers and people interested in open learning on Friday. But time is not on anybody's side. Friendly and efficient progress is made.

Dash back to North London to the first governing body meeting of the local girls' comprehensive of the new municipal year. As I arrive, there are more observers than governors: well under half the possible numbers. Minutes and matters arising take over an hour. The main discussion (very valuable) is about the teaching of languages – but how different from Switzerland. However, numbers in the 6th Form have dropped and so therefore have exam passes. Are they going out to other boroughs? To school or tertiary? The lack of resources and proper teaching space that new curriculum initiatives demand are a constant worry and drain on the morale of the teachers. Back home to finally bid farewell to sons.

Tuesday

Up early to go to Television South at Southampton to view rough cuts of 'The idea of Europe', a personal essay by Richard Hoggart about Europe and its cultural and political identity. Designed as a curtain raiser for the EEC elections next June. Richard Hoggart and Douglas Johnson are writing the book and we are also planning a study guide. The producer at TVS, John Miller, is an old friend from OU days. We reminisce about ACACE and continuing education and ask where the new Gurus are.

Blissful peace on the train back to London, and catch up on some of the heap of accumulated mail. Agree Press Release about OC commissions. No final farewell from sons: they must have finally gone. The house has been refilled with their surplus junk. Continue until midnight on accumulated mail.

Wednesday

Dash into Channel 4 to drop work and pick up the wherewithal for two speeches in Glasgow. I go up early to be able to visit a brilliant animator, Lesley Keen, who is working on a very demanding film for us. She wins awards for everything she makes and is now moving from Greek myth (Orpheus) to ancient Egyptian myths – the God Ra. This is a happy link for me as my stepfather held the Egyptology chair at Oxford and through this link we have found a friendly and extremely knowledgeable specialist in Egyptian art and culture, Geraldine Pinches. Her knowledge provides sympathetic expertise for Lesley's creativity. The work is astonishingly beautiful and requires astonishing patience. It is a collaboration of three people and will take two years.

To the hotel to change and thence to SCET, the Scottish Council for Educational Technology. It is Midsummer's Day, the first with no rain and a penance for any to spend that beautiful sunlit evening talking about Open Learning and the Open College. But the group was a large and interested one and stayed until nearly 10 p.m. It was their second meeting to consider the Open College: the timescales are even more difficult for Scotland than England and Wales because the Open College has not yet identified its centres and Scottish colleges close for the summer at the end of this week. In many ways Scotland is in advance of England and Wales and scarcely needs an Open College. Their guide to Open Learning started seven years ago and now has 600 courses. They have already rationalised their qualification system through Scotvec and have a consortium of colleges working on open learning materials for modules of the National Certificate. And C4 of course broadcasts nationally. What they really need if they want 'Scottish' materials are programmes on BBC Scotland or STV and Grampian. The unresolved issue at the end of the evening went as follows: 'If Scottish education is distinctive and requires its own materials, is its distinctiveness in the institutions or in the education. If, with open learning, the importance of the institution diminishes, does the Scottish distinctiveness diminish and therefore the need/justification for Scottish materials?' A good evening, but to miss the final instalment of Porterhouse Blue ...?

Thursday

A lie-in in the hotel and a good Scottish breakfast with porridge. SIACE's annual conference is focussing on Adult Learners and I have to kick it off with the keynote speech. Given the current emphasis on vocational education and training, it is not a particularly good time to be alive in general adult and continuing education. However, the conference is the best attended yet even though the Minister has declined to come and there are enough familiar faces to encourage me. I am, and they are, concerned about the increasing divide between education and training. And who is going to pay for the unemployed? Will the Open College be for the employed who can pay and traditional adult education be for all the rest, if it can survive? It was put to me that the Open College and the Open University are at the extreme end of the philosophical spectrum.

Per Himmelstrup, the head of the Danish Cultural Institute has brought a party of Danish adult educators over to join the conference. We still have a lot to learn from the Scandinavian traditions. It was at a conference he ran that I worked out the ACACE ideas about educational entitlements. Back on the shuttle from sunny Glasgow to rainy London and drive back to C4 just in time to pick up another pile of mail. Can't the Post Office go on strike?

The Open University years: researching for action

Introduction

Naomi joined the Open University (OU) in 1969 as a Senior Lecturer in Research Methods. She, along with Tony Bates, had been hired to carry out a study of prospective OU students who had enrolled on specially designed preparatory courses. The first intake of undergraduates began their studies in 1971. By the time she left in 1981, she was Professor of Applied Social Research and Head of the Survey Research Department, and she had served a term as Pro-Vice Chancellor (Student affairs).

Naomi brought to the OU her research skills that had been fashioned and honed in the somewhat harsher world of market research (she spent 12 years working for Social Surveys Ltd and three years teaching the subject at Enfield College of Technology). These skills, allied with her crusading spirit, made her a formidable champion of lifelong learning. She designed and carried out the necessary research and she made sure that the results were listened to.

Back in the 1960s very little was known about higher education (HE) in the UK. The Robbins Report, which was published in 1963, managed with basic statistics on student places or commissioned its own research to fill in the gaps.

When Naomi joined the OU she was one of the first to realise that the university would need more and better information about itself if it was to succeed. The following is an edited version of a paper that she delivered to the Society for Research into Higher Education in 1972.

Research for a new institution: the Open University[1]

Introduction

In its early stages, the Open University faces a variety of problems for which there are no easy solutions, and for which it must endeavour to find comprehensive and cost-effective answers. It has no precedent, and little existing information to guide it.

These problems include:

- the devising of an integrated multi-media system, suitable for teaching degree-level courses;
- the problems of teaching effectively at a distance;
- the problems of teaching mature students with a wide range of educational backgrounds, experience and ability, as well as varying home situations.

Each of the problems is daunting in itself. Collectively, they present a formidable challenge.

The resources available for higher education in Great Britain are inevitably limited, although pressure for expansion is great. The Open University provides the possibility of expanding higher education by an amount more than commensurate with its cost. Since the majority of students are in employment while studying, it follows that the net cost to the country is proportionately less.

It is important that this new educational system be adequately evaluated both at the level of effect on the individual student and at the level of total impact on the country as a whole.

---

1. Sargant, Naomi (1972) 'Research for a new institution: the Open University', in *Innovation in Higher Education*, Society for Research in Higher Education, London, 1972.

If solutions are found to the problems posed by the undertaking, the benefits to this country, and to other less developed countries, will be great.

Procedures are already in hand within the Open University for the accumulation of essential data – both for administrative purposes, and to provide the basic feedback and monitoring necessary for the efficient functioning of the system. These procedures have enabled the University to set up individual student records, course records, tutor and counsellor records, and so on. The University has also financed, within its current budget, a number of individual projects – e.g. to process and analyse the results of computer-marked and tutor-marked assignments and to index the success of individual students, tutors, counsellors and course units. Unfortunately, this information will not on its own be sufficient to answer all the problems and questions likely to arise. It will be available, however, for correlation with any information gained through subsequent research and evaluation projects.

Constraints of time and money

The University has to operate within limited resources, and within very stringent time-scales. The scale of its operation causes it to resemble at some stages a production plant rather than an academic institution. The budgets are large. The number of people involved is very large. The penalties for bad decisions are very great.

At the same time, existing information is scarce. The degree of uncertainty attaching to some of our early decisions was very high. We are constantly surprised by how accurate some of these decisions proved to be. The University was in the conflicting situation of recognizing the need for information, knowing there was no time to wait for it and also knowing how little money there was available to get it. Academic and organisational demands had to have priority over the needs of research and evaluation. Funding for such ancillary activities, although desirable, had to be sought from elsewhere.

Research information from administrative records

3 a) Early hopes of substantial outside funding for a major seven year research project did not materialise, and even before this time the need for close co-ordination with the academic administration of the University was realised. Such basic documents as the student's application form had all to be seen as part of the overall research and information system. Information was sought on this form to enable the University:
   (1) to make decisions about the actual admissions process;
   (2) to discover which applicants were most in need of personal counselling.

A set of algorithmic procedures was devised by Professor Brian Lewis of the Institute of Educational Technology to assist in this process, which in the event in our first year, was used mainly for the second of these objectives, to allocate priorities for counselling. These algorithms looked at such factors as study circumstances, motivation and educational preparedness.

They had one other limited use which was to control the number of students whom we allowed to commence studying two courses. Some 60 per cent applied to study two courses in our first year, and we allowed only 20 per cent to do so. The constraints on this were financial, the total number of course places we could afford.

Realism has set in for 1972 and only about 26 per cent have applied to do two courses, of whom we have offered places to about 20 per cent.

In designing the application form, the Admissions Committee of the University faced two sets of conflicting problems:

(1) That this form, the key piece of paper seen by the applicant, had to be viewed against the background of our public commitment to 'open' entry to the University, but at the same time had to give us enough information about the students' backgrounds to help us in the procedures outlined earlier in this paper.
(2) It had to be clear, unambiguous and motivating for the applicant, but at the same time had to be available both for immediate microfilming for the records, and translation on to punch-cards, since the admissions process of necessity, owing to its time scale and volume, had to be computerised.

Occupational categories are a particularly thorny problem. The University does not have the resources to postcode these. We therefore devised groupings which we listed on the back of the application form, with examples, and into which we asked applicants to place themselves. In addition we asked them for their job title etc. Testing out these groups showed a high degree of correct self-completion. The groups finally arrived at are designed to admit of overall comparisons with the Registrar General's Occupation Orders.

3b) The second key administrative document, which is also an integral part of the overall research plan, is the student registration form. Students fill this form in as they accept their place and pay their 'provisional' registration fee of £10 in October. This form, as well as updating the administrative records, contains two main areas of information: (1) possible predictors of student difficulties; (2) more detailed information about the student's personal and educational background.

This information had to be limited, for resource and space reasons, to data considered essential. Of course what administrative staff and academics consider essential will not necessarily coincide with what researchers consider essential. Suffice it to say that after much argument the information so obtained forms a basic part of the student record file for all students and as such provides a very solid database for all subsequent projects.

Why did we adopt this strategy?

A major objective of the Open University was and is, the extension of educational opportunities. To be more specific, it is to offer degree-level courses to adults who would not otherwise be able to pursue such courses. Unfortunately, the mere provision of a new educational opportunity is not enough. The Open University cannot by its mere existence, and on its own, put right the inadequacies of decades of educational disadvantages. Potent factors militate against certain categories of people being able to grasp new opportunities opened to them. In addition to offering new opportunities, we have to search out those factors which have prevented such people from taking advantage of educational opportunities offered in the past.

Unless this is done, and done early, the very factors that prevented people from benefiting from earlier educational opportunities may ensure that they are unable to embark on an Open University course, or to see it through to completion. In this case, the University will have failed to achieve one of its main objectives, and the personal and psychological cost to many individual students will be great. We considered, consequently, that there was an urgent need:

(a) to identify those factors that had prevented students from taking advantage of previous educational opportunities;
(b) to identify current difficulties in the environment and in the University's study arrangements that might impede the full utilisation of the new opportunities offered;
(c) to identify resources that might assist the learning process, and
(d) to distinguish difficulties which were remediable by the University from difficulties which were not.

Our first priority, therefore, was to endeavour to identify such possible difficulties. At the same time we considered that just **because** the University has no formal entrance qualifications, it was important for us to know something of the previous educational experience of our students.

Another section of the student registration form, then, asked in greater detail about the students' previous educational experience, both full- and part-time, but only **after** they had already been offered a place.

The initial resource commitment to fund this level of research activity as part of the basic information system was made by the University at an early stage and clearly it provides our necessary minimum monitoring and information flow.

The monitoring of the system

Turning now to the student, and it is the student-based research for which I am responsible and to which I am addressing myself in this paper, it is necessary to analyse in some detail the student's progress through the University system. (Other research is being carried on by my colleagues into the tuition and counselling system, effectiveness of the media, developmental testing etc.).

This analytical process has to start even before the student enters the system. An interesting category of students known particularly to those involved with part-time and correspondence education is the category of what has come to be known as 'non-starters' – those people who apply, sometimes even pay their fee and then do not study at all. The very act of registering appears to fulfil for them some need.

For planning purposes, it is important to isolate this group and try to eliminate it, since it represents at minimum:

(a) a personal cost to the student;
(b) a financial cost to the University;
(c) a disadvantage to an unknown rejected student who might successfully have entered the system.

Looking at the planning of the Open University year, then, it is possible to discern milestones in a student's progress through the system...although perhaps it would be more appropriate to call them hurdles or even obstacles.

At each event, the student either remains in the system or leaves it for a variety of reasons. The characteristics of students who leave at each point, and their reasons for leaving require close monitoring and a regular statistical analysis has been planned to produce this.

Predictions in our first year, of necessity, were 'pragmatic' or 'intuitive'. One early problem, which although we did foresee, we could not allow for was the size of the group of 'non-starters'. Unlike airlines or the Dover-Boulogne ferry, with our limited resources we could not risk over-booking.

In the event, some 5, 000 of the students who had applied and to whom we had offered places did not pay their provisional registration fees, and other students from the reserve list were therefore offered a place instead. The figure for this year is much the same, so clearly this is a noise in the system that requires early attention.

Looking at the calendar in more detail, I want at this stage only to comment on parts of it. The first and very important point to make is that we planned the University year and allocated its resources to allow the students a provisional registration period of three months, (extended to four months in 1971 because of the postal strike) for which they paid an initial ten pounds, to give them a chance to try out this new educational experience to see if it was suitable for them, and to see if they could fit it in with their other commitments. This was a crucial part of our planning – not just because we were catering for a heterogeneous group of adult students who had chosen to study in a new way, but also because it enabled us to concentrate the bulk of our financial resources on what we call our 'final' students, those who paid the final registration fee after three months of study with us. Existing available evidence, such as it is, on part-time or correspondence study at university and other levels, indicates that wastage is particularly heavy in the early stages of a course. It is clearly important to do all that we can to support students in this provisional registration period, but it is equally important to minimise the expenditure on students who are not going to continue for reasons that have nothing to do with the University.

Our baseline figures for all our pass rates therefore are our *final* registration figures. The overall figure of credits for courses based on our final registration figure was 75.3 per cent.

Provisionally registered students

Coming back to the 'provisionally' registered students – a very significant group for planning purposes – some clear differences have emerged between those groups who 'finally' registered and those who did not. Overall, 80.8 per cent of our 'provisional' students finally registered. The variation between courses was already marked at this stage.

A large number of students who had started to study two courses preferred to drop one of them and concentrate their studies, rather than leave the University altogether. Thirty per cent of students who started studying two courses had dropped to one course by 7 May. Part of this drop was undoubtedly caused by the award of credit exemption to some students, but in the main it reflects the sheer work load involved in two courses.

Longitudinal studies of Open University students, their educational and occupational background and their progress through the system

So far, so good, but the information flow discussed so far only meets short-term objectives. In order to evaluate the impact and effectiveness of the Open University as a whole, one needs to set up criteria against which to judge it. These criteria could be absolute ones, in terms of the value of the University to the individual student, and to society. Alternatively, they might be relative criteria, making comparisons, for example, with alternative methods of higher education. In this area problems of definition for the purpose of valid comparisons become acute.

It is beyond the scope of this paper to do justice to this problem. Suffice it to say that it is one that is exercising our minds considerably, as, I suspect, it is the minds both of other educationalists and politicians.

a) To complement the information the University is gathering, the SSRC* has funded the start of a long-term project, directed by myself, which is

---

* Social Science Research Council.

designed to follow the progress of the first generation of students through the University. This project has already started with an initial questionnaire to *all* students as they began their studies, covering, in some detail, their educational and occupational backgrounds, their work and leisure patterns and their future plans.

The Open University expects its students to spend ten to twenty hours a week on study, over a period of three to six years. Most of these students are doing a job as well as studying with the University. A commitment to study on this scale is likely to shape, and also to be shaped by other major areas of the students' lives, notably their work, their family life and their leisure. In order to obtain a degree, changes and sacrifices will almost certainly have to be made by individuals both in their work and in their leisure. They may have to forego promotion, for example, or give up special interests.

Open University students need to structure their non-work time in very specific ways. Time previously available for leisure or family life may have to be re-allocated to study – in particular to serious reading and to disciplined television viewing and radio listening, or to spending time on home experiments! Previous reading, viewing, listening and social habits may have to be broken. The Open University is asking its students to change previous patterns of leisure and media consumption. In many cases, students' families also have to make adjustments and sacrifices; and there may be significant repercussions within the family group.

There will clearly be an interaction between study habits and patterns of life, including patterns of work. The areas of work and non-work, leisure, and social and family life are so fundamental and so interrelated that it is desirable to integrate them into one study.

The initial questionnaire, funded by the SSRC, covers these areas and in addition includes a detailed section on occupational and social mobility and will tell us much about the social class of our student population – a subject that has been the cause of much speculation in the press. I would here repeat the point, made before, but not taken by some people, that to make valid comparisons with existing students what we need to know is the occupation of our students' parents at the time when our students would normally have started on higher education. That is how students are classified conventionally – by their father's occupation.

This information will be available shortly – but, as you all know, any social class analysis dependent as it is on variations of occupational and other analyses, is a time consuming game, and open to much question and discussion – yet another paper!

b) Initially, we decided to gather base-line data about *all* students and to cast our informational net wide and shallow rather than narrow and deep. To this end, we may have had to gather more data than seems initially to be justified so as not to pre-judge what are and what are not the critical factors in the learning process. It is impossible at this stage to know which students, group of students and types of learners will adapt and progress or fall out early, or fall out late. Much post hoc analysis will need to be done of significant groups which emerge at later intervals in the learning process. A unique opportunity would have been thrown away if inadequate baseline data about these students had not been obtained before they started their studies.

The first stage of this project could not be planned to test specific hypotheses. It has had to be planned to provide a firm basis on which specific hypotheses could later be tested.

Built into this first stage also are a number of sub-studies designed to look at, in detail, the most urgent problems facing the University in its early years, for example the factors affecting students who decided not to 'finally' register.

A questionnaire has already been sent to a sample of students who did not finally register to discover the problems they faced, the reasons that caused them to withdraw and above all to discover what in all this was within the control of the University and what was not.

The baseline questionnaire, previously referred to runs to 14 pages and 65 questions. It has, as with the application form, to be clear and unambiguous and motivating for the student. It has to answer short- and long-term informational needs. An immediate early problem was the scheduling of broadcast times.

Other sections of the baseline questionnaire will give us indicators of occupational attitudes, leisure activities, motivation etc. Constraints of time and money dictated a two stage strategy of analysis. A one in four sample of all questionnaires has been coded and punched for early analysis. The remainder are being banked for the future when resources permit their use.

Methods of data collection employed

The universe to be sampled and the nature of the information to be sought pose particular problems for the researcher attempting to decide among alternative forms of data collection.

The geographically scattered sample, the size of the student population and the longitudinal nature of the study would make the cost of personal interviewing very high. On the other hand response rates to postal questionnaires are variable, depending on the nature of the population and the subject under study. At first sight, the information that we are seeking may look too complex to be safely and validly collectable via postal questionnaires. Nevertheless, we have decided to use postal questionnaires for the majority of our studies, on the following grounds:

(1) The organisational structure of the Open University virtually guarantees a higher-than-usual response rate. Respondents who are highly motivated to follow a course, which is itself based mainly on the use of the postal system, respond well to this approach, provided that the questionnaires are carefully designed, and are administered with sensitivity. Above all,

students need to be brought into the confidence of the researcher and kept informed about the results of the research and the uses to which it is being put. This we are doing.

(2) As a further guarantee of high response rates, our administrative system maintains a constantly up-dated mailing list, and we also have an easily invoked system of postal or mass media 'reminders'.

(3) Evidence from our previous University research into the BBC/NEC preparatory courses shows that questionnaires, administered to similar students following similar multi-media courses, produce response rates of 75–90 per cent.

(4) We wished to obtain baseline data on **all** Open University students and the cost of personally interviewing such numbers would be prohibitive.

We have the resources, in addition, to make personal interviews with selected samples of Open University students for piloting purposes and to verify the reliability of the data. Telephone interviewing is also proving useful.

Response rates

The mailing of our baseline questionnaire hit the researcher's nightmare, the postal strike of last spring. We despatched 24,000 odd questionnaires the week before it started and received 5,000 back by that first week-end. We then had to wait in agonised suspense wondering how many had been thrown away, hidden in cupboards or just lost.

Extraordinarily enough, completed questionnaires are still arriving. By 1 May we had received questionnaires from 61 per cent of all students. We then sent out reminders in June. The current response rate is now 69 per cent over all students who started with us in January 1971.

The significant fact, which confirms my previous comments about the characteristics of our 'provisional' students, is the difference between the response rates of those students who finally registered and those who did not.

Table 1 Summary of response rate on baseline questionnaire (SSRC)

No. of provisionally registered students – 10 January 1971 (24, 010)			
No. who finally registered (8 May) 19.600 (81%)		*No. who did not finally register* 4410 (19%)	
Questionnaire returned 15.126 (77%)	Not returned 4474 (23%)	Questionnaire returned 1514 (34%)	Not Returned 2896 (66%)

A response rate of 77 per cent for all students who finally registered is clearly satisfactory. The comparison with the response rate for those who did not finally register (only 34 per cent) is fascinating. A unique early predictor of student withdrawal!

We have in addition the possibility of checking the characteristics of non-respondents from the comprehensive information already described on our student records.

We are also encouraged by the response rates for what we have called the 'drop-out' study – these are our 'provisional' students who did not finally register. We wrote to them only in October, but as many as 63 per cent who had previously completed the baseline questionnaire replied, and 47 per cent overall – a reasonable figure for a most difficult group.

The course unit reporting system

We have carried out numerous ad hoc projects during the year, at the request of individual faculties or departments and funded out of their own budgets, which included, for example, a questionnaire to social science summer school students, a questionnaire to arts students about the logic component of their course etc.

In addition one other major project has occupied us. This project, which services all the sections of the University, is a regular reporting system that we have devised to monitor the way in which the students are studying and are reacting unit by unit to the course materials.

A sample of one in three of all students formed a reporting panel, starting the year with a pad of report forms, one for each course unit, and sending them in at intervals over the year. We have experimented this year with an advanced optical reading system which allows the student simply to under-line in pencil their answers, with the minimum of effort. We have been able to feed information back to the faculties within a few weeks of the students studying the unit, and in time for the academic 're-make' teams to utilise the information in their planning for 1972. (Although every foundation course is designed to run for four years, each faculty has the resources to remake a limited proportion of it each year.)

This project, as with most of our projects, had to be multi-purpose. It is designed firstly for short-term information for the course teams, the BBC and the administration, both central and regional, of the University.

For example, we have asked students about their attendance at study centres, a network of 200 of which are available for students to attend over the country, on a voluntary basis.

Another fundamental question was to discover how many students were managing to watch and listen to the TV and radio programmes. These figures have been surprisingly and consistently high, although reactions to different programmes, of course, vary.

Science, where TV is advised as compulsory, has consistently the highest viewing figures although not much higher than Social Science. More students, however, watch the Science programmes twice than they do for any other faculty.

Radio listening is also high – particularly so for Humanities. This may be a reflection of the fact that slightly more arts students do not have access to BBC 2 and are therefore more concerned to use the medium that is available to them.

One of the most important problems facing both the University and the student was the level at which the work load was pitched. The University aimed at an average of ten hours per course, per week. In the event, students across all faculties have worked longer hours than was anticipated. There is some variation between courses and some variation between units. Understanding Society averaged 11.3 hours and was fairly consistent over its units. Humanities was more varied, but this figure excluded the logic component which averaged about another hour a week.

Maths took consistently more time (an average of 13.1 hours per week) as did science, averaging 14. 8 hours. Clearly for both of these courses, this was more time than had been anticipated. With Science some of this was due undoubtedly to home experiments, particularly when students had to unpack and repack their kit after each experiment, due to inadequate study space at home.

Looking at one faculty in detail, the Science faculty, it is worth noting the fact that remedial action has already been taken on the basis of this information for 1972's students. Several changes have been made. An example of this is the fact that Unit 10 on this course has now been spread over two weeks for 1972 and Unit 13 has been made 'optional' material. All units now have a detailed study guide directing students to timetable their work, and telling them which part is essential, which is desirable and which part is optional and so on.

Another major purpose of the course unit reporting system is to allow us at the end of the year's course, to analyse the study habits of different groups of students, with different patterns of learning and reactions, and see how their study patterns relate to their progress. Have for example, 'high' study centre attenders got consistently higher grades than 'low' study centre attenders? How does previous educational experience relate to study patterns and results? Here we are mainly looking for group differences.

A further and more long-term purpose is to individualise the results and see if we can, for individual students, discern a pattern of reactions, multiple indicators, perhaps, of difficulty, interest and time taken on study which may enable us to predict for that student the likelihood of his getting into trouble and needing individual help. A consistent negative correlation, for example, between difficulty and interest might lead to a student withdrawing. If we could, in future years, detect this tendency as it was developing, we might be able to forestall it by action at regional level.

We are involved in a system which has to be continually critical and self-improving if it is to survive. As with all research, each set of results produces some of the answers, but in its turn throws up new problems. We look forward to the day when other institutions are equally involved in such a self-monitoring system. The whole of higher education may benefit.

The Social Science Research Council-funded study of the first intake of OU students that was referred to above resulted in many research papers and fed into numerous policy-making processes at the OU. The major academic output was the book A degree of difference. *This volume described the OU students in meticulous detais – their motivations, their previous education, their occupational histories, their hobbies, their access to media, etc, etc.*

Here we present the concluding chapter. It shows how Naomi worked with the data and interwove it with information from many other areas and with the underlying philosophy of the OU. Some of her ideas were remarkably prescient.

Establishing a baseline[2]

Demand now

The first year of applications in 1970 showed quite clearly that the planners' faith was justified. In a period of six months, from January to July, 40,817 people applied to study with a new and totally untried organisation. For many, it was an opportunity for which they had been waiting all their lives. The backlog of pent-up demand, particularly among older people, showed up clearly in that first year. Applications declined in 1971 and 1972, particularly among men. 1973 brought a significant increase in the numbers of women, at whom publicity had been particularly directed. But the real surprise was the amazing increase in sheer numbers in 1974, which has been maintained in 1975. And this increase in demand comes at a time when demand for conventional universities is decreasing. Figure 1 shows the level of applications in each year so far for men and women separately.

We can only speculate as to the reasons for this increase. There is no doubt that the visible output of graduates must have given the university credibility to some who were still doubting. Publicity through the mass-media has been widespread and encouraging. Limited advertising campaigns using mass circulation dailies for the first time have been directed at population groups who would not normally have thought of university education. The level of awareness of the OU in the country as a whole has increased steadily, though it is still uncomfortably low among the working class, as Table 1 shows.

2. Sargant, Naomi and Calder, J. (1982). *A degree of difference: A study of the first year's intake of students to the Open University of the United Kingdom.* London: SRHE; New York: Praeger.

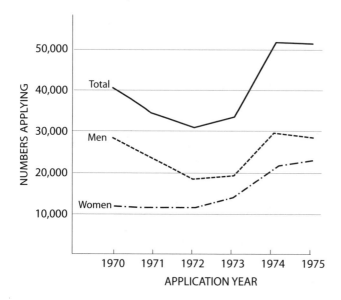

Figure 1 Sex of applicants 1970–1975

Table 1 Proportion of the adult population aware of the Open University (1971–75)

| Year: | Total %| Sex | | Social Class* | | | |
		Male %	Female %	AB %	C1 %	C2 %	DE %
1971	31	37	26	66	50	21	17
1972	40	43	37	78	58	30	22
1973	44	47	42	78	61	38	26
1974	54	58	51	82	71	49	37
1975	55	60	50	86	70	53	32

*The social class categories used are as defined by the Institute of Practitioners in Advertising.
Source: Survey commissioned from Louis Harris International

Demand: occupation and age

Over the initial period to 1973, the greatest proportional increase in demand came from housewives. In part this reflected the fact that teachers were not applying in such large numbers as in 1970, but this was not the only factor. There was a real increase in the numbers of housewife applicants reflecting the increasing awareness among women of the existence of the OU. Over the latter period (between 1973 and 1975) the proportion of housewives dropped marginally, but the numbers applying increased just as they did among other groups.

In the period as a whole, the proportion of applications from manual workers and clerical and office staff also increased. It was especially encouraging that the proportion of applicants from these groups increased most sharply in 1974, the year in which there was the great upsurge in demand for places.

The figures for teachers show how the data can tell a different story depending on whether absolute figures or percentages are used. In 1970 teachers accounted for 38% of applicants and this proportion dropped steadily year by year to a figure of 23% in 1975. (The decrease was largely due to a drop in demand from male teachers). But though teachers were a proportionately smaller group in 1975, they were applying in greater numbers than in any year other than the first one.

Except for engineering, where there has been no change, the proportions – and indeed numbers – of women applicants in each occupational category increased. But though women represented 41.8% of applicants in 1975 compared with 32.9% in 1971, they are still applying in significant numbers in only four of the OU's fourteen occupational categories.

These are 'housewives', 'education', the 'professions and arts' and 'clerical and office staff'. Women in these groups represented 13.8%, 10.8%, 5.2%, and 6.9% respectively of the total applicants in 1975.

Apart from a limited experimental intake of under 21s in 1974 and 1975, sponsored by the Department of Education and Science, the OU was set up and designed for adult students. It has attracted applicants up to the age of 91, and has students of 75 who have already graduated successfully. It could be argued that to allow older students to take up scarce places is a waste of resources, but on the other hand the University is 'open' in the sense that it makes no judgement about the worth and motivation of individual applicants. Increasingly, older people are needing to change course, and early retirement may well stimulate a demand for more of such opportunities.

The first year saw a backlog of older unqualified students applying to study. The age-range then dropped slightly. Table 2 compares the ages of student applicants in 1971 and 1974. The average age was 34 years in 1974, which is comparable to the average age of students at Empire State University (Empire State, 1975), a similar experiment in the United States.

Demand: which courses?

Arts and Social Sciences have been the subject areas consistently in most demand at foundation course level, as Figure 2 shows. Arts has now overtaken Social Science as the favourite, but this almost certainly relates to the decrease in the percentage of teachers applying. Education Studies has no

Table 2 Applicants in 1971 and 1974 compared in terms of age

	1971	*Year of Application* 1974
Base – all applicants = 100%	34,222	49,550
	%	%
21 – 25	22.0	23.3
26 – 30	28.0	28.4
31 – 40	29.3	27.8
41 – 50	15.7	14.2
51 and over	5.0	6.2

foundation course, and Social Science turns out to be the preferred method of entry for teachers.

Course applications appeared higher in 1970, but more people then were applying to study two foundation courses. Additionally, the Technology foundation course did not become available until 1971, and a further elementary mathematics course was added to the array in 1972. Demand has now been stable for two years, but there is no reason to suppose it will stay stable (Figure 2).

Demand: a specialist or generalist degree?

The Planning Committee was clear that the Open University should not set out to compete with established Universities in the provision of 'specialist' degrees, (Planning Committee, 1969). The degree was to be a 'general degree' in the sense that it would embrace studies over a range of subjects rather than be confined to a simple narrow speciality. They envisaged a degree structure that would be as flexible as possible, allowing students maximum reasonable choice from among courses offered. Since people commence their studies from a wide range of educational backgrounds, it was also accepted that the first year or 'foundation course' had to be designed to suit a wide variety of preparative backgrounds, and to familiarise mature students with modern concepts in the main lines of study.

All students, except those with credit exemptions, are required to study two foundation courses. After that, within available courses, and with a few limiting prerequisites, they are free to specialise or range across faculties as they wish. In practice, large numbers of students have made use of this facility. Indeed early students wishing to graduate quickly have needed to do so, as the full range of courses is not yet available. By 1974, 63 courses had been prepared. This figure rose to 74 in 1975, and it will reach 96 in 1976.

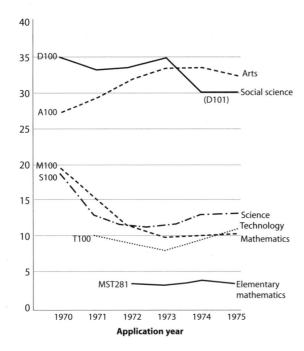

Figure 2 Course applications – 1970–1975

On current planning the full undergraduate profile of 134 courses will not be available until 1984.

But the view of the Planning Committee that there was a great need and demand in the country for the extension of facilities for general degrees was matched by the demands of the early students. The majority, nearly two thirds, of students surveyed in 1971 did not see themselves as specialising, but wanted to cut across faculties. About one third intended to specialise, although in Social Science in particular this covered significant proportions who, as we noted earlier, planned to move over to specialise in Educational Studies (Table 3).

Teachers formed a significant section of this first cohort, and it is interesting to look at the group of students, with credit exemptions, mainly teachers, and consider their pattern of choice over their first three years of study. The patterns are surprisingly different. Arts and Mathematics bear out the 'intentions' data and show the highest degree of loyalty, with 38.4% and 40.2% respectively sticking to the faculty of their foundation course over three years. For Science and Social Science the figures were very different. As few as 10.1% studied only Science and 8.5% only Social Science. 40.7% of Social Science foundation course students were studying Social Science and Education, and a further 21.4% were studying Education only. The comparable figures for Science were 22.9% studying Science and Education, and

Table 3 Proportion of 1971 students intending to specialise or cut across faculties

| | Total | Foundation course on entry | | | |
		Arts	Social Science	Maths	Science
Base – all respondents					
= 100%	4199	1214	1492	988	1014
	%	%	%	%	%
Intend to specialise in:					
Faculty of foundation					
course...		21	13	18	13
Other faculty		12	23	6	7
All specialising:	30	33	36	24	20
Intend to cut across ...	58	58	54	66	69
Don't know yet	9	8	10	10	10
No answer	3				

6.5% studying Education only. Among students without credit exemptions and therefore doing two foundation courses, Arts and Maths again showed a higher retention level (Figure 3).

It will be interesting to see whether the majority of students still wish to cut across faculties when a wider range of courses is available. Even in the 1980s, however, the profile will not allow for specialisation in the traditional sense of the word in many subject areas.

Demand in the future

The OU was designed initially to operate at degree level: its remit was to provide 'higher education for adults'. It could equally well have been designated an Open Polytechnic or an Open College, but it was not. The designation of 'university' is, in itself, less important than the level of new opportunities it was planned to provide. It was set up for adults, but it was not set up for 'adult education' as we know it, and there are problems about financing non-undergraduate education which require to be solved if the University is to enter this field effectively.

Initially the University set out to provide an undergraduate programme, and there is no sign of the demand for this reducing in the foreseeable future. Although current demand for conventional higher education is slackening, it is a fact that significant numbers of qualified school leavers are not at the moment going on direct to higher education. The DES Planning Paper No.2 1970 (HMSO, 1970) gave the following figures:

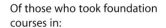

Of those who took foundation
courses in:

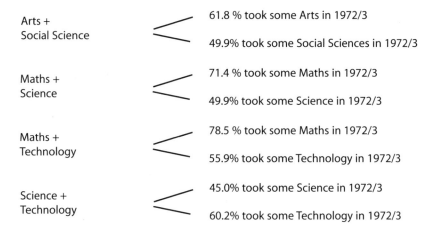

Arts +
Social Science

61.8 % took some Arts in 1972/3

49.9% took some Social Sciences in 1972/3

Maths +
Science

71.4 % took some Maths in 1972/3

49.9% took some Science in 1972/3

Maths +
Technology

78.5 % took some Maths in 1972/3

55.9% took some Technology in 1972/3

Science +
Technology

45.0% took some Science in 1972/3

60.2% took some Technology in 1972/3

Figure 3 Paths of study taken by 1971 students doing two foundation courses.

Table 4 Proportions of qualified boys and girls not going on to full time higher education

	Boys %	Girls %
3 'A' levels or more	10	17
2 'A' levels	32	39
1 'A' level	62	75
5 or more 'O' levels (no A's)	98	95

This group undoubtedly provides a pool of potential applicants on which the OU is likely to draw for a long time to come.

As long as there is no central record for applications to polytechnics it is difficult to make a clear estimate of total demand for higher education. DES estimates of demand by 1981 have been progressively reduced from the 1970 estimate (Planning Paper, No.2) of 835,000 to the 1972 White Paper estimate of 750,000 (HMSO, 1972) and to the current estimate announced in November 1974 of 640,000 by 1981. These changes take into account the reduction in the birth-rate and the slowing down in the growth of the percentage staying on at school and gaining qualifications. But the DES also notes (Forecast, 1974) a new factor affecting the participation rates, i.e. a decline in willingness to take up places, which has manifested itself over the last few years. Lord Crowther Hunt, speaking at the same conference as Forecast, stated that the government was still fully committed to Robbins, and that the latest forecast was simply the application of that principle to the latest available numbers. But the new figure does assume a continued decline in the numbers qualifying and in participation rates, and it is interesting to consider whether or not this assumption is likely to prove justified. Armitage (1974) argues cogently that current forecasts are too sanguine, and that demand may well turn out to be much higher.

There are four imponderable factors at least:

1) Nobody can really yet tell what effect ROSLA is likely to have in the longer term on the number of children staying on to take A levels.
2) Despite the move towards comprehensive schooling, large numbers of children are still being educated in secondary modern or similar schools. As the move to comprehensives continues, more children are likely to stay on into the sixth form and gain A levels.
3) The number of people who got two 'A' levels in further education increased over the decade. The increase was appreciable, from 3,000 in 1961–2 to 11,000 in 1971–2.
4) The pressure for the extension of mass higher education may become a reality for Britain. The example of other countries is increasingly before us.

These factors all point to a substantial continuing pool of qualified students who will not immediately be able to continue on into existing institutions of higher education. And the education system is not likely to become perfect over night in guiding children into the routes that are best for them. Large numbers of children will continue to discover too late that they have the capacity to study and may well turn to the OU.

Demand: from teachers

Significant numbers of teachers are continuing to apply to become OU students, as we noted earlier. Though they form a smaller proportion of applicants than in the early 1970s, absolute numbers have been higher in the last two years than in any year other than the first. Initially, one might expect this demand from teachers to dry up, but Armitage (1973), basing his projections on figures from the White Paper of 1972 shows that, despite the fact that the proportion of trained men graduates will have increased by 50% in 1981, and that of women by 100%, it seems unlikely that more than one in four teachers overall in 1981 will be a trained graduate. Looking further into the future, he predicts that:

'fewer than three in ten will be graduates in the mid-eighties, and a completely graduate profession will not come about for many years!'

So apart from any contribution the University may make to the in-service training of teachers planned within the framework of the recent White Paper, there is clearly going to be a continuing demand for degrees from non-graduate teachers for many years to come.

Demand for post-graduate degrees

The University accepts a modest number of post-graduate students, some of whom study full-time (11% in 1974) and others part-time. The current plan is to build up to 700 registered post-graduate students over the next triennium. But it is already clear that there is likely to be an appreciable demand for part-time higher degrees which, within current resources, the OU is not able to meet. The additional demand that will stem from OU graduates themselves is just starting to make itself felt, particularly in the area of Education. As far back as 1973, 94 such students were turned away, not because they were not suitable but because the University did not have any additional supervisory capacity.

Post-graduate work is an area currently under pressure in the country as a whole. In times of economic pressure, the expansion of opportunities for part-time post-graduate work seems like enlightened self-interest both for the country and the university, even if not for the students. (Certainly the educational lockstep evidenced in America poses a warning for Great Britain about the over-development of full-time post-graduate course work as a ritual.) There is little provision for part-time higher degrees in conventional institutions. This may be an area they turn to as the pressure from undergraduates lessens.

The increase in sheer numbers in demand for postgraduate places which the graduate output of the OU is likely to generate provides a quantitative challenge both for the OU and the country. It may well require a positive decision from government as to whether or not the country can afford to expand opportunities at this level; and if so at what rate and through what type of institution.

Certainly, as it is currently funded, the OU cannot meet the needs it is bound to stimulate.

Courses, not degrees

The credit structure was designed to be flexible, to allow people to stop and re-start or to change stream. In the future it may well be an increasing advantage for people to be able just to take courses and not register for a degree, particularly as the country moves to increasing leisure, shorter working hours and earlier retirement. It is more sensible to fit courses to people, than to force people to decide if they are degree students or 'post-experience' students. Some people wish to be both and this type of demand may well increase.

The boundaries between undergraduate, post-experience, post-graduate and extra mural courses become more difficult to define. One problem is the academic one of certification and legitimacy. The other is financial. The undergraduate programme is subsidised, the post-experience one is not. Adult education, though, is subsidised by local authorities, which comes to much the same thing. In the long run, if the country moves towards recurrent or continuing education where all people expect to go on studying as adults and get time off work as a right, then grants for all such educational courses will need to be made, and such distinctions will probably have to go. The dual system at the moment creates both financial and organisational problems. In the long run it might well be much more constructive to look at the University as a course-providing institution, providing a wide variety of courses, some of which are designed for undergraduate programmes, some for certificates, some for diplomas. Many would be dual purpose. A student would choose the ones he wanted, and build up to a degree or a certificate or just take one only. The emphasis on the undergraduate 'degree' would then lessen, and the University would extend its role to 'the education of adults'. This trivial change of phrase conceals a very significant shift of emphasis.

Demand and flexibility

A shift towards recurrent or continuing education is likely to bring with it increased pressure for modular courses. The model of initial education ending with a three or four year degree will need to change if recurrent education becomes a reality. Adults will need education in 'smaller chunks', and will want it to be made available in ways that can be fitted in to their working and family lives. Younger students, not yet bothered by job or family, can study where they wish. Older students are constrained by the availability of jobs, and often have to move with them. Over one in ten of all families move house in any one year. Over a five year part-time degree, the chances are high that half the students may be forced to move, usually to another area. In the past this has often meant giving up studies. With the current increase of modular degrees, particularly in polytechnics, provided institutions are prepared to accept transferability of credit, students can take their credits with them and continue their studies. Added pressure for this is likely to come from the Diploma in Higher Education, if it really gets off the ground.

The OU has led the way both in pioneering a credit exemptions policy and in outlining a more radical policy for transferability of credit between itself and other institutions of higher education. A specific reciprocal agreement has already been negotiated with Lancaster University, and discussions are in progress with Birkbeck, Liverpool Polytechnic, Bulmershe College of Education, to name only a few. It is clear that adult students in particular need a policy of transferability of credit. But the tradition of university academic autonomy dies hard, and many institutions are reluctant to allow students to transfer between courses, let alone to accept students transferring from any other institution with advanced standing. For polytechnics, which are only just tasting their freedom as course designers under the CNAA after years of the straitjacket of the London External syllabus, the timing is particularly inopportune.

Any genuine extension of educational opportunities for adults at whatever level, will have to allow for people who need to move from one institution to another for a variety of reasons. A particular strength of the OU is that people can move geographically. However its main mission initially has been to provide an undergraduate degree programme, and people cannot therefore move sideways or to a lower level. If many people are not to drop out, it will be important to extend the range of opportunities available for part-time study either by extending the range of courses available through the OU, or by extending the range of institutions serving adults in this way, or indeed by doing both. It is no longer adequate for institutions to deal with this problem independently. It is a luxury that neither the country nor potential students can afford. Hopefully the OU will be a catalyst in this respect.

On the assumption that the University adheres to its three basic remits of:

1) adults studying part-time
2) independent home-based study
3) a multi-media learning system

there are five main groups of people who seem likely to form its continuing student population, some for a second chance at initial education and some for continuing education. These are:

1) the students who for reasons of time or money or lack of a place have not been able to go to college
2) the 'drop-outs' and returners, e.g. student drop-outs and housewife returners, who require a second chance
3) people who need to move sideways or re-enter the labour force
4) people with increasing leisure, including the retired, who may wish to study for personal reasons
5) people who need to up-date their knowledge.

It is no accident that in America, where there has already been a high level of investment in educational plant, other material resources and staff, educationalists are not only translating the Open University idea into a 'new' institution – the University of Mid America – as Britain did. They are also using the idea to deliver existing courses in new ways, ensure access for minority groups, extend access to 'new' groups, and so on. In the late 1980s, Britain's problems may be more akin to theirs, but in the meantime it has a different problem.

The most recent bulge in the birth-rate, which the reviled DES planning target of 640,000 places in higher education by 1981 is designed to accommodate, shows no sign of being repeated. The birth-rate had dropped steadily since 1964. After 1983 the number of 18 year olds will decline gradually until 1989 and then fall sharply to 1993. Government inevitably will face the question of how to meet that peak of demand at the turn of the decade, particularly since at the moment it appears a one-off demand. Should it and can it afford to meet that peak demand, and if so through what institutions?

In 1970, the Department of Education and Science asked the Open University to consider the contribution that it might make to the development of higher education provision in the future, the suggestion then being that the OU should admit a group of qualified 18 year olds. The current experiment has changed somewhat from the original proposal, and some unqualified students are being admitted alongside the qualified ones. But demand from such students is currently voluntary demand, made in the full knowledge of available places in conventional universities. If by the end of the decade places are not available, because it has not proved possible to meet the one-off peak of demand with additional bricks and mortar, the Open University may well be under renewed pressure to look on a larger scale at the question of admitting qualified school-leavers and the demand might become enforced demand. It is interesting that the White Paper of 1972 was notable for its omission of any reference to the Open University in this respect.

It is, however, one thing for the OU to provide an additional opportunity for that age group. To provide it as the only opportunity would provoke much concern.

The first of the many

In this volume, we have looked at the 1971 intake of Open University students, their current preoccupations and backgrounds. We have shown that although many of them are not 'educationally deprived' in the more obvious sense, they have certainly not had as much education 'as they can turn to advantage, or as they discover sometimes too late that they need' (Crowther, 1969). Many students are characterised not only by inter-generational mobility but also intra-generational mobility. The Open University appears to be, for many, another step rather than the first step in this process. For women, the University is providing an important additional opportunity. Many very able women precluded from going on to further or higher education for a variety of reasons are choosing to study through the OU and doing so very successfully. How the labour market will react to those women seeking to enter it for the first time or to re-enter after a long period will be a critical question.

Indeed the general question of the recognition of OU graduates and of the OU degree is emerging as a major candidate for concern and for research. It is not just a question of recognition by employers, but also by professional bodies and by other educational institutions, since many students wish to use their 'credits' as a passport for entry into conventional institutions either to complete degree programmes or to embark upon further qualifications. Education appears to breed an insatiable desire for more education. And there remains the problem of students who fail to continue their studies, who have dropped out and would have wished to continue.

For some, the level at which the university provides its opportunities is not the appropriate one. For others the physical barriers to access are too great: availability of time, money, access to educational support systems are all limited for many people. Shift workers are one obvious category. Other barriers are less obvious. Some students are not even able to start because of the assumptions about verbal and numerical facility, the use of language and cultural background that are embedded often unconsciously in the way the courses are structured.

It could be argued that these are not problems for a university, but that they are the responsibility of the rest of the educational system. This is a seductive but irresponsible view. Even if such students' paths back to education should not lie only through the OU, the University undoubtedly has an important role in stimulating the rest of the educational system into an awareness of the gaps in provision below and surrounding it. The real gap in provision is between sixteen and nineteen. It is idle to expect an institution located at university level to bridge this gap on its own. Indeed it would be wrong of it to attempt to do so, since this would eventually only produce an alternative educational ladder. It is for this reason that moves made by the University in the area of the provision of preparatory courses or materials are inevitably attended by ambivalence.

In our ongoing research programme we are continuing to follow the progress of the first, and also other, cohorts of students through the University and on into their subsequent careers. It is clear that they are not an isolated phenomenon, but, indeed, the 'first of the many'.

References

ARMITAGE, P. (1973) Facing facts and jumping to conclusions, *Higher Education Review*, Spring 1973.

ARMITAGE, P. (1974) The White Paper – a step in the dark, *Higher Education Review*, Autumn 1974.

CALDER, J. and McINTOSH, N. E. (1974) Student drop-out, wastage and withdrawal, *Higher Education Review*, Autumn 1974.

EMPIRE STATE COLLEGE (1975) *Selected Background Characteristics of Empire State College Students – Fall 1974–Spring 1975*, New York: Empire State College. In mimeograph.

LORD CROWTHER (1969) Inaugural address on the occasion of the Charter Ceremony, 23rd July 1969. Reproduced in: Open University Prospectus. Open University, 1971.

FORECAST, K. (1974) From a speech delivered at North East London Polytechnic Conference: 'What happened to the students?', November 1974.

HMSO (1970) DES Planning Paper, No.2, London: HMSO.

HMSO (1972) Education: a framework for expansion. White Paper presented by Secretary of State for Education and Science, London: HMSO.

THE PLANNING COMMITTEE REPORT (1969) Report of the Planning Committee for the Open University to the Secretary of State for Education and Science, London: HMSO.

The next paper was published in 1975 and can be read as updating 'Research for a new institution'. It addresses more of the problems of embedding and funding institutional research. It also includes examples of questions faced by the OU and how the Survey Research Department approached them.

The sub-title for this paper was 'Why do we need all these forms?' She notes that data processing staff saw this research as 'irrelevant academic research'. Her files were allegedly labelled NAOMI which stood for 'Never Access, Only Marginally Important'. This is Naomi's spirited defence.

Institutional research: needs and uses[3]

The growth of the demand for higher education and the move towards 'éducation permanente' pose problems for educationalists, administrators and politicians all over the world. Universities, traditionally a law unto themselves, have now to accept public scrutiny, be responsive to public demand, and are having to become more cost-conscious and cost-effective. The extension of the use of the mass-media for educational purposes brings advantages in terms of economies of scale, but disadvantages in terms of cost, flexibility and distance. The normal luxury of 'eyeball-to-eyeball' contact is one which distance learning is denied.

In particular, conventional institutions with students on site can obtain feedback in a variety of formal and informal ways. As one colleague said 'If the students didn't like my lectures, they went to the library!' Informal feedback in a two-way learning situation is easy to obtain and is usually all that is seen to be either necessary or desirable, though increasingly some institutions are trying to supplement it in more formal ways. Informal feedback in a distance learning situation is more difficult to obtain. Immediate reactions to the learning materials are usually private ones. Tutorials are an additional, but not integral part of the learning system, and may be removed in time from when the learning takes place. Unlike the lecturer, the television screen cannot watch the attentiveness of the audience and wake it up when it has gone to sleep.

Letters, phone calls, contacts with tutors and counsellors all provide valuable, informal and speedy feedback. This 'shriek' system as it has become known, can at least be relied on to convey the gross failures and difficulties

3. McIntosh, N. E. (1975) *'Institutional research: needs and uses'*, printed in *Teaching at a Distance*, number 2, pp. 35–48.

'*Wake up. The Open University's finished*'
(From the *Times Educational Supplement* 11 February 1974.)

of the system. It is, however, noisy and not very reliable. Some people shriek louder than others and their ability to shriek may not relate to the validity of their case. So other methods of obtaining information have to be devised.

Since students are studying at a distance, one major source of information about the students themselves and how they study has been survey research, which has provided an input to academic decisions and planning on a scale which is new to education, and of a nature to which academics have not been accustomed. The programme of research carried out by the Survey Research Department in the Open University, which is discussed in this paper, includes a longitudinal study of students' educational and occupational backgrounds. Sample surveys of drop-outs show the University where it is failing to meet student needs. Panels of students report weekly about their study habits and reactions to the educational materials. Some 100 000 questionnaires have been through the department to date.

With thousands of students learning at a distance, using the media in a new way, informational needs are acute. The institution has to know how the students are using the educational resources it puts out. At the same time academics and administrators do not always understand that they have these needs, or that there is any possibility of resolving or even of reducing them. How is it possible to overcome this problem in the Open University situation?

Most educational research has traditionally looked *within* the educational process, at what is being learnt, and in a tidy way endeavoured to test and measure whether or not anything has been learnt. It has developed its own language and its own inner logic. It has frequently become identified with curriculum evaluation, and has drawn heavily on experimental and psychometric techniques. This 'test and measurement' model which Parlett and Hamilton (1972) describe as the 'agricultural-botany' paradigm of evaluation may have been adequate for some traditional classroom situations. They themselves found it inadequate, particularly for innovatory programmes, and have developed a new approach, 'illuminative evaluation' based on what they describe as a 'social anthropology' paradigm. Their approach is based on a very different research technique, participant observation. In both cases, one could argue, it is the technique that has dominated the development of the paradigm and not the nature of the programme or the purpose of its evaluation. Attempting to apply either model to the particular situation of the Open University shows up the limitations of both approaches. The problem of producing controlled experimental conditions involving before and after testing of samples of the Open University's population of scattered independent learners is immediately clear. (McIntosh, 1973) The problem of using participant observation as a research form when the majority of the learning, is carried out alone in people's homes is again clear.

The research problem

So other means have to be sought. It is not, in my view, the particular tech-niques that are used that are important, but the nature of the research problem and the purpose of the research. Indeed the techniques all belong to the general domain of survey research—observation, the use of documentary sources, personal interviewing (with or without structured questionnaires), self-administered questionnaires, discussion groups and so on. Some are obviously more suitable within the Open University's particular circum-stances than others. Personal interviewing is good but expensive in time and money. Telephone interviewing rules out those without telephones. Self-administered questionnaires are practicable, but need to be carefully designed if the information obtained is to be unambiguous and usable. Discussion groups concentrate on those who can get to study centres, and so on. (The Open University handbook on institutional research provides important guidelines for anyone involved with the Open University who is thinking of researching into it/us or them!)

One apparently obvious suggestion, to use our own counsellors and tutors as interviewers, is not as ideal as it seems. They are, after all, both involved with the student in his learning, and sometimes his assessment. Even if trained and experienced it would be virtually impossible to rule out the like-lihood of the student's answers being affected by his knowledge of this rela-tionship. And they would need to be paid if they were involved on a large scale, so it would be no cheaper.

Internal or external research?

This leads to one final, but critical, point. If research is to be effective in an institution like the Open University, should the research be carried out inter-nally or externally? This 'make or buy' decision is one that industry shares. But the decision in industry, except where secrecy is involved, is usually made on financial grounds. In an institution in the public sector like the Open University, there are other constraints, such as that of impartiality. If impar-tiality is, in fact, the critical criterion then undoubtedly research should be bought outside. At the same time, it is then easier to ignore its results.

What happens if the institution or department decides to 'make' its own research? It is open to the charge of bias, it is true, but it is more difficult for the institution to ignore it. It is worth distinguishing here between what Scriven (1967) describes as 'formative' and 'summative' evaluation. 'Formative' evaluation is usually conducted in conjunction with the develop-ment of new educational programmes, and 'summative' evaluation is used to assess ineffectiveness of existing programmes. Much of what we tend to describe as 'feedback' could alternatively be described as 'formative' evalua-tion. It is concerned with improving the system while it is still developing.

Particularly if the system is complex (and ours is) it is difficult for outsiders to be intimately enough involved for this type of research to be effective from outside. The requirement for impartiality is less because one is not judging the end product. 'Summative' evaluation, on the other hand, a final judgement of the worth of the programme, needs to be impartial. But it may well be idle for researchers to come along from outside at the end of a programme to try to make such judgements since much of the information they may need may not have been, or be able to be, collected.

What we have at the moment settled for is a compromise. The unit doing the research is located within the institution, but is independent of the main faculty and administrative groupings, the results of whose activities form the main subjects of its studies.

It is becoming less unusual to have research units in social and community services. It is still unusual to find them in educational institutions. Frequently the necessity for research is only realised after the institution has been under way for some years. Perhaps the significant difference at the Open University was that institutional researchers were appointed to the staff at the beginning of its life and well before any students arrived. Additionally, instead of being part of the administration, they were accorded academic status and membership of Senate. Although this posed problems in their relationship with the data processing staff, who saw their research as 'irrelevant academic research' and gave it no priority, it provided compensating benefits in their relationship with the academics, who found it more difficult to ignore the research results produced and argued by academic colleagues. In the middle were to be found the key group of administrators, who had to be converted first. But they were, many of them, the most easily converted, because the contributions to better management decisions are more easily demonstrable in this area.

Research in action

The remainder of this paper will look at some examples of the way in which institutional research has been used at the Open University. In general, the methods employed are not remarkable. Given the scattered nature of the population under study, and its commitment, heavy reliance has so far been placed on self-administered questionnaires. Research in a public institution has a particular necessity to be cost-effective. We have been fortunate in having the goodwill of the students. Good communication with them, our respondents and customers, is as important as good communication with our clients.

Example 1

Problem: to forecast the demand for the Open University. Initially there was no way of accurately forecasting the level and nature of demand for the University. In its own terms the Open University needed not only to achieve an adequate overall level of applications, but also wished to ensure that it reached those persons, previously educationally disadvantaged, for whom it had been set up. The first year saw a large number of applications from teachers and other apparently 'middle class' occupational groups.

An early national poll on knowledge and awareness of the Open University, commissioned from Louis Harris International, and followed up each year, immediately put this in perspective. (See Table 1a.)

Table 1a

% knowing of the OU		Sex		Social class				Terminal age of education		
	Total	Male	Female	AB	C_1	C_2	DE	15 or less	16–18	19 or more
1971	31	37	26	66	50	21	17			
1972	40	43	37	78	58	30	22	29	68	90
1973	44	47	42	78	61	38	26	34	68	92
1974	54	58	51	82	71	49	37			

Although knowledge in the country as a whole is steadily increasing, we still have a long way to go, particularly with those who have missed out on previous educational chances. The group who left school at fifteen or earlier, of whom only one in three 'knows', forms, after all, seventy-five per cent of the British population. To reach them in larger numbers almost certainly means expensive advertising campaigns, with budgets which a state-funded university does not have. Looking at an analysis by newspaper readership makes this point forcibly. Knowledge is already high among readers of the serious dailies, where we get more (free) editorial coverage, but of course these papers are read by relatively small groups of people. The mass of the population read the popular dailies. (See Table 1b.)

Table 1b

% knowing of the OU	Total	*Guardian*	*Telegraph*	*Times*	*Daily Mail*	*Daily Express*	*Daily Mirror*	*Sun*
1972	40	79	73	72	48	46	34	35
1973	44	74	77	73	53	53	38	37

'Clients' for this research are the Director of Information Services, the Public Relations Committee, and the Admissions Committee who are concerned with the process from application to admission. The first poll was commissioned, without a budget, by the research group. Now Information Services pay the bill from their, albeit small, advertising budget. Lately advertising has been directed at women and lower middle and upper working class groups, and in 1974 space was taken in two popular dailies—the *Daily Express* and the *Daily Mirror*.

Example 2

Problem: to provide regular information on the progress of students from application onwards. Essentially this became a problem of building up internal statistics to provide the basis of a management information system. Both the student's application form and provisional registration form, as a result of close co-operation between the survey research department and the administration, were devised to provide not just basic administrative data, but also research data for planning purposes. The more information that could be collected from all students in this way, as a matter of course, the cheaper and more accurate would the monitoring system be. The key problem was to gain agreement to include questions on the application form and registration form which met administrative and organisational needs, but could be coded and recorded in a suitable form for later analysis. A more detailed discussion can be found in McIntosh (1972).

One example suffices to show the way in which analyses of existing statistical data enabled the University to detect an area in which administrative procedures were not ensuring that policy objectives were being met.

The admissions procedure operates within quotas on a 'first come first served' basis. But teachers, in fact, obtained proportionally more places. A retrospective analysis of the application statistics by the Survey Research department showed teachers applying much earlier in the application period. All other things being equal, they got far more places. Decisions about quotas for the subsequent year were taken in the light of this knowledge.

Analyses of student survival for each course are now provided at all major milestones of the students' year. These show for key indicators such as sex, age, region, previous education, occupation and mother tongue, which groups of students are more vulnerable than others, and on which courses. In 1974 these analyses were extended to show the relationship of survival to current continuous-assessment grades, and to past course performance. These analyses need to be quickly and clearly available for busy and often non-numerate academics.

Again the impetus for providing this regular monitoring came initially from the survey research department with no earmarked budget. More people are now aware of the necessity to have regular statistics and the administration is accepting more responsibility, both financial and organisational, for producing some of them.

Example 3

Problem: to discover how the students were using the wide variety of educational materials open to them, and what their reactions were to them. The student receives his instruction in several ways, of which the main substance is provided through written course correspondence texts and these are essential. Large sums of money are also invested in making television and radio programmes, in home experiment kits for science, in providing local study centres and so on. It is vital to know, at minimum, whether these resources are even being used. Preferably we need to know something about their relative use and effectiveness. Ideally we need to know in detail how much more effective one method is than the other and for what purpose.

If television, for the sake of argument, costs £1000 per half hour programme and radio costs £100, does it convey the same concept ten times as well as radio? Alternatively does it convey some concepts better than others? Are all students able to learn equally well from all the media, or do some learn better from one or two and not from others? We do not know whether the media work in isolation, or in co-operation or even in antagonism to each other. The problem is particularly acute at the Open University, as students are trying to gain a qualification. Differential ability to learn from different media may therefore affect the person's success and therefore their future work and life. We are not, of course, anywhere near solving these problems. But there are also intermediate problems, no less important, with which we have to be concerned. Students' ability to view the programmes is constrained by their work and domestic arrangements. For example, an early pilot study showed only sixty-two per cent of students are back home from work by 17.30. But already with 42 courses in 1973 we had to start broadcasting at 17.30. We chose therefore, to schedule education courses at this time as teachers finish work sooner, and form proportionally more of the student audience available at this time. Now of course we are having to use early morning time slots.

At the moment we are still in a position to broadcast each programme twice, once on a weekday evening and once on a weekend morning. On the face of it one would expect there to be regularity in viewing patterns across students which would depend on their family and work circumstances, not on the Open University programming. One early finding which took all the planners by surprise was that the opposite was the case. Rather than preferring to watch in the evening or at the weekend, students chose to watch the first showing of the programme, irrespective of time of week. The academic motivation of watching it 'first' and also presumably, of retaining the possibility of viewing it twice, appeared to be stronger than work or home constraints.

In fact, an extraordinarily high percentage has consistently watched and listened to the programmes, although the numbers listening to radio in our second year started to drop on maths and social sciences courses. This poses more critically for these faculties the problem of how to utilise radio in future years. This is clearly an area where experience in different countries will be affected by the attitude in that country towards radio. In America some students using Open University materials on an experimental basis have found it virtually impossible to utilise and learn from our radio programmes, as in their cultural setting they are now unused to listening seriously to radio.

To obtain this sort of information regularly week by week from large numbers of students when resources are limited posed a serious problem. Students, on a sample basis, in 1971 and 1972 were asked to report regularly on their study patterns, and were provided with a pad of report forms (designed to be easily completed by them and easily read by an optical scanner on return). All the problems of panels – non-response, conditioning, attrition – arise, and although we have in some ways a bonus of committed students, in other ways we lose because we cannot provide incentives, use personal follow-ups etc. To rotate the panel might improve response rates, but would preclude the possibility of later longitudinal analyses. Response rates over the later weeks of the year drop inevitably. We cannot detect, however, any gross distortions from non response and attrition over the year, and a repeat of the same study with new students in 1972 replicated 1971's findings closely. (McIntosh and Morrison, 1973)

Initially, we had hoped to build this feedback automatically into the student assignment system. This proved too complex. It was, therefore, planned *ad hoc* as a research project and funded by the university out of budgets allocated by the Planning Board. It is a co-operative research project which has to meet the needs of many different clients at the same time –faculties, the administration, the regions, the BBC, and the planners. But it would be impossible to bother the same set of students with five different questionnaires. The department attempts to co-ordinate and service the disparate needs.

Example 4

Problem: to discover the take up of opportunities made available for students at the 250 plus study centres. The decision to provide a network of local study centres was made early on. Indeed it figured in the *Report of the Planning Committee*. (Open University, 1966), Attendance at study centres is not compulsory, although some academics considered that it should be for some courses, for example in science. The centres are like resource centres, but ones where many of the resources are human ones! It is up to the student to decide to take advantage of the facilities made available, but since they all cost money, which might be spent on other forms of support, it is important to know how much the resources are used. Attendance was higher in 1972 than in 1971, and did not tail off towards the summer as it had done in 1971. In 1972 the counsellor became course-based for foundation courses and most class tutors became the people who also marked the students' assignments. These changes had marked effects on students on mathematics and science courses who went to tutorials more and visited their counsellors more. Television viewing and radio listening are clearly seen as *primarily* home-based activities. A reasonable proportion of students watch or listen to live programmes at centres, but very few use the playback facilities (Table 4). The decision to attend the study centre, then, is more critically related to the 'people' experience there. Although other students are a factor it is obviously the counsellors and tutors who are most important.

Table 4 Attendance at study centre and reasons for visit. 1971 and 1972 compared

Question: Have you visited a study centre this week? *If yes:* for what reasons did you visit it?

| | Arts | | Social Sciences | | Maths | | Science | | Technology |
	1971	1972	1971	1972	1971	1972	1971	1972	1972
Base—all Respondents = 100%	15,094	13,931	14,559	16,871	9,965	14,287	10,433	18,662	10,793
	%	%	%	%	%	%	%	%	%
% visiting per week	39	46	41	46	47	55	41	53	53
Reasons Class tutorial/seminar	17	26	18	24	25	30	24	31	29
To meet counsellor	20	21	21	22	18	28	17	26	28
To meet other students	18	20	19	21	13	19	15	20	21
To watch TV	12	20	12	13	13	16	12	15	14
To listen to radio	8	5	8	4	6	3	3	6	2
Library purposes				1		1		2	2
Computer terminal					11	9		2	6
Other purposes	2	1	2	2	2	2	2	2	2

Example 5

Problem: dissatisfied customers. A critical problem for us is to discover what has caused students to drop out. Is it our fault or is it due to circumstances over which we have no control? From their point of view to drop out is costly, both in terms of money and morale. For us it is a waste of a place, a matter of educational responsibility and, on top of that, potentially damaging to the reputation and survival of the University. Of the first 10 000 applicants in 1974, thirty per cent of them heard about the Open University from somebody who was already a student. Publicity can work both ways!

Sample studies have been carried out, therefore, of students who have withdrawn at different stages of their degree studies. Two groups of students have been compared so far—those who began studying foundation courses but decided not to register finally after three months, and those who studied for one year and have decided not to continue.

The University commits a lot of effort to providing some face-to-face support for students at local level particularly in the form of counselling and tuition services. Above all, these should be valuable at critical times such as when students are considering whether or not to withdraw. These studies showed some early problems in developing this new role. Either students did not know where to go for help, or some may not have felt able to ask for help or indeed many may not have felt they needed any help. This third alternative, although happier from the student's point of view, is not so happy from the University's point of view, since it implies a misjudgement about allocation of resources.

Example 6

Problem: the Open University in society. These sample studies form part of a separate longitudinal study, funded initially by a grant from the Social Science Research Council, which is designed to examine the educational and occupational backgrounds and progress of the students who entered in 1971. For many, the University has an implicit social objective, that of providing opportunities for higher education to the working class. Despite the greatly improved provision for education at all levels over the last century, inequality of opportunity remains. Douglas concluded, in a quotation that was referred to in the *Report of the Planning Committee*, 'in the population as a whole...the middle class pupils have retained, almost intact, their historic advantage over the manual working class'. (Douglas *et al.*, 1968). It is important to attempt to assess whether or not the University has done anything to cancel out this advantage. As the Universities Central Council for Admissions and the Open University both use categories based on groupings of the Registrar General's occupation orders, some comparisons can be attempted. These are discussed in detail elsewhere; (McIntosh and Wooley, 1974) the main points of interest can be seen from Table 5.

Table 5 The occupational background of students at the open university and at conventional universities

OU occupational categories	Registrar General's occupation orders	Students entering conventional universities 1971	Open University students 1971 intake		All economically active males aged 45–59 in Great Britain	
		Father's occupation %	Own occupation* %	Father's occupation %	1951 Census %	1966 Census %
8 Electrical, engineering etc. 9 Farming, mining etc. 10 Communications & transport	I–XX	29	5	52	70	64
2 Armed forces 11 Clerical and office	XXI–XXIII, XXVI	27	14	28	21	22
12 Sales and service	XXIV	14	6	6	5	6
3 Administrators & managers 4 Education 5 Professions & Arts 6 Qualified scientists & engineers 7 Technical personnel	XXV	30	76	14	4	8

* Open University students not economically active are not included.

The Registrar General's categories I—XX (Open University categories 8–10) contain the majority of manual workers. The 1966 census showed 64% of all economically active males in this category. The figures for conventional university entrants show 29% with fathers in this category in 1971, while 52% of Open University students' fathers were in this category.

It is not just that our students have been upwardly mobile from their parents, they have also been extremely mobile within their own working life. It is clear that teaching has provided the main route for upward mobility and many went into teaching late having started in a different field. Looking just at those Open University students with fathers in manual occupations, 27% of them started work in those same manual occupations, but only 8% are still in them. The proportion who started as teachers was 20% compared with 40% who are teachers now. (McIntosh and Woolley, 1974).

At the start of the University's life, funding for such 'interesting' but 'non-essential' research could not be found within its own budgets, and external grant aid had to be sought. Now the University is continuing to fund the longitudinal studies itself, and demanding more of them. They are also proving of increasing interest to the Department of Education and Science and educationalists elsewhere in Britain and abroad. And it is not just the nature of the work that is creating interest, but the nature of the relationship between the research function and the institution.

The fact that the research has consistently been used in educational planning and decision making within the Open University finds little precedent in any other educational institution. It will be interesting to see if the relationship can be maintained. As the institution ceases to grow and starts to stabilise the nature of the relationship should change. A basic monitoring system providing, effectively, management information should be established and accepted within the University. Current plans are that responsibility for organising this should lie with the administration who will routinely provide it to all potential users. The Survey Research department will be relieved of much day-to-day work enabling it to pay more attention to *ad hoc* problems thrown up as areas for further attention by the routine monitoring process. In theory, this should lead to better information and better decision making.

References

DOUGLAS, J. W. B., ROSS, J. M. AND SIMPSON, H. R. (1968) *All Our Future*, Peter Davies, p. xii.

MCINTOSH, NAOMI E. (1972) 'Research for a new institution—the Open University' in *Innovation in Higher Education, Society for Research into Higher Education*.

MCINTOSH, NAOMI E. (1973) *Evaluative Research for Out-of-school Multi-media Educational Systems*, Strasbourg, Council of Europe..

MCINTOSH, NAOMI E. and MORRISON, V. (1973) 'Students' study patterns and their reactions to course materials', Open University internal paper.

McIntosh Naomi E. and Woodley, A. (1974) 'The Open University and second-chance education', Germany, *Paedogogica Europeaea*, Autumn.

Open University, (1966) *Report of the Planning Committee to the Secretary of State for Education and Science*, HMSO.

Parlett, M. and Hamilton, D. (1972) *Evaluation as illumination, Centre for Research in the Educational Sciences*, University of Edinburgh.

Scriven, M. (1967) 'The methodology of evaluation' in *Perspectives of Curriculum Evaluation*, AERA Monograph series on Curriculum Evaluation, Chicago: Rand McNally.

The next paper was commissioned for the very first issue of the new journal Distance Education. *It was also chosen by Sewart, Keegan and Holmberg to go in their seminal edited book* Distance Education: international perspectives.

It was published in 1980, the year before Naomi left the OU, so it was almost her swansong. It certainly summarises an awful lot of research. It also reflects the 'cradle to grave' approach adopted by the department in that it covers everything from hearing of the OU through to graduation.

Student demand and progress at the Open University – the first eight years[4]

Introduction

'But what would happen in a university of the air? The numbers attracted to it would certainly be out of all proportion to the numbers that stayed the course. Can we really afford the fantastic cost that this would entail? The government give no estimate. It is just as well. This is one of those grandiose schemes that does not bear inspection while so much else that is already begun remains half done. We shall need to be very sure that it is necessary before we commit ourselves to the expense.'

This quotation taken from a leader in *The Times Educational Supplement* under the heading 'Pipe Dream' was typical of the scepticism that greeted the original proposals for a 'University of the Air' or an 'Open University' as it later became. This scepticism was shared by a wide range of educationalists, politicians of both parties and informed commentators. Among many, the scepticism was accompanied by hostility, clearly documented by Perry in his account of the University's first years (Perry, 1976). Demand was not proven, students would not stay the course, degree-level work could not be taught in such a way, there was a vast array of existing educational opportunities – the criticisms were numerous, and strongly argued. Now, ten years after the granting of the University's charter and eight years after the first students

---

4 McIntosh, N. E., Alan Woodley and Val Morrison (1980) *Distance Education*, 1(1) pp. 37–60. Also in Sewart, D. Keegan, D. and Holmberg, B. *Distance Education: international perspectives*. London: Routledge, 1988.

commenced their studies, it is possible to start to make some assessment of how far the University has confirmed the prophecies of its early critics and how far it has confounded them.

Early attempts to study the progress of Open University students and to make comparisons with the graduation rates of other relevant groups have been limited and fragmentary. The problems stemmed both from the difficulties of making comparisons (Calder and McIntosh, 1974) and from the fact that the majority of students were going to need several years to complete their studies (McIntosh and Morrison, 1974). In this paper we propose to look at the pattern of demand as it has built up over the years, and then to concentrate on the progress and graduation patterns of the early intakes, as it is only for these that we are able to display a nearly but still not complete picture. Inevitably this paper will cover much of the same ground as an earlier one on the same topic (McIntosh and Morrison, 1974). However, we propose to repeat the data where appropriate, thereby providing a more complete picture of the University's first years.

Before commencing our discussion, it is worth reminding those unfamiliar with the detail of the Open University's structure what its key characteristics are, and how it differs both from other conventional and other distance learning institutions. It was set up specifically as a distance learning institution, and

1. it is designed for adults of all ages who are normally working, and study is expected to be part-time
2. its educational opportunities, initially, were provided at degree level only
3. its study is designed to be mainly home-based
4. it uses open-network BBC television and radio in addition to written and other materials
5. it requires no formal educational qualifications for entry

Unlike other institutions providing degree studies in the United Kingdom at that time, the Open University decided to use a credit structure, allowing students to study at their own pace and take years off from their studies if they so wished. Six credits are required for a BA Ordinary degree and eight for an Honours degree. Additionally students who have previously successfully completed other 'higher' education courses are allowed to claim exemption from one to three credits. Originally it was anticipated that each credit would require an average of ten hours study a week for thirty-six weeks of the year. In practice it is now generally agreed that most courses require, and most students spend, twelve to fourteen hours a week on each full-credit course, and many courses now run for thirty-two to thirty-four weeks. The University currently offers around 120 different courses. They range in difficulty from foundation to fourth level and many have been designed as half-credits.

Although the University is now extending its range of courses into the area of continuing education, this paper confines itself to a discussion of the undergraduate programme, the University's first mission. For a more detailed account of this programme readers are referred to the Open University's BA Degree Handbook (Open University, 1979a) and Courses Handbook (Open University, 1979b).

The level of demand

At the time of its inception there was little firm evidence of demand which could be drawn upon to back the case for setting up the Open University. The Planning Committee quoted estimates of the potential pool of adults who had been born too soon to reap the benefits of increasing educational opportunity (Open University Planning Committee, 1969). They suggested that applying Robbins' targets retrospectively indicated a pool of such people of at least one million, of whom 10% (at least 100,000) might apply. Similarly they estimated that some 10% (i.e. 25,000) of the pool of 255,000 non-graduate teachers in the UK might be interested in up-grading their qualifications. They also commissioned a study of the adult population which asked people about their degree of possible interest in such an institution. About 5% indicated that they would be 'very interested', and 0.9% said that they 'would certainly be one of the first students'. Inevitably these survey figures were subject to wide limits of error. Applied to the country as a whole the 0.9% yielded a figure of total possible students ranging from 34,000 to 150,000. However what nobody could foretell was exactly what the demand would be and whether or not it would be a continuing demand. In a very real sense, then, 'supply' preceded 'demand' rather than the other way round. In the event, applications in the first year were high enough to satisfy the hopes of the planners, and although the characteristics of those who applied were not necessarily what everyone had expected, there were far too many applicants for the places available. Consequently admissions procedures had to be devised to choose the first 24,000 students. The basic procedure adopted was one of 'first come, first served' with early applicants being favoured over late applicants. However, there were also course and regional quota restrictions to ensure that there were viable numbers of students taking each foundation course in each geographical area.

Figure 1 shows the absolute number of applicants for each application year since the University started. After the high number in the first year, the number of applicants dropped in the second and third years. The figures for 1973 showed a slight rise but the largest increase came in 1974. Applications reached a peak in 1975 with large numbers of potential students having to be turned away, and since then there has been a gradual decline. However, there is still no sign of the pool of applicants drying up and in fact the provisional figures for 1979 show an increase of four thousand from the previous year.

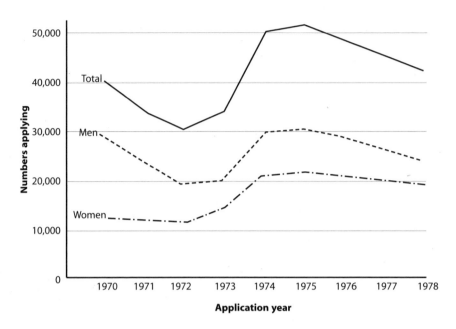

Fig. 1 Open University applicants 1970–78 – overall numbers, and men and women.

We can offer no conclusive explanation for the pattern of applications in the early years. We assume that the first year represented a build-up of demand among people who had been waiting for the OU to be set up. However, it was still a new and untried institution from which no students had graduated and few courses were yet available to display its academic quality. The end of 1972 saw the first small number of students graduating and it does seem that the media coverage of their success in early 1973 added to the credibility of the University and stimulated demand. The gradual decline in applications in later years may be due to one of a number of factors. The cost of OU studies is known to deter a large number of potential applicants (McIntosh and Woodley, 1975) and therefore the increases in student fees may have reduced demand. What is of interest is that the number of 'fresh' applicants has remained fairly constant in the later years. Although many unsuccessful applicants re-apply in subsequent years there has been a decline in the proportion who do so.

Table 1 shows the pattern of enquiries, applications, places available and places accepted over the years. Each year many thousands of people enquire about the OU but then decide not to apply for admission. Their reasons for taking such a decision have been reported elsewhere (Woodley and McIntosh, 1977). Here we merely note the general increase over the years in the ratio of applications to enquiries. The situation is complicated by re-applicants who will not usually count as 'enquirers', but it does seem that the proportion of 'serious' enquiries is increasing.

Table 1 Enquiries applications, places available and acceptances (1971–78)

	1971	1972	1973	1974	1975	1976	1977	1978
*Enquiries	123,556	77,722	71,757	81,392	109,858	86,433	75,541	87,335
Total applications	43,444	35,182	32,046	35,011	52,537	52,916	49,956	45,293
Applications transferred to computer file	40,817	34,222	30,414	33,220	49,550	50,340	48,234	44,839
Places available	25,000	20,500	17,000	15,000	20,000	17,000	20,000	21,000
Provisionally registered (new) students	24,220	20,501	16,895	14,976	19,823	16,311	19,886	20,882

* This line represents the number of formal written enquiries received in the Admissions Office and does not include contacts made with other University offices nor with Open University students or staff. The figures contain an unquantifiable but not very large number of those who enquire more than once.

The OU has to take into account two factors when deciding how many places are offered in a given year, namely the number of places available and the rate at which applicants decline the offer of a place. The number of places the University has been able to offer from year to year has varied according to the resources made available by the Department of Education and Science, who have usually indicated both the number of students they expect to see admitted in any one year and the total number overall within the University. From 1975 the DES have approved an increased intake at a level of approximately 20,000 which has gone some way towards reducing the backlog of applicants waiting for a place. In 1976 the University reached the permitted plateau of student numbers and had to limit that year's intake. However the intake was raised in 1977 and again in 1978 and this together with the slight decrease in the number of applicants meant that the chance of being offered a place improved during this period. In fact the OU offers many more places than there are available because over a quarter of the places offered in a given year are declined by applicants. The acceptance rates vary from occupation to occupation and region to region and these rates together with the reasons for non-acceptance are documented elsewhere (Woodley, 1978). This over-offering of places meant that only one in three applicants in 1978 were not offered a place at all.

To improve our knowledge about demand we have commissioned year by year a study of the awareness of the Open University among the adult population in the United Kingdom. It is clear that people cannot be expected to apply to an institution if they have not heard of it. Not surprisingly, the level of knowledge in the country as the OU started was quite low among the general population, although higher among the better educated and middle class groups. Over the years the numbers who know of the OU have increased from one in three to over two in three of the population, and in some social class groups it is obvious that saturation point has been reached in 'advertising awareness' terms. The phenomenon that marked the early years of applications – the fact that the middle class and particularly teachers applied earlier and therefore were earlier in the 'first come, first served' queue (McIntosh, Calder and Swift, 1976) – still occurs, but is now less marked, as more people have learnt about the OU and how its admissions system works. Table 2 shows how awareness has increased over the years.

Table 2 The percentage of the population who had heard of the Open University (1971–79)

| Year | Total | Sex | | Social class | | | |
		Male	Female	AB	C_1	C_2	DE
1971	31	33	29	66	50	21	12
1972	40	43	37	78	58	30	22
1973	44	47	42	78	61	38	26
1974	54	58	51	82	71	49	37
*1975	55	60	50	86	70	53	32
1976	45	49	42	68	57	42	29
1977	67	71	63	90	81	63	51
1978	72	76	68	93	85	69	57
1979	70	74	66	92	79	69	54

* The break in the trend between 1975 and 1976 was due to a change in research agency. The research was carried out by Louis Harris Research from 1971–1975 and by Social Surveys (Gallup Poll) Limited from 1976 onwards

The nature of the demand

We turn now to the types of people who were attracted to the Open University and the courses they wished to take. While our basic concern here is with applicants to the OU some of the relevant information is not available for the early years and we have therefore had to use student data. This does not present great problems as the OU's admissions policy ensures that the student profile is very similar to the applicant profile. However there are slight differences which should be borne in mind. For instance, those with low educational qualifications are more likely to decline the offer of a place and therefore form a smaller proportion of students than of applicants.

There has also been a decline in the proportion of women at this stage in some years. This is because women apply predominantly to take Arts or Social Science and are therefore less likely to be offered a place due to course quotas which restrict admission to the most popular courses.

The occupation of applicants

In Table 3 we show the occupations and sex of those who applied to the Open University in 1971, 1974 and 1978. The figures for 1970 have not been included as unfortunately no sex breakdown is available. However, in that first year 36% of all applicants were teachers. This fell to 30% in 1971 and continued to fall so that by 1978 only one in five applicants were in this occupational category. With the national decision to make teaching a graduate profession, and given the large pool of non-graduate teachers remaining in the country, it looks as if teachers will continue to form an important though declining group for many years to come. With the exception of an increase in the retired and unemployed, the rest of the occupational groups show very little change.

The OU has attracted relatively few applicants from 'working class' occupations. Between 1970 and 1975 manual workers increased their share of the applications from 5% to 10% but since then the figures have levelled off and may even be declining. It has to be remembered that the educational opportunities being applied for are at degree-level, opportunities in the UK which are normally only available to a highly selected 10% of school leavers. The barriers to access – educational, financial and cultural – are formidable and unlikely to be overcome by many other than the most able and motivated of people from such disadvantaged backgrounds. These questions have been discussed at greater length elsewhere (McIntosh and Woodley, 1975: McIntosh and Woodley, 1974).

As is clear from Figure 1 the number of women who applied to the OU in the first years was quite low and certainly lower than many people had expected (McIntosh, 1975). However, Table 3 shows that the proportion of women has continued to increase steadily over the years. By no means has all of this increase been in the expected category of 'housewives'. There has been an important increase in the clerical and office group and female teachers continue to form 10% of all applicants whereas the proportion of male teachers has declined. However, the OU has continued to fail to attract female manual workers.

Table 3 Occupational analysis of applicants in 1971, 1974 and 1978

No. of applicants = 100%	1971 34,222			Application year 1974 49,550			1978 41,321		
	Total %	Male %	Female %	Total %	Male %	Female %	Total %	Male %	Female %
Housewives	11.0	0.1	10.9	14.3	0.1	14.2	14.4	0.0	14.4
Armed forces	1.6	1.6	0.0	2.5	2.4	0.1	2.5	2.4	0.1
Administrators & managers	4.6	4.3	0.3	4.3	3.8	0.5	4.6	3.8	0.8
Teachers & lecturers	30.2	19.8	10.4	24.0	13.0	11.0	21.3	11.1	10.2
The professions & the arts	12.6	8.0	4.6	11.1	5.9	5.2	11.9	6.1	5.8
Qualified scientists & engineers	4.4	4.3	0.1	3.1	3.0	0.1	2.9	2.8	0.1
Technical personnel: inc data processing, draughtsmen & technicians	11.9	11.1	0.8	10.0	9.0	1.0	10.2	9.1	1.1
Electrical, electronic, metal & machines, engineering & allied trades	3.0	3.0	0.0	4.0	3.9	0.1	3.7	3.6	0.1
Farming, mining, construction & other manufacturing	2.3	2.2	0.1	3.4	3.2	0.2	2.9	2.7	0.2
Communications & transport: air, sea, road & rail	1.3	1.2	0.1	2.1	1.8	0.3	2.0	1.7	0.3
Clerical & office staff	9.4	5.3	4.1	11.7	4.9	6.8	11.6	4.1	7.5
Shopkeepers, sales, services, sport & recreation workers	4.4	3.8	0.6	5.4	4.5	0.9	5.0	3.9	1.1
Retired, independent means, not working (other than housewives), students	3.1	2.2	0.9	3.9	2.5	1.4	6.9	4.3	2.6
In institutions, e.g. prison, chronic sick, etc.	0.1	0.1	0.0	0.2	0.2	0.0	0.1	0.1	0.0
Total	100.0	67.1	32.9	100.0	58.2	41.8	100.0	55.7	44.3

Previous educational qualifications

In Table 4 we show the educational qualifications held by new students at the time they entered the Open University. Students in recent intakes have tended to have lower qualifications than those in earlier years. For instance, 34% of those who entered in 1978 held no qualifications higher than GCE O-levels compared with only 25% of the 1971 intake. Over the same time period the proportion of students with qualifications which would entitle them to credit exemptions declined from 52% to 44%. However, most of these changes occurred in the first few years and the patterns have been relatively stable for the last four years.

On the face of it, over one-half of new OU students have the qualifications necessary for admission to a full-time degree course. However, it should be remembered that many of these students were 'unqualified' at the time of leaving school. A great number of the teachers, for instance, gained entrance to a College of Education on the basis of their GCE O-levels.

Course choice

Every new Open University student begins by taking one of the foundation courses in Arts, Social Science, Maths, Science or Technology. Students with little or no previous experience of higher education must study two foundation courses before they can graduate, while those with two or more credit exemptions are only permitted to study one. Students can take two foundation courses in their first year or one foundation course plus a half-credit course in elementary maths, but the great majority settle for one foundation course. The actual pattern of course applications over the years is shown in Figure 2. (The figures for 1970 have not been included as the Technology foundation course was not available then.)

The dominant trend has been the decline in applications for the Social Science foundation course. Though the rate of this decline was arrested somewhat in 1975 by the introduction of the new Social Science foundation course D101, this was only temporary. The explanation is not, however, that it is a poor or unattractive course, but the more mechanistic one that it is the course predominantly chosen on entry by teachers and the fall in numbers is very closely correlated with the decline in the number of teachers. The numbers applying for Arts increased initially and is now fairly stable. Many who have no qualifications at all choose the Arts course as their point of entry. The most encouraging sign is the increase in applications both for Science and Maths which appear to have been helped rather than hindered by the introduction of the new Science and Maths foundation courses in the application year 1978.

Table 4 The highest educational qualifications held by entering students (1971–78)

No. of students = 100%	1971	1972	1973	1974	1975	1976	1977	1978
	24,220	20,501	16,895	14,976	19,823	16,311	19,886	20,882
	%	%	%	%	%	%	%	%
No formal educational qualifications	6.8	8.6	9.1	8.5	11.2	10.7	9.3	9.8
CSE, RSA, or school leaving cert. in 1 or more subjects	1.8	3.8	3.8	2.9	3.6	3.3	3.4	3.5
GCE 'O' level, SCE 'O' grade, school cert. or equivalent in 1–4 subjects	5.9	7.6	8.1	8.0	10.2	9.9	9.8	10.2
GCE 'O' level, SCE 'O' grade, school cert. or equivalent in 5 or more subjects	10.8	12.8	12.3	10.8	12.9	12.3	11.5	11.4
GCE 'A' level, SCE 'H' grade higher school cert. or equivalent in 1 subject	3.5	4.2	4.1	4.3	4.7	4.8	5.0	4.9
GCE 'A' level, SCE 'H' grade, higher school cert. or equivalent in 2 or more sub.	9.5	9.3	9.4	10.2	10.8	11.4	11.7	11.7
ONC/OND	3.8	5.1	4.4	3.8	3.8	4.0	4.2	4.2
HNC/HND	10.7	10.6	9.2	7.7	6.7	8.0	7.7	7.6
Teachers cert. or equivalent	28.9	24.0	25.8	27.7	24.6	24.6	25.0	24.9
University dip. or equivalent based on at least one year's full-time study	8.6	7.4	7.1	7.8	7.6	8.1	8.2	7.6
University first degree	4.1	5.3	5.8	6.3	2.7	2.8	3.6	4.1
No information	5.5	1.1	0.9	2.1	1.1	0.3	0.6	0.6

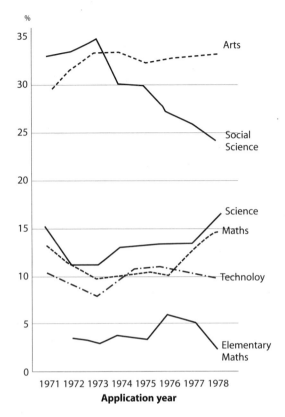

Fig. 2 Course applications 1970–78: percentages.

We do not have information available which separates out course choice by sex, at application stage, but it is clear from the student figures that the early reluctance of women to apply for Science and Maths courses is being gradually overcome, and the increase in Science and Maths applications is likely in some part to have been helped by the increase in the proportion of women applicants to the University. However, Arts is still the most popular course for women and they now outnumber men by two to one on this foundation course.

First year progress

Applicants who accept the offer of a place at the Open University pay a provisional registration fee. After three months study during the 'Provisional Registration' period the new students decide whether to pay the final registration fee which will entitle them to receive teaching materials for the rest of the first year. This decision is made entirely by the student and none are debarred from continuing on academic grounds.

Table 5 The foundation courses taken by men and women (1971–79 intakes)

	1971	1972*	1973*	1974	1975	1976	1977	1978	1979
Base - all students = 100%	6274	5477	5176	4301	6187	4916	6004	6024	6080
Arts	%	%	%	%	%	%	%	%	%
Male	55	48	49	42	38	35	36	32	33
Female	45	52	51	58	62	64	64	68	67
Base - all students = 100%	6188	6689	6156	4886	6395	4801	5747	5846	5728
Social Science	%	%	%	%	%	%	%	%	%
Male	66	59	57	55	52	52	50	48	49
Female	34	41	43	45	48	47	50	52	51
Base - all students = 100%	4778	3827	2701	2099	2960	2475	3039	3613	3559
Maths	%	%	%	%	%	%	%	%	%
Male	89	88	87	82	80	78	79	75	74
Female	11	12	13	17	20	21	21	25	26
Base - all students = 100%	5087	3629	2904	2355	3005	2423	3029	3449	3421
Science	%	%	%	%	%	%	%	%	%
Male	87	81	77	70	72	67	69	67	68
Female	13	19	23	30	28	32	31	33	32
Base - all students = 100%		3319	2663	2238	2202	2632	3071	2837	2905
Technology course not available%		%	%	%	%	%	%	%	%
Male		95	93	92	89	88	90	90	89
Female		5	7	8	11	11	10	10	11

*New and continuing students are included in these figures

In 1971 some 81% of the first intake proceeded to final registration (Table 6). This proportion declined somewhat in the next two years but has since remained remarkably constant at around 75%. These later figures are particularly encouraging given the changes in the student population over this period which were noted earlier.

Table 6 also shows the progress made by students on each of the five foundation courses and here there have been interesting changes over the years. In recent years the final registration rates for Maths, Science and Technology have all improved and in 1978 it was the Social Science foundation course that lost the most students.

Table 6 The proportions of new students who finally registered for each foundation course (1971–78)

	1971 %	1972 %	1973 %	1974 %	1975 %	1976 %	1977 %	1978 %
Total students	80.8	76.7	75.1	75.7	74.8	75.0	75.3	75.0
Arts	80.9	76.5	77.2	77.1	75.5	78.7	78.6	76.2
Social Science	77.6	72.4	76.1	75.5	74.5	71.3	74.0	69.2
Maths	69.2	66.6	62.0	62.4	65.9	68.0	69.7	72.5
Science	74.9	69.2	69.1	73.7	70.1	72.1	70.8	76.3
Technology	–	69.3	69.0	71.9	68.1	72.7	71.3	78.2

The great majority of finally registered new students proceed to gain some course credit at the end of the first year. The actual proportions have varied between 75% and 81% but there have been no clear trends over the years. Those who have taken two courses in their first year have generally passed both or neither of them.

Student performance in second and subsequent years

In Table 7 we show the percentage of students registered in a given year who successfully obtained some course credit. The patterns for each intake were found to be very similar. Performance drops slightly in the second year of study, rises again in the third year and then steadily declines in subsequent years. The greatest proportion of each intake graduates at the end of the third year and this is a possible explanation for the peak in performance at that time. The decline in performance in later years would suggest that the remaining students find it increasingly difficult to cope with their OU studies.

Table 7 The percentage of registered students gaining some course credit in each year of study (1971–74 intakes)

	Year of study							
	1st	2nd	3rd	4th	5th	6th	7th	8th
Intake	%	%	%	%	%	%	%	%
1971	80.0	74.0	79.5	73.5	67.0	64.3	57.7	54.0
1972	75.1	74.8	75.2	70.4	68.2	64.1	57.0	
1973	79.6	71.9	74.0	72.0	69.2	64.9		
1974	80.0	72.4	75.4	71.5	67.5			

Percentages based on the number of finally registered students in each year for each intake

Graduation rates

From the early days the Open University has attracted large numbers of visitors from overseas who want to find out more about this new distance-teaching system. Their questions have varied according to their specialist interests but few left without asking 'What proportion of your students graduate?' It was pointed out to them that no satisfactory answer could be given as the OU's credit system allowed students to take as many years as they wanted to obtain a degree. Ultimately everybody might graduate, it was too soon to say. However, the OU is now in its ninth teaching year and graduation patterns have begun to emerge. We are now in a position to make realistic estimates of eventual graduation rates.

In Table 8 we show the cumulative graduation rates for each of the first six student intakes. By the end of 1978 54% of those who had finally registered as new students in 1971 had obtained an Ordinary degree from the OU. For those students who were awarded two or three credit exemptions it was possible to graduate after two years of study and almost nine hundred managed to do so. The third year marked the peak with 3,318 obtaining a degree. Students continued to graduate in subsequent years but in decreasing numbers. When the cumulative graduation rates are plotted as a graph in Figure 3 it can be seen that the curve is beginning to flatten out and although extrapolations are always dangerous, it appears that the final graduation rate for the first intake of students will be slightly over 55%.

Table 8 The cumulative proportions of Open University students graduating over time

	Year of entry to the Open University					
	1971	1972	1973	1974	1975	1976
Base – all finally registered students = 100%	19581	15719	12680	1 1336	14830	12227
	%	%	%	%	%	%
Graduated by:						
1972	4.6					
1973	21.5	2.0				
1974	35.0	16.6	2.0			
1975	43.4	27.7	16.6	1.9		
1976	49.8	36.3	28.4	16.8	1.5	
1977	52.7	43.4	36.8	27.9	13.8	1.4
1978	54.3	46.8	43.5	35.0	22.5	12.8

The graduation rates for the second and subsequent intakes have been very similar to each other but somewhat lower than those for the first intake. This is shown graphically in Figure 3 where we have plotted the cumulative graduation rates for the second, third and fourth intakes.

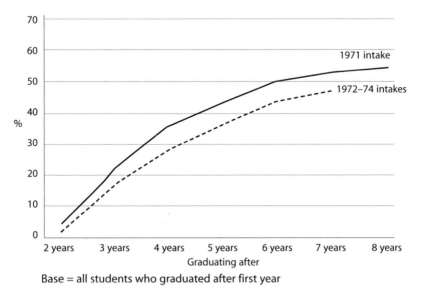

Base = all students who graduated after first year

Figure 3 The cumulative proportions of Open University students graduating over time

From the evidence presented earlier in this paper, the slowing down of graduation rates was only to be expected. Changes in the student population, such as the declining number of teachers, have meant that fewer people enter the OU with credit exemptions and we also know that, on average, students are attempting fewer course credits per year. This results in a slower 'through-put' of students and hopefully the final graduation rates for later intakes will be at least as high as those for earlier ones. At the moment we can only say that it seems that at least 50% of each intake will eventually graduate.

While the factors outlined above may account for a general slowing down of graduation rates, they are unlikely to explain the markedly superior performance of the first intake. In the absence of other evidence one is tempted to suggest that here was a group with a particularly high motivation to succeed. They were the ones at the head of the queue to join the new institution and they were very much in the public eye as the 'experiment' was observed with great interest by the media.

We can now look at graduation rates among certain sub-groups of the student population. As the OU operates an open admission policy one obvious area of interest is that of prior educational qualifications. Did the OU provide a real opportunity for those students who did not possess the entry requirements for a conventional degree course? In Figure 4 we have plotted the cumulative graduation rates for students from the 1971 intake both with and without the normal degree entry requirements. Those in the 'qualified' group graduated much faster in the first few years but then the rates began to level off. By the end of 1978 62% of them had graduated. Among the 'unqualified' group graduation rates picked up in later years and by 1978 40% had obtained a degree. As the 'unqualified' students were unlikely to have any credit exemptions, this pattern was to be expected. However, as the two curves are now almost parallel it seems unlikely that the 'unqualified' will catch up with the 'qualified' group. Nevertheless four out of ten of those students who, judging by the educational qualifications, were not 'university material' had obtained a degree.

In Figure 5 we compare the progress of men and women from the 1971 intake. In the early years men graduated slightly faster than women. However, by the end of 1978 women had overtaken the men with 62% having graduated compared with 52%. This pattern seems to be repeating itself among later intakes.

There is great variation in graduation rates between the fourteen occupational categories used by the OU. In Figure 6 we show the cumulative graduation rates for students from the 1971 intake in just four of these categories. The teachers fared best and around seven out of ten are likely to graduate. Housewives graduated at a slower rate in the early years but the proportion who eventually graduate is unlikely to be far below the figure achieved by teachers. Among the clerical and office workers, slightly over

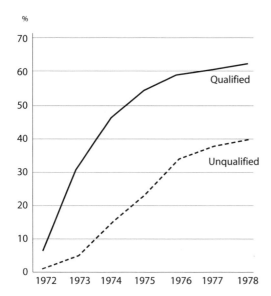

* A 'qualified' student is one who holds two GCE A-levels
or their eqivalent, or some higher qualification.
Base = all finally registered students in 1971

Figure 4 The cumulative proportions of 'qualified' and 'unqualified' Open
University students from the 1971 intake graduating over time)

Base = all finally registered students in 1971

Figure 5 The cumulative proportions of men and women from the 1971
intake graduating over time

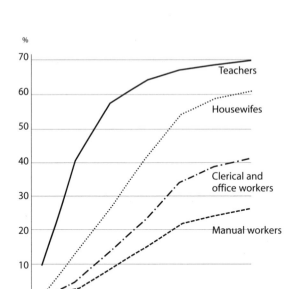

%

Base = all finally registered students in 1971

Figure 6 The cumulative proportions of Open University students from the 1971 intake in selected occupational categories graduating over time

four out of ten are likely to graduate. The picture is least encouraging for manual workers. Although small numbers of them continue to graduate it is unlikely that more than three out of ten will eventually gain a degree.

The Open University has now produced almost thirty-three thousand graduates with ordinary degrees. Over six thousand of this group did not possess the entry qualifications for a conventional degree course at the time they began their OU studies. Each year between five and a half and six thousand new graduates are added to the total. This means that of all the first degrees awarded each year in the United Kingdom, around one in twelve are from the OU.

Many of the OU graduates have proceeded to study for an Honours degree with the OU. To obtain an Honours degree a student has to gain eight credits, two of which must be at third or fourth level. By the end of 1978 one in ten of the 1971 intake had gained such a degree but the final figure is likely to be much higher than this as the numbers awarded each year are still rising. All we can say at the moment is that the OU has already produced over four thousand Honours graduates in total.

Patterns of 'dormancy' and 're-entry' among Open University students

Students who have finally registered with the OU in their first year of study are entitled to re-enter in any subsequent year without negotiating the normal admissions procedure. Thus while there were 58,788 students registered on courses in May 1978 there were also over 40,000 'dormant' students who were not currently studying with the OU. A small proportion of these students were Honours graduates but the great majority were people who in theory might resume their OU studies in some future year. For planning purposes it is important to know what proportion of this group is likely to re-enter the OU. We approach this problem by looking at the registration patterns of 1971 entrants up to 1977.

For some 84% of the 1971 entrants their study with the OU could be described as 'continuous'. That is, at no stage did they resume their studies after one or more rest years. The actual numbers of years of continuous study undertaken by this group are shown in Table 9. We turn now to the 16% who studied 'discontinuously' and Table 9 also shows rest periods taken at some point between 1971 and 1977. Among this group, the most common pattern was to have one study-free year. Some students did return after a gap of four or five years but they were comparatively few in number.

Table 9 Patterns of continuous and discontinuous study among the first intake of Open University students (1971–77)

Finally registered students in 1971 who studied:

Continuously		Discontinuously	
16,402		3,179	
%		%	
Period of continuous study		*Rest year patterns*	
First year only	27	Single rest period of 1 year	66
2 years	9	' ' ' 2 years	16
3 years	12	' ' ' 3 years	8
4 years	13	' ' ' 4 years	3
5 years	11	' ' ' 5 years	1
6 years	11	Two or more rest periods	
7 years	16	of at least one year	6

The present evidence would therefore suggest that the great majority of students do not take rest years but study continuously until they have obtained their Ordinary degree or until they have studied as many courses as they want. Some students do take rest years, often before proceeding from an Ordinary to an Honours degree, but they are unlikely to take more than two years off from their studies. However, just as successive intakes are attempting fewer credits each year, it may prove to be the case that a higher proportion will elect to take rest years. Even if the proportion remains the same, it does mean that the number of students who are returning to the OU studies after a gap of one year or more will continue to increase at least for a number of years.

Student workload

Each course offered by the Open University represents one full credit or one half credit. Students can take up to a maximum of two credits per year through any combination of full and half credit courses. In their first year students must register for one full credit foundation course but in subsequent years the minimum requirement is one half credit course. In Table 10 we show the number of credits attempted by students from 1973 to 1978.

It is clear that students are now attempting fewer courses than in earlier years. In 1973 only 4% were attempting a single half credit course but by 1978 this had risen to 15%. Conversely the proportion taking the equivalent of two full credits declined from 10% to 3% over the same period.

Table 10 The number of course credits attempted by Open University students (1973–78)

	1973	1974	1975	1976	1977	1978
Base – all registered* students = 100%	38,424	42,636	49,358	51,035	55,127	58,788
	%	%	%	%	%	%
Number of course credit attempted						
Half	4.0	8.3	11.1	13.6	14.6	15.4
One	74.0	73.0	73.1	72.4	73.1	73.6
One and a half	11.5	11.3	9.4	8.8	8.3	7.5
Two	10.5	7.5	6.1	5.2	4.0	3.4

*In the case of new students this means finally registered.

This decline in the number of credits attempted, coupled with the fact that students are now slightly less likely to successfully complete a given course, means that students are accumulating credits at a slower rate. As we see in the next section, student survival rates do not seem to have been affected but what has happened is that students are moving more slowly through the system. In part the OU has become the victim of its own success in attracting more students with low educational qualifications. As they have no credit exemptions these students have to study for more course credits to graduate and at the same time they seem less willing or able to take on a high workload in any one year.

'Student survival'

As a final indicator of student progress we look at 'student survival' patterns as measured by the percentage of finally registered new students who registered for OU courses in subsequent years. In Figure 7 we have plotted the 'survival curve' for the 1971–75 intakes up until registration in 1978. (This method does not allow for discontinuous study patterns but, as we have seen, these were relatively infrequent.) The survival rates for the five intakes were almost identical. Slightly over one-half of the students registered for courses in their fourth year and less than one in five were still studying by the eighth year.

For a complete picture we need to couple 'survival' rates with graduation data. We therefore conclude this section by summarising the progress up until 1979 registration of those who finally registered in 1971 (Table 11). Some 12% were still taking courses in 1979 of whom over one-half had already obtained an Ordinary degree and were aiming for an Honours degree. The majority of those who were not studying had already graduated and 10% of all students had gained an Honours degree. Only 41% of the first intake appear to have given up any plans to graduate, at least for the present.

Table 11 The status of students from the 1971 intake as at February 1979

	Finally registered students in 1971
Base – all students = 100%	19,581
	%
Still studying: Ordinary graduate	7
Non-graduate	5
Not studying: Honours graduate	10
Ordinary graduate	37
Non-graduate	41

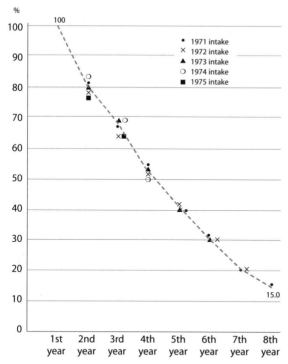

Figure 7 Survival curve for the 1971–75 intakes up until 1978

Conclusions

We have shown in this paper that the basic beliefs held by the Open University's founders have proved to be true. There was a great demand for degree-level studies among working adults and this demand has continued as evidenced by the application figures over the years. The information on student performance has also demonstrated that great numbers of people can study successfully at a distance. Every year three out of four admitted students proceed to final registration and over eight out of ten who do so gain some course credit. Approximately one-half of all finally registered students will eventually graduate.

Now that the Open University has established its credentials it must concentrate its efforts on becoming more 'open'. While its early years saw some increase in the proportions of students with low educational qualifications and in the manual trades, little progress has been made since then. Also those students from 'disadvantaged' groups who were attracted have found it more difficult to cope with the demands of OU study. There are no easy solutions to these problems but the tasks which face the OU over the second eight years are clear. We hope to return to these topics in a later paper.

References

CALDER, J. and McINTOSH, N. E. (1974) Student Drop-outs Wastage and Withdrawal – some problems of comparison between the Open University and other educational institutions, in *Higher Education Review*, Autumn, pp. 61–68.

McINTOSH, N. E. (1975) Women and the Open University, in *Women in Higher Education*, University of London Teaching Methods Unit.

McINTOSH, N. E., CALDER, J. and SWIFT, B. (1976) *A Degree of Difference – A study of the first year's intake to the Open University of the United Kingdom*, London: Society for Research into Higher Education; New York: Praeger (1977).

McINTOSH, N. E. and MORRISON, V. (1974) Student Demand, Progress and Withdrawal – the Open University's first four years, in *Higher Education Review*, Autumn, pp. 37–60.

McINTOSH, N. E. and WOODLEY, A. (1974) 'The Open University and Second Chance Education – an analysis of the social and educational background of Open University students', in *Paedagogica Europaea*, Vol. X, October, pp. 85–100.

McINTOSH, N. E. and WOODLEY, A. (1975) 'Excellence, Equality and the Open University', paper presented at 3rd International Conference on Higher Education, University of Lancaster, September, 1975.

OPEN UNIVERSITY (1979a) *The Open University BA Degree Handbook*, Milton Keynes: The Open University Press.

OPEN UNIVERSITY (1979b) *The Open University Courses Handbook*, Milton Keynes: The Open University Press.

OPEN UNIVERSITY PLANNING COMMITTEE (1969) *The Open University*: Report of the Planning Committee to the Secretary of State for Education and Science, London: HMSO.

PERRY, W. (1976) *The Open University – a personal account*, Milton Keynes: The Open University Press.

The Times Educational Supplement (1966) Leader, 4 March.

WOODLEY, A. (1978) *Applicants who decline the offer of a place at the Open University*, in mimeograph, the Open University.

WOODLEY, A. and McINTOSH, N. E. (1977) 'People who decide not to apply to The Open University', in *Teaching at a Distance*, No. 9, pp. 18–26.

The OU attempts to combine equality and excellence. It does this by having an open door policy, so anybody can enrol, but carefully monitored academic standards so that its degrees are comparable to those from other universities. An inevitable consequence is student drop out. In this paper Naomi addresses the problems and suggests necessary changes to the educational system.

Open Admission – an open or revolving door?[5]

The commitment of the Open University to opening up access to higher education is well known. It is exemplified in the following quotations.

We took it as axiomatic that no formal academic qualifications would be required for registration as a student. Anyone could try his or her hand, *and only failure to progress adequately would be a bar to continuation of studies* (Report of the Planning Committee, 1966).

We are open, first, as to people. Not for us the carefully regulated escalation from one educational level to the next by which the traditional universities establish their criteria for admission (Crowther, 1969).

The Open University demolished, at a stroke, the long tradition of regulated academic selection. Perhaps it is too soon for the full impact of this act to have been felt. Thousands of students who had not previously been selected, for whatever reason for higher education, are showing conclusively that they can study at degree level. But at the same time thousands cannot, and are leaving their studies. What does open admission involve and how open, educationally, can the Open University be?

America advanced earlier towards the expansion of opportunities in higher education, and 'open-door' admission to public supported colleges is widespread. The principle of equal opportunity in America requires that all who want to try should have access to higher education. Great Britain is very far from that stage, nor by any means do all the British agree on it as a goal. Of course, the base on which higher education builds in America is very different to that in Great Britain. A recent survey quotes 75% of American 18 year olds as still in school compared with 45% in Sweden and only 20% in Great Britain (International Association for the Evaluation of Educational

5. McIntosh, N. E. (1975) Open Admission – an open or revolving door? *Universities Quarterly*, Spring 1975, pp. 171-81.

Achievement, 1973). But American experience has shown that the extension of opportunity does not ensure that the opportunities are taken. The extension, in particular, of 'open-door' admission has not adequately increased the proportion of minority groups continuing on to and remaining in higher education. Certain factors militate against minority groups being able to take advantage 'equally' with majority groups of opportunities opened to them. This situation is not restricted solely to American higher education as an OECD report *Group Disparities in Educational Participation and Achievement*, Vol. IV (1971) shows. Within their member countries they see much of the selection of students for higher education taking place before the final, decisive school examinations are taken—for the students reaching eligibility to sit those exams are mainly members of the upper ranks of society. Crosland (1971) provided a cogent summary of the barriers to minority access to higher education in the United States. He discussed the testing barrier, the barrier of poor preparation, the money barrier, the distance barrier, the motivation barrier and the racial barrier. The majority of these also apply to working class students in Great Britain. Even the racial barrier may well become significant in Britain over the next decade as more second generation immigrants become qualified for and expect access to higher education as of right.

The problem has become acute in America because the great expansion in higher education in recent years has taken place in those institutions where the drop-out rate is highest, and these are also the institutions which are unselective. Newman (1971) makes this point forcibly and his figures are reproduced here (Table 1).

Table 1: Variation in graduation rates according to selectivity of institutions

Type of institution	% of students graduating within four years at initial institution	% graduating within 10 years at same institution
Fifteen most selective private universities	80–85	90–95
Large state universities	35–45	60–70
State colleges	15–25	35–50
Public junior colleges	20–25*	15–30†

* Graduation from the two year programme in a two year period.
† Graduation with a four year degree after transfer.

In Britain the selective nature of the educational system means that the process is more like that found in the most selective private universities in the United States. The rigorous admissions procedures employed by conventional universities, in effect, screen in only those who are likely to succeed. At such institutions 'dropping out' occurs effectively, before admission. The majority of people never have the chance to 'drop-in'. But the expansion of opportunities in Britain together with the current slackening in demand for places is leading to less rigorous admissions criteria particularly in some subject areas. UCCA, for example, reporting the range of acceptable qualifications for the different courses within their 'clearing' system indicated that the engineering, technology and science courses in general were accepting the equivalent of a 'C' and a 'D' in 1971 but by 1972 had dropped their minimum to a 'D' and an 'E' (UCCA, 1972–3). The more popular Arts and Social Science courses continued to require higher qualifications than these. Many of the innovative CNAA degree programmes at polytechnics only demand the minimum requirements necessary for a mandatory grant, i.e. two 'A' levels of any grade. The CNAA is also prepared to accept the ONC and OND as suitable degree entry requirements, though, in fact, the numbers of those entering for science and technology courses with an ONC or OND are decreasing (21% in 1969/70 compared to 14% in 1972/73). In the arts and social sciences a very high percentage of entrants (96% in 1969/70, 91% in 1972/73) hold 'A' level qualifications. There are supposedly no rigid requirements for a CNAA degree course as their Annual Report for 1970 stated: 'The Council has always made it perfectly clear that it is prepared to be flexible on the admission of students to courses leading to its degrees' (CNAA, 1970). This is of particular help to unqualified 'mature' students.

Apart from the Open University, selection is the rule rather than the exception in Great Britain. The wastage rate of 13% quoted by the UGC (University Grants Committee) (1971) is similar to that given in the table quoted above for selective private universities in America (Newman, 1971).

Evidence from polytechnics is less easy to come by. Since many of them are by no means as selective as conventional universities, but do still select by 'A' levels, in itself a formidable selection device, one might expect their rate to come somewhere between the private universities and the large state universities in America.

The clear implication of extending access is that it increases drop-out. Without entering the arena of 'more means worse', and preferring the alternative thesis of 'more means different' (Ashby, 1973) it is still necessary to answer the possible charge of irresponsibility in apparently offering people an opportunity which is not in fact a genuine one. If large numbers of students who enter an 'open' door discover that it is in reality a 'revolving' door and all that they are doing is entering it in order to be carried round and out again, then both the educational institution *and* society could be held to have erred.

Newman (1971) commented on this dilemma in the following words:

In interpreting these findings, we *can* assume that society fulfils its obligations simply by providing the opportunity for as many people as possible to enter college. Success cannot and should not be guaranteed. High drop-out rates are not inconsistent with our commitment to broad access, but rather reflect the maintenance of rigorous academic standards and our insistence that a college degree represents real achievement. *Or* we can assume that society's obligation (and its own self-interest as well) is to provide more than just the chance to walk through the college gate. There must also be access to a useful and personally significant educational experience.

These two assumptions are not, of course, mutually exclusive. Some perfectly competent students choose to drop out for valid reasons which are not academic in nature. Some students should never have entered college in the first place. And colleges vary in the strategy that they adopt in dealing with the problem.

Clark (1960) in a classic study of one open-door college analysed the same dilemma over a decade ago. He noted:

A major problem of democratic society is the inconsistency between encouragement to achieve and the reality of limited opportunity. Democracy asks individuals to act as if social mobility were universally possible; status is to be won by individual effort, and rewards accrue to those who try. But democratic societies also need selective training institutions, and hierarchical work organizations permit increasingly fewer people to succeed at ascending levels. Situations of opportunity are also situations of denial and failure.

Equality of opportunity, narrowly interpreted, could be taken to mean selection according to ability without regard to any extraneous considerations. In theory, this is the British system. In America, it is popularly interpreted to mean 'unlimited access to some form of college', and as Cheek (1971) commented 'America has been committed in principle to universal access to higher education for some time'. To deny access to college is therefore to deny equal opportunity.

Provided resources are available, society can then fulfil its obligations simply by making enough initial places available for all who want them. What happens after that is, arguably, not its affair. Thus the conflict is moved into the institution itself. But higher education, while responding to external pressures for wider admission is also subject to other pressures. In particular, academic standards must be maintained. It is vital both to the academic faculty and to external educationalists and laymen that standards of performance and graduation are equivalent to other comparable institutions. Indeed the students themselves would be done a disservice if this were otherwise. Clark (1960) commented:

The conflict between open-door admission and performance of high quality often means a wide discrepancy between the hopes of entering students, and the means of their realization.

While a few students who show little initial promise are successful, many are inevitably faced with standards well beyond them. Their rejection instead of taking place at the admissions stage, takes place within the college. This places the onus fairly and squarely on the institution which has to make difficult choices about how rejection is accomplished. Clark (1960) distinguished between two types of response—a 'hard' response and a 'soft' response. The 'hard' response is found in the state university which accepts the policy of broad admission, but then protects its standards by weeding out the incompetent in the first year. As many as one third may have to drop out in the course of the first year, and their failure is psychologically and academically more destructive than if they had never commenced the course. Additionally there is the financial cost involved which is also great, and the possible negative cost to other students who may have been de-barred from entry. The alternative, delineated by Clark (1960), is the 'soft' response where an institution does not dismiss a student, but provides him with an alternative course. He may be counselled on to an easier field of study, or on to more vocational studies. The provision of such an alternative is obviously more constructive for the student, but it is costly and requires either that an institution provides a wide range of courses at a variety of levels, or that there is easy transferability between institutions. How the person being disappointed is handled by those responsible for the disappointment is critical.

Clark's thesis is that educational institutions perform a 'cooling out' function for society. Students who are failing or barely passing have to have their expectations disappointed. This is not only difficult for the students, but difficult for the persons in the institutions who have to do the disappointing. An institution cannot fulfil its 'cooling-out' function adequately without a degree of concealment. Obviously if all students were to understand the function, they would be unlikely to continue to apply to study at the institution. So it is necessary for other successful functions to be highlighted instead. Clark (1960) comments 'the other side of cooling-out is the successful performance in junior college of students who did poorly in high school or who have overcome socio-economic handicaps, for they are drawn into higher education rather than taken out of it'.

What is the relevance of this experience for Great Britain, and in particular for the Open University? In the halcyon days of the late 60s when the binary policy had just been adumbrated, polytechnics were seen to be the new comprehensive institutions of higher education. Within one polytechnic it was envisaged that students would find available a range of provision of educational courses of a wide variety and at different levels. A good student starting on an HND might move on to a CNAA degree. A student struggling on an Honours degree might transfer to an Ordinary degree or change from full-time study on an HND to part-time on an HNC. This was indeed a rational and constructive proposal, particularly for the individuals concerned who otherwise might have entirely wasted their study time so far.

In practice this ideal has not been reached in many polytechnics and nor indeed are many still striving to achieve it. Lower level courses are being seen rather as the function of technical colleges and many polytechnics are reducing their involvement in part-time courses. Burgess and Pratt (1974) in their recent study comment on this. 'A quite clear trend of the polytechnics has been to become less comprehensive in the most important ways. The substantial growth of full-time and sandwich advanced students has been at the expense not only of non-advanced students, as the policy implied, but of other groups, not implied in the policy. Part-time students are struggling to retain their position in the colleges, and those on HNC courses are steadily being shed.' As their increase in advanced work has been at degree level (from just under 15,000 students in 1965/66 to nearly 25,000 students in 1968/69) and the decline has been in part-time and National Diploma and Certificate courses, the polytechnics are seen as suffering, perhaps deliberately, from 'social academic drift' excluding more working class students as the choice in *level* of courses decreases. If the early ideal had been achieved, the polytechnics would have been the best able of all British institutions to provide opportunities for mass higher education. This was clearly what Crosland envisaged in his Woolwich speech (1965). 'There is an ever increasing need and demand for vocational, professional and industrially-based courses in higher education—at full-time degree level, at full-time just below degree level, at part-time advanced level and so on...In our view it requires a separate sector with a separate tradition and outlook within the higher education system.' Their admissions criteria, already wider than universities, could have been wider still, and institutions would have been able to provide a range of opportunities at a variety of levels such that the cooling-out function in so far as it had to be performed could have been done 'softly', and as constructively as possible.

Instead, ironically, it is an institution located initially at degree level *only* which has had the task laid on it, and indeed has accepted the task, of expanding educational opportunity. The O.U. demands no educational qualifications at all. Not only has it denied to itself the possibility of selection, it also has ruled out by its philosophy many of the features that institutions have conventionally used as an aid to 'cooling-out'. The O.U. cannot currently provide alternative, but lower status avenues of achievement. Since it is based on voluntary independent learning, it would be inconsistent with this principle to cause students to *have* to be in touch with counsellors empowered to exercise a role in the cooling-out process. Contact with counselling and tutorial staff is entirely voluntary.

The strategy adopted by the O.U. does not fit easily into the hard/soft dichotomy outlined by Clark (1960). Nor indeed was it designed to do so. It has behind it one guiding principle—that of providing 'independent learners' with as much information as possible on which to base their decisions, but having done so, to leave decisions about the continuation of their studies up to them. To this end, the first year of students' studies starts with a provisional registration period designed to allow them an opportunity to test out the course and its materials, to see if it is suitable for their needs, and if they can fit it in with their lives. During this time, they have access to counselling advice and tutorial help if they wish it. More important though is the fact that the University has built in a system of continuous assessment. Marks from tutors and computer-marked assignments completed throughout the year are conflated with an exam mark, and on some courses a summer school assessment as well. Students, in addition to their subjective reactions to the course, have an early opportunity to see what sort of grades they are getting. Some, of course, withdraw without completing any assignments. Summer school with its opportunity to meet and make more direct comparisons with other students provides another occasion for reappraisal, as does the decision to actually sit the exam. Many students make their own decision to withdraw during the course of the year. This shows up particularly at exam stage, when a very high proportion of those with low continuous assessment grades, although still registered as students, 'cool themselves out' and choose not to turn up to sit the exam.

Thus it could be postulated that the strategy employed by the O.U. does inadvertently fulfil the same 'cooling out' function, but 'softly'. Arguably, it does it in a more acceptable way, since the student may gradually realise for himself that he is likely to fail, and choose of his own accord to withdraw himself from the system. The responsibility is shifted from the institution to the student. However, it must be said, that the strategy was not settled on with any of these considerations in mind! It was seen to be more constructive for adult students than traditional final examinations.

At the end of the day the Open University, of its own structure, has no option but to adopt a 'hard' response. Given that it has been set up within an educational system where parity of esteem and parity of standards are desired both by students and faculty alike, then academic standards at some point have to be met. Since the University has adopted a credit structure with equal weight for credits, then effectively standards have to be set at the termination of the first credit. So we return to the words quoted at the start of this paper.

Anyone could try his or her hand, and only failure to progress adequately would be a bar to continuation of studies (Report of the Planning Committee, 1966).

The open door into the Open University is an open door into the foundation courses, and students can re-enter and retake foundation courses as many times as they wish. But for those who fail or are not suitable, the University does not have an infrastructure of alternative courses available. Neither are suitable courses always available through the rest of the educational system since by definition, many students who have chosen the O.U. have chosen it because conventional educational institutions for a variety of reasons cannot meet their needs.

In the short-term, the O.U. must rely on and work with the rest of further and adult education to provide alternative opportunities. In the long run provided resources are forthcoming it is likely to wish to extend its own provision to complement these opportunities in order to meet the needs of a wider variety of students as constructively as possible. It must ensure that the initial opportunity provided for these students is a continuing opportunity and that the open door does not turn out to be a revolving door.

Until that time comes, the O.U. will continue to be faced with the dilemma posed by open admission. Society's needs are apparently being met, students are apparently being given an opportunity—but for many it is not a real opportunity.

One final point is worth commenting on.

There is clearly a great and continuing demand for open admission to the O.U. from adult students which the university is attempting to meet within available resources. The suggestion that the O.U. should also accept conventional qualified school leavers was made arising from a letter from the Department of Education and Science (August 12th, 1970).

'The government wish, however, in the context of their continuing examination of public expenditure, to consider, in consultation with the university authorities...the contribution that it can make to the development of higher education provision in the future.'

The suggestion of the then government was that the O.U. should admit a group of 'qualified' 18-year-olds. The current experiment has not taken the form of the original proposal, and some unqualified 18–21-year-olds are being admitted alongside the qualified ones. Even the qualified ones tend to have good non-academic reasons for not going to conventional institutions, and not to be immediate school-leavers. As long as the demand from under-21s is voluntary, demand for an additional opportunity, the dilemma may be kept in abeyance. At such time as demand becomes enforced demand, when no alternative opportunities for higher education are available, then the danger that the O.U. may be used by society to perform a 'cooling out' role will be great.

And current forecasts of the demand from school-leavers may well be too low. The full impact of comprehensive reorganisation and ROSLA has not yet been felt. The most recent bulge of births, building up to 1964, will hit higher education at the end of the decade. Recent DES figures show that the proportion of school-leavers with two or more 'A' levels has risen from 11.8% in 1961–2 to 20.1% in 1971–72. The number of other children who got two 'A' levels in *further* education increased over the decade from 3,000 to 11,000.

If current forecasts are wrong and demand for higher education increases, the pressure put on the O.U. to meet it, if only for a temporary period, will be great. The O.U. might be put in the position of *apparently* providing opportunities which, for many, were not genuine or continuing, or might effectively be only second best for those who were forced to utilise them.

The Open University is, of course, technically well placed to perform a cooling out function effectively, but currently only by adopting a hard response—and this is not the most constructive for students. We can assume that demand for open admission in Britain is likely to increase rather than decrease. The current debate about the admission of more mature students to conventional universities is only the tip of this iceberg.

As new sectors of higher education tackle the problem of open admission, the educational system as a whole will have to face up to the necessity for the provision of genuine alternatives at different levels. The question then will be how can such alternatives best be provided. Should they be within an institution or within a range of institutions cooperating with each other? One likely implication for Britain will be an increased demand for transferability of credit. Added pressure for this is likely to come from the Diploma of Higher Education, if it really gets off the ground. But the tradition of university academic autonomy dies hard, and many institutions are reluctant to allow students to transfer *between* courses, let alone to accept students transferring from other institutions with any advanced standing. Cooperation on structure and syllabi is likely to be particularly hard for polytechnics who are just flexing their academic muscles having gained a degree of independence through the CNAA.

But any genuine extension of open admission, particularly if it involves mature students, will have to allow for people who need to move from one institution to another for a variety of reasons. It is no longer adequate for institutions to deal with this problem independently. It is a luxury that neither the country nor potential students can afford. A concerted attack across the board, both in higher and further education, is called for. Until such time many students will discover that the open door is simply a revolving door.

References

ASHBY, E. (1973) 'The structure of higher education: A world view', *Higher Education*, Vol. 2, No. 2, May 1973: Elsevier.

BURGESS, T. and PRATT, J. (1974) *Polytechnics: a report*, London: Pitman.

CHEEK, J. E. (1971) Foreword to *Minority Access to College*: Ford Foundation Report by F. E. CROSSLAND, New York: Schocken Books.

CLARK, B. (1960) 'The "cooling-out" function in higher education', *American Journal of Sociology*, Vol. LXV, No. 6, University of Chicago, May 1960.

CNAA (1969–73) *Annual Reports of the CNAA*.

CROSLAND, A. (1965) Speech at the Woolwich Polytechnic by Secretary of State for Education and Science.

CROSSLAND, F. E. (1971) *Minority Access to College*: Ford Foundation Report, New York: Schocken Books.

LORD CROWTHER (1969) From the inaugural address on the occasion of the Charter Ceremony, July 23rd, 1969, reproduced in the Open University Prospectus 1971.

HMSO (1971) *U.G.C. Statistics of Education*, London: HMSO.

INTERNATIONAL ASSOCIATION FOR THE EVALUATION OF EDUCATIONAL ACHIEVEMENT (1973) *Survey of International Educational Attainment and Achievement*.

NEWMAN, F. (1971) *Report on Higher Education*, Washington: U.S. Government Printing Office.

OECD (1971) *Group Disparities in Educational Participation and Achievement*, Conference on Policies for Educational Growth, Vol. IV.

The Planning Committee Report (1966) *Report of the Planning Committee for the Open University to the Secretary of State for Education and Science*, London: HMSO.

UCCA (1972, 1973) *Annual Reports of the UCCA.*

There have been several references to the government pressure on the OU to admit 18-year-olds. The experiment that became known as 'The Younger Students Pilot Scheme' was comprehensively evaluated from within the Survey Research Department. The results are detailed in the book The door stood open *and show that, on the whole, the OU was not a popular option for school-leavers and that the progress of younger students within the OU was relatively poor.*

However, here I want to include an extract from Chapter 9 'Younger students who persisted with their OU studies'. The chapter was written by Naomi and was based on the transcripts of face-to-face interviews with twenty successful younger students. In its entirety it shows a researcher who is comfortable with qualitative data and who is skilled at pulling out telling quotes. Here there is only space for the conclusions.

The door stood open: an evaluation of the Open University younger students pilot scheme[6]

These interviews although small in number are rich in information. Several important themes emerged, some expected and some unexpected, which shed further light on the question of younger student performance at the Open University.

Very few of the students had failed academically at school. Several had A-levels, while the majority had numerous O-levels but had not gone on to take A-levels. Those who had actually failed exams at school could point to external causes and did not regard themselves as failures. Some students had got onto the wrong educational track, taking the wrong subjects at A-level or ending up in the wrong institution. Others had left school early because they had got married, were pregnant, had had enough of school or had simply not considered the possibility of more education. What many of them did share was a dislike of, and a disillusionment with, the conventional education system. Several of them resented being shunted along the expected route through O- and A-levels to university. The OU for them, then, repre-

---

6 Woodley, A and McIntosh, N. E. (1980) *The door stood open*, Lewes: Falmer Press, pp 246-248

sented a conscious choice to opt back in but on their own terms. It gave them the chance to study while continuing with their lives: their family life, their working life or indeed, for a small number, their other educational life. The OU was not offering them 'second best' but rather exactly what they wanted.

Not surprisingly, those who had survived that far were aiming for a 'degree' and the possession of a degree was very important to them. They were able to be philosophical about the length of time it would take, noting however that many younger students were in more of a hurry, and the length of time to get an OU degree was for them a deterrent. Similarly, few of the surviving students appeared to care about whether their degree was specialist or general in nature. They had been able to chop and change their areas of interest as they themselves developed and matured, and had found enough to interest them within the wide range of courses offered by the OU. Presumably those who sought greater specialisation figured more highly among those who had left to continue their studies elsewhere, or had indeed dropped out. Certainly some of the highly motivated students following two educational programmes at the same time had decided to drop the OU rather than their other one. Very few had been able to continue both successfully.

Apart from their self-evident interest in their studies, what other factors appeared to contribute to their success? One very important one appeared to be their family environment. Many students were encouraged to apply by parents, or by their spouses and the majority had continued to have a family which was supportive of their studies. Not only were they living in an intellectually stimulating academic or professional atmosphere, but they were usually actively supported by their family, who shared their academic values. At minimum, the family was not actively opposed to their studies. Those few, particularly the less qualified single men, who did not have this intellectually supportive environment, were noticeably struggling.

Many people had assumed that younger students would feel the need for personal contact more and be more concerned about access to study centres and tutorial and counselling facilities. This was not true of successful students who after their foundation courses made little use of these resources, not so much because they did not wish to but because they were not able to. They were similarly able to survive without regular access to TV and radio. Undoubtedly the less organised and less secure students who were unable to obtain access to study centres or the media would have suffered because of this.

Perhaps the most important thing which emerged was what can only be described as an 'ability to cope'. As we have seen, younger students were at a stage in their lives when their work or family circumstances were likely to change dramatically within a short space of time. Finance was also a problem. For many younger students these pressures were too great and they dropped out, as we showed in Chapter Eight. It became clear from these interviews that successful students were not free from these pressures, but were able to cope with them better. They appeared to have done this by keeping their studies with the OU in perspective. They were philosophical about them and did not let them dominate their lives. Many of them had accepted that there was a hierarchy of priorities in their lives, and that the OU came pretty low on that list. With this acceptance came the ability to keep 'cool' about their studies, letting their level of work fluctuate, dropping it when they were under pressure, but not panicking when this happened. They had developed to a fine art what one student described as an 'organised capacity to work in small bites'. They preferred to study at a low level to keep in touch, even if this meant failing the odd course, rather than drop out. To adopt such a strategy successfully required that they had enough ability to cope with the course academically. There was a small number who although they were still studying had not been able to gain any credits after foundation level. There were usually good external reasons to explain this, but possibly these students were also academically weaker. What distinguished these academic failures from those who had actually dropped out appeared to be the characteristic labelled by one student as stubbornness.

Trying to make comparisons between those who were successful and those who dropped out in these subjective areas is not easy. The successful students were certainly academically able, probably more so than most of those who dropped out, but this academic ability was coupled with an ability to manage their lives at what was undoubtedly an unstable time – their OU studies were important to them and they were very determined to graduate but they were also mature enough to realise that the path would not be a smooth one and to stay cool under pressure. While drop-outs were more likely to have seen the OU as an alternative route into higher education, and indeed many of them had dropped back into the conventional system, successful students had chosen the OU for positive reasons either because of personal circumstances or because they were disillusioned with the conventional system. They had welcomed the chance to combine study with their work and family life and had obviously benefitted from the opportunities opened to them. While they were very realistic about the difficulties of distance study, and generally considered that the OU was more suitable for older people, they did believe that younger students who were settled and motivated should not be deprived of this type of opportunity just because they were young.

Good institutional research is about getting things changed and changed for the better. However, this is rarely a straightforward matter. In this final paper Naomi lays out some of the problems that intervene.

Barriers to implementing research in higher education[7]

Summary

The paper* is concerned to discuss why so much institutional research activity is carried out at such a cost and has apparently made so little continued impact on so few institutions. It argues that the problems relate not so much to inadequacies in methodology as to the nature of the decision-making process and the relationship between decision-makers and researchers in education. The paper discusses some of the barriers to the effective use of research and relates this discussion to the experience of institutional research at the Open University.

Preamble

This paper will not attempt to differentiate between the activities variously described as institutional research, evaluative research and evaluation. It is concerned rather to discuss why so much activity carried out at such a cost has apparently so little continued impact on so few institutions. Previous papers (McIntosh, 1976) have noted the way in which the historical dominance of the test-and-measurement tradition has been replaced by new developments such as the illuminative approach and the decision-making approach to educational evaluation. The illuminative approach has become fashionable in Great Britain, particularly among curriculum evaluators working at school level. The decision-making approach has in the last five years gained widespread currency both in America and in Europe, particularly in the field of post-school education.

7. McIntosh, N. E. (1979) Barriers to Implementing Research in Higher Education, *Studies in Higher Education*, 4(1), pp. 77–86.
* An earlier version of this paper was given to the 1977 Annual Forum of the Association of Institutional Research, Montreal.

It is now generally accepted that no one technique or paradigm is likely to be adequate to meet all the needs of institutional research. An analysis of the problem and the decisions that are to be made must precede the choice of research strategy, which should not be dictated by intellectual fashion. It is not the availability or adequacy of information that is the real problem. The range and variety of research techniques and evaluation strategies is great. Problems relate rather to the nature of the decision-making process and the relationship between decision-makers and researchers in an educational institution. The paper will concentrate on a discussion of some of the barriers to the successful implementation of research findings in institutional decision-making.

Other authors have attempted similar analyses (Gooler, 1976; Gilmour, 1976). I propose to extend the discussion and relate it to experience at the Open University, where there was from the outset a significant and effective commitment to institutional research, but where those of us in the Survey Research Department continue to be dissatisfied at our ability to have an impact on many major problem areas.

One definition of educational evaluation is 'the process of delineating, obtaining, and providing useful information for judging decision alterna-tives' (Stufflebeam, 1971). Despite the emphasis on utility, many institutional researchers have found that when the decision is finally made, their findings and recommendations have been ignored or rejected. I do not, of course, want to imply that all research findings *should* be implemented. Undoubtedly, many incorrect decisions have been made as a result of the uncritical acceptance of naive recommendations based on unsound research. The intention behind this paper is not to bring into view a series of barriers simply in order that they can be bulldozed down or avoided by the institu-tional researcher. Rather the intention is that, once these barriers are recog-nised, researchers and clients can work cooperatively to dismantle them.

Institutional research in the Open University

The Open University was set up in 1969 to provide degree-level courses for adults studying in their own homes. The teaching system involves the use of correspondence texts, television, radio and other media. No educational qualifications are required for entry. It currently has 60000 students enrolled, and 30000 students have already graduated.

Institutional research in the Open University setting covers a wide range of research activities. On a microlevel it can be concerned with evaluating a specific component on an individual course such as a single television programme, a student project or a summer school. Moving up a stage, we might wish to evaluate the educational impact of a whole course with a view to re-making it. On a macrolevel we might well be trying to evaluate the Open University system as a whole. In studying the subsequent careers of OU graduates, for instance, one is concerned with the perceived value of the OU degree. The 'younger student' research project on the other hand is trying to determine whether the system as it stands is more or less suitable for students in the 18 to 20 age-group.

Institutional research staff, of whom there are now over 20 working full-time, come from a variety of academic backgrounds such as sociology, psychology, statistics and mathematics and tend to work in inter-disciplinary research groups. Any given piece of research may have been commissioned by an individual academic, by a course team, by a faculty, by an Open University committee or by the Vice-Chancelloriat. Alternatively, it may have been initiated by the researchers themselves.

The implementation of research findings may involve a group decision, say, of administrators or of a committee. Equally the Chairman of a committee or the Vice-Chancellor or another line manager may act on research findings. Institutional research, then, is commissioned or initiated by many different people to inform many different types and levels of decisions. This paper is primarily concerned with the Open University's experience of the barriers to implementation of the results, in the confident expectation that many of them will be common to other research projects in different institutional settings.

First, catch your hare!

A decision is a very elusive animal. Who takes decisions? When will a decision be made? What constitutes a decision anyway? Is it one 'big' decision, or a series of small ones? Is it a consensus decision or a coercive decision? Is democracy at work? Unlike industry, few decisions in an educational institution are likely to be 'tidy' ones, with a clear decision-maker, an over-riding objective and reasonably measurable outcomes. Much information may similarly not be 'tidy' and rather than providing detailed specific answers for one particular decision, may simply be absorbed into the general stock of background knowledge of decision-makers, ensuring that it is taken into account in planning.

In education there are at least two distinct sets of people involved in decision-making whose interests may not necessarily coincide, namely the academics and the administrators. Although the majority of decision-making is based on a participative democratic committee structure, the sheer scale of the OU, as of other universities, and the pressure under which faculty works, ensures that the administrator's role is often the formative one. There is a third force—data processing—which cannot be ignored, and may in certain cases become dominant: without the computer, the OU could not operate.

The question of who takes the decisions is intimately related to their timing. Sometimes it is possible to forecast or to determine that a decision will be taken at a given time. In such cases, provided people are aware of their needs, it may be possible to commission research well in advance. Until recently, OU funding was on a triennium and the University redeveloped its overall plan on a triennial basis, thus giving reasonable warning of the time-scale for any changes.

Development of a policy for higher degrees is a case in point. It was given a low priority in the triennial bid submitted for 1976–78. Work in this area had to wait for the next triennium, and research evidence of student demand became a significant factor in the OU's decision to give it a higher priority in the current triennial bid. At the time of the last major review of summer school policy, nobody had even thought what the appropriate questions were to ask, and the only research input was a collation of information already available from existing sources (McIntosh, 1975). No new research could have been commissioned as there was no time. We should now be researching to prepare information for the next review. We are not, since nobody has yet put a date on the next review and we have not sufficient resources to do it as a 'philanthropic' gesture. Our summer schools researcher has his work cut out in studying the day-to-day impact of summer schools, and cannot lift his head up to look at long-term policy.

If decision-makers were more sensitive both to the fact that they seldom have perfect information and to the fact that institutional research might provide some information to reduce their area of uncertainty, then they might be more likely to think of possible research questions earlier, to commission research and eventually to be interested in the results. Researchers are not normally in a position to affect the timing of the deci-sions. Timeliness is a major barrier which can only be overcome by building up a good relationship between researchers and decision-makers, so that wherever possible research can be initiated early enough for its results to be of use.

Two questions arise from this, one of which concerns the location of the research function, and the other of which concerns the nature of the research strategy.

The status of the research function

Should institutional researchers within an institution be appointed as academics or as administrators? Lyons (1976) describes the conflict clearly. He notes 'Few of us can afford the luxury of doing nothing but basic research, and few of us wish to be relegated to the role of basic efficiency expert.' There are arguments, of course, on both sides. If academics are the main decision-makers, then they are the ones who need to be persuaded that the research is valid. Shared academic status is more likely to achieve this. On the other hand 'academic' researchers are not accustomed to working to deadlines and to producing data which are 'good enough' for the decision to be taken. The audience for whom they normally carry out and write up their research is composed of their fellow academics. They choose their language and style accordingly.

On balance, the fact that institutional researchers at the OU were from the beginning accorded academic status, appears to have been of major significance. They became members of Senate, and therefore of its committees. This enabled them at an early stage to feed both the need for, and the results of, institutional research into a number of critical discussions of such bodies as the Admissions Committee and the Planning Board. It has proved relatively easy to produce information for overall planning decisions and to create the necessary relationships with administrators and top management. Research for course design and curriculum development is a more complicated problem, to which we shall return.

The nature of the research strategy

Most researchers have been brought up to believe that it is necessary to start with a particular hypothesis and then to develop a research design to test it. This assumes that we know not only what the problem is, but also when and by whom the decision will be taken to tackle that problem. In a complex system, decisions are not likely to wait for hypotheses to be developed and tested. The consequent failure of researchers to deliver the goods does little for their credibility.

There is no easy answer to this problem. The OU Survey Research Department has approached it in various ways. The first has been to attempt in cooperation with the administration to build up a collection of routine data as a by-product of administrative processes. The second has been to adopt from the outset a catholic research strategy which allowed an initial purchase on a variety of uncharted problems.

The combination of these two approaches has provided a broad data base which can be scanned to give a swift reaction to a variety of general questions. For example the basic monitoring of student progress, course by course, at several stages in the academic year, enables us to pinpoint with a fair degree of accuracy whether an unexpectedly high failure rate is due to changes in student characteristics, changes in the course assessment, gross problems in course content or some other factor. In itself this pin-pointing does not, of course, provide any explanation. But it shortcuts the research process, eliminating a variety of candidates for research, and provides an automatic warning of major areas of trouble.

In addition to the strategies used to build up a broad base of data, we have kept some part of our available effort both to initiate research in areas we believe will turn out to be significant and to enable us to respond to clients' requests for research.

Research findings which are rejected by decision-makers

Many competent research findings sit on bookshelves and are never used. It is possible to identify various factors which inhibit their use. Although they may seem trivial, they are sufficiently widespread to justify giving them some attention.

'My technique is good, your technique is bad'

Within universities, research groupings are usually built up within one faculty or discipline area. The majority of institutional researchers have been trained as psychologists (whether experimental or interpretative), or as sociologists or anthropologists, and tend to believe that only their own disciplines and techniques are appropriate or usable. The necessity to protect academic empires reinforces this insularity and makes it difficult for many people to accept that an inter-disciplinary grouping may be more appropriate.

'My data are hard, your data are soft'

This problem follows on from the previous one, but is more difficult to deal with since it operates at a more personal level. Every academic believes that he or she is a competent researcher and can do better research than anyone else. If a survey is quantitative, then it cannot offer explanatory ideas. If it is qualitative, it cannot be generalised. An early OU questionnaire was condemned by a psychometrician because it contained only 'nominal scales': in fact, they were not scales at all, but merely a set of reasons pre-coded on to a questionnaire. Any given methodology can be attacked in a variety of ways (the response rate is too low, the sample is unrepresentative etc.).

'The student I met at summer school told me...'

Clients, both academics and administrators, always have their personal theories and experiential anecdotes with which to contradict the most carefully carried out piece of research. Nothing can persuade a Dean that the three or four students who happen to bend his ear at summer school are not typical of the 'silent majority'.

The language barrier

As Gilmour (1976) said, 'Institutional researchers and decision-makers sometimes do not speak the same language, literally and figuratively. A major problem in recent years has been the growth of technical or jargonistic language in the social and management sciences.' In his very next paragraph,

Gilmour offers an unconscious example of exactly this problem. He describes 'linkage', as a possible factor for removing conflict, in the following terms: 'Linkage is the degree of interpersonal connection and collaboration between the decision-maker and the institutional researcher and the extent to which mutual communication exists between the two'; or presumably, in plain language, how closely the two work together.

The phenomenon of professional/academic jargon is a curious one, designed to make those who can use it feel superior, and those who cannot, inadequate. At best it provides a more accurate and speedy communication system. At worst it can make some perfectly competent people believe they are lacking in understanding, and therefore persuade them to opt out in self-defence.

The barrier of numbers

Much research contains statistical information. Very often this is presented in ways which are not easily comprehensible to non-numerate decision-makers. The use of elaborate statistical tests may be designed to impress fellow academics. It is likely to be a barrier to the majority of decision-makers. Many OU staff have commented, in pleased surprise, that they have found our reports interesting and readable: by the same token fellow researchers have complained at the lack of statistical tests in them. We take the view that statistics are not an end in themselves, but only a means to an end.

The over-use of statistical tests often gives a spurious impression of accuracy. Providing the basic sample is well-drawn and the sample size adequate, the most obvious differences are likely to be the most important.

Caveats and defence mechanisms

All researchers are only too aware of the imperfections of their art, and endeavour to protect themselves against possible attack by spelling out the limitations of the data. By doing so, they often display such a lack of confidence in their own work that it is not surprising that potential users also lack confidence in it. Gooler (1976) quotes a typical caveat:

> The following data should be used extremely carefully. The reader should not extrapolate the findings of this study to any other setting, at any other time or any other way. These data are based on a limited sample, possibly not representing the total population involved. The statistics used herein are valid only under certain conditions and assumptions. More studies must be done to replicate the findings of this study.

We need first of all to have reasonable confidence in our own work. Greater accuracy can always be obtained but at a greater cost, and often only after a longer time. Sometimes greater precision is necessary, but often it is not. Sometimes the demand for greater precision is really a defence to avoid a decision. The judgment about how precise the information needs to be is difficult.

The data explosion

A more catholic approach to institutional research and evaluation, combined with the increasing complexity of many post-school educational systems, has resulted in more data from a wider variety of sources. The interpretation of a classic piece of experimental design (a pre-test/post-test, for example) was relatively simple. The approach developed at Empire State University (Palola and Bradley, 1976) provides an illustration of a complex situation where multiple observers and multiple standards are planned to be components of an evaluation strategy. Interviews, rating forms, survey instruments, content analysis, observation and tests are all used as tools for obtaining a full picture of what is happening to students.

A similar richness of data can be found at the Open University. Information is available from students, tutors, counsellors and academics both inside and outside the university. It comes through 'the shriek system', through letters, phone calls, through analyses of assessment material and student performance, through observation, through questionnaires and interviews, and through information from the administrative system. But its very richness and profusion has become a barrier to its use. The problem is a serious one of organising and storing it in such a way that it is accessible. Given the relatively long time-scales for the production and life of an OU course, the collection of some of the data may need to take place at an early stage, to give an opportunity for short-term remedial activity, but the data may also need to be banked and collated to aid later decisions about retaining the existing course, remaking it, or going for an entirely new course. Personnel who collected and understood the data may not be around when it is needed for use. We are working on a model (McIntosh, 1976) which relates possible research activities to decisions over the life of a course, the key being the development of a planned bank of information. The group concerned with the planning of the new OU science foundation course are building up such an information bank, together with an accessing system to aid in the production of the course itself (Melton, 1976).

Multiple standards

As Gooler (1976) noted, multiple standards clearly exist, at a variety of levels. The most obvious one is that individuals often do not agree on what data are acceptable and what they mean. Different people tend to examine and interpret data in terms of different standards. They may have different standards of what constitutes a good course. For some, a good course may mean one with a high pass rate. Others may believe that a high drop-out rate indicates a good (i.e. 'tough') course. Some people may place greater weight on information stemming from tutors than on information from students. Some may only be concerned with objective data and not allow a role for subjective information. Such diverse viewpoints are difficult to reconcile: so it is not surprising that some decision-makers find it easier to ignore the information and stick to their own convictions. Even the best information will not resolve the perennial dilemma: is a course designed for students or for the staff who produce it? The OU's foundation course in Social Science was written entirely anew not because existing students had reacted badly to it, but because a new generation of young academics wished to write a new course and not just to tinker about improving the old one.

The 'creative' imperative

The fact that academics see themselves as exercising creativity increases the problem. The provision of research information is threatening to the creative process, in so far as it may appear to diminish it. While some academics are resistant to the use of empirical data, others may simply be ignorant of their potentialities or inexperienced in their use. Even if academics do not reject the findings of research, they frequently complain that they cannot act on them because they are too general and not prescriptive enough. Too often evaluation is retrospective, and can only be used negatively to point out what has gone wrong or what has not worked. In one sense an evaluator cannot win: if the report shows the course was good, the academic is reinforced in his blind confidence. If it shows it as bad, the academic will complain that he should have been told earlier.

In course and programme evaluation we have found—and this experience is shared by the University of Mid-America (Gooler, 1976)—that if we work closely with the course team from the very beginning, the research will be both better planned and more likely to be used. Such an approach is, of course, more time consuming, but it highlights what types of data academics *can* use and interpret. Indeed, some faculties have gone so far as to suggest that evaluators should be located, perhaps on a secondment basis, within the faculties themselves (on the grounds that if they are not, they will never get close enough to the real problems). Other faculties argue that their members can, as academics, evaluate better than professional evaluators, since course-related knowledge is more important than the possession of evaluative research skills.

Relationships in the OU with television and radio producers are similarly affected by the problem of creativity. Obviously, producers must use their artistic judgment: but the problems with them are if anything greater, and relate in some way to the structure and mode of work of the media. Whereas most academics know that they are going to continue to teach a course, or at least a subject area, for several years, and therefore have some incentive to improve their performance, many producers will move on immediately to a totally different subject and often a totally different audience. There is no merit in producing a series rather like, but better than the previous one. Merit comes from doing something new and different.

Not surprisingly, the role of research in improving performance for next time is not necessarily acceptable. The comparison with research carried out into television commercials makes the point more forcibly. There is an obvious incentive to develop and use research techniques to improve television commercials, since the finished commercial may be shown hundreds of times and each showing of the improved film may result in some thousands of pounds more sales. A typical BBC adult education course is likely to be made to be run two or three times at most—afterwards it will not be replaced, the fashionable subject of 1976 and 1977 now having been overtaken by the new subject for 1978. A producer may well have to change from poetry to gardening, and is unlikely to think, therefore, that any research information from the previous series will be relevant. At least in the OU set-up the BBC producers continue to work at one level of education and within one faculty. But subject-matter may still vary very widely, and the available resources are not sufficient to remake very many television programmes. With a five-year course life, any lessons learnt from a previous course can either just be forgotten, or perceived as irrelevant. Generalisations from one type of programme to another are almost the most difficult to accept. 'My course is different, special, difficult...' 'You just don't understand!'

Evaluation as politics

Evaluation is very often a highly political act, being built into the decision to make a change. Brickell (1976), in an entertaining paper, describes 10 different cases where politics played a major role. These were all contracts where external evaluation was commissioned, and this may be significant. The demand for evaluation to be rigorous and objective is great, particularly if government money is being spent. It is almost always taken to imply external evaluation. At the same time, it is clear that all of the barriers and problems we have been discussing are multiplied and exacerbated if the evaluators or researchers are external to the institution. Time barriers, the identification of decision-makers, language barriers, vested interests: all those are more difficult to tackle from the outside.

On my first venture into the American evaluation scene, as an internal adviser, I was introduced to the external formative evaluation team who had been at work for five months. In response to a question about what they had been doing, they replied, 'How could we have done anything? Nobody has

Naomi presenting Harold Wilson with the honorary degree of Doctor of the Open University, Free Trade Hall, Manchester, May 1974; and with the honorary graduand

formulated their objectives yet.' The idea did not seem to have dawned that part of their job might have been to help the team to formulate their objectives, or at least to clarify what they were trying to do.

Mielke (1974) differentiates between formative and summative research and argues that although background and formative research should be done in-house, policy and summative research should not. I certainly share his views that formative research should properly be done in-house: it does not seem realistic to suggest anything else, given that much research has proved unusable just because it is too distanced from decision-making.

I am not, however, clear that summative evaluation needs to be done externally—unless its only objective is to prove some political point. It will always be difficult for external evaluators to come along and engage in adequate summative evaluation unless there has been adequate preparatory work and data-gathering. The solution at the OU has been to set up an Institute, external to the groupings that it is mainly researching into, but within the University. This seems to work quite well. Academic status protects the integrity of the research, which is made available to all interested parties.

The tradition of external evaluation is rare in the United Kingdom, as, indeed, is the tradition, common in America, of building in evaluation, usually external, as a required part of the educational programme. It is interesting that the first example of this nature in the OU is the experimental intake of 'younger students', which has an evaluation component required and funded by the DES and which is being carried out within the University. The protection, both political and professional—and it is a very real and helpful one—is an Advisory Body containing national representatives of all the bodies, universities, polytechnics and local authorities who may be interested in the outcome of the research.

What can be done to make research more effective?

It may be that some of the barriers discussed here are inherent in educational institutions, particularly where participative democracy purports to be the method of government. Many of the problems appear on the surface to be trivial. The fact that they continue to occur leads me to believe that they are important, and may be more important than those which have until now preoccupied people more.

Perhaps the single most important, and cheap, improvement is to simplify language and avoid unnecessary jargon. One of the questionnaire-writer's rules is: 'never use a long word when a shorter one will do'. Use common-sense, everyday language. Do not be afraid that people will not think you are clever enough if you do.

Improvements will not come about through the efforts of researchers alone: researchers and clients need to cooperate in identifying and removing obstacles. Some of the following ways may help.

(1) Researchers should work to build up an awareness among their clients of the possible contributions that research might make.
(2) Better planning by administrators and academics is, in itself, likely to generate more opportunities for the effective use of research. As policy is discussed more overtly and with recognised time-scales, more decision-makers will be encouraged to discuss possible choices and their results, thus identifying information gaps earlier.
(3) Both sides must find ways of breaking down the 'us' and 'them' gap. Researchers must get, or be allowed to get, closer to the problems, and be prepared to work to decision-making deadlines rather than 'perfect world' time-scales. Decision-makers should learn more about the research process in order that they may become better clients, commissioning better research.
(4) A corollary of this in education is that researchers should have the same job security that academics and administrators possess. They then need not worry about unpopular research findings, and are not under pressure to concentrate on short-term results with easily recognisable objectives at the expense of building up a solid base for the longer term.
(5) Researchers should get clients politically, emotionally and financially committed to the commissioning and outcome of the research. They are then more likely to take notice of its results.

Conclusions

There is obviously no easy way forward. Researchers and decision-makers will have to continue to try to develop good mutual working relationships, neither promising too much on the one hand nor demanding too much on the other. Researchers will have little effect if they try to keep their hands too clean; on the other hand, they cannot lower their professional standards and integrity if they wish to keep the respect of their clients and to do effective work.

Researchers based in institutions may occasionally be fortunate enough to produce new earth-shattering revelations. More often, they can expect one or two significant bits of information to be absorbed into the general stock of knowledge, so that the next decision may be taken on a slightly better base. Perhaps the final point is the important one: unlike external evaluators, institutional researchers are there to stay.

References

BRICKELL, H. M. (1976) The influence of external political factors on the role and methodology of evaluation, *Evaluation Comment*, 5, 2.

GILMOUR, J. E., Jr. (1976) *Sources of conflict between institutional researchers and decision-makers*, paper presented at AIR Forum, Los Angeles.

GOOLER, D. (1976) *A pragmatic examination of the uses of research and evaluation data in decision-making*, paper presented at the CEREB Conference, Milton Keynes, April.

LYONS, J. M. (1976) *Memorandum to a Newcomer in the Field of Institutional Research*, Florida, Association for Institutional Research.

McINTOSH, N. E. (1970) Evaluation of multi-media systems: some problems, *British Journal of Educational Technology*, 15, 3.

McINTOSH, N. E. (1975) The place of summer schools in the Open University system, *Teaching at a Distance*, No. 3, Milton Keynes, The Open University.

McINTOSH, N. E. (1976) *Evaluation and institutional research: aids to decision making and innovation*, paper presented at OECD Third General Conference on Institutional Management in Higher Education, Paris.

MELTON, R. F. (1976) *Course evaluation at The Open University: a case study*, paper presented to the EARDHE Congress in Louvain, Belgium, September.

MIELKE, K. W. (1974) Decision-oriented research in school television, *Public Telecommunications Review*, Vol. 2, No. 3.

MUNRO, R. G. (1977) *Innovation: success or failure?* London: Hodder & Stoughton.

PALOLA, E. G. and BRADLEY, A. PAUL, Jr. (1976) *Multiple perspectives evaluation; a strategy for dealing with conflicting pressures*, paper presented at AIR Forum, Los Angeles.

PHI DELTA KAPPA NATIONAL STUDY COMMITTEE ON EVALUATION. STUFFLEBEAM, D.L. (CHAIRMAN) (1971) *Educational Evaluation and Decision-Making* (Ithaca, Illinois, F. E. Peacock).

A footnote

If Naomi was writing about the OU today she would be rejoicing in the capabilities of Excel to draw graphs so quickly and she would not be referring to the OU student as 'he'! Above all she would be describing a University that has changed in many ways (several of which she predicted). Readers requiring an update should start at **http://www.open.ac.uk/**

Postscript

What I hope that has emerged from these extracts is not only Naomi's creativeness and farsightedness, but above all her professionalism and passion. One might ask 'Can you be both objective and committed?'

Back in 1961 Gouldner had attacked what he took to be the dominant professional ideology of sociologists: that favouring the value-free doctrine of social science. In 1968 he returned to the fray because he feared 'that the myth of a value-free social science is about to be supplanted by still another myth, and that the once glib acceptance of the value-free doctrine is about to be superseded by a new but no less glib rejection of it' (Gouldner, 1968, p. 103). He took to task Becker and others in the Chicago School who sided with the 'underdogs' in their studies of deviant behaviour (see for example Becker, 1963). They did so on the grounds that it is impossible for a social scientist to do research uncontaminated by personal and political sympathies. Work must be written either from the stand-point of subordinates or superiors because one cannot do equal justice to both. Gouldner, on the other hand, while recognising the inevitability of bias and partisanship, notes 'the fact remains that two researchers may have the same bias but, nonetheless, may not be equally objective' (Gouldner, 1968, p. 111) .

He goes on to outline three possible conceptions of sociological objectivity. 'Normative objectification' is the objectivity of the court judge which 'requires his explication of the moral value in terms of which his judgement has been rendered' (Gouldner, 1968, p. 113). 'Personal authenticity' is a form of objectivity that involves 'the capacity to acknowledge "hostile information" - information that is discrepant with our purposes, hopes, wishes or values' (Gouldner, 1968, p. 114). A third component of objectivity is 'transpersonal replicability' which means that sociologists have described their procedures with such explicitness that others employing them on the same problem would come to the same conclusion.

Gouldner, then, did not see partisanship as incompatible with objectivity. 'The physician, after all, is not necessarily less objective because he has made a partisan commitment to his patient and against the germ' (Gouldner, 1968, p. 113). However, Gouldner did not address the question of the researcher's position in relation to the different factions. For example, how would it have affected Becker's research if he had been doing the research for the police force, or even if he was part of that police force? As an institutional researcher for the Open University, and as a full academic member of that University, Naomi and her colleagues had three sets of constraints acting on them: the need to be a professional, objective researcher; the need to act responsibly toward, and to seek improvements in the institution of which they were members; the need to act in accordance with their own values.

I have written elsewhere of the need for an institutional researcher to 'Respond', 'Alert' and 'Provoke'. To me these summarise the three key tasks of the effective, professional and committed institutional researcher.

In institutional research you have to 'respond' to the needs of policy-makers. To achieve impact you need to be 'where the action is' and you need to be accountable. However, this does not mean that you have to agree. Your independence as a researcher can give you the freedom to dispute whether the policy-makers are asking the right questions or interpreting the data correctly.

The needs of policy-makers tend to be short-term and affected by pressing circumstances. It should be the duty of the institutional researcher to be aware of wider issues, research findings elsewhere, theoretical developments, trends in institutional statistics, etc, and to 'alert' policy-makers to their implications.

It is also the duty of a good institutional researcher to be a trouble-maker. He or she must be able to point out the things that are going wrong and to 'provoke' action within the institution to put things right.

To perform these three tasks well the institutional researcher has to become what I termed a 'partisan guerrilla'. I hope that this chapter has shown how well Naomi took on that challenging role at the Open University.

References

SEWART, D., KEEGAN, DESMOND J. AND HOLMBERG, B. *Distance Education: International Perspectives,* Hardcover, Croom Helm Limited, ISBN 0312213190 (0-312-21319-0)

BECKER, H. (1963) *Outsiders,* Free Press, USA

GOULDNER, A. (1968) 'The sociologist as partisan: sociology and the welfare state', *The American Sociologist,* 3 (2), 103-116.

Channel 4 and afterwards: a continuing commitment to individual viewers

By any standard, the 1980s were extraordinary years in the history of broadcasting in this country. Channel 4 was born and had influence far beyond its size. Its establishment broke the duopoly of the BBC and ITV. It pioneered the concept, now regarded as normal, that broadcasting organisations could be the publishers of programmes as well as their originators. It positively encouraged new voices on and off air; among them was Naomi Sargant, senior commissioning editor for education from 1981 until 1989, who brought to the infant channel a highly distinctive set of insights from the worlds of market research and education, which had not hitherto been much heard in the corridors of broadcasting.

Naomi responded most positively to Jeremy Isaacs' (founding father and first chief executive) vision of Channel 4 as a broadcaster which would give space to needs and interests which were not then being catered for by other channels. Her starting points for the translation of that vision into programmes were often radically – but, in principle, creatively – different from commissioning colleagues who were concerned to refresh the medium of television itself. She was far from uninterested in that, but her primary concern was with 'the other end', with the Channel 4 audiences themselves in all their heterogeneity. She rejected – passionately – estimations which showed contempt for everyday interests and preoccupations; she rejected, equally passionately, proposals or programmes which she felt were driven by ideology. She was lucky, of course, to have a great many broadcasting hours to fill; this gave her scope to commission programmes on a fascinating variety of subjects, from the very serious (numeracy, media literacy, contemporary history, consumer education, and, yes, marketing) to the very pleasurable (the history of art, pottery painting, bee keeping, and, her own personal passion, gardening).

Naomi, Carol Haslam (Commissioning Editor for Documentary Series) and I (Educational Liaison Officer and Editor, Programme Support) were also given the opportunity to take educational programmes out of the ghetto in which they had hitherto resided. They took their rightful place alongside politics, the arts, sport and documentaries, not only in terms of the slots which they earned the right to occupy – no small thanks to Naomi – but also because colleagues in those years regarded it as a mark of status that programmes in all these other areas might be named educational in intent and were glad to have them followed up through the printed word and the telephone.

'What happens if it works?' is a question which she repeats again and again in these pages, referring to the absolute necessity to go beyond counting the number of people watching a programme, to ask how it was received, whether it stimulated fresh interest, what people did when the television was turned off. It was perhaps because she did not have a television background that Naomi appreciated the enormous potential of the medium. As she related, she did not discover Lady Bridget Plowden's bon mot 'television is democratic; there are no reserved seats' until after she had left Channel 4 in 1989. But it is implicit in everything she did and said through nine very creative years. What a far cry from the populism now so dominant on all mainstream channels, even, alas, Channel 4.

A short extract from Peter Catterall's interview with Naomi, conducted on 30 July 1998.

My appointment[8]

Catterall: How did you come to be appointed to Channel 4?

Sargant: I'd been working at the Open University for about 11 years. I ran the survey research department and then became Pro-Vice Chancellor in charge of student affairs. Then, under the 1974–79 Labour government, I was appointed to the Advisory Committee for Adult and Continuing Education (ACACE), which was chaired by Richard Hoggart, and was given the task of chairing the group which did the planning nationally for continuing education. So I had been setting out a structure of opportunities of education for adults as a process continuing throughout life. Related to that, I had been part of and commissioned a major study of education and leisure interests amongst adults – and that is the context in which I think Jeremy Isaacs thought I would be appropriate for the job of Senior Commissioning Editor for Education.

Catterall: So he contacted you?

Sargant: Well, we knew each other, but that went back 20 years or so. I had always been very admiring of his work, for example *The World at War*. We had shared a number of friends and we had frequently discussed the educational power of television. I remember us discussing the educational effect of *The World at War*. He said, 'I suppose you think *The World at War* isn't educational.' I said, 'Nonsense, of course it is extremely educational' and he described a lovely occasion when he'd been asked to go and talk to the 'War and Society' summer school at the Open University, and he sat next to a woman who turned out to have developed her first interest in history from watching *The World at War*, and she'd gone to enrol in the Open University, and here she was on a second level course.

Then, at one point over dinner, when we knew that Jeremy was going to get the Channel 4 job, and we were congratulating him, he sat there and said, 'but I've got this amazing responsibility to do all this educational programming, and I have no idea what to do about it'. Of course, to have a Channel with 15 per cent of the output mandated to be education was extraordinary. And I cheerfully banged the table and said, 'I know exactly what you should do about it' and proceeded to talk about what could be done. We went on with this conversation and towards the end of the dinner he sort of looked

8. Catterall, P. (1999) *The Making of Channel 4*, London: Routledge, pp. 134–61

at me, and said, 'If I was to advertise a job which looked like this...how likely would you be to apply for it?' Prickles went up the back of my neck, and I suddenly thought he could be serious.

A few days later the phone rang, and it was Jeremy. He said he'd gone 'nap' on getting me appointed without interview, but that they wanted to interview me. I sort of gasped, because I hadn't taken him *that* seriously, and I had to phone him back that night and say if *I* was going to be serious. Clearly, you wouldn't turn down a chance like that, even though it was a bit frightening, and later on, I went and got interviewed by Edmund Dell (former Labour cabinet minister and first chairman of Channel 4) and Anne Sofer (then a member of the Inner London Education Authority, and a founding member of the Channel 4 board).

Catterall: So you had a clear vision of what you wanted to do with this per cent of the Channel?

Sargant: Well, I knew it had to be done differently from the basic educational programming on other channels, because to fill 15 per cent we had to cast it more broadly.

Catterall: You did believe strongly that television can be an effective means of education?

Sargant: Well, we already had, at the higher level, the OU on the BBC, which had opened up opportunities as well as providing knowledge for people. At the other end, we'd already had adult literacy programmes triggering lots of responses, and more recently, I had been running the evaluation of a numeracy project which had been done by Yorkshire Television. We knew the power of all this ...

Catterall: So you had a vision of education for different age groups and levels?

Sargant: Yes, I was chairing the National Gas Consumers' Council, and serving on the National Consumer Council. The notion of consumer education, of adults having better information and being able to make better decisions about their lives and being stimulated into a wider variety of activities – that was all in my head. We had a more precise thing we wanted to do as well, though it wasn't the main thing at that stage, which was to offer some lower level analogue for the OU, to do something like an Open College, which might reach people who had left school at 16 ...

We were saying we needed a range of levels where people could come in and out. And one of the interesting things was to think about the simple outcome that people's imaginations might be stimulated, when educational broadcasting wasn't conceived as formal, sequential and curriculum-led (as it had hitherto). We had a number of clear goals, such as reaching the unemployed, consumer education, political education (which I conceived of as active democracy), health programmes and programmes for the over 60s. But a brilliant thing about the freedom which Jeremy gave me was that there were also a number of areas which didn't need to be treated as a piece of curriculum...

Catterall: Was the 15 per cent always a boon, or could it be a straitjacket?

Sargant: I think it was very much resented and worried about, because there never had been a commitment of that kind. The person who didn't worry was Jeremy. If you go back to my appointment I think there were large numbers of people who would have given their back teeth for my job. I was of course dead scared of it and I went to the person who would be my opposite number at the BBC, a man called Don Grattan, whom I knew very well through the OU. One Friday evening I asked him about the idea that I should go for the job. He said, 'What a brilliant idea. If you don't go for it, tell me, and I'll go for it myself'. So it was a deeply coveted position. But the honour ought to go to Jeremy who was completely idealistic about it. He gave me, as he said, not the best, but a very decent budget, and the best of all was that he didn't tell me, in any way, that it had to be any particular televisual form. The limits were my own imagination....It was an extraordinary time.

Naomi was appointed in early 1981. She quickly realised that her job included careful discussions with the Independent Broadcasting Authority (IBA), to whose Educational Advisory Committee (EAC) Channel 4 was accountable for the quality, range and penetration of its educational programmes. By November 1981, she had drafted for them and for the Channel 4 board the following account of what the channel had in mind for education.

Groundwork[9]

It is not the purpose of this paper to embark on a discussion of what constitutes 'educational television'. Other people have trodden this ground before, and to attempt to put boundaries round it is likely to act to exclude rather than include. Kim Taylor's (then Head of Education IBA) simple formulation is a helpful one; he wrote that an educational broadcast is simply a 'broadcast used educationally'. It can be used by individuals, or by people in groups, informally or in formal institutions. Sometimes it will stimulate them into other activities, sometimes they may simply be wiser or better informed. Ultimately, the decision is made by the person who chooses to use a programme to learn.

What will be different about Channel 4's education output?

Channel 4 will add to the range of choice available to people. It is worth recording the charge laid on the Channel by the Broadcasting Act, 1980:

'As regards the programmes (other than advertisements) broadcast on the Fourth Channel, it shall be the duty of the Authority:

(a) to ensure that the programmes contain a suitable proportion of matter calculated to appeal to tastes and interests not generally catered for by ITV
(b) ...to ensure that a suitable proportion of the programmes are of an educational nature
(c) to encourage innovation and experiment in the form and content of programmes.'

---

9. Sargant, N. E. (1981) Education on Channel 4 (Board Paper, unpublished).

Channel 4 will also add to the quantity of educational output available. 15 per cent of airtime more than doubles the amount of adult education currently available on ITV, and is likely to put the two independent channels' contribution to post-school education as high as that of the BBC (discounting the BBC's OU output).

Thirdly, the hours available for educational programmes will be in peak, or near-peak time, and will continue week-in, week-out for 52 weeks of the year. This should enable Channel 4 to reach new audiences in larger numbers.

It is not likely that these challenges can be met by continuing to provide educational television in its historic form. Channel 4 will have to break new ground, in range, variety, level and structure. Traditional distinctions between what is or is not educational are already changing. As the number of those not in jobs increases, so creative leisure becomes more important. What is vocational and job related for a young person may be an important part of active retirement for the elderly, or of increased leisure for those with a shorter working week. Anything which people want to learn, or which makes people want to learn, should be part of the canvas.

Run-up, back-up, follow-up

Some people define educational television in terms of what it causes people to do. The notion is that people are stimulated into activity by programmes. Proper follow-up to them must be provided if people are not to be infinitely frustrated.

There are, however, an enormous range of ways in which people can follow up programmes, some more active than others, and some more private than others. Some series do not need complicated follow-up involving other parts of the community, but back-up at a much simpler level – books, leaflets, etc. 700,000 people wrote for a recent Health Education Council leaflet. Other series would benefit from better 'run-up', or advance warning, particularly where plans need to be made to use the programmes for learning in the community.

Since Channel 4 is a national channel, it is likely that more of its follow-up will have to be provided nationally, through print, for independent learning. Where local or regional follow-up at community level is desirable, then it is anticipated that Channel 4 may be able to call on the time of the ITV community liaison officers (or community and continuing education officers, CCEOs), employed by each of the regional companies. Obviously, this will only be possible for a very limited number of series at any one time. Sometimes it may be possible or desirable to work closely with other organisations – the Health Education Council, Age Concern, the Women's Institute, the Sports Council are all examples of the kind of organisations with whom we have already talked. Where linkage/follow-up is of a more formal kind involving links with a range of educational organisations, then the educational liaison officer to be appointed by Channel 4 will play a key role.

Target audiences

With a small number of exceptions, Channel 4 proposes to concentrate on the education of adults and young people rather than school children – and not to enter the field of children's programming. The reasons for this have to do mainly with our planned airtime and quantity of resources. The Channel will not start its daily broadcast until 5pm.

There are a number of obvious target groups: the elderly, youth, the disabled, mentally handicapped, etc. The difficulty is that over any two or three year time period everyone will be identifying the same 'fashionable' target groups. This year it has been the disabled, a previous year it was child-minders, next year it looks like being the elderly and youth. The government has recently asked the Advisory Council on Adult and Continuing Education (ACACE) to look at education for the unemployed. There are two difficulties; firstly that even such groups as these are very heterogeneous, and secondly the avoidance of overlap with the BBC.

We have received proposals for such groups as the elderly, parents, the mentally handicapped and the disabled where regular strands of programmes would be appropriate. It is particularly important to avoid overlap where programmes are aimed at 'disadvantaged' groups and involved limited resources in the community. We should, however, be able to make a longer continuing commitment to some areas of social need, over two to three years, although, being realistic, we would not anticipate taking on more than a couple of such areas at any one time.

Relationships with ITV

Relationships with the BBC have been touched on. It is equally important for the two independent channels to gain the greatest mutual benefit. There will, essentially, be three options open through ITV: regional programmes, programmes networked on ITV, and programmes shown nationally on Channel 4. Different types of programme will sit more happily in different locations. At the same time, Channel 4 has to meet the requirement that a given proportion of programmes should be made by independent programme makers. It is necessary to balance these interests; liaison and coordination will obviously be very important to all parties.

Relationships with the Manpower Services Commission (MSC), including the Open Tech

Discussions are continuing with the MSC, predominantly about the possible use of broadcasting space during the day when Channel 4 will not otherwise be on air. Approaches have also been made about the possibility of education for management, and such professional areas as architecture. Such approaches might also involve collaboration with the OU. It is too early to comment on these in any detail. The main point to note at the moment is that if we are to spend daytime on some of these areas, then it might affect the judgement about the balance of content in the main programme areas.

Content areas

It is possible to list content areas in a number of ways. Two main alternatives are to analyse subject areas, or to look at the needs of people in their different roles. ACACE, in its discussion paper, takes the first approach, and lists, among others, adult basic education, industrial training and re-training, social and community education, education for individual development and family life, and education for general qualifications. It is probably sensible, unless it is part of some Open-Tech-type programme, for Channel 4 to stick to what the mass media can do best, i.e. non-certificated content areas. An alternative approach, which cuts across ages and more orthodox descriptors, is to approach people in their various roles as consumers, as parents, as tax and rate payers, as workers/bosses.

With the quantity of space and regularity of approach available to Channel 4, no one approach is likely to be adequate on its own. A number of priority areas and target groups have been identified, and these have been matched with the very large number of proposals received from a wide range of providers. In some important areas there have been fewer proposals, and in these we are actively seeking more submissions.

At the moment we expect to be eclectic in our choice of formats, using a magazine or miscellany approach where this suits, or a series or strand of programmes where this is appropriate. A main objective over the first two or three years will be to experiment with a wide range of approaches and monitor their effectiveness for different types of target groups and different types of educational objectives.

The main areas which have emerged are listed below for discussion, together with some indication of their possible slots. It is not possible for us to deal with all areas at any one time, or to give all areas equal weight. In some areas where we are clearer about our goals and the needs to be met we have started to commission developmental work. In other areas we have reached a long list stage. We need to move ahead quickly with commissioning in all areas, and we envisage a major round of commissioning before the end of the year.

Programme area 1: Children with Special Needs. (5.30–6 pm)

The aim is to select one or two areas of programming for the children themselves, which may then be complemented with limited programming for parents and concerned third parties, supported by ITV Community Liaison Officers and possible links with Independent Radio News (IRN) at local level. It is unlikely that more than two such 'campaigns' could be carried through at any one time. The two areas being looked at are the mentally handicapped and English for non-English children.

The suggestion is that two series of ten parts each should be commissioned in each area. In the second area, a pilot has been commissioned from Telekation, entitled *Everybody Here*, which is now being tested out with children from a range of ethnic backgrounds and appropriate adults. A book will be published to accompany the series. A second area is less advanced. An idea has been submitted and a pilot script has been commissioned from David Wood. The initiative is supported by Mencap and the adviser is Dr C, Kiernan of the Thomas Coram Foundation. Both possible providers are independent production companies.

Programme area 2: The Elderly (5.15–6 pm)

A regular weekly magazine is planned. Designed to educate, inform, involve and entertain, it will include such matters as health, diet and rights. It will involve elderly people in the programme, linking them together. Discussions have taken place with Age Concern, Help the Aged, the Centre for Policy on Aging, the Health Education Council and the Scottish Health Education Council. The proposals are in line with their thinking and they are very supportive. The run-up and follow-up for the magazine will take a variety of formats. The provider is an independent company.

Programme area 3: Active Sport (5.30–6 pm)

Many people are already active in one or more types of sport or physical recreation, and many others feel that they ought to be, but never quite get going. Programmes in this area would have two main aims: first to cater for a much wider range of sporting interests than existing channels, giving news and information to enthusiasts in such fields as swimming, cycling, fishing, dancing, climbing, canoeing, etc; and second, to motivate the less active sector of the population to take up at least one kind of physical activity by providing guidance on how to pursue new interests. This area of educational programming will be distinguished from ordinary sports coverage by its emphasis on individual sporting activity, accessible to people with limited resources. Follow-up information and advice will be provided.

Programme area 4: For People with More Time than Money. (5.15–5.45 pm)

The aim here is to interest the whole age range, but with special emphasis on unemployed youth. Programmes will be designed to introduce people to new activities and new skills, using resources around them, including their own resources. These offers come mainly in reasonable length series from both ITV and independent production companies. A strand or slot might be decided between a number of independents and a main provider.

Programme area 5: Basic Education, Living in a buff-envelope world (6.30–7 pm)

We believe Channel 4 should make a continuing commitment to the basic educational needs of adults, including numeracy, literacy, coping skills, rights, Plain English, and English as a Second Language. There are minimum estimates of up to 5 million adults with inadequate basic education, broadly defined. We hope to approach basic education in two ways: firstly, by building on and adding to Yorkshire Television's (YTV) existing series *Make it Count* and *Numbers at Work*. YTV will improve/update the two existing series where necessary and add a third series, to which we will then make a continuing commitment over two to three years; secondly, we will feed in, during holidays as it were, a number of other series covering a spectrum of coping and basic survival skills.

Programme area 6: The Way the World Works (6.30–7 pm)

In order to take an active part in the society (and the world) in which we live, we need to understand more about the way in which society is organised: the function of the government, the legal system, the economy, the role of pressure groups, trade unions, the media, and so on. Such an understanding depends on seeing Britain in relation to the rest of the world, and in particular in the context of relations between the developed nations and the Third World. In a regular weekly slot many of these subjects will provide a focus for different programmes and series, which will aim to throw light on some of the social, racial and sexual divisions which threaten the social order both within societies and between them. The fundamental aim will be to help individuals or groups to be more active citizens, voters, tax-payers, rate-payers, consumers of the welfare state and neighbours.

Programme area 7: Culture and the Arts (6.30–7 pm)

In this programme area we wish to provide opportunities for people to participate in culture and the arts in literature, poetry, history, archaeology, music, drama. We expect to emphasise heritage and to use programmes to open people's eyes to new areas that they have hitherto thought of as not for them. We would expect the programmes to make conscious linkage to other areas of arts output. The range of offers has been very strong, especially in the area of history. The problem here is that we have too many contenders rather than too few.

Programme area 8: Living and Looking (6.30–7 pm)

This is not one area, but several. In order to fit in a number of creative areas to do with people's lives, home and work situations, and wider environments, we propose to feed in four separate monthly strands. The first pair is close to home: gardening and DIY. The second pair has wider implications – the impact of new technologies, art and design on our lives and work.

Programme area 9: People as Consumers (8.30 pm weekly)

Here we will concentrate on choosing what's best for you in an increasingly complicated society. A regular weekly magazine will provide consumer information and education covering not just goods but services, public and private – e.g. the law, nationalised industries, leisure, social services; it will also include money management, energy, etc.

Programme area 10: Ways of Seeing

Television is essentially a visual medium, but hitherto it has not made a substantial contribution to visual education. Channel 4 would like to explore different ways of making people more aware of their physical environment and more sensitive to visual imagery of all kinds. Such subject areas as architecture, planning, photography, art, design, film, video might be covered. The aim, once again, is to inspire viewers to use this visual awareness in their own lives, whether in the design of their own homes or clothes, or in the creation of artistic and photographic images. There is room for considerable innovation and experiment in this area of programming. We expect contributions to range from five minutes to one hour, and to 'pop up' unexpectedly all over the schedules!

Programme area 11: Keeping Abreast of New Technology

Engineering, science, energy, resources, industry, business are all involved. At the moment, this area is the least advanced, as it depends both on the emphasis of Channel 4 news and current affairs, and also on discussion with the Open Tech. A pilot on business gaming has been commissioned.

Programme area 12: Feeling Good (10.15–11 pm)

There are many areas that determine how we feel about ourselves – both physically and emotionally – and these are closely related to our overall state of health. Channel 4 intends to define health in broad terms and to present a range of programmes and series that address health-related issues from a wide spectrum of perspectives. Some programmes will look at what individuals can do to improve their own health chances by making informed decisions on medical issues – by facing and coping with personal crises, difficult relationships and turning points in their lives; and by evaluating and implementing possible changes of lifestyle. Other programmes will look at social, economic and political factors that affect the life of the community, including discussion of medical practice, social policy and legislation in this area, as well as analysis of changing patterns of social interaction and the role of marriage and the family in contemporary society.

By April 1982, it was possible to draft an initial policy for the 'valida-tion' of some parts of Channel 4's more general output as having educational intent. In a further paper, an extract of which appears below, Naomi summarised the principles involved.

General programming and educational output[10]

Channel 4 is committed to the utilisation of a substantial quantity of its general output for educational purposes. It is appreciated that if this is to be achieved effectively, arrangements have to be made for run-up information, and back-up or follow-up materials where these are appropriate.

To this end, Channel 4 has appointed an Educational Liaison Officer, Derek Jones, who, as part of his job, will plan for such utilisation. The Channel has also set aside a substantial sum of money to cover the provision of follow-up where neither commercial publication nor sponsorship are appropriate alternatives.

There are a number of areas of programming which are confidently expected to be educational in the broad sense. Some are obviously so impor-tant and relevant as to need little discussion, e.g. Science and Society. A commitment to this monthly strand, and to the weekly Industry show, goes some way to explain the otherwise inexplicable omission of these areas from the regular weekly programming commissioned by education editors.

Implicit in the decision to allocate to one commissioning editor (Carol Halsam) responsibility jointly for documentary series and for some part of the educational programming is the understanding that the majority, if not all, of the documentary series are likely to be educational in purpose and appropriate for educational exploration. A large number of series has already been commissioned which could represent an hour a week of programming over the next two years or so.

Another regular programme area is designed to give able individuals a platform for their intellect. *Opinions* will present important points of view in a simple lecture format, which will probably be published afterwards as a collection of essays.

From current affairs we expect a number of programmes of great impor-tance dealing with Science and Society (13 one-hour programmes in maga-

---

10.Sargant, N. E. (1982) How educational programming and policy is developing on Channel 4 (Board Paper, unpublished).

zine format;), a weekly half-hour slot devoted to industry, including the trade unions, and, not least, a series of 12 two-hour programmes, *Report to the Nation*, during which the nationalised industries will be called to account for their policies and actions. All these are clearly within Channel 4's educational remit.

The Channel is committed to the display of the best films from Europe and further afield. The need to place these in critical context is obvious, as is the desire to be equally constructive in criticism of the newer medium, television. There will be a regular media show looking at both cinema and television, though the provider has not yet been settled upon. A number of plays are also amenable to exploitation, for example, *The Nation's Health*, *Nelly's Version*, and *The Red Monarch*. Arts performances and programmes are obviously of considerable educational importance; an important contribution in 1982–83, will be *Music in Time*, 16 one-hour programmes describing the history and development of western music, to be complemented later by a history of reggae, (six 50-minute programmes).

We are confident that there is no shortage of additional material which is genuinely educational in nature.

A *further extract from Peter Catterall's interview with Naomi carried out on 30 July 1998.*

Changing the image[11]

Catterall: Did the IBA ever come back to you about the educational content?

Sargant: Oh yes. They had an Education Advisory Council with very posh people on it. They had Geoffrey Holland from the MSC, Peter Newsam from the Inner London Education Authority, and so on. The guy who was scrutinising my first set of proposals was Sir William Taylor (Director of the Institute of Education, University of London, 1973–83). I remember that vividly, because he was looking quizzically at headings like 'for people with more time than money', and I said to him, 'If I had called these strands for the unemployed or consumer education and so on you wouldn't be arguing with me now'. He said, 'No, I suppose not'. It was an attempt to change the image. If we were to have such a large chunk of the Channel devoted to education, it couldn't have been presented as education in a formal way. That would have been death for the Channel. So I had to find a way of opening it up and presenting it. The key thing was that Jeremy, in giving us good slots, had been honourable about the handicapped, the over-60s and so on. Showing the IBA that we had these good slots and proper goals meant that that they, in turn, agreed to extend their definition to include basic skills, cookery or gardening. We had some of the most serious gardening programmes, for example, about seeds and propagation, *Plants for Free*, which got 4.2 million viewers on Friday evenings at 9pm, much to the chagrin of the entertainment commissioning editors on the Channel. It was the trick of, at the same time, facing the IBA with your conscience and facing the audience with life-enhancing stuff which worked. Much of this has now become the model for the current infotainment programmes, and my work was really the beginning of that.

11. Catterall, P. (1999) *The Making of Channel 4*, London: Routledge, pp. 134–61.

Flesh on the bones[12]

Channel 4 went on air on 2 November 1982 with the first transmission of Countdown, *the longest lasting of all its programmes and one of the most popular.*

Immediately afterwards, at 5.30pm, came Book Four, *presented by Hermione Lee, which was destined to become a validated education programme. Two days later, the first edition of* Tom Keating on Painters, *was transmitted, in which a man best noted for faking the work of great masters was employed to show us how it was done, not so that we could all go and do likewise, but so that we could appreciate the principles involved in creating a great work of art, surely one of the most imaginative programme ideas to have emanated from Naomi's stable.* Gardeners' Calendar *took off and so did* Coping, Years Ahead, *for retired people, and the first of YTV's numeracy series to be transmitted on the new channel.* For What it's Worth, *made by Thames Television, launched Naomi's consumer strand, and* Well Being *launched Carol Haslam's health strand; Carol also initiated the long running* Fragile Earth, *and* The Heart of the Dragon, *six penetrating programmes on everyday life in China, produced by Peter Montagnon and colleagues, already famed for* Civilisation *and* The Long Search, *transmitted by the BBC during a previous golden age.*

Channel 4 education was well and truly in harness. Each year, while she was Senior Commissioning Editor, Naomi compiled and edited a thorough report for the IBA's Educational Advisory Council. We reproduce one here. It conveys the atmosphere of a channel, which, well aware that it does not have all the answers, is yet finding its feet, producing a distinctive educational schedule and looking forward to an equally interesting future.

Annual Report 1983–84

As befits a new Channel, the pattern of educational programming has not yet settled down. Let us hope it never will. Previous papers to the EAC have outlined the overall policy framework, structural objectives and the constraints within which educational programming on Channel 4 is planned and implemented. These discussions will not be re-iterated here.

---

12. Sargant, N. E., with Carol Haslam and Derek Jones (1984) Educational Programmes on Channel 4, 1983/4, a report for the IBA's Educational Advisory Council (unpublished).

What we now have is a full year's experience to work on, and a year in which it is reasonable to suggest that Channel 4 has become a better understood and increasingly accepted part of the broadcasting landscape. Inevitably, the increasing success and audience reach of the channel as a whole has a beneficial effect on the reach of educational programming, though, at the same time, it shows up areas which will continue to be of only specialist and minority interest no matter how much the overall Channel audience grows. It is worth comparing the reach and penetration of the Channel in summer 1983, as compared with summer 1984, since this provides the overall audience framework in which educational programming is located. (The figures are from mid-June.)

Table 1.

| | C4 | | BBC2 | |
	1983	1984	1983	1984
Audience share				
	4.8%	6.0%	10.8%	9.9%
Average hours watched per week				
All individuals	53 mins	1 hour 12 mins	1hour 58 mins	1 hour 59 mins
Average hours viewed by C4 viewers	2 hours 10 mins	2 hours 13 mins	3 hours 4 mins	2 hours 50 mins
% watching in a given week	41%	54%	64%	70%
% watching in four weeks	67%	80%	87%	90%

It will be seen that an increasing number of people are prepared to turn to the Channel, but they visit it for a limited number of specific programmes. There is, effectively, an inheritance effect from programme to programme. ITV's scheduling strategies are not applicable to Channel 4 and Ehrenberg's Laws do not necessarily therefore apply!

Channel 4 and ITV

Before considering Channel 4's programming in more detail it is worth briefly reminding ourselves of the nature of the ITV system and where Channel 4 fits in to it. We say this because Channel 4 is charged with 'catering for tastes not otherwise catered for on ITV', and there are some educational objectives which, by definition, it cannot cater for, which should be catered for on a mass channel rather than a specialist channel: adult basic education is the most obvious example of this.

ITV and Channel 4 do not have access to the same audience, and the two audiences have different habits and interests. It is also the case that the nature of the commitment to educational programming inevitably differs on the two channels. Channel 4 has a particular educational mandate, and while it does have access to better times of day for programmes, it does not have any access to the mass audience which has greater educational needs.

However, within this simple generalisation there are choices to be made. On each channel there is scheduling time which is accessible and desirable (e.g. peak time), times which is accessible but not desirable (e.g. Sunday mornings) and times which are only accessible to those who are at home during weekdays. The ITV system can choose only which output to transmit nationally, and therefore does not have this added flexibility.

As far as the EAC is concerned, an additional factor has to be remembered, which is that Channel 4 is required to take programming from independent production companies as well as from ITV. Many of these are small companies, sometimes coming together simply to make one programme or a series of programmes. It is not feasible, with these companies, to plan so far in advance as ITV needs to do, both for its own production and for Channel 4 production; nor is it possible to be as public in response to their proposals in advance of their commissioning. Their commissions are in competition on Channel 4 with commissions from ITV. At this point, production ability, efficiency and price all enter into the equation to be balanced against educational purpose.

The educational vehicle available to us, and our audience

It is also worth reminding ourselves that, in contrast to schools programming, or the OU, we are not providing an *integrated* multi-media learning experience. Nor are we providing programmes primarily to a 'closed' audience, learning either directly or through an intermediary, where we could more directly assess the needs and measure the benefits. We are aiming at an open audience where contact with any intermediary is optional, and the degree of commitment to study or to pursue the subject rests entirely with the motivation of the learner.

The majority of our series do not aim to provide cumulative sequential subject matter. They aim to encourage, stimulate, open the eyes, and increase the curiosity of the viewers who are then offered ways of pursuing these stimuli if they wish. Sometimes the suggestions may be for individual activities, e.g. booklists for reading or going to art galleries. Sometimes a network of informal groups may be available, e.g. through the International Broadcasting Trust (IBT). Sometimes the back-up simply provides information for better personal decisions, e.g. *For What it's Worth*.

The current exception to this has been the numeracy project, where the content is sequential in nature, and a workbook and learning quizzes are available through the National Extension College (NEC). The audience, particularly for *Counting On*, stood up very well against other programmes transmitted at the time. The series that was out of line was the first transmission of *Numbers at Work*, which suffered from being moved to 6pm from 6.30pm. A renewed campaign with the Adult Literacy and Basic Skills Unit (ALBSU) – Numeracy Week in September 1983 – paid dividends, and ALBSU records attendance at numeracy classes as being 10 per cent up on the previous year.

The major systematic educational experiment, again to be carried out with Yorkshire Television (YTV) and the National Extension College (NEC), is a distance learning course, *A Question of Economics*. This provides an important new opportunity for adults since the course is geared to a BTEC continuing education credit. If this experiment proves successful, it opens the way to collaboration over a number of subject areas at a sub-degree level, which would go some way to replace the lost opportunity to meet national needs represented by the decision of the MSC not to proceed with training-related programming on Channel 4. The *Economics* model is very similar to the original BBC/NEC preparatory course model, documented elsewhere. It makes a variety of inter-related, but not inter-dependent educational elements available to potential students with a minimum number of barriers to access, and allows people to engage in the learning enterprise to the extent that they are able and willing to do, i.e. on their own terms.

Quantity of programming

We planned our educational output on the assumption that five and a half hours a week would be directly commissioned as educational and that a further one and a half hours would be achieved by the wrapping round of general output in particular of the major documentary series. In the event, the quantity of output so organised has averaged around eight hours a week, rather than the seven hours required by the IBA. This is due in part to the wide range of informative programmes commissioned by colleagues, and their interest in its wider application.

It is important to note that our resources, both financial and human, have stretched too far in this area in our first year. And we shall need to be more selective in this regard in 1984/85. However, we have used the time period to good advantage in learning what type of wraparound is most effective and needed for what types of programme.

Audience reaction

Apart from a small number of in-depth surveys on individual projects and 'shrieks' from the Duty Office, there are three main sources of systematic information available to us about our audience's reaction: (a) the Broadcasters Audience Research Board (BARB) measurements of the size of the audience and its appreciation of programmes where the audience is large enough, (b) regular series-based research commissioned by the Channel from the British Market Research Bureau (BMRB), which can include questions on content, knowledge of the availability of back-up, etc, and (c) take-up of back-up provided. With as many series as we have, it is not feasible to report individually on each one. However, an idea of the range of reaction can be gained from Table 2, where we have compared the average audience for a number of series, with the relevant audience appreciation mean and noted against it, as an indication of educational penetration, the percentage of the audience leaving school at 14 and under.

We can argue forever about whether or not it is the size of the audience or the level of their appreciation that matters here. It is, on the one hand, satisfying that the quality of *The Heart of the Dragon* was so appreciated, and, on the other hand, also encouraging that *Years Ahead*, for example, is reaching efficiently an older and less well educated audience.

We have been able to discover from such surveys whether the programmes are moving at the right pace, contain the appropriate number of items, and are covering content areas which match audience needs. Copies of the reports are made available to producers for feedback and, particularly if they are working on new series, the research is able materially to assist future planning.

Requests for back-up and the accompanying letters provide our third major source of information, although we are not staffed to read these individually and rely on Broadcasting Support Services (BSS) to pass them through to programme producers. We have not been able to predict the demand for back-up, or the lack of it. The variation in demand continues to surprise us. It is easy to theorise about the instrumental nature of people's interest, and to discover that people are much less interested in arts and culture than in health. However, we then get contradictory evidence, with the demand for the second Keating programme, *Tom Keating on Impressionism*, continuing at the same high level as its predecessor, *Tom Keating on Painters*.

Table 2

	Audience Appreciation Index	Penetration (% watching series)	(% leaving school at 14)	
Jack's Game	69	27	29	Apr'84
Heart of Dragon	79	26	24	Apr'84
Amateur Naturalist	78	23	33	Dec'83
Fragile Earth	78	22	22	Dec'83
Gardeners' Calendar	76	20	40	Apr'84
Wellbeing	70	20	21	Apr'84
Good Food Show	69	20	31	Apr'84
Picture of Health	71	17	26	Dec'83
For What it's Worth	70	16	27	Dec'83
Spice of Life	76	13	24	Dec'83
Flashback (Family)	68	12	32	Apr'84
Flashback (Media)	66	11	27	Dec'83
The Arabs	70	10	26	Dec'83
Built in Britain	72	9	30	Apr'84
Years Ahead	68	9	46	Apr'84
Cautionary Tales	67	8	32	Apr'84
Years Ahead	70	7	39	Dec'83
Anything we can do	66	6	20	Apr'84
Today's History	66	5	35	Dec'83
Making the Most of	66	5	33	Dec'83
Book 4	62	5	15	Dec'83
The Enthusiasts	67	3	34	Apr'84
Fanny Waterman	64	3	23	Dec'83
Counting On	62	3	29	Dec'83

The schedule

Our output in 1983–84 has followed very much the lines that we adumbrated this time last year. We worked within a framework of educational objectives matched against a range of scheduling slots, some of which were extremely well matched and some of which were less so. Sometimes this was because the programming was too good for the slot, and sometimes we just didn't know quite how to schedule some new material.

We have been completely caught up in the unsatisfactory argument about the best way for Channel 4 to build up to the 7pm News. On the one hand, it is necessary to give the news a good build up, and education, it is argued, does not provide this. On the other hand, it is possible to argue that people who are more likely to watch *Channel 4 News* are also more likely to watch arts, culture or political education. There is no question that 6.30pm, especially in the North of England, Scotland and Northern Ireland, and for the working class, is an appreciably better time than 6pm, and several quite valuable series have suffered simply by being put half an hour earlier. The audience figures for Numeracy make this point very clearly, as did the audience for *Gardeners' Calendar*, when it was moved to 6pm for a few weeks.

However, autumn 1984 sees a change in scheduling policy which will bring with it advantages and disadvantages for educational programming. It will not now be possible to plan and operate within a given number of known slots, but programmes will be scheduled as and where they are felt best placed. While initially this is, in many ways, a tribute to the quality of educational programmes and audience response to them, it will be important to monitor it to ensure that series are appropriately and responsibly scheduled in relation to audience needs.

The main effect of the additional opportunity provided to the Channel by opening up for longer hours is to place *Years Ahead* at 3.45 to 4.30pm (before *Countdown* rather than after it), and to move the children's strand to Saturday lunchtimes. An additional bonus is that the live magazine programme to be provided by Thames A Plus team twice a week to Channel 4 – to be called *A plus 4* – is consciously to build some major elements of its content to be of appeal, interest and support to those not in employment. In this, they will have the support of their Access Unit.

The overuse of repeats is not a problem for us – we have quite a queue of new programming jostling for proper scheduling time.

The 'quality' of the audience

The effects that we are seeking to achieve are, in the main, not easily measurable. We are not working in an evaluative situation where the agricultural/botany paradigm is the appropriate one, nor can illuminative evaluation be of much assistance when most of the effects are likely to be individual ones, usually private and personal, and ones which cannot be observed or measured through intermediaries. Whereas macro measurements of size of audience can be obtained for most programmes or series, qualitative or appreciation figures can only be obtained where audience sizes are large enough to provide adequate sub-samples. These systems are rarely adaptable enough to permit detailed investigation of audience effects.

Where more detailed studies of viewers' reaction have been carried out, e.g. *For What it's Worth, Staging an Opera, Years Ahead, The Heart of the Dragon, Well Being*, they are inevitably based on a sample of viewers: those who have already displayed an above-average interest in the subject by joining a study group, for example, (as in the case of IBT output), or sending off for back-up material. Statistically, they do not represent the 'open' audience.

These problems are not new, of course, and have been discussed elsewhere. They are technically soluble enough, given enough time and money, but such resources will never be available for the majority of projects. It would be worth selecting a specific number of areas/projects each year on which to concentrate research effort in order to gradually increase our corpus of knowledge. It would certainly make sense to collaborate with the ITV system to do this, and it might even be appropriate to mount a joint bench-mark study of needs and utilisation with the BBC, now that strategies between the two systems are becoming less dissimilar and we have agreed that we should liaise over areas of social need, e.g. basic education and handicap.

In the meantime, we continue to draw on research from such bodies as ACACE and NIACE to inform our assessment of people's needs and interests, complemented by the voices of such bodies as the EAC, the Channel 4 board, the Department of Education and Science, Manpower Services Commission, etc.

What happens if it works?

This question, first used in that form on the satellite demonstration in the Rockies, is not one that general output broadcasters have usually bothered with. The work of the Media Unit and the designation of some kinds of broadcasting as 'social action broadcasting' have made many more broadcasters conscious of the possible powerful effects of their work. We start from the premise that we *expect* all our educational broadcasting to have some effect – whether we can entirely predict it or not is another matter! We do not find the distinction between social action broadcasting and educational broadcasting a helpful one. We would argue that all educational broadcasting has a 'social' goal. Whether the goal is an individual one or a community one, whether the goal is personal or familial change, are not critical distinctions. We also *take for granted* the fact that much general output broadcasting is educational in effect. It is for all these reasons that we do not draw hard and fast lines round different types of programming. We have continued and extended our major commitment to providing a wide variety of possibilities for run-up, back-up and follow-up to just about every sort of programme the Channel has transmitted – from entertainment to opera, from current affairs to dance, from health to archaeology and gardening. Discussions are even taking place about providing forms of back-up to some aspects of *Channel 4 News!*

The forms of activity are also very varied as later sections of this paper demonstrate in more detail. While the majority of printed materials are aimed at individuals for their own personal use, many are also designed for group use; and there is no question that *SEE 4*, now in its seventh edition and with a print-run of 160,000, provides a vital link between the Channel and the wide range of educational and social intermediaries interested in utilising our general and specifically educational programmes. We all meet frequently with community groups to ensure that we are addressing people's needs as well as possible, and we maintain contact with the majority of the main educational organisations. Some idea of the scale of this side of our work can be gained from the fact that we broadcasted around 90 educational series in 1983–94 and look to broadcasting some 80 in 1984–85.

We are extremely grateful to our colleagues, the ITV CCEOs for their valuable work on back-up to 'common list' programmes and to individual officers who take on the responsibility for backing up their own companies' programmes for Channel 4. We would also like to thank the triumvirate of BSS, Network Scotland, and the Educational Guidance Service for Adults (EGSA) in Belfast, who play a vital role in working with us and our production companies across an incredibly wide range of programming.

Copying off air

A major breakthrough this year has been the establishment of a modest voluntary licensing scheme for copying some parts of Channel 4 output off air. It has not been easy to explain to people accustomed to free copying of educational programmes why Channel 4 could not similarly grant such rights to users.

It is now our policy, wherever we can afford it, and owners (actors, musicians, etc) agree, to negotiate for copying off air rights at the initial contract stage for all programmes commissioned as educational. We are also endeavouring to identify some areas of general output which may have educational value and include them in the scheme; examples are *Opinions, Voices,* and *A Week in Politics*. We are extremely grateful to Guild Learning for their continued stimulus and support in getting the scheme off the ground. We are also pleased that the Independent Television Companies Association (ITCA) is now able to extend copying off air permission to the educational programmes the ITV companies produce for Channel 4.

A Review of education areas

The arts and culture

1983–84: Programming for this area presents us with a similar problem to that faced in all educational programming: those who already appreciate the arts have benefited from education and will find easily find arts and culture programmes; those who have been denied access to these areas of life will not find their way to them or believe they are for them. The distinction between programmes commissioned by Michael Kustow, Commissioning Editor for Arts programmes, and our art education programmes is that we try to make arts and culture available in an accessible and demystified way. Perhaps the two key examples of this were the two Tom Keating series, which had an impact way beyond their audience size, encouraging 20,000 people to send for booklets which were not free. We work closely with Michael Kustow, in the hope that people so encouraged – for example by *Design Matters* – will also watch his current major series on design. We have not set out, at this stage, to reproduce 'popular' culture on the screen, but to make more available the best of our cultural tradition. A clear example of this is *Six Centuries of Verse*, where a representative anthology of poetry is spoken superbly, but simply, providing the audience with a quality of performance they otherwise could not have. Such series have been complemented by programmes which demonstrate and encourage individual creativity; the best example of this is *Everyone a Special Kind of Artist*, presented by Ken Sprague.

It is fair to say that, while virtually all the series in this area have been strong on screen, they have not, for some of the reasons just discussed, been major audience-pullers. A most interesting and challenging area has been to discover what is the most appropriate format for dealing with books. There have been three series of *Book Four* so far, the first one in a half-hour slot on a Wednesday early evening, and the next two in an extended and more varied and accessible format and slot on Sundays in the late afternoon. The audience figures are not encouraging at either time, although the programme does reach a motivated audience and achieved critical acclaim. Reading is, as we know, a major leisure activity among the population as a whole. Maybe it is simply that people who are really keen on reading prefer to read about books rather than watch them being discussed on TV

1984–85: The coming year sees a strong and continuing commitment to arts and culture with a second series of *Six Centuries of Verse*, a new series of *Book Four*, and an important new series on the Spanish guitar, *Guitarra*, with Julian Bream. Visual education maintains its presence with a new series on architecture, *Space on Earth*, and a further run of *Design Matters*. We are also experimenting with a quiz format in the area of art education – *Gallery* asks two panels of contestants to identify and discuss a range of painters and paintings, all of which are on view to the public.

1985–86: We wish here to repeat those early arts series which were strong but suffered in audience impact from the generally low audience early in the life of Channel 4. (They also need to be repeated before the rights run out!) The two new series to note are *A Love Affair with Nature*, presented by Edwin Mullins, which will, we hope, feature for back-up on the common list; and a new initiative of modest collaboration with the OU Centre for Continuing Education, where a new course, *Looking into Paintings* will be launched in tandem with a television series of the same title to be made for Channel 4 by an independent production company.

The pains and pleasures of presentation

Writing and thinking – and an all-woman line-up for her own honorary degree at the Open University, April 2005: including Peggotty Graham, presenter, and Brenda Gourley, Vice Chancellor.

History and archaeology

1983–84: History and archaeology have been and continue to be major features of our educational programming. It is also an area which the audience clearly appreciates. Perhaps the most important point to make is that we have chosen to adopt an eclectic attitude to history, not only in the level to which different series are pitched, but in differing intellectual approaches and television formats. Those whose demand is for unashamed 'naked intellect' find it in the lectures to camera from brilliant historians in *The Making of Britain*. Those who have learnt little history, but are interested in a broader view of the world, find *The World – a Television History* an accessible entry point; extremely innovative computer graphics show ill-understood inter-relationships over space and time. The most challenging series to make was *Passage to Britain*, a historical survey of the waves of immigration to this country designed to provide a perspective against which current issues could be assessed. All of the historical series have been complemented by some form of back-up literature, most of which has been intellectually successful, but none of which has been numerically very successful. We have used the TV medium itself to provide an update, both historical and political, on the now famous series, *The World at War*, whose executive producer was Jeremy Isaacs; the four programmes were designed to punctuate the repeat of the series, identifying new information and interpretations which have emerged since the series was first produced.

1984–85: This year's main history series are lineal descendants of *The World at War*. Jeremy's last major series before the establishment of Channel 4 was *Ireland – A Television History*. The suggestion that histories of Scotland and of Wales should now follow was irresistible, and it is these two series, *Scotland's Story*, presented by Tom Steele, and *The Dragon has Two Tongues*, with co-presenters Wynford Vaughan Thomas and Gwynn Alf Williams, who have radically opposed political positions, will occupy pride of place in this year's schedules. *The Making of Britain* will continue its chronological survey, as will *The World – A Television History*. Also to be transmitted is a personal *tour de force* by A.J.P. Taylor, *How Wars End*.

1985–86: After all this, one may well ask, what more can we possibly do? It is true that there will be less new commissioning for this area , and some good early series may well be repeated, e.g. *Flashback*. We have decided to transmit an important new series made by WNET, New York, *Heritage: Civilisation and the Jews*, presented by Abba Eban, first shown in the US this autumn. The educational wraparound being prepared for this in the US is a telecourse, which is very impressive and should prove of major interest to educators here. There is also likely to be a major series on the history of Poland. Two new ten-part series, using archive film, but contextualising the material for future generations, will be based on *The March of Time* archives.

Basic skills

1983–84: The commitment we have made to numeracy in our first live year has already been discussed. The repeat of *Counting On* this autumn completes two years of this work. The current demands on the schedule mean that it is not realistic to move on immediately to a third run of the three series; nor has there been any major demand for us to do so, although the individual audiences for the programmes continue to hold up perfectly well in the slots in which they have been scheduled. We need to have a clearer assessment of interest and priorities quite soon, if we are to consider a third year's provision, which could then more appropriately commence in autumn 1985 to coincide with the start of the education year.

1985-86: Our second major commitment to basic education will continue to be in the field of consumer education, with *For What it's Worth* carrying on its blend of informative and investigatory programming. Winter 1985 sees an extension of its range into holiday choices, and, dependent on audience reaction, this may or may not be continued in 1985/86. *For What it's Worth* has continued to justify its position in peak time, featuring in the Channel's Top Ten on a number of occasions. It has also enabled us to engage with the OU and the Department of Energy in providing an unusual Home Energy Audit and conservation service to viewers. The programme is unique in that it not only provides detailed information free to any viewer who wishes to send for it, but the programme's staff also respond to individual consumer enquiries and requests for help in a most conscientious and effective manner.

The successful formula developed in the first two series of *Coping* will be used to look at the problems faced by the unemployed. We will also endeavour to find a similarly successful formula to that used by *Energy Matters* in the area of personal money management and family finance – where basic information is complemented by individualised advice.

The environment

1983–84: Programmes in this broad area have been spread over various slots, with varying degrees of success. For a period of months last winter, a Sunday afternoon slot gave viewers an opportunity to see programmes on different aspects of the British countryside. Subjects ranged from rural vernacular architecture (*Built in Britain*) to field sports (*Jack's Game*), although whether there was much overlap between the large audience for both series is uncertain – but unlikely.

There is no doubt that the series *Fragile Earth* provides our most prestigious natural history output. The exceptionally high quality of these films is not only acknowledged by the specialists (three of the four entered for the Wildscreen Festival have reached the final), but the general audience appreciation index averages 90 per cent. The problem we face in future is trying to find a steady, if small, flow of films of this calibre, since they are exceptionally expensive to produce. However, other high quality films in the same slot were also well received, including Naresh Bedi's *Ganges Gharial*, Derek Bromhall's *Kitum*, and a couple of Oxford Scientific/Anglia films; some of these lack the strong conceptual framework that distinguishes *Fragile Earth*.

Following the purchase of Gerald Durrell's *Ark on the Move* series, *The Amateur Naturalist* was a specially commissioned series, made as a co-production with a Canadian independent, aimed at encouraging ordinary people to observe and conserve the natural world. This aim was supported by a national competition to find Channel 4's own 'amateur naturalists'; the winners have now been identified and have taken part in a film 'special', visiting the Durrells at their zoo in Jersey. The 'special' will precede a repeat of the series. *The Amateur Naturalist* pack, prepared in association with the Conservation Foundation, was well subscribed to, although it cost well over £1.

Border Television's series *Land of the Lakes*, written and presented by Melvyn Bragg, was transmitted on consecutive evenings in Christmas week. This was the first documentary series to be made by Border and it received a warm response. The films traced the geological, social and cultural history of the English Lake District, featuring those who live there now and the many representations of the area in art and literature.

BMRB research has revealed some interesting characteristics about audiences for environment programmes. For example, *The Amateur Naturalist* was considered a very attractive series for young people, but drew a relatively 'old' audience profile. Recent BMRB research on *Jack's Game* shows a significant percentage of viewers opposed to some or all field sports. Only 10 per cent of viewers thought their attitudes had been changed by the programme, and those of the vast majority were less favourable than they had been before. Fears that the series might encourage viewers to participate have not been substantiated; well over 90 per cent of viewers have done nothing to increase their involvement, if any, in field sports. The implication of this finding for more acceptable sports and activities is worth further research. Appreciation indices for all series in this area , as mentioned earlier, were particularly high, and the main reason quoted for not viewing was 'not knowing that the programme existed'; this is a common finding for most Channel 4 programmes, but it is particularly frustrating in this area because of the extremely high ratings gained by similar programmes on other channels.

1984–85: Motivated by this particular finding, it was agreed to schedule environment programmes according to a coherent plan with improved 'packaging', follow-up and promotion to a wider public. This will take the form in the first half of 1984 of a Conservation Season, featuring programmes about both the natural and the built environment. Programmes for the season will consist of relevant films already in production, plus singles and series due for a good repeat run. Appropriate projects from other commissioning editors' output will be included in the promotional material, and the whole season will be accompanied by appropriate print material and will encourage viewer participation and feedback from around the country. The season will start with an *Amateur Naturalists of the Year* special, to be transmitted in Christmas week, and end with a live evening of entertainment and conservation activities on Whitsun Bank Holiday.

1985–86: We already have many films in production for this period – programmes in this area often take many years to make. These include a major series on the natural history of China, more *Fragile Earth* films from Central America and possibly Africa, two more films on Indian wildlife, and some *Survival* films shot in Europe. From Britain, there will be films shot in Cumbria, Dartmoor, and the Shetland Islands. If our conservation season is successful, we hope to repeat the event in 1986.

For and about disabled people

We have adopted a catholic approach to programming for and about disabled people – accepting proposals both from integrated production companies, and, more unusually, from a production company whose members are entirely disabled. The definitions and interests have been heterogeneous. The results have been interesting and varied. Some groupings which came together have not proved robust, and it is not yet clear to us that we should be giving time to a regular magazine programme covering disability generally. In 1984–85 we are concentrating on the needs of the deaf and hard of hearing, and we shall build on this in 1984–85 if it works. *The Listening Eye* is a current affairs programme for those whose first language is British Sign Language (BSL). We shall also continue, if practicable, the pattern we have built up of obtaining a double advantage from our regular educational repeat strand – by selecting them in discussion with the deaf organisations, and re-transmitting them with subtitles and/or sign language, whichever is most appropriate. It was particularly gratifying that this year's coverage of the Paralympic Games was produced by a disabled company, Interface – commissioned by Adrian Metcalfe, Commissioning Editor for Sport, as part of his coverage of athletic events.

Pre-retirement and the retired

It is helpful to remind readers of the regular commitment, made over two years now, to the interests and needs of the over 60s. Particularly since they are not homogeneous – at all! – as a group, the problems of content, tone of voice and pace were great. It is a tribute to the independent company who suggested the idea that the programme has grown in strength as well in the size and loyalty of the audience – as the BMRB surveys show.

How long we can and should continue with the same formula will always be a subject for discussion. Current commitments run through to mid-1985.

We have delayed further commitments hoping that the valuable work of John Willcocks, the IBA research fellow studying this area, can inform future decisions. To have the possibility of formative evaluation is rare in television; too often evaluation informs only after the event. Obviously there are still many older people who do not even know the programme exists, but then many older people do not even know that Channel 4 exists! What we hope for from the IBA report is the illuminative dimension which may add depth and imagination to straight numbers and attitudinal measurements which have so far confirmed and comforted us in our planning.

We have decided *not* to engage for the moment in pre-retirement education, or in child or parent education. These decisions relate less to any agreed view of the importance of the subject matter than to a practical view of the types of scheduling times and educational priorities that exist in the Channel. Accident prevention, another IBA priority, represents a further example of the type of programming we do not feel is best placed on Channel 4. Accident prevention and home safety are mass, basic concerns which should be provided in peak time on ITV, as the BBC does on BBC 1. The contribution we could make to this extremely important area on Channel 4 would be, dare we say it, derisory in terms of national needs. We prefer not to *pretend* to be doing it.

Health and family

1983–84: The Friday night slot has continued to attract large audiences for a wide range of health related programmes. The more individualist approach of some programmes was balanced in the autumn of 1983 by two series on the social and political determinants of health. In September 1983, an attempt was made to construct an educational package linked to a major drama series. N.F. Newman's *The Nation's Health*, transmitted on four Thursday nights, was followed by a discussion programme on Friday nights, which picked up important issues and examined the arguments more explicitly. A Programme Guide was prepared to accompany the package and provide background information for discussion purposes. The dramas caused considerable debate, particularly within the health service, and the follow-up programmes were well-supported. Take-up of the guide, however, was disappointing. The whole project took place at a time of much concern about the future of the NHS – a debate which still continues. Next, a series about the politics of health turned out – unexpectedly, it has to be said – to win a substantial audience, reaching the Top Ten on a number of occasions. It emphasised in particular the class and gender factors in health inequalities and devoted time to occupational health and to similar analyses of health in Kenya and Bangladesh. In addition to its wide general audience this series was popular with health professionals and is much in demand for non-theatrical and educational use.

Well Being has continued through the second year with another series and three specials – on Heart Disease, Diabetes and the *Sunday Times* Getting in Shape experiment. The success of the presenter, Pam Armstrong, was confirmed when she was lured away to ITN! A range of different approaches and programme forms were explored in the second series, some with more success than others. One programme focussed on Walsall in the West Midlands, containing a film report on the town's poor health record with a public meeting where health professionals and local residents met to discuss problems, policies and priorities. The programme was prepared in cooperation with the National Association of Community Health Councils and a special guide to assessing the health of your community, written with them, was produced. The series as a whole was planned in association with the Royal College of General Practitioners, who have expressed a high level of satisfaction with this form of collaboration.

An interesting experiment was carried out following a film about women's experience of, and ambivalent feelings about, abortion. Working with the caring agencies in this field and funded from health education sources, a network of counsellors was set up to respond to requests from women viewers to join the kind of self-help group featured in the programme. A postal and telephone referral service organised by BSS acted as intermediary; BSS also worked with the Family Planning Association (FPA) to recruit and train the coordinators. Although a significant number of women used the referral service, the success of the subsequent group work varied from region to region. The focus on abortion caused inevitable concern among anti-abortionists, although all agreed that there was a serious unavailability of support and counselling in this area.

The best publicised (or should we say 'most widely publicised'?) series came from YTV. *Sex Matters* enabled ordinary people from many walks of life to talk openly and unselfconsciously about their own sexual relationships – both the pleasures and the anxieties. The series was well received by both the general public and health professionals working in marriage guidance and psycho-sexual counselling. The published book sold well, although the take-up of the free factsheets was rather disappointing.

This strand continues to generate the highest average ratings on the Channel in the factual area – this year averaging just under 2 million viewers per programme. We have three main sources on audience reaction: (a) BARB gives us basic demographic data, (b) BMRB research commissioned by Sue Stoessl, Channel 4 head of Marketing, provides more detailed information from a cross section of the audience on various issues, (c) in depth research has been carried out by Robin McCron, of the Centre for Mass Communication Research, on *Well Being*. The last report was published before production on the second series began and various recommendations were noted and implemented. In addition, numerous meetings with health professionals across the country have generated considerable informal feedback about the perception of the programmes and their strengths and weaknesses. There is no doubt that the Channel has established a reputation in the health world for making a modest but valued contribution to public knowledge and understanding of health-related issues. Expressions of support and encouragement are frequently received from the field and articulated at meetings and conferences.

1984-85: The coming year will include a similar mix of subject areas, starting in the autumn with a major series on food and nutrition, *Food for Thought*. This is the first project to be co-funded by the Health Education Council (HEC) and we have worked closely with them to publicise and promote the series and the accompanying booklet throughout the country.

This will be followed by another series on attitudes to sexuality, commissioned as a pair with *Sex Matters*. *Just Sex* explores the social determinants of our ideas and feelings about sex. Once again, it relies heavily on first-hand accounts of individual attitudes and feelings, but is richly illustrated with examples from the mass media and with quotations from those who have written on the subject over the last couple of centuries. It aims to analyse the origins of our ideas and expectations and to match these against realities.

Relationships also form the basis of other series in the first half of 1985 – a series on *Families* with Mavis Nicholson, and a sequel to *Mothers by Daughters* in which Bel Mooney talks to men about their relationships with their fathers. For those who prefer to live by themselves, there is a four-part series, *A Life of My Own*, in which the negative and positive aspects of single living are explored.

The crisis in the health service is likely to continue through 1985 and the public debate on Government moves towards privatisation will also impinge on NHS policies. A series which makes a contribution to this debate has been planned, offering viewers a comparative study of health care systems in different societies with various political and economic orientations.

1985–86: Finally, one area which has not received adequate attention in this strand, so far, is mental illness. A number of projects have been commissioned to remedy this omission, starting with a three-part *Well Being Special* on the treatment of the mentally ill in March 1985. Further series are planned for 1986, including a major series on counselling and psychotherapy, a short series on the history of mental hospitals and the treatment of 'madness' and a three-part look at schizophrenia. Meanwhile our commitment to general health issues continues.

In and out of work

Euphemisms for our shared concern about increasing unemployment take a number of forms and a number of different descriptors. Can broadcasters do anything to ameliorate the problems, nationally, locally, or at an individual level? Obviously they cannot do anything structural about the lack of jobs in this country. Channel 4 had hoped that it would have been able to work with the MSC on broadcasting designed to support a range of adult and youth training initiatives on a systematic basis, rather as the BBC works with the OU at the level of higher education. It has been a decision of the current government that such broadcasting initiatives should not proceed. Therefore the only immediate options are at the macro/current affairs level to endeavour the cause people to be more thoughtful about, and understanding of, the nature and relationships of work and non-work, and, at the micro level, to offer to people the skills, insights and encouragement to pursue new paths for themselves whether through work in the conventional sense or through happy and creative activities.

We have not, heretofore, commissioned much programming which could be classified as 'in and out of work' with the exception of the *Be Your Own Boss* programmes. We have preferred to concentrate on providing opportunities and ideas for people about how to use their leisure (enforced or voluntary) creatively. The result has been a valuable strand of programming called 'for people with more time than money'. There is a still a need and demand for such programmes and we repeat many of them with good effect. However, we shall this year and, in 1985–86, increasingly endeavour to focus on the problems of being 'in and out work' from a variety of aspects. For those who are young there is a series called *I Could Do That* to encourage them to get going on their own. In 1985–86, as indicated above, the *Coping* team will look at coping with unemployment, matched with a series discussing *How to Survive at Work*. In another point/counterpoint, a series on the role of the multi-nationals will be balanced by one on the role of Trade Unions, and another on the patterns of international labour migration. We are also planning a series designed to look at the changing nature of work/non-work.

Leisure

As we came on air in 1982, we distinguished between active leisure and creative leisure, and did what educators would call PE in our educational output.

Active leisure: Increasingly, and mainly due to the imagination of Adrian Metcalfe, we have turned this area of programming over to him, where it is in very good hands. Whether or not it is now validated as educational is immaterial. It will continue to exist, be valuable to people in extending their skills and ambitions and frequently gain large audiences. The new areas to be given coverage in 1984–85 include squash and climbing. We shall certainly continue with the re-legitimisation of walking (as in Alistair Hetherington's *Six Great Walks*) – that great non-competitive, accessible and free sporting activity – that we decided would form part of our output from the beginning. We also plan to repeat on a regular basis series already made on swimming, tennis, exercise and fitness.

Creative leisure: There will continue to be, as we have observed earlier, an extremely important role for programming in the area of creative leisure.

The fact that we have given it an identity which is dictated by the phrase 'for people who have more time than money' does not change its essential purpose. It points up the irony that the rich who have money have always known about the value of leisure and have never had any qualms about using it to good effect. That knowledge and confidence has now to be shared among a much wider number of people. Therefore this area of programming covers a very wide area of content: it is dictated by the need to use one's own resources and abilities as well as possible to take effective advantage of the resources available in the community. There are, not surprisingly, a wide variety of exciting series jostling for a place in this area and future programming, while continuing such old favourites as gardening and cookery, will also cover such subjects as looking after pets, sewing, flowers and their arrangement, the decorative arts and Low Tech projects. Second series of *As Good as New* and *Make it Pay* are also planned.

Science and technology

These areas have not so far been covered within educational programmes, since it has been assumed that they were to be dealt with by other commissioning editors. While this has been in part the case with extended coverage of science and technology, including on *Channel 4 News*, there has clearly been a lack of material, which *Earth Year 2050* has now started to make up. John Ranelagh, also commissioning editor for religion, has been asked to take particular responsibility for science programming and has commenced commissioning series, which we anticipate will be educational in effect, to start in winter 1985; the format is a current affairs science magazine. We are planning series in the areas of astronomy and geology. A major series on human anatomy, *The Living Body*, has started transmission this autumn.

Computers and new technology

We took a decision early on not to attempt to compete with the massive and very effective investment that the BBC has made into computer education. We shall, in winter 1985, make a modest venture into this area, but we shall aim at younger viewers in an early evening slot. It is the young who are the intellectual leaders in the computer world, and *4 Computer Buffs* is designed for experts. It will be preceded by a repeat of the valuable series teaching BASIC, *Me and My Micro*. We expect to use the experiences of these two series to guide us in our future commissioning decisions in this area.

Social and political

Given the nature of Channel 4, a significant proportion of factual programming falls into this area. It is therefore sometimes difficult to draw a clear distinction between educational and general output programmes in this respect. Much of our news and current affairs output is more educative than that on ITV, and we certainly regard most of our documentary output as educational (see below). However in the first couple of years we devoted one strand to the educational priority 'political literacy' and a report follows on the second of those years.

1983/84: A second series from IBT on development issues, *Utopia Ltd*, was generally felt to have been an improvement on the first series, and the educational network of viewing groups and supporting print material was highly regarded. The series covered major topics like food, health, energy and arms, and locations included Peru, Sri Lanka and Malaysia.

Country Crisis, a series on rural political issues, was widely expected to fill a gap in television's service for rural communities. Unfortunately, it was not as well received by many of the organisations that had welcomed its arrival, as it was by the relatively high audience who watched. The demand for the related booklet was exceptionally good.

From the earliest planning stage, *Cautionary Tales* was produced in collaboration with agencies active in the field of legal rights. It was always intended to assist advice-givers – possibly in a training context – as well as to provide basic civil rights information for a general audience. How far it has succeeded in combining these twin objectives is not yet clear, but there is some evidence to suggest that it did; the telephone referral service provided was well-used and take up of the first class booklets on each topic was very rewarding. Feedback from the specialist field suggests that it was a useful series, worth repeating and updating regularly.

Whose Town is it Anyway? was commissioned as a twin series with *Country Crisis*; it covered current urban issues, particularly in relation to inner city problems. It had an interesting origin, the original idea emerging from a group of community development and voluntary action specialists. In liaison with the production company, and drawing on their extensive network of community contacts throughout the country, the team covered a range of community initiatives and related them to local and government policies. Funds were raised from the Gulbenkian Foundation to sponsor various forms of follow-up activity. Viewing figures, on the other hand, were disappointing, reflecting a general lack of interest in local politics and over-exposure of inner city crises since the riots of 1981. Informal feedback, however, suggested that the opportunity to hear firsthand accounts from people about their own local projects, on a national rather than a regional network, was welcome, and the unusual variety of related local activities certainly broke new ground.

This is not an area where a high level of audience response is expected, nor do producers expect to reach a broad general audience. The only in-depth data we have is on *Utopia Ltd*, where Channel 4 and the IBT commissioned special research projects. The main conclusion from both was that the audience was youngish, well-educated, predominantly male and already fairly committed to international concerns. These viewers were appreciative, although not in an uncritical way; they wished to see further programmes on development issues, listing topics they felt should be covered.

Other series in this area were on the whole well received by those viewers who made a point of tuning in, but the average ratings rarely exceeded half a million; nevertheless it is worth noting that these ratings compare very favourably with current affairs programmes – since these often cover similar topics, there seems to be some evidence that people welcome a more systematic, series approach to those topics in which they have a personal or professional interest.

Documentary series

1984–84: The most distinctive feature has been the sequence of three major international series. It was interesting that, although they shared a common aim – to explore in depth the history, culture and current state of a particular nation or group of nations – the production companies each adopted a completely different approach to their task. *The Arabs* was structured around an Arab presenter, who focused on a social analysis related to one Arab country. In *The Heart of the Dragon* the producer/directors alone were responsible for shaping the material in each film, drawing on extensive research and expert opinion; the commentary was written by them, but spoken by an actor. By contrast, *Africa* was very much Basil Davidson's account of the history of the continent; although the production team worked with him over a period of years to translate his ideas into televisual form, he was a strong presence in each programme, talking both to camera and over film.

Each of these techniques attracted praise and criticism. *The Arabs* was praised for enabling authentic Arab voices to explain themselves and their world direct to the viewer, but criticised for being occasionally dull and didactic and not sufficiently challenging of the Arab perspective, particularly on recent history. *The Heart of the Dragon* was praised for its detailed and uncluttered look at everyday life in China and for the fact that, in many programmes, commentary was only used to give basic information; viewers could draw their own conclusions from the first-hand accounts of the Chinese themselves. It was, on the other hand, criticised when commentary included value judgements, particularly since the voice presenting the interpretation was anonymous, and, in some sense, authoritative. Some also felt that the technique of allowing a story to unfold before the camera led occasionally to rather too long, slow and sometimes boring sequences. *Africa* was praised for its clearly constructed storyline, seen to reflect the views of a highly experienced and respected scholar, who could offer insights and knowledge to a predominantly western audience; being a white 'outsider' himself, he commanded credibility and authority with that audience. The opposite view was that Africa's story should have been told more through the voices of Africans themselves, and, in contrast, that this particular white man identified so closely with Africa that he failed to present those aspects of the story that were less favourable to Africans.

All three series were acclaimed for the quality of their photography and their high production values. Everyone agreed that they offered real insights into cultures that had previously received little television attention. The criticisms raise questions and issues that are of fundamental importance in documentary film-making and are worthy of much fuller discussion.

At other points in the year some very different series attracted interest and comment. Angela Pope's films on *Childhood* attempted to capture the essence of individual children's lives and their views and experience of the world. They did this partly by 'fly-on-the-wall' techniques and partly by reconstruction, but with no commentary and no interviews. The result was four fascinating and moving profiles of four very different children growing up in different circumstances in contemporary Britain. In that respect, they told us as much about social class, rural and urban environments and the education system, as they did about the children themselves.

Another remarkable series, called *Survive,* was made by Nick Downie. Its theme was the apparent fragility of the human mind and body and the ability of some individuals to cope with the most extreme forms of physical and mental stress. The first three films focussed on extreme climatic or geographical conditions – jungle, Arctic, and ocean; they drew largely on the experiences of individuals who had been pushed to the limits of their own endurance but had managed to survive. In the second half of the series, Downie turned to suffering inflicted by man, and looked at prison, torture, concentration camps and war. The final programme – on the notion of survival after a nuclear war – was obviously not based on actual individual experience, but looked instead at the conflicting arguments from experts about the facts of nuclear aftermath, and at the various preparations individuals and governments have made to deal with such an event. The main impact of the series lay in the strength of the individual stories, often told for the first time in any detail, and the common factors that emerged from all these experiences. The film on the concentration camps in particular was felt to offer new perspectives on a much covered subject.

The audience for documentaries on Channel 4 has grown over the last year, as part of the overall growth. *China, Africa,* and *Survive* all averaged 1.3 million viewers, although this could vary from over 2 million one week to less than 700,000 another for no obvious reason.

Another barometer of interest and appreciation – the purchase of books and take-up of free leaflets – indicates that the major series won a committed audience, a substantial proportion of who wished to take their interest further. This was particularly the case on China and Africa where IBT prepared a study guide and organised viewing groups throughout the country. The impact of *The Heart of the Dragon* on British attitudes to China was the subject of a special study, commissioned by Sue Stoessl, from a market research company. The results suggested that, in those areas that were clearly featured in the series, attitudes had been influenced and knowledge increased. About half the audience were surprised by what they had learnt, the majority favourably. A little over a quarter of viewers felt that the programmes had encouraged them to find out more about China.

1984–85: In the coming year the only major long-running documentary series will be Granada's *End of Empire* (14 parts). This leaves room for more unusual, shorter series that rely on co-funding; we need to keep funds available for series of special interest to Britain, or of a particularly experimental and innovative nature. This year, Britain itself will receive the kind of scrutiny that other continents received last! *Scotland's Story* starts transmission this autumn, and *The Dragon has Two Tongues* on the history of Wales will follow, then four one hour documentaries on *The Land of England* in the spring.

Further away – both in space and time – the autumn will see the arrival of *Ancient Lives*, written and presented by John Romer, about the people who built the tombs in the Valley of the Kings, and the village where they lived, Deir el Medina. At Christmas, Gore Vidal will trace the history and legacy of the Venetian Empire in a two-part film. In complete contrast, *Africar* is a series which combines a critique of the growth of the family car in the west and its export to the Third World, with the development of an alternative low resource car that has recently successfully completed a trial run from the Arctic to the Equator.

1985–86–87: There are a number of major series being made, but the production period for such series makes it difficult to anticipate the year of transmission. In autumn 1985, a social and political history of Britain during *The Seventies* will start. Other projects include a short series on *The Politics of Food*, another aspiring to present the definitive story of oil, and a fascinating series on the concept of insight and the evolution of human consciousness, devised by Cambridge psychologist, Nick Humphrey.

Our reputation for transmitting series on major wars will be sustained by further series on the Franco-Algerian war, *The People's War*, the Korean War, and a series about the Greek resistance. We very much want to balance this output in a small way by commissioning a short series on the history of pacifism!

Some years later, after she had left Channel 4, Naomi compiled a series of brief summaries of programmes she commissioned, with details of educational purpose, target audience, audience size and back up. They are included here to deepen the analysis already begun in her annual reports.

Case studies[13]

All Muck and Magic (1987)

Description: The first organic gardening series based at the Henry Doubleday Research Association's green-field site at Ryton, near Coventry. Fronted by Ryton's own young staff, it demonstrated organic techniques and recorded the site's development.

Production Company: HTV West. Producer: Derek Clark. Director: Sebastian Robinson.

Educational Goals: To demonstrate how gardens and the environment can be protected and healthy plants and food produced by organic methods.

Target Groups: Existing and potential gardeners, those (especially young people) interested in the environment, and the general public.

Schedule: Saturdays, 8.30pm, repeated Friday 9.30pm.

Audience Size: Average 1,079,000. Repeat, 2,193,000.

Back-up: Booklet, price £1.50, to provide additional information about organic methods and encourage viewers to adopt them. Numbers requested 45,872.

Repeat, 28,346

There is little doubt that this series influenced the build up of interest in organic gardening. Despite the fact that the first series was transmitted in a poor slot for gardening programmes and did not achieve a high audience, the number requesting the booklet was astonishingly high, virtually the highest in relation to the size of audience that had hitherto been seen. Both its repeat, and the second series, *More Muck and Magic*, transmitted on what was then to become the regular gardening slot (Friday evenings) more than doubled its audience to over two million. The third series, *Loads More Muck and Magic*

13.Sargant, N. E.(1993) *Adult Learners, Broadcasting and Channel 4*, London: Channel 4, pp. 124, 150, 160, 81, 69, 155, 95, 105.

sadly, did less well. Media pressures won over the idea of intelligent gardeners being their own presenters, and the agenda was broadened to look at organic farming. The home audience noticed the difference. More important, organic gardening is now less novel, and many other series touch on it.

Another Way of Life (1987)

Description: It was current policy to encourage mentally handicapped people to live in the community and to close many of the long-stay hospitals and hostels in which they had been living. This moving and controversial series (three 60-minute films) followed a year in the life of three mentally handicapped adults, David, Pat and Michael, who, at the beginning were resident at a local authority hostel in Hereford. The three films were a frank observation of events as they unfolded, made without comment, in *verite* style, maintaining a close sense of involvement with people whose uninhibited friendliness gave us a vivid and positive insight into their lives. During the 1992 Channel 4 Disability Season, *People First*, there was a follow-up visit to David, Pat and Michael to see what had happened since we had last met them.

Production Company: Compass Films. Producer/Director: Simon Heaven.

Educational Goals: To examine the implications of the government's policy of *Care in the Community*, and to provide support for social workers, carers and families involved with and affected by the policy.

Target Groups: Social workers, carers, local authorities, families of the mentally handicapped and the general public.

Schedule: Fridays 10.30pm.

Audience Size: 1,723,000, 1,763,000, 1,544,000. Average 1,677,000.

Back-up: Free booklet produced with the Central Council for Educational and Training in Social Work (CCETSW), produced by Learning Materials Design, to assist social workers and carers involved with these issues.

Numbers Requested: 1,887. A video was made available through Guild Learning.

These films gained astonishingly high audiences for late night Fridays in August, maintaining their audience over all three programmes – a tribute to their power and sensitivity.

Art of the Western World (1989)

Description: A chronological survey of the history of western art from Greece and Rome to post-modernism, examining the way life and culture have shaped art. The programmes provided visual access to art, sculpture, and architecture in an unparalleled way.

Production Company: Television South and WNET New York.

Producers: Andrew Snell, Tony Cash. Series Editor: Perry Miller Adato. Presenter: Michael Wood. International art experts were also involved in the production.

Educational Goals: To provide a visual foundation for a major telecourse at undergraduate level, funded by the Corporation for Public Broadcasting's Annenberg Project.

Target Groups: The general public, adult education and home learners wishing to study art history and art appreciation systematically.

Schedule: Sundays 5.30pm. Repeated Fridays, 2pm.

Audience Size: Average 533,000, repeat 309,000.

Back-up: A booklet to encourage people to study the subject further, numbers requested 3,825. The trade book, *Art of the Western World* (Boxtree, 1989) did extremely well and went into paperback to tie in with the repeat transmission (28,500 hardback, 19,000 paperback). In Britain, the Open College of the Arts developed its own telecourse to accompany the series.

Citizen 2000 (1982 and continuing annually)

Description: This series followed up children born in the first year of Channel 4's life, who became citizens in the year 2000. The children were chosen to reflect the breadth of social, ethnic, and occupational groups living in the British Isles. Themes included: fathers, going away to boarding school, siblings, coping with bereavement, methods of teaching the three Rs.

Production Company: Thames TV and Dove Productions. Producers: Catherine Freeman and Annie Macdonald.

Educational Goals: The structure was that of a longitudinal social research study, using the camera to form the record. The intellectual structure focussed mainly on social, cultural and ethnic determinants; they include religion, language, class, handicap, parenting. Some filming was carried out each year, but the individual programmes did not follow a regular pattern, and indeed the development of the series depended on the future of the children.

Target Groups: Social workers, education and child care students, teachers, parents and the general public.

Schedule: The pattern of programming varied year by year, usually in half-hour slots, but originally in a one-hour slot. Originally scheduled in the evening, they were later usually shown in the late afternoon at weekends, so that families can view together.

Audience Size:

Thursday 8.30pm		Sunday 4.30pm	
30 Dec 1982	611,000	24 Sept 1991	1,742,000
23 Jan 1983	488,000	3 March 1991	817,000

Back-up: When the themes had implications for current needs and interests, e.g. pre-school care, or fathering, booklets were produced for the general audience. The first one was entitled *Action for the Under Fives*. Another was devoted to *Starting School*. Videos of the series could be obtained from Dove Productions. Programmes have been selected for showing at the New York Film Festival.

The significance of a project like this grew as the years progressed. Obviously, such a series could not be made without the commitment and collaboration of the children's parents, and it says much for the sensitivity and competence of the production team that nearly ten years after the series started all the families were still participating, and actively involved in meetings and discussions about the future of the series.

The Heart of the Dragon (1984)

Description: A major 12-part documentary series presenting a unique view of modern China set against its history, observing, through first-hand accounts experiences of contemporary life: marriage, the law, child-rearing, food, political life, etc.

Production Company: ASH Films. Executive Producer: Peter Montagnon. Directors: Mischa Scorer, Nigel Houghton.

Educational Goals: To present a comprehensive portrait of life in contemporary China, and the continuity of Chinese culture.

Target Groups: General public.

Schedule: Mondays 9pm, repeated Sundays 7.15pm.

Audience Size: 1,343,000 (average), 774,000 (repeat)

Back-up: Study guide produced by IBT to encourage individuals and viewing groups to follow up the programmes. Numbers requested: 8,500.

Book: *The Heart of the Dragon,* by Alistair Clayre, (Collins/Harvill, 1984). Sales, 14,000.

The series was a good example of the Peter Montagnon 'Trojan Horses' principle – 'you must leave "education", construct a Trojan Horse, trundle it into some hospitable (BBC) department and set up shop. There were two simple rules, do not call your horse by a name that smacks of either education or of religion, and, if at all possible, come bearing gifts of money from foreign broadcasters'. One of the earliest of Channel 4's commissions, this was a prime example of a major documentary series asking to be exploited for wider educational purposes; this goal was also assisted by the commissioning of an on-screen discussion of the series at the end of its transmission. A number of regional seminars were also organised by IBT and Channel 4 to enable viewers to discuss the films with the programme makers.

Tom Keating on Painters (1982), Tom Keating on Impressionism (1984)

Description: Series in which artist and restorer Tom Keating shared with viewers his enthusiasm for the old masters and his practical understanding of how they painted, and achieved their effects. In the first series, the painters were Titian, Rembrandt, Turner, Constable and Degas (in pastel). In the second series, he focussed on the early impressionists, then Manet, Monet, Renoir, then the post-impressionists Van Gogh and Cezanne.

Production Company: The Moving Picture Company. Producer: Richard Beighton. Director: Richard Fawkes.

Educational Goals: To demystify techniques of painting and to encourage people to visit art galleries and take up painting themselves.

Schedule: *Painters:* Thursdays 6.30pm, audience size average 458,000. Repeat, Wednesdays 8pm, audience size 1,286,000.

Impressionists: Tuesdays 8.30pm, audience size 668,000, repeat 1,443,000.

Back-up: Booklets (£1.25) to recapitulate Keating's insights into technique, to encourage people to paint and give information about where to see the paintings featured. Numbers requested. Series I, 13,000. Series 2, 19,578.

To place a series with a controversial character in the first week of Channel 4's life was a gamble, but one which paid off. Jeremy Isaacs was to describe the series as one of the successes of the first schedule. The series was also an educational success with a level of demand for the booklet that has rarely been surpassed – and clear educational effects recorded by the Channel's market research. Most importantly, its success and the complaints about its early evening schedule helped the argument for education to gain a regular 8pm slot for its arts and culture programming. The increase in audience when both the series was repeated in an 8pm slot speaks for itself. Few arts programmes on any channel get as high audiences.

Make it Count (1983)

Description: A determined attempt to help those who find numbers incomprehensible.

Production Company: Yorkshire Television. Producer: David Wilson. Presenter: Fred Harris. (Made in 1977, and updated for Channel 4.)

Educational Goals: To teach basic numeracy skills.

Schedule: Mondays 6.30pm, repeated Monday 1pm, (Open College), 1989.

Audience Size: Average 423,000, repeat, 127,000.

Back up: Workbook and individual computer-based feedback, produced by NEC, providing an interactive means of helping people with numeracy problems. Numbers requested, 40,000.

The total numeracy project, including this series and subsequently *Numbers at Work* and *Counting On* was carried out with the collaboration and support of ALBSU.

Years Ahead (1982–88)

Description: The over 60s may watch a lot of television, but there never has been a great deal designed for them in the medium, apart from a few short series. Channel 4 provided the first week-in, week-out service in a topical 45-minute magazine programme looking at issues from the over-60s point of view and responding to the wishes and requests of its audience.

Production Company: Sidhartha Films. Producer: Steve Clark Hall. Editor: Rosemary Forgan. Presenter: Robert Dougall.

Educational Goals: To provide a forum within which issues affecting the audience would be raised; to act as an information channel for financial, sociological and health information; to generate a relationship with the audience that would create a harmony between the programmes and the viewers, allowing the programme content to be responsive to the audience's needs and wishes.

Schedule: Series I, Thursdays 5.15–6pm, audience size average 349,000.

Series 7, Tuesdays 3.45–4pm, audience size average 1,176,000. By 1986, the team has built up the audience to just touching two million at 3.45pm, of whom 50 per cent were in the target age group.

Back-up: Free factsheets were provided covering information in programmes. The programme did not attempt to drum up response for the sake of numbers, but it is clear that it did touch on important needs and interests, such as arthritis (536 requested), claiming benefits (1338), hearing loss, pensions from the 1940s (3661), tracing family trees ((878). There were 11,733 requests for leaflets in 1983/84.

A book, *Years Ahead: Getting the Most from Retirement* was published by Ward Lock in 1984. (ISIS Large Print Edition.)

It is difficult to explain to younger people that older people may feel most comfortable with older familiar faces and without constant change. Unfortunately, the over 60s lost *Years Ahead* and *Getting On* (Central Television) at around the same time, and then found the successor programme *Third Wave* moved to 2pm.

*In an interview with Gemma Moss for Women: A Cultural Review,
carried out in 1991, Naomi discussed how being a woman and coming
to Channel 4 with no previous direct experience of broadcasting made
a difference to how she tackled the job. The interview represents one
of the few descriptions we have of the commissioning process.*

Women at the top in television[14]

Moss: How did you see your job?

Sargant: I think that what was different in my approach... is that firstly I
had been working on educational planning, and that secondly I came from a
market research background. I had recently been representing consumers on
the National Consumer Council (NCC), as well as chairing the National Gas
Consumers' Council. I was quite preoccupied with how big bodies like this
were accountable and served people's needs. Having come out of that side of
politics rather than the other, I always start where people are, and with what
they want, and what their lives are like, and what will help them. We had
been talking a bit on the NCC about the lack of accountability in broadcasting. I had also, as part of my ACACE work, directed and written up the
first major study about adults' educational experience and needs – 2500
interviews all over England and Wales. So, in a sense, I had, quite acciden-
tally, done the market research... I had figures which actually showed what
people were watching, what they would do if you gave them five to seven
more hours of spare time a week, all the things they would like to learn
about that they hadn't already learned about. All of this was mapped out in
a very decent and proper piece of research.

Moss: How did you set about using that information?

Sargant: The next stage was more practical. We went into discussions. To
start with I wondered how on earth I would be credible to all the media
people. I think it needs to be said quite clearly that the media, in particular
television, is extremely arrogant, inward-looking, incestuous and emotional
in its decision-making. Academics are like that too, though they don't admit
it. Both the media and academia had generations who believed that they had
got a production-based right to 'do things to people'. The media believed it
knew what to give audiences, just as academics believed they knew what is
right to teach people and the way to teach them. I don't actually agree with
that. I come from a learners' perspective, and I don't believe that anybody
has a God-given right to make these programmes with all these resources

14.Moss, G (1991) Interview with Naomi Sargant: Women at the top in Television,
Women: A Cultural Review, 2(1), pp. 29–39.

without thinking about it that way...I began at Channel 4 as somebody who was already a professor. I had been the first woman Pro-Vice Chancellor in the country. I had a serious educational reputation. But television people were so arrogant that none of them even knew that I had a previous reputation. It was irrelevant to them. For the first year or so, some of the people, particularly in the big ITV companies were incredibly scornful of both Liz Forgan (who had been Women's Editor of *The Guardian*, and also had no previous broadcasting experience) and me.

Moss: Because you were women, or because you came from outside?

Sargant: Predominantly because we came from outside...but I think the hidden thing was that we were women. Mike Scott, (chief executive at Granada Television) simply refused to meet us at the beginning and would only agree to talk to Jeremy Isaacs. It was very uncomfortable until, firstly, I started getting some of the programmes I had commissioned back, and secondly, I saw on screen that some of them were going to be among the first successes of the Channel. I have had similar experiences in the academic world. It requires holding your nerve, being totally committed and believing absolutely that's what you have got to do.

Moss: Do you feel that it was then you had proved yourself in broadcasting?

Sargant: There was no question. Once we went on screen, some of my programmes were among the serious early successes, including Keating, and, in the next summer, Jancis Robinson and *The Wine Programme*. Everyone knew that they were very, very high successes. That was it. But there was still a problem about the label 'Education', and also that I did have such a large chunk of airtime...It took people a long time to understand that education meant something broader than usual, and that many of the things that would elsewhere have been described as informational, or features, or factual, would actually find a home in my lot, rather than in Liz's.

Moss: So initially they defined education very narrowly?

Sargant: Everybody still does – there's this knee-jerk reaction that education equals learning, not even that, *schooling*. If you think about it, the majority of the bosses in the media are – not exactly uneducated – but they have not, by and large, come through the graduate tracks. Like computing, it's an industry where you can make your way up. It is very good for creativity, but it does have some other problems. It allows people not even to understand when they are being irrational.

Moss: But what about attitudes to you as a woman?

Sargant: Well, let's say clearly that what Jeremy Isaacs did was quite unique. He had a different channel to set up and he was determined to do it differently...His view was that he was more likely to find unrecognised talent among women than among men. There were no women in senior broadcasting jobs at all at that time. So he made these first three senior commissioning editor appointments, effectively heads of department, appointing two women, and one man (David Rose, Head of Fiction). That was extraordinary at the time. And neither of these women…was in television. But that wasn't it. We very quickly had a woman Head of Marketing (Sue Stoessl), a woman Head of Presentation (Pam Masters), two more woman commissioning editors, Sue Woodford in charge of multi-cultural programming and Carol Haslam in charge of documentary series. Then we rapidly had a large number of other women…I think it's arguable that the fact that Channel 4 did do something different, and for much of that period had almost half of its management structure female, actually led to a totally taken-for-granted different way of behaving and thinking about things, and a lack of poncing about, a lack of all these other structures and hierarchies. Instead, for many, many years there has been, in Channel 4, a culture which allowed you to expect these matters to be dealt with properly, without being made to feel that you were being perverse in raising the issue yet again, or that you were making a point or a special case.

Moss: What difference did it make to your work that you'd come from outside the television industry?

Sargant: Once I was inside and looking at the space I had and the needs I had identified, I saw my task differently from people who had come out of production, many of whom, whether men or women, continued to master/mistressmind productions themselves as Executive Producer. I always saw myself as a creator of space for particular needs and I found the best ideas which fitted a need and a slot. I then encouraged and challenged and stimulated that production team to make the programme in the best possible way…

We would, for example, have a need for multi-cultural programmes, and there would be a proposal, and we would say, 'Right, let's talk to this company who has proposed it. Is it good enough? Do we want to go with it?' Much later on, if we had a need but no proposals we might occasionally put the area out to tender.

There was one early proposal about archaeology, which became a series called *The Blood of the British,* where a production company had come in with the idea. I was interested in the waves of immigration into Britain both pre-historically and later, and I kept on looking for proposals which would represent this in multi-cultural *and* archaeological terms. The proposal came in with a standard white, upper-class name attached to it, a safe BBC voice. I said, 'Lovely idea, can't stand the presenter…look, go away and find a bright young archaeologist, preferably female'. He came back with wonderful Catherine Hills from Newnham College, Cambridge…So we got a very good new personality, an intelligent personality, and therefore, and this is an important part of the strategy, she got more out of the other archaeologists she talked to, a much higher level of interaction and intellectual exchange than she would if she was simply a standard presenter. That became for me a serious piece of policy…

The Jancis Robinson programme is an exactly similar example. Jancis knew everything about wine and therefore was lovely and witty and intelligent and got this buzz out of the interchange.

It doesn't only happen with women. It happened in a different way with Tom Keating, and Chris Frayling (then professor of Cultural History at the Royal College of Art). This is not precisely a feminist point, but retrospectively, all of these points about somebody unorthodox coming in, who doesn't accept the orthodox rules, proceed from Jeremy Isaacs' determination to do things differently, and so having women.

Moss: What is interesting is that you had a kind of real intellectual respect for intellectual content and expertise and professionalism in a way that previous programmers hadn't.

Sargant: The content has to be the most important thing. When you know what you are trying to convey, you then think about the best possible, or the most exciting or exhilarating way of communicating this. You then put another layer of filters on, which is that you have got to choose content areas which are very important to Britain, or which the camera can communicate best. That was the brilliant thing that Jeremy did... I argued with him that we hadn't allowed to produce 'things visual', that we had a visual medium, that Britain was profoundly under-educated visually, so that we should actually use television for visual education. He came back next day and gave me another £1.2m and told me I could spend it in any way I wanted. It didn't have to be for one slot, it didn't have to be in a particular form, it could be anything as long as it used the medium for visual ends. This led into programmes like Tom Keating, to *Every Window Tells a Story,* which was about stained glass, *Tudor Miniatures,* Edwin Mullins doing *A Love Affair with Nature, Paintabililty,* that wonderful *Pottery Ladies* series on the old women who painted all the original designs for Charlotte Reade, Clarice Cliffe and Susie Cooper – in that series you had a fantastic combination of feminism, oral history, skill, design, all in one series. The other curious example was Kaffe Fassett; that knitting series he presented was not about knitting but about colour, and going round and looking at things which had inspired his imagination.

Moss: What other criteria did you work on in deciding which proposals to accept?

Sargant: We knew we wanted to do obvious things like health, which Carol Haslam covered. We got amazing proposals from men, which were entirely about general health, ignoring any particular women's health issues. Classic – a team without a woman on it, and not a mention of cystitis or breast cancer, the menopause, or any of these things. And when you sat there saying, 'but what about some of the women's issues' they responded, 'why does it matter?'. I remember one team who were deeply affronted by this and never came back. We never censored their proposals.

We had these two things...I had women fronting *For What it's Worth* (Sally Hawkins, Penny Junor) and Heather Couper, *The Planets.* The second thing was content. When we were doing *Today's History,* for example, Juliet Gardiner, then editor of *History Today* magazine, did a particular programme about women's history; after the issue of ensuring that the content covers women, there is then the issue about whether you do special programmes about women.

Moss: What did you feel about that?

Sargant: Well, when we were doing the long-running series, *Today's History*, it seemed perfectly sensible to do a programme about women's history, along with a number of other things which weren't adequately covered...I never, on the other hand, determined that I would separate out a whole slot for a women's magazine. I had separated out a whole slot for the over 60s magazine *Years Ahead*. That seemed to me to be a specific and different group, although many of them were older women, but that is a different point. Women's viewing habits are different from men's and older people's viewing habits are different from younger people's...

Moss: What about women in the power structure of the industry?

Sargant: It is worth distinguishing between the management power structure and the general production structure, because what we have got, increasingly, are quite a lot of women at the professional level, working in production teams as producers and directors of series and programmes. If we start from the bottom up, I think there has been a big advance for women as professionals, as producers, directors, quite a lot of editors, slightly less with cameras. There aren't the professional barriers there that I think were there ten years ago. It seems to me that that structural advance has been made mainly because of the breakdown of the big integrated production monopolies of the BBC and ITV, with their teams' solid structure and union agreements about their size. The manual work...was almost entirely male, and they would go off to their hotels together or they would go and work together...But once you break that down and start to have lots of small independent production companies, then you find many more women and everyone can choose who they want to work with...I think there is evidence to show that they were actually more interested in being flexible, innovative and creative than in a tidy career track...that level of space has now been loosened up...A lot of women were helped in their careers by their stints at Channel 4...; the fact that we had a more open policy over those ten years has actually infiltrated into or irrigated the BBC and ITV, but you will still see a great area of editorial heads, or heads of departments, the equivalents of commissioning editors, where are very few women...

I sat on a committee chaired by Paul Fox, a big representative steering group for the Royal Television Society's (RTS) Biennial Cambridge Convention (the only woman)...I started to do my statutory thing about 'Please can we have some women speakers'. After a bit, when I had said it twice, he said, 'Naomi, if you want any women you will have to find them yourself'. That's Paul Fox. The result was that I chaired a session and got Pam Mills from the BBC to speak, and everyone agreed that it was one of the best sessions of the conference. Paul is a good guy, but everyone is brought up as a liberal, and everybody thinks that we don't have to do anything active about it. But we do.

By the late 1980s, a new, government-driven deregulated broadcasting landscape was on the horizon, one which was less hospitable to educational broadcasting. Channel 4 too was changing and it became clear that Naomi's educational passions fitted less well with the new, more commercially oriented regime. Undoubtedly she felt keenly the loss of an arena in which she could put her principles into practice; her anxiety about the future of educational broadcasting in general is reflected in the first of the post-Channel 4 papers reproduced below, an extract from a major report on her Channel 4 years, commissioned and published by the Channel in 1992.

The end of a golden age?[15]

It may be that we will look back on the 1980s as the golden age of educational broadcasting. A typical week in 1988 (12–18 March) contained 42.4 hours and 94 individual programmes of educational output for adults on four channels; this included the Open University, the Open College, strong series on Network ITV, BBC and Channel 4, but not the variety of local programmes on regional ITV. The audiences for educational programmes in this one week totalled over 32 million people.

The 1990 Broadcasting Act has set the legal and financial framework for broadcasting on commercial channels for the next decade and removed the obligations from ITV to provide educational programmes for adults. While a number of companies have promised some education for adults within their output, their ability to deliver this nationally is dependent on central scheduling and it is too soon to see what the results will be.

As the ITV companies approach the end of their franchises, it is not surprising that their commitment to education series has diminished, particularly in evening slots. The last two years have, however, seen educational elements made by a number of different providers in the regular live Granada programmes *This Morning*. There was some concern, especially among CCEOs, that ITV's educational impact in the daytime schedule could be diminished by the short duration of each item. However, a report on the first year's experience of *This Morning* showed that over 130,000 items of printed back-up had been requested on a wide range of topics, and that there was a heavy demand for the telephone helplines. (*This Morning: Viewers Reactions to the Programme and its Educational Inserts*, Granada/ITV, 1990).

---

15. Sargant, N. E. (1992) Adult learners, broadcasting and Channel 4, London: Channel 4, pp. 72–5.

Detailed findings showed that two-thirds of those who sent for the booklets were prompted by the programme itself to find out more about a subject in which they had little previous interest. The rate of request for support materials was high and over half had never sent off for anything like them before. The programmes reach all age groups and over half the people who sent for booklets had finished their formal education at the minimum age.

The drawbacks are, of course, that only a third of the adult population is available to watch television on weekday mornings, and that the audience inevitably contains a disproportionate number of women. If this new strategy was an addition to the existing ITV commitment, there would have been cheers all round. The problem is that it has replaced much of their other work and working people clearly miss out.

It is, as noted earlier, too soon to know whether the new franchise-holders will maintain any of these activities after 1992. There is already concern that the cutting back of education staff, who formerly worked for the IBA, by the new Independent Television Commission (ITC); its lighter touch will mean that the two remaining professional staff will, of necessity, shift from their previous pro-active role to a more passive one. The concern is that 'the inception of ITC...came as part of the drive to market-place values in broadcasting, a move that has always threatened to damage vulnerable non-profit-making areas of programming such as education' (*Times Educational Supplement*, 27 March 1992). Any further disengagement of commercial television from education risks existing structures and brings forward the prospect of moving more education into down-time, or on to satellite services.

Current debate about the renewal of the BBC Charter, due in 1996, reveals clear difficulty nowadays to agree what constitutes educational broadcasting. The Director-General of the BBC, Michael Checkland, speaking to the Annual Conference of the Voice of the Listener in November 1990, said that, as he saw it,

'Public Service Broadcasting has three main elements – range, quality and universality. It must cover the whole range of programming, not just the 'minority' or highbrow kind. We are all members of minorities, even when we listen to *The Archers* or watch *Neighbours*, because there are always more people who are listening or watching something else, or not listening to or watching anything at all'.

He did not, in this speech, refer to any specific types of programmes, such as children's, educational or religious programmes.

As it approaches the Charter Review, the BBC's continuing commitment to educational programmes for adults is not yet clear. Inevitably, the government's failure to maintain ITV's obligations in this respect provides the commercial channel with an additional competitive edge, which may threaten the BBC's mass national educational campaigns. Recent valuable examples of these have been Anneka Rice's *Play it Safe*, *Tomorrow – The World* and *Sum Chance*.

The celebration of Adult Learners' Week in March 1992 was planned and supported by all four television channels, with BBC 1's *Second Chance* initiative as a fundamental part of the project. If the BBC is forced into competition for ratings it may not be able to maintain this sort of commitment in the future. And BBC Education could not have undertaken the quality and quantity of programming for its *Second Chance* initiative if the programming as well as the back-up had not been supported by the Department of Employment (ED).

It is clear that the boundaries round the BBC's educational programming are being drawn more tightly, whether for philosophical, political or economic reasons. Now called Continuing Education and Training, the department is working on more vocational areas, assisted by funding from the ED and the Department for Education (DFE), as well as focusing on a more limited set of strictly educational priorities. The 1992 catalogue includes new series on training and business, information technology, languages, science, access to education and equal opportunities, and a small number of 'general' series: *Advice Shop, Bazaar, Europe by Design, Spain on a Plate, See Hear* and *Sign Extra*.

The tighter definition mirrors somewhat the Conservative government's philistine intent to separate the funding for vocational and qualification-bearing adult education from what it incorrectly terms 'leisure' courses. The point is that the majority of adults choose to use their leisure time for study, whatever they are learning, be it immediately related to their work or not; this is one reason why television is so important as a door-opener. What is now missing from the BBC list are many of the life-enhancing areas – the stuff of traditional adult education – which feed the imagination and creativity as well as helping with life's everyday demands.

Earlier this year, Sir Michael Checkland announced that BBC Schools Television and Radio were to be amalgamated into a single, multi-media department, promising a more efficient and flexible service, and including, in the same department, publishing sections currently under the aegis of BBC Enterprises. This will mean that new series can be published on their own as programmes or with books, videos and audio cassettes accompanying programmes. A clear concern is that it is only one step further to expect the new structure to be financially independent, and therefore, as has been recently rumoured, to be available for privatisation. What is not clear is whether it will have protected slots in the schedule; if it does not, then the whole debate about 'educational' and 'educative' will come back into play, and 'educational' programming may be as vulnerable to market forces on the BBC as it has become on ITV.

Additional pressure on television provision for adult learners may also come from the government's decision to make Channel 4 responsible for carrying ITV schools programming as well as their original remit of programming for adult learners. It would scarcely be surprising if carrying both these obligations was not entirely welcomed by those in the Channel who will soon be responsible for selling its advertising space, even if there were arrangements which allowed the Channel to maintain its independent status under the Broadcasting Act 1990.

Previous funding arrangements protected commissioning editors from direct commercial pressures, and indeed there was often little relationship between the placing of the commercials by ITV and the specialist audiences targeted by Channel 4. The full potential for selling specialist advertising space will only emerge as the Channel takes control of this. Theoretically, it should be better for the halo-effect of the programming if the space-selling strategy bears some relationship to the schedule's content, provided that no undue pressure is brought to bear on commissioning editors to select more popular programmes for commercial reasons.

The first sign of this has indeed already arrived in the educational area. Until now, educational programmes, like children's programmes, running in half-hour slots, have not been allowed a centre advertising break. When such programmes are likely to have a pro-active educational agenda, and may also be advertising helplines or other follow up activities, to break the structure of the content with non-related advertising may well impair its message and its educational effectiveness. Apparently, the new ITC regulations have failed to maintain this protection, though it does not seem to have been a matter for discussion with the education advisers or with Channel 4 at the time. An obvious example such as gardening makes the point. Channel 4 wishes to promote its Gardening Club. There are likely to be advertisers for products and magazines who will have messages which are competitive with the Channel's own educational promotions.

The ITC has also developed a new licensing framework for Channel 4, to be implemented from 1993. The requirement to provide seven and a half hours a week of educational programming for adults will be maintained. In the early years, the Channel provided the seven hours through a combination of directly commissioned educational programmes and around two hours of general output material which was particularly appropriate for educational wrapping around.

In 1988, under budgetary pressure, the Channel took a decision to reduce the quantity of directly commissioned educational programming, increasing the amount that was to be validated as educational from general output commissioned by other editors. There is clearly no dearth of informative, mainly factual, material on Channel 4, and much of it can be readily enhanced with support materials. Significant recent examples are booklets to accompany the *Equinox* series such as *Unravelling the Universe*, as well as *Fragile Earth*, *Fin de Siècle* and *Talking Liberties*.

Another valuable strategy, which potentially provides a broader and richer effect, is to incorporate into a *season* a wide variety of programmes, including films, drama, documentaries, interviews, all of which would carry appropriate generic back-up. *Soviet Spring*, on the extraordinary recent events in the USSR, and *Banned*, a season on censorship, were notable examples of this. A further option, currently favoured by the Channel, is to encourage the commitment to educational programming to be taken on more widely by other commissioning editors. *Orchestra* was commissioned by the music editor, the arts editor introduces educational elements into the arts magazine *Without Walls*. One benefit of this, arguably, will be to improve the professional quality of the content. The danger, as always, will be that voiced by John Robinson, that the educational becomes 'secondary and incidental' rather than 'primary and fundamental'; educative wins over educational.

The distinction is clear to educational producers, but is not understood or accepted by general output people. A polite explanation for this is that it is not their professional background and they are ignorant of its real meaning. A less charitable view is that they do not wish to know, as they prefer to keep education in its place.

Behind this issue lies the national schizophrenia about education. Finally, the country is starting to accept that we are profoundly undereducated and undertrained in comparison with our neighbours in Europe and with much of the rest of the world. Education and training, particularly for adults, is moving up the political agenda. Yet, television, in particular is deeply uneasy about education.

Undoubtedly, the media are most powerful communicators. The conduct of contemporary elections makes this point clearly. Since television is so powerful, and the country has such great educational needs and deficiencies, the obvious conclusion would be to use broadcasting more rather than less. It has been argued that television does not teach well. There is abundant evidence, however, to show what it can do, particularly when planned in combination with other learning resources. The normal reaction, when something is not working as well as it might but is clearly needed, is to work at improving it, not to stop making it altogether.

It is difficult to know whether the prejudice against education on television comes from people's own less-than-good school experiences, or from the implicit threat that many people may need more education or updating as adults from their locked-in commitment to face-to-face teaching. It is clearly not a rational reaction.

In many ways the nineties are quite different from the eighties. In particular the increased accessibility of new technologies, together with the increased introduction of market forces, is changing the electronic environment in which we live. What is not changing so fast is our social and cultural environment. Unemployment is as significant a problem as it was in the early eighties. Many people are poorer. Old people form a higher proportion of the population. Broadcasting will remain the most effective educational medium to reach large numbers. The task of educating people for active citizenship and helping people to get more out of their lives is still as important for Channel 4 as it was at its inception and probably more so now that other broadcasters are giving it less priority. It is a task that Channel 4 should continue to carry with pride.

Naomi was now in campaigning mode. With educational broadcasting under serious threat across all channels, she submitted the following personal view to the Department of National Heritage in response to the Government's Green Paper on Digital Broadcasting and, en passant, to the BBC's Extending Choice document (1992 and 1993)

Digital terrestrial broadcasting[16]

1. The Green Paper is curiously limited in its reference to educational programmes given the historic importance of education as one of the three 'legs' of the BBC. It refers to programmes for schools and those who have left school, and goes on to note that with the availability of cassettes and other material, some of this output may no longer be necessary.

2. Policy-makers still tend to equate education with schools and the formal educational system, and not to appreciate the increased need for continuing education and training throughout life, delivered both in formal and informal ways. Most adult learning is part-time, and much of it is home-based. Broadcast television will continue to play a vital role in delivering such education, while it remains the most accessible form of broadcasting financially and geographically for most people. It is free at the point of use and need, and reaches people with special needs and in rural areas. It will also still be the most important way to reach the under-educated, as the adult literacy campaigns and now the Adult Learners' Weeks are showing.

3. Research shows one-third of people studying formally or learning informally now or within the past three years. One in ten is engaged in some form of current formal study, and one in six is trying to learn about or teach themselves something informally. These are large numbers and much of this learning is going on at home.

4. As the local provision of traditional liberal education in Britain comes under increasing pressure, and charges for it are raised, television's importance as an educational and cultural provider will increase. Indeed, for some people, especially in rural areas, it may become all there is.

16. Sargant, N. E. (1993) Response to 'Extending Choice', unpublished letter.

It will continue to play a key role in keeping people informed, sensitising them to change and alerting them to new opportunities and new ideas. It will allow them to 'attend' performances and view artistic and cultural events in their own homes. Lady Plowden, when chairman of the IBA, used the evocative phrase – 'Broadcasting is democratic – there are no reserved seats'.

It is the large and generous educational and social role that public-service broadcasting has played which is under pressure. Recent history on other channels has not been encouraging. The requirement for the other mass TV channel, ITV, best for reaching the least well-educated, to provide 'adult education' was removed under the 1990 Act. Inevitably this has tempted the BBC to move its education for adults from its mass channel, BBC 1, in order to be more competitive.

Channel 4 has also over recent years decreased the quantity of educational programming that is directly commissioned by educational staff and includes more of its factual and other programming validated under an 'educative' rubric. At the same time, the ranking of education staff has been reduced.

5. The BBC has, over the last few years, narrowed its definition of educational programming to a list of specific and overtly educational and vocational areas of work, which includes mainly foreign languages, information technology, science, business and training, access to education and 'equal opportunities'.

At the same time, BBC's educational programmes for adults have been moved off the mass channel on to BBC2 and into daytime or late at night.

6. BBC Education has recently been structured into one Directorate, coordinating education's activities across all media, including print and BBC Select. Its recent launch and the size of the budget are encouraging. However, its Director is not included in senior management and there is a concern that while such unification provides strength, it can also pave the way for a requirement to make the new structure financially independent, and maybe even available for privatisation.

7. Neither does Education have any guaranteed schedule time, perhaps its most significant vulnerability.

8. *Extending Choice* discusses education both in terms of its broad principles in Section 2 'A Clear Public Purpose for the BBC' and in Section 3, 'High Quality Programmes'. Most of the statements in Section 2 are admirable in their general intent. However, in Section 3 'Creating Opportunities for Education' does appear to switch the emphasis from providing education programmes which are intrinsically educational in themselves to 'creating opportunities' for education from other general output programmes.

What is needed is both. They are not in competition with each other. The difference lies in the intent of the producer and the primary purpose of the programme.

9. It is the fine print of Section 3 which gives more cause for concern. Three points emerge:

   a. Reference is made to sustaining output for primary schools, secondary schools and the Open University, but not to the expanding sector of further education, or indeed to higher education generally.

   b. No reference is made to future strategy for general adult education or indeed to continuing education.

   c. Programme emphasis is heavily on vocational, professional and qualification bearing programming.

   Of course it is correct to say that these are important need and current government priorities. However, these are already the areas most generously funded by government, and achieved through local institutions. It is the general curriculum of adult education, which is being cut elsewhere, which television is so well able to deliver, and which enhances opportunities for all adults, including opening up access and progression routes to more systematic learning opportunities.

10. Of course, the Green Paper is correct in noting that some educational programming really is 'narrow-cast' and could be delivered in other ways where audiences consist of specialist groups who are motivated and appropriately funded. However, other delivery methods all impose new barriers to access, usually financial ones.

   The main argument for continuing to do so is borne by the provider/delivery system and not the user, and therefore does not increase barriers to access.

11. BBC Select and the increasing use of down-time for downloading schools programmes at night is the most narrow-cast use of the terrestrial system. It is worth noting that Channel 4 is also researching the use of down-time for what used to be ITV Schools.

   OU programmes are also obviously a candidate for down-time, as over 90 per cent of programmes are already recorded off-air for later time-shift viewing. It is in many ways a better candidate than schools for night-time transmission, since there has always been an interested audience of daytime viewers for schools programmes, and for parents and teachers to have easier access to schools material is an informational benefit. Research also shows more staffing, technical and security difficulties with night-time copying.

12. Using broadcasting at night-time, as noted earlier, is the most specialist use of the terrestrial network. Its virtue is that if programmes are broadcast unencrypted, its basic advantage over satellite is that, at marginal cost, it can continue to reach more people freely, without cost of dishes or decoders.

   Its disadvantage is that it hides itself, when more knowledge of and access to education would be of benefit nationally. 'Out of sight, out of mind' was a major factor in the previous decision to move ITV schools on to Channel 4 rather than into down-time.

13. What is not clear is why neither the government nor the BBC are yet looking at the next obvious step of a satellite channel for more targeted education and training. Much narrowcast specialist material would be more appropriately served by satellite rather than by cassette, since it allows not just delivery of live or pre-recorded programmes, but also live interactivity and data-broadcasting. Such channels are now taken for granted in North America, and are operated both publicly and commercially.

14. The opportunity offered by Marco Polo satellite would have provided an important experimental period, at very low cost, which would have housed both schools, OU, and training materials from both the BBC and the commercial sector. That opportunity was ruled out by the ITC, under the terms of the 1990 Broadcasting Act, and apparently the DFE and ED were not involved in discussions as to the desirability of a modest amendment to the act to allow non-commercial imperatives to be brought into play. A satellite channel is already being considered by the OU, partly to deal with the shortage of terrestrial air time and partly to facilitate transmission to Europe.

15. It would be in the public interest for these discussions to be held across the different sectors of education and training, and involving all the government departments which have a major interest in education and training provision as well as the regulatory departments with a financial interest.

16. Technology is changing fast. By the end of the Millennium, compression will provide many more channels. The day of the desktop university at home and the wired-up campus are effectively with us. In this review, broadcasting and the BBC's educational role need to be looked at not just rather conventionally and in the shorter term as an extension of its current activities, but more imaginatively, considering its role at the end of the Millennium as we move towards the learning society.

Again and again, in her post-Channel 4 writings, Naomi referred to the insights of three seminal figures, who, she thought, understood better than most both the continuing potential of broadcasting, but also the radically changed social context in which it was received, and its place alongside many other delivery systems. The three were Lady Bridget Plowden, formerly chairman of the IBA, Michael Young, social entrepreneur, and, perhaps surprisingly, Rupert Murdoch, international business tycoon.

A global cornucopia with no reserved seats[17]

'Broadcasting is democratic – there are no reserved seats', Bridget Plowden, *Shrinking Employment: What role can broadcasting play in the future?* The Roscoe Lecture, 19 April 1980, quoted by Naomi at the head of her review of Channel 4 educational programming, *Adult Learners, Broadcasting and Channel 4* (Channel 4, 1992).

Small and private

We tend to think of the breaking down of the duopoly as politically motivated, and as an attack on public service broadcasting. This is not strictly the case. New technologies which are bringing new choices to consumers are the engine of the breakdown and we cannot be Luddite in keeping these technologies back. Ultimately, adding more choice removed power from producers, whether paternalistic or not, and placed it in the hands of the consumers. We then need to make sure, as in other areas of our life, that consumers have proper protection.

Michael Young, and I have been grateful to him for the power of his observation, has come to the same issue from a different perspective. He pointed, in a speech to the Fabian Society Centenary New Year School in 1984, to a related set of changes that had already taken place. There has already been a shift of scale of people's lives outside work. The small (and private) has increasingly replaced the big (and public). The watch has replaced the public clock. The fridge has replaced the ice factory, the washing machine, the public laundry, the private bathroom, the municipal baths, the

17.Sargant, N. E. (1990) Access and the media, Chapter 10 of G.Parry and C. Wake (eds) *Access and alternative futures for higher education*, Sevenoaks: Hodder and Stoughton).

television, the cinema, the car the bus or train. And even so, he suggested, the new home computer and teletext replace the newspaper...The most important thing is that all these changes have to do with accessibility, freedom and choice. Evidently the small and private are more accessible to the individuals who *possess* them than the large and public. This is the nub of the matter.

Of course the better-off had access to their own bath houses and ice houses several centuries earlier than they were made available to the community. Victorian philanthropy and enlightened self-interest coinciding with the industrial revolution led to the development of much municipal provision in the nineteenth century, including the foundation of many universities.

The provision of these services developed into near monopolies of supply, more because of their scale and nature than for any philosophical reasons. The Victorians, indeed, would not have agreed with Mrs Thatcher when she said that there is no such thing as society. A side benefit was the universality of provision, and a major characteristic was the fact that the user did not normally pay at the point of use. A negative was that these structures did not allow much flexibility and individuality in use, particularly in relation to geographical location.

The point of this discussion is that there are parallels between the provision of education and broadcasting. With both of these we have taken for granted the principle of universality of access – though nobody, of course, can guarantee equality of outcomes.

What changes, in Michael Young's scenario, is that those who can afford the small and private maintain their access while those who cannot are increasingly denied it, or may only be provided with a lower standard of service; the obvious example of this is the increase in car ownership, which has led inevitably led to a reduction in demand for public transport such that the standard of service on trains, tubes and buses is now lower; increasingly, its main users are those who have little choice – the old, the young, and the poor.

Infinite libraries

Broadcasting is just one of many delivery systems and it is not realistic to talk about broadcasting as if it is somehow separate from other delivery systems. Our existing broadcast channels already engage in narrowcasting for part of the time. Just as they increasingly make programmes which are designed *ab initio* to have a broadcast life and a video life. The same programmes may be available for direct copying off-air or on video, or even re-edited in a different structure for mediation by teachers.

And the *broadcasting television set* is no longer just that. As Rupert Murdoch said in his 1989 McTaggart Lecture at the Edinburgh Television Festival:

'Perhaps surprisingly, television has so far been unaffected by this information revolution, for that revolution involves digital technology, while the TV set has remained a doggedly analogue device...All this is about to change. The television set of the future will be, in reality, a telecomputer linked by fibre optic cable to a global cornucopia of programming and nearly infinite libraries of data, education and entertainment. All with full interactivity.'

Current arguments about broadcasting, he stated, will soon sound as if they belong to the Stone Age:

'These telecomputers will bring a huge variety of television channels including the ability to order up whatever you want to watch...(they) will revolutionise the way we are educated, the way we work and the way we relax.'

Of course we are not yet at that stage and most of us will not live to see it, though our children will, but it is clearly on its way, and the successful launch of the Olympus satellite last July marks a punctuation point of some importance. I have chosen to quote Murdoch since he reiterates, in an important forum, what a number of us have been saying for nearly ten years. What's more, he refers positively to the significance of education in the new dawn.

Naomi continued her preoccupation with delivery systems. In a further extract from Access and alternative futures for higher education, she explored future institutional uses of new technology, with special reference to satellite technology.

The new technological landscape

Using the media for the delivery of education

The media are themselves value free. They are merely delivery systems to be used for appropriate purposes. In far too many projects, people have mistaken the medium for the message and planned totally inappropriate purposes and content for particular delivery systems. The current example of this looks like being Olympus, the European Space Agency's newly launched high-power communications satellite. A recent example, closer to home, was the Open College, which, despite clear warnings, expected at its inception to be broadcast-led. It is one thing to have access to the medium of broadcasting and to use it intelligently and effectively, it is quite another for an *educational* institution to be broadcast-led. The Open College was first named 'the College of the Air' just as previously the Open University had been named 'the University of the Air'. Of course, they both use television, but it forms only a small part of the learning process.

Neither are the media necessarily cheap or expensive to use. Print still remains an invaluable, cheap and flexible medium as does the delivery system of the postal service. Of course, some media are more expensive than others. However, while the cost of face-to-face teaching tends to increase in proportion to the number of learners being taught, the cost of using the media for distance learning is capital intensive at the front of the system. Once the up-front investment has been made, the marginal cost of extra students is low in relation to the fixed cost. There is every incentive to expand the number of students studying each course, and indeed to sell the course materials to other countries. OU materials are widely used in many countries, not just in English-speaking ones. Other initiatives, such as the Commonwealth of Learning and the American National Technological University, expect to use materials across national boundaries. Satellite communications will make the academic village smaller, encouraging links between learning projects on different continents.

New options

Cable is clearly not, and never will be, a major player in the educational field, except, perhaps, locally. In terms of access, cable will only ever cover perhaps half of urban areas, and the level of take-up is not, so far, encouraging. The developing model for general viewing, which is probably more realistic, looks like this, though it obviously depends on cost, marketing and programming.

Urban	*Rural*
Satellite/some cable	Satellite
Rich	Rich
Urban	*Rural*
Broadcast/some cable	Broadcast only
Poor	Poor

Murdoch's current satellite strategy is, however, extremely practical, low-cost and overcomes geographical barriers. Its take-up curve is likely to rise faster than the pessimists suggest if it provides enough different programming of the sort people want: golf, cinema films, 'soft' pornography are all good examples.

It is a pity that most recent discussions of the possibility and desirability of a dedicated education and training channel on satellite were so closely related to the future of ITV schools programming, and were therefore not given a proper airing except in *The Times Educational Supplement*. The proposition is that, while much educational broadcasting is properly aimed at everybody at home and needs to stay on broadcast channels (access to the arts and sciences and consumer education are examples), much of it is effectively narrowcasting, targeting to closed groups. School Television and the OU are both of this kind, curriculum-led and often designed to be mediated by teachers or tutors. Closed audience groups, who know what they want, can be asked, and will indeed want, to organise their viewing and recording off air in advance. A recent estimate showed nearly 60 hours of educational programming for closed audience groups being broadcast each week in term time. The cost of dishes is not high in relation to other costs, particularly given the flexibility and extra resource that will accrue.

There is no reason why a single channel cannot carry programming from a variety of sources. If the channel is operated as an open carrier for education and training, anyone who wishes to deliver narrowcast or targeted learning could buy the requisite number of slots on it as though they were buying advertising time. Good, or more accessible, time slots could command premium prices. Less accessible time slots can be cheaper and be used for specific and highly motivated target groups, particularly those that are geographically scattered but homogeneous in interest.

It is possible to plan a structure which can accommodate private interests and the community at large. For example, employers wishing to update employees on a number of scattered sites could buy the time they need and encrypt the material if it was confidential. One television guide for educators and trainers would be a bonus and make the organisation of recording by institutions easier. The programming is likely to acquire more status when it is promoted on The Learning Channel and not hidden away in the corners of other channels. Schools, the OU and the Open College all work on a high proportion of repeat programming which, with agreement, could be carried over. Such a channel could also systematically provide more programming accessible to the deaf and hard-of-hearing.

Two educational experiments using satellite channels will start to transmit in Europe in 1990. It is significant that the first of these, the EU-funded experimental Channel E, the Knowledge Channel, will transmit on an Astra satellite transponder number 9, sharing it with TV10, a Dutch commercial company. Due to start transmitting on 7 December 1989, it will have three regular time slots each weekday (6.30–7am, 10–10.30am and 3.00–3.30pm) and probably a midday slot at the weekends. In the experimental phase, Channel E is planning to use existing education or training programmes and learning materials from any source, provided they meet educational standards and the rights have been cleared. The programmes may have originated in any European language and will then be subtitled into one another. The experiment will be closely monitored to provide information on costs, structure and programme availability, since the aim is to put in place a European Open Learning Channel, which uses existing sets, Astra dishes and also links into cable, represents a financially cheaper and more practical proposition than Olympus.

The other major development is the launch of Olympus, the European Space Agency's (ESA) satellite, which started test transmissions in autumn 1989, and begins regular transmission in 1990. Described as the most powerful communications satellite in the world, it will carry nine hours a day of education and training programmes on its high-power European direct broadcast beam. They are planned to be originated through Eurostep, a users' association of 300 organisations from 16 countries. The BBC has, of course, in the shape of BBC Enterprises, a major role in the provision of peak-time programming on Olympus, and will undoubtedly include in its scheduling some of the BBC's continuing education output.

What is interesting is the fact, that neither Channel E on Astra nor Eurostep, the grouping of European Olympus users, has included the possibility of using conventional *broadcast education* programmes in their plans. On Olympus, control of allocation of hours, scheduling, content and production is in the hands of the educationalists and trainers. Programmes will come out of television studios and audio-visual centres in schools and colleges and in higher education. The schools network is already very active and the Training Agency is a major player in this ambitious and exciting project; but, while they have maintained their virginity at this point, it is quite clear that they are having to learn many lessons from scratch and rein-vent some wheels already invented and broken on previous satellite demon-strations. Some of this should have been preventable in a proper partnership and will have a cost.

The importance of Olympus, apart from its European dimension, is that it is the beginning of a new generation of larger satellites with the possibility of interactivity through two-way audio. On the negative side, it will require a different and probably more expensive dish only likely to be affordable by institutional users, and it will transmit in DMAC or D2MAC rather than in PAL, so it faces an immediate difficulty in the current lack of availability of DMAC receivers. A further negative aspect is that one of its two tubes has already burnt out, and it therefore has no back-up.

Learners will need to view at centres rather than at home, though, of course, centres can be in hotels, medical schools, clubs or workplaces, as well as in educational and training establishments. Much of the programming, in order to obtain the benefit of interactivity, is expected to be live from studios with conference call bridging. Most of the participants from post-school education have quite specialist, i.e. narrowcast, educational goals and target groups.

It is interesting that these plans are almost diametrically the opposite to the way in which programming is increasingly being planned for the OU, for instance. The most recent analysis of viewing rates and VCR access from the OU shows the continued maintenance of an encouragingly high viewing rate for programmes in spite of, the authors note, a deterioration in the quality of broadcast transmission times (Crooks and Kirkwood, 'Video Cassettes by Design for Open University Courses', *The Journal of Open and Distance Learning*, Vol. 3, Issue 3, November 1988). The maintenance of these high rates is attributable to compensatory increase in video viewing at more convenient times. The volume of home recording now accounts for all but nine per cent of the total viewing figure for post-foundation course programmes. Overall access to video equipment among OU students had already reached 86 per cent in 1988 and will continue to increase. The OU, of course, already chooses video cassette as the appropriate medium for some courses and also has a broadcast loan scheme to back up broadcasting. However, it is still more economic for them to transmit programmes for home recording for large population courses than to distribute programmes on video.

An associated OU recommendation notes the substantial educational advantages of video format programmes, i.e. programmes designed for video cassettes from the start, over those designed for transmission only. An obvious policy issue for the BBC (rather than the OU) will be to determine for how long it will be prepared to make airtime available even for high population courses, simply as a method of distribution, particularly made in video rather than in a broadcast format.

Funding is as yet only a partial problem for Eurostep users on Olympus, as the ESA is providing time on the satellite free for three years, and is also providing a professionally staffed play-out centre. Participating organisations will obviously need to fund programme production and delivery to the play-out centre, but do not have to fund transmission costs. The project is, as noted earlier, another example of technology-led rather than a needs-led enterprise.

The ESA's philanthropy is much to be welcomed and it behoves us all to make the best of this experimental period, as it does to make the most of Channel E's experimental time. They are not in competition with each other. At the same time, it raises again the issue of the feasibility of a more broadly-based UK education and training channel, on which a variety of users, both publicly and privately funded, could buy time for a variety of programming. A second Astra satellite is due to be launched providing more spare channels. A transponder on Astra, unlike Olympus, on costs around £5-6 million and the cost of dishes is well within the competence of most schools' and colleges' management arrangements. Obviously BSkyB's higher picture and sound quality and telesoftware/digital data capacity would have been of greater benefit, particularly to schools, but the price would have been higher and might only have got off the ground with the sort of injection of government stimulus and support which Kenneth Baker put into the micro revolution in schools when at the Department of Trade and Industry. Obvious candidates for such a channel already exist, even apart from schools: the Open College, the OU, the Training Agency, the Open Polytechnic and any business or industry grouping with education and training needs where learners and/or sites are scattered.

It would be important to ensure that all the provision was not in the vocational area. For many people, non-vocational programmes are just as important. Indeed, the Open College of the Arts would be an appropriate participant. Large numbers of older people, people taking early retirement, or changing stream, are interested in arts, culture and social studies and not just in vocational areas. The OU is a candidate since, as we have seen, it has been moved to less favourable transmission hours and is mainly recorded at home. The Open College is a candidate since the transmission it was offered by Channel 4 was predicated on the unemployed being a main target group, which they are now certainly not. The Open College of the Arts has a particular need for the delivery of visual content.

It will, however, be ironic if the educators and trainers get their hands on a channel just at the time when broadcast education is being forced off the important ITV channels. We need to fight to keep space for the educationally and socially disadvantaged (the wantless) on the broadcast channels, but we must also fight to gain new appropriate space on the new channels.

Previous essays in this section have demonstrated again and again the importance Naomi placed on whether or not broadcasting 'worked' as a tool for adult learners and general viewers. In a final consideration of this question, part of the transcript of a speech she made to an international audience in Munich in April 1996 she returns to her central preoccupation, the necessity for broadcasters to research, continually, the receiving end of mass communications, and to analyse and act upon their findings.

Broadcasting and the adult learner: a review of current research and research needs[18]

... (It) is striking to discover how little research into the effectiveness of educational broadcasting, as such, now appears to be carried out. This cannot, of course be because of the lack of appropriate methodology. Advertising research using much of the same methodology continues as a major industry, with vast expenditures and continuing refinement of techniques. Many of these provide lessons for educational broadcasting, and many of them are already affecting programme making. Telecommunications research is also advancing apace.

A simple explanation of the lack of interest could just be lack of resources. More cynically, it could stem from arrogance on behalf of educators, who think they know best what to do, or arrogance on behalf of education producers who prefer their own 'creative imperative' to learning from what has worked for other producers or other audiences...The imperative to increase the effectiveness of Coca-Cola's advertising message and increase its market share by 1 per cent translates into millions of dollars. Neither the educator nor the education producer share this imperative...

18. Sargent, N. E. (1996) broadcasting and the adult learner, A review of current research and research needs; paper prepared for the IZI International Conference 'Educational programmes on television: What do people want?

Educational effects of general output

It is important to note that much general output broadcasting, sometimes planned for, sometimes unplanned... A US study of the incidental learning of ageing adults noted that:

'... not only can intentional learning occur from purposely watching educational programmes, but incidental learning can result from casual viewing or commercial television. Ageing adults not only watch more television proportionately than their younger counterparts, but they also actively seek educational broadcasts. Little research, however, has been done on the amount that ageing adults actually learn from commercial television' (Stokes and Panowski, 1988).

Barry Gunter, formerly Head of Research at the IBA commented in a paper *Learning from Television*:

'...it is difficult to dispute one consistent and over-riding finding: viewers can and do learn from television. What is really intriguing, however, is how much and what kinds of things they learn while viewing, and whether they learn from television when they are expected to do so' (Gunter, 1992).

He went on to highlight two key issues. First that learning from television depends on the ability of viewers to follow and identify with programmes, and second, that viewers often learn from programmes not primarily intended to impart information, while at the same time failing to learn from programmes which are designed to inform.

Focussing on learning from television news, Gunter reported that political knowledge levels of young children and teenagers has been found to be positively associated with reported levels of television news watching. However, he went on to say:

'Although, with much of the evidence on this subject, it can be difficult to disentangle whether watching the news leads to better knowledge, or better knowledge leads to more news watching, at least two studies have indicated that the influence flows primarily from television news viewing to enhanced political knowledge.'

The positive association between political knowledge and levels of television news watching is reported in more detail by Lukesch (1992). He shows that boys watch more television news than girls, and older boys watch more than younger ones. Boys have greater political knowledge than girls and older boys than young ones. He suggests that information from the media carries more weight than personally communicated information.

Gunter records other factors which affect learning from news:

- having a sound background knowledge about, say, politics or economics can significantly increase the extent to which news stories on their topics were understood
- the production features, such as sequencing, packaging stories and use of pictures can affect learning

- items with negative consequences for those involved were well remembered
- the use of film footage can distract attention away from what the newscaster is saying
- news pictures must be supportive of the narrative.

This last factor is also noted as in important in a paper on experience in Sweden by Hoijer (1991), who comments that '...the correspondence between the verbal and the visual information is important as well as the tempo'. She summarises research which is related to popular education as one of the main programming goals for Swedish public service television; the agreement is that 'the supply of programmes as a whole shall be characterised by an ambition to provide popular education'. She notes that:

'Popular education may be related to current affairs programmes like news and news magazines as well as to factual or expository programmes or documentaries. The former usually reached very high audience ratings while the latter categories have lower audience sizes. On the other hand they often receive high appreciation.'

Hoijer provides summaries of some main findings of the research on news experiments, on analyses of the news and on studies of audience comprehension of expository programmes focussing on programme strategies and reformulations and visual illustration. Several findings match those referred to by Gunter: the need for adequate background information to the news, the need for a unifying theme, too many items presented too fast, texts devastated by irrelevant pictures. Her conclusion was that it was 'news for the initiated'.

Research on expository science programmes showed that viewers found abstract themes more difficult to understand than concrete ones, and that the viewers can relate concrete themes to their own life and experience. Viewers primarily assimilate or pay attention to themes or content which are psychologically close to them. They are helped by good verbal and visual presentation, with experts who use everyday language, and with mental time to interpret the visuals and relate them to the verbal information.

Hoijer concludes by noting that the audience is not of course homogeneous and that background is largely related to social position, and especially the level of formal education:

'The segments among the citizens who have a long education have naturally received a broad background of knowledge which makes it easier to understand and assimilate information from the media...For television with popular education as a programming goal, it is a big challenge to overcome this tendency and to catch sight of the perspectives of the ordinary, not so well-informed audience groups which, in fact, constitute the broad majority of viewers.'

Hoijer also makes a vital research point, commenting on the combination of long-term research goals aiming at general knowledge with more short-term research goals of the evaluation of specific programmes and the need for such research to be undertaken within an overall theoretical perspective of cumulative knowledge about viewers' incidental learning processes.

While this section has focused on learning from news and factual programmes, learning from television drama and from performance is also particularly important, especially for those who are housebound, or who live in rural areas, and there are excellent examples of educational work building on major drama series and operas for this purpose.

Use of television for direct educational broadcasting

The classic educational strategy is to use the mass medium for mass popular broadcasting to speak to anyone in the community who is interested in watching. Such educational programmes may be on general or specialist topics and should be transmitted at accessible times for the general population. Such programmes are, however, in competition with general output for good slots and decisions about the scheduling will not usually be in the hands of educational producers...

More often, education programmes are allocated slots at the edges of the schedule, in the early morning, late at night, or on Sunday morning. By definition, these times are not attractive to the general public; although they are adequate for motivated target groups who know what they are interested in, they are unlikely to attract large audiences or to bring in newcomers to the subject area. Their subsequent low audiences are seen as a self-fulfilling prophecy, justifying even further cuts in budgets. Occasionally, such slots can be turned to good account; for example, scheduling *Years Ahead*, a magazine programme for the over 60s, at 3.45pm when a high proportion of the target group was available to view.

The research issues behind these strategies have less to do with the content of individual programmes and more to do with the overall pattern of audience behaviour and competition with other programmes (educational programmes need to look as good as other general output, or people will not bother to watch). To obtain information about the general audience it is necessary to have access to a large sample of people, probably requiring the collaboration of the national broadcasting system. It is usually management, advertisers or regulators who own the relevant research and they may not be prepared to make it available, as it often involves information of competitive advantage. For example, while quantitative audience ratings are publicly available in the UK, the qualitative measures of audience appreciation, often, as Hoijer noted, are not. An argument that is being pressed in the UK is that since the national broadcast research organisation, BARB, is, to a large extent, funded from the licence fee, the public is entitled to have access to its findings.

Examples of research information which is relevant to the planning of educational output and which act as the frame within which programmes or series are viewed include: studies of the public's attitudes to types of programmes; research into people's use of time; profiles of audiences for different programme types; profiles of audiences for different time slots; the effect of using repeat programmes or series; and the effect on the audience of changing schedule slots. The crude measures of effects are provided by the audience ratings. Broadcasting management is unlikely to provide the resources for much *ad hoc* research on the effects of specific programmes or series, though several such surveys were carried out in the early years of Channel 4, and the BBC has conducted several programme-specific studies using their TOPS panel.

What has proved of increasing interest is the body of information arising from the provision of various forms of programme back-up and follow-up. While some producers are still taken unawares by the unexpected effects of programmes, in principle, the idea that programmes can and should have an effect, and an afterlife, is now understood and accepted across a wide range of programmes and not just educational ones. The provision of telephone helplines, dial and listen advice lines and a wide variety of follow-up information provides informal feedback to programme-makers, which is in turn becoming the subject of evaluation...

A specialist channel?

Europe has not so far seen fit to support an entire specialist channel dedicated to education and training though there are a number of encouraging precedents in North America. Two projects are of interest here. Glikman (1994) describes extended research into the history of continuing education in France, which became timely again as the country renewed its interest in the educational roles and functions that educational television could specifically fulfil.

In 1993, the French government decided to create, during the daytime, a terrestrial (Hertzian) learning channel on the fifth network, on which ARTE, a French-German cultural channel, was already broadcasting during the evening. The issue was not to develop precise programmes, but to 'clarify the channel's global design, targets and purposes'.

Glikman proposes that significant differences are less between styles of production, content and so on, but rather between the ways the programmes are related to educational systems and social goals. She distinguishes three types of use of Hertzian educational television:

1. When television is used as a promotional tool for face-to-face educational systems, for example in relation to the BBC's Adult Literacy campaign in the 1970s, its role is then to sensitise underprivileged groups and to

encourage them to contact appropriate organisations. The recent BBC Family Literacy campaign, which used short 'commercial-style' programmes devised with the assistance of an advertising agency, is similar in its strategy.

2. Its oldest use, she describes, is using television at the centre of an open multi-media system, in which television is the driving force. Programmes, usually in series, may cover a range of topics and offer 'additional or deepened knowledge'. These series usually reach people who are already quite 'advantaged', but who are willing to learn more. They have, however, no impact on the general social situation.

3. The third type is as a component of a distance learning system in which television participates in a complete curricula supported by media and other resources and is sup[plied by educational organisations in partnership with broadcasting companies. These include the OU/UK, the Telekolleg in Germany and A Saber in Spain. Since they allow people to obtain better qualifications, they contribute to a policy of ascending mobility.

Glikman's paper is a strong restatement of the importance of terrestrial broadcasting, free at the point of use. Other media, either for individuals or in groups, can only reach already motivated audiences, ready to register for courses, prepared to go to resource centres or to buy necessary equipment.

Only Hertzian television allows education to meet new populations: those who are not spontaneously motivated by knowledge or willing to enter a learning process. Particularly being the link of underprivileged people...television is the best if not the only way to reach these groups, which spend more time looking at it than all others. Met by chance, in the flow of information or entertainment programmes, promotional programmes can break down psychological blocks and activate a demand for action.

A second important piece of policy research stems from the activities of the EBU itself. Following on a preliminary piece of research by Gwynne-Jones and Hasebrink (1995), a more detailed feasibility study has been carried out on the potential for a European Educational Television Channel. The study considered availability of programmes, distribution, the audience/market, other funding, and proposed a short to medium way forward for EBU members to pursue.

Such studies as these go well beyond the research normally carried out and described by educators and academics, and have more to do with projects normally carried out by management consultants.

Television as one component of a distance learning system

Glikman's third type, where television acts as one component of a distance learning system, is of course, an increasingly common model, and is more frequently the subject of academic research, as the educational institution has more interest in its monitoring and evaluation. An interesting case, where the partnership is between the US Public Broadcasting Service (PBS) and a wide range of American institutions of higher education, is the PBS Adult Learning Service, the first national effort to provide coordination and focus for adult learning via television. Brock's (1990) paper sets out an agenda of research needs for adult learners via television, assuming that some learners must, or wish to, study for credit through such distance institutions of higher education.

What is helpful is that she assumes that 'television has proven itself as an important delivery mode to meet the educational needs of adult students at a distance'. Coming at it as a manager, she chooses to focus on research needed for 'pragmatic' purposes. She lists as topics: the awareness of the public of such opportunities; awareness on conventional campuses of such options; better and comparable profiles of current and future students; learning styles; student retention and comparisons with conventional students; student support services; counselling and access to library services; faculty training; and the need for a national clearing house for information about adult learning through television:

'...Since current research clearly demonstrates that television is an effective teaching/learning medium for a variety of adult learners, the main point...is that a high priority should be given to research which serves the pragmatic purposes of supporting television course development, improved management of such courses, and advocacy for their greater acceptance and use.'

Russell (1992) is less tolerant of what he variously describes as slick production, broadcast quality and interactivity. He is, however, a strong proponent of instructional television and its effectiveness. He has reviewed, he says, 44 studies and 21 research summaries, and argues that there can be a high degree of confidence in such a number:

'No matter how it is produced, how it is delivered, whether or not it is interactive, low-tech or high-tech, students learn equally well with each technology and learn equally well as their on-campus, face-to-face counterparts, even though students would rather be on campus with the instructor, if that were a real choice.'

Russell is a supporter of the VideoClass System, a variety of the Candid, or nowadays, Virtual Classroom, and argues that, by heeding the research and downsizing the technology, it is possible to lower costs, increase course offerings and reach many more learners with confidence...He reminds us that 'the media are mere vehicles that deliver instruction but do not influence achievement...it is only the content of the vehicle that influence achievement'.

The message itself

Hence we return to the message itself. It is here that the research is thinnest. It depends, of course, on what one means by research and whether we are sticking with research into educational programmes on television. Is it research into the content of one individual programme, into the effectiveness of a series, or into the socio-economic benefits of a project?

As noted earlier, there is little new research at the macro-managerial broadcasting level, though there is some awareness of its desirability among educational producers. There are few institutes or academic departments...who have concentrated on research into educational broadcasting. Sadly, educational broadcasting is itself too narrowcast to be of interest to most mass communication researchers.

Among educators and academic researchers, interest has mainly moved to work on newer technologies. Even though the term 'educational television' is still used, it is not used in the Hertzian sense (e.g. the UK *Journal of Educational Television* does not address itself to broadcasters, or even to distance educators, but mainly to people producing a variety of video and multi-media-based materials for use inside institutions).

Perhaps the most interesting new research which links the forms of Hertzian television with the new multi-media courses is that of Diana Laurillard on multi-media, education and narrative organisation. Arguably, one of the most important characteristics of broadcast television has been its linear structure. The much-vaunted benefit of the new media is their interactivity. Laurillard's proposal focuses on the difference:

'For interactive media, one of the key benefits is seen as being the *lack of imposed structure*, giving much greater freedom of control to the user. However, in the context of instruction this benefit runs counter to the learner's need to discern structure if there is a message to be understood. We have found from observation that learners working on interactive media with no clear narrative structure display learning behaviour that is generally unfocused and inconclusive...Thus one of the key benefits of interactive media, the greater learner control it offers, becomes pedagogically disadvantageous if its results in mere absence of structure' (Laurillard, 1995).

It is clear that the importance of educational programmes on television needs to be restated, to broadcasters, to educators, and to the community, if broadcasting which is accessible to all, is not to be forgotten about in the rush to drive on the information superhighway. It is particularly necessary to ensure that educators look beyond the confines of their own and their institution's needs, and use and research into all the technologies, both old and new, which are at our disposal for the educational benefit of the whole community.

References

BROCK, D. (1990) Research needs for adult learners via television, in Moore, M.G. *Contemporary Issues in American Distance Education*, pp. 172–180.

GlIKMAN, V. (1994) *Research and Policy: Which Design for the future French Learning Channel?* Paper presented to the ETA conference on Media and Learning Designing for the 21st Century, Bournemouth, 1994.

GUNTER, B. (1992) *Learning from Television*, paper presented at the British Association Science Festival, 1992. Mimeograph, London, ITC.

GWYNNE-JONES, E., Hasebrink, U. (1995) *European Educational Television: A Feasibility Study*, Hamburg: Hans-Bredow-Institut.

HOIJER, B. (1991) *Research Related to Popular Education for the Swedish Public Television Service*, Sveriges Radio, Stockholm, 1991.

LAURILLARD, D., *et al.* (1995) *Multi-media, Education and Narrative Organisation*: description of and proposal for an ESCR-funded project, Mimeograph, Milton Keynes, The Open University.

LUKESCH, H. (1992) 'TV learning: Incidental or a systematic process?' *Communications*, Vol. 17 No 2, pp. 205–214.

RUSSELL, T. L. (1992) 'Television's indelible impact on distance education: What we should have learned from comparative research', *Research in Distance Education*, Vol. 4. Athabasca University, Alberta, Canada.

As noted earlier in this volume, media literacy was among Naomi's programme priorities as a senior commissioning editor at Channel 4. In a further exploration, prepared for NIACE in 2004, she takes account of the vastly increased range of media where literacy is an increasingly practical necessity.

What is media literacy?[19]

The OED describes it as a 'condition in respect to education, especially the ability to read and write'. There is, as yet, no agreed definition as to what constitutes media literacy, nor is the idea understood by most people, or thought of as a problem to be addressed. At its simplest, it can be described as 'the ability to access, analyse and respond (critically) to and benefit from a range of media'.

Media literacy is taking its place in the array of literacies increasingly recognised as necessary for participating in democracy, or, indeed, in day-to-day life; financial literacy is another current example. Transferring the concept to the electronic media adds the question of the range of the media and their different forms.

There are two sides of media literacy to be considered. The enabling side is concerned with empowering people, giving people the opportunity to gain more from all the media in terms of education, information and entertainment and total communications potential. The protective side is concerned with ensuring that people, particularly children, are protected from harmful, unwanted or inappropriate messages.

The Office of Communications (OFCOM) has been given the duty, under the Communications Act 2003, to promote media literacy. This is described in the Act's Explanatory Note on Section 11, as follows:

'...To bring about increased public awareness and understanding of material published by the electronic media, the processes by which such material is selected or made available for publication, the available systems by which access to such published material can and should be regulated, and the available systems by which persons to whom such material is available may control what is received. OFCOM are also required to encourage the development and use of technologies and systems for regulating access to such material and for facilitating control over what is received. These could

---

19. Sargant, N. E. (2004) *What is Media Literacy and Why Does It Matter?* Leicester: NIACE.

include internet filtering systems, rating systems by which, for example, programmes can be given a classification which indicates the nature of their content, and other technical devices such as PIN-based systems to control viewing. Promotion of the use of such systems could include OFCOM participating in the development of related materials.'

While the Act covers all electronic material, television broadcasting is likely to be its public face initially, as OFCOM is already engaged in a one-year review of public service television broadcasting and the Department of Culture, Media and Sport (DCMS) has launched its consultation on the review of the BBC Charter.

The tension underlying the Act is between protective regulation for control and prevention and positive regulation to enable and empower and to maintain and enhance, in particular, in the first instance, public service broadcasting. There are also urgent issues about universal access and digital switchover since fewer older people have access to multi-channel TV and fewer older people, as well as poorer people, have access to the internet. Positive regulation is necessary to keep a generous and uncensored offering of on-screen broadcast provision. The digital divide tends to reinforce the learning divide.

As with other literacies, it is necessary not to be judgemental, patronising or paternalistic about the need for media literacy. The concept of 'rational ignorance' is an important one, and many people do not feel 'the need to know', or wish to bother to do so. The assumption being increasingly made, particularly by broadcasters, that everyone has access to the internet is far from the truth, and even if people do have access, it is almost certainly not yet at the same time, let alone in the same room, as their TV set or radio.

The DCMS has produced a Media Literacy Statement (2001) in support of a general statement of policy on media literacy and critical viewing (and listening) skills, laying emphasis on the 'ability to think critically about viewing...and to take greater responsibility for viewing choices and the use of the electronic media'. While focusing on content skills, the DCMS added a requirement for technical competence in terms of navigation skills for the new electronic media landscape and production content.

The Broadcasting Standards Commission (BSC)/ITC/NIACE working group offered, in 2001, a working definition of media literacy as follows: 'media literacy exists when the user not only has access to a full range of electronic media, but is able to comprehend the choices available and evaluate them'. The literature review, *Assessing the Media Literacy of UK Adults* (2003), commissioned by the same working group, focused specifically on the question, How media literate is the adult population in the UK?, and looked for empirical evidence... including the identification of gaps or inequalities. It concluded that 'in the context of these lively debates...and strong expressions of support for media literacy, it is undoubtedly both curious and disappointing that little empirical research on media literacy has been funded or conducted in the UK. The report noted that the majority of research has been to inform about the place in the school curriculum and the resources available to it.

Their text then offers helpful suggestions as to what may be involved in attempting to measure media literacy: access as a prerequisite to literacy, informal/formal learning, existing curricula in audio-visual media/ICT, etc.; it notes that much academic research is medium-specific despite growing media convergence. The review then returns to the issues of 'technical competencies' (access and the ability to use the equipment), 'critical reception practices' (to understand the content and view it critically) and actual 'content production' as the areas for assessment.

Tessa Jowell, Secretary of State for Culture, Media and Sport, spoke eloquently at the first major seminar, *Inform and Empower: Media Literacy in the 21st Century,* (BBC/UKFC/BFI/Channel 4) held at BAFTA, 27th January 2004. She suggested that the definition of media literacy must embrace at least three different strands:

'First, that people must have the means to understand the potential of all the new communications technologies that are becoming available...second, that it is the content delivered that matters to people. In particular, people need to be aware of the way in which large corporations and other institutions use the media to promote their products and shape the way people see the world... So we want active, informed consumers, able to take decisions for themselves based on judgement and understanding. But, thirdly, we recognise that people are more than consumers. They are citizens, and to be citizens they need to have an understanding of the world around them and how they engage with it. Most of the information they need to be able to act as informed citizens does actually come from the media. It's not only the big corporations that are sophisticated in their use of the media.'

The same could be said of political parties, pressure groups, NGOs, and, you might even say, government too.

Research, evaluation and public policy

Naomi had started to worry about the practical and theoretical constraints on her Open University research at an early stage. She wrote a paper on the subject for the Council of Europe in 1973, and refined and expanded it in this contribution to the British Journal of Educational Technology *in October 1974. Her starting point is the limited scope of existing educational evaluation, which had been normally in one medium and inadequate to the complex demands made by the OU.*

The evaluation of multi-media educational systems[20]

Traditionally educational evaluation has been identified with curriculum evaluation. And within the field of curriculum evaluation, the 'test and measurement' model of evaluation has been dominant. However, Eraut (1972) lists as many as eleven alternative evaluative models, all of which have at some time been applied to curriculum evaluation. Parlett and Hamilton (1972) in their discussion of one of these alternatives comment on the dominance in conventional approaches of the experimental and psychometric traditions in educational research. They introduce 'illuminative evaluation' based on anthropological research as an alternative research paradigm and emphasise that they are interested in the study of a programme as a whole.

Increasingly the traditional approach to evaluation, characterised by Parlett and Hamilton (1972) as the 'classical' or 'agricultural-botany' paradigm is found to be inadequate as evaluators are confronted by innovatory educational programmes of a wide variety. It is quite clear, in particular, that the evaluation of multi-media educational systems cannot even confine itself to curriculum evaluation, and certainly cannot confine itself to the 'test and measurement' model.

One important characteristic is shared, however, both by the new 'social anthropology' paradigm and the traditional 'agricultural botany' paradigm – the concentration on one research technique.

---

20. McIntosh, Naomi (1974) 'Some problems involved in the evaluation of multi-media educational systems', *British Journal of Educational Technology*, 3(5), 43–59, and from a longer unpublished manuscript version of the article.

Educational researchers, frequently psychologists by training, inherited the mantle of the physical scientists and continued their scientific attempts to measure under controlled experimental conditions. The 'social anthropology' paradigm as its name implies has replaced the mantle of the physical sciences with that of the social sciences, and uses research techniques stemming from social anthropology, in particular, that of participant observation. But in both cases, the technique has dominated the development of the paradigm and not the nature of the programme or the purpose of its evaluation.

This paper cannot attempt a comprehensive discussion of educational evaluation and will concentrate therefore on the special problems involved in evaluating multi-media educational systems, particularly as they affect researchers.

Within this, it will work to the broad definition given by Astin and Panos (1971) of an educational programme as 'any on-going educational activity which is designed to produce specified changes in the behaviour of the individuals who are exposed to it. Thus an educational programme could be a particular method of instruction, a single classroom lesson, a complete course of study, a programmed textbook, the environment of a college, a special remedial programme, an apprenticeship or internship, or an entire school system'.

Suchman (1967) takes a broad view of evaluation as referring to the general process of assessment or appraisal of value. Astin and Panos (1971) take a more specific view which is now gaining currency in the area of educational evaluation, and appears particularly applicable to the evaluation of multi-media systems where the educational and financial penalties for bad decisions are greater than for conventional educational programmes.

'...It is assumed that the fundamental purpose of evaluation is to produce information which can be used in educational decision making. These decisions may be concerned with the continuation, termination or modification of an existing programme, or with the development and possible adoption of some new programme.'

By definition, at this stage in their development, the majority of multi-media programmes are innovatory by nature. Although this innovatory nature poses additional research problems, it is the fact that the courses are multi-media which is dominant. Parlett and Hamilton discuss the evaluation of innovatory programmes as if there is something intrinsically special and different about it. The variety and number of new programmes in America, listed by Valley (1972), for example, makes it clear that innovation can take many forms – a new student audience, new instructional techniques, new settings and so on.

Some of these forms may be marginal to the evaluation, while some may be critical. The main fact about innovatory programmes no matter how marginal the innovation, is the obvious one – that we do not know how they are going to work. How can, then, the researcher know which techniques are likely to be most appropriate? Indeed the main technique favoured by illuminative evaluation is singularly inappropriate for any multi-media educational programme which is based on independent learning, as many are. The example of the Open University makes this point clearly. Participant observation as a research form can find little place in a mass home-based learning system. The 'learning milieu' concept (Parlett and Hamilton, 1972) could perhaps be applied to face-to-face sessions at study centres, but these are not participated in by all students and form only a small proportion of their total learning even for those who do attend. To accept as dominant any technique may be to pre-judge or prejudice the outcome of the evaluation. Ideally a researcher should select from a total armoury of techniques those that are suitable for that particular research problem within that particular research environment.

Multi-media educational programmes are not, of course, all of one kind. They can range from on the one hand a limited course internal to one institution which simply uses some hardware, to, on the other hand, a major educational series designed to go out to the whole country on open network television. Either the course may be using the *mass-media*, or it may be using some sort of *media* for *mass* education or it may simply use the media for education. It may be that we should exclude the last of these from this discussion. On the other hand, it is on such courses that evaluators in this field have traditionally concentrated (Campeau, 1972). Of course it is tempting to stick to their 'test and measurement' model, and this, of necessity, would limit the scope of our work. But Parlett (1972) contrasts forcibly the 'tidy' ideal world of the 'test and measurement' type of evaluation with the 'untidy' reality more usually found.

'The chief deficiency of a testing-type of evaluation is that the restriction and pre-structuring required for it are so formidable...Where are the large-scale innovations, with samples of hundreds of students? The colleges who are willing and able to co-operate in some joint experimental venture? The heads of departments who are prepared to countenance dividing students into experiments and controls?'

The 'tidy' and 'controllable' world of the experimental psychologist, and the natural scientist before him, find less and less parallel in the untidy world which is likely to make up the environment of a multi-media system. It is interesting to note that it is educational psychologists who have concentrated on and found it possible to concentrate on curriculum evaluation, and sociologists and others who are now more concerned with extending the scope of evaluation. For an educationalist *within* an institution, the system with which he is concerned may be permitted to end at the boundaries of the institution. Mass multi-media systems, in particular, are unlikely to be so confined. If it was only a question of the additional cost involved, this would be relatively simple. But it is becoming clear already that multi-media systems have social and even political implications. It could indeed be argued that the evaluator should not be concerned with these and should confine himself to the educational content. All the indications are that this argument is no longer acceptable. The Open University in Great Britain provides an obvious example of a multi-media educational system set up with objectives which were both educational and social. The fact that the system is also cost-effective is an additional bonus. As pressure for expanded educational opportunities increases, so does the necessity to be cost-effective. It is not surprising that countries as diverse as America, Iran, Spain and India are looking hard at the contribution that educational technology and Open University type systems can make to solve their educational problems. The causes of this could be said to be semi-economic and semi-political.

Another danger is worth noting at this stage, one that could be described as semi-political and semi-educational. Multi-media systems, particularly if nationally-available have more potentiality of centralised control of content and standards. This may be a good thing, or it may be bad. It could lead to raising of standards, or to uniform mediocrity, or to misuse. All of this is likely to have implications for the evaluator that go well beyond that of curriculum evaluation.

The boundary line between what constitutes a research study and an evaluative study often becomes blurred. Research has an important role to play in the overall set up, design and evaluation of multi-media courses. Some of this research may be evaluative in nature, some may not. It is in our interest, at this stage, not to try to draw the demarcation line too clearly. Several points at which research or evaluation of one type or another can make a contribution can be distinguished:

a) In discovering whether there is a need for a course
b) In locating, defining and characterising the target group of the course
c) In pre-testing the course or its components
d) In providing short-term remedial feed-back while the course is running
e) In determining whether or not the course works both in terms of
   – The needs of the student
   – The needs of the course producers and conveyors
f) In determining whether or not the objectives of the resource-provider have been met

The research techniques which can be brought to bear on these problems are many and varied. They will come mainly from the areas of social, psychological and educational research.

The objectives of multi-media educational systems

It is first necessary to comment, albeit briefly, on the nature of the objectives of such systems. Each system will undoubtedly have multiple objectives. Different objectives will be specified by different persons or organisations within the educational process. There may also be different objectives for different components of the course. Some of these may be interdependent – some may not. Some of these may be in conflict with each other. Some may be short-term and some may be long-term. This complex of objectives is likely to be hierarchical in nature, and different values may attach to different objectives. It is not always possible to define all objectives adequately at the start of a programme, even with the assistance of pre-existing lists such as Bloom's. More importantly, the dogmatic use of the 'objectives' approach assumes that the only likely outcomes of a programme are those anticipated by its Statement of objectives (Eraut, 1972). Should any unspecified outcomes be ignored when the programme is evaluated? They may turn out to be more significant, either positively or negatively, than the specified outcomes. And all this pre-supposes that the objectives themselves are worthwhile.

Assuming that we are able to determine adequately the objectives of all the parties involved in the decision to set up a multi-media educational system, we may distinguish sets of people with differing objectives.

a) Society as a whole
b) The institution/group that makes the course
c) The designer of the course
d) The institution that runs the course
e) The student who is the 'user' of the course
f) The employer of the student, if any
g) Other people who may be affected by the student's participation in the course

Not all of these categories will be present for any particular course.

Implicit in the establishment of these hierarchies of objectives is the attempt to measure their attainment. This, in turn, implies agreement on the criteria against which attainment of these objectives should, be measured. The major distinction to be made is between criterion- referenced and norm-referenced measurements. Sometimes measurements of both kinds may be desirable and may or may not be possible. For example, we may wish to try to measure the absolute benefit to the student or to society as a whole. Alternatively, we may wish to make relative comparisons between alternative methods of teaching the same material, or between alternative types of institutions providing the same courses. There is frequently no *absolute* yardstick available, and relative comparisons with fellow students may be all that is possible.

Two major problems inherent in evaluating multi-media systems

Before we can go any further we need to make two fundamental distinctions which arise from the nature of multi-media systems for out-of-school education and affect the selection and use of evaluative techniques in this area. These primary problems are:

1) The nature of the student population. Is it an 'open' or a 'closed' group?
2) Is the teaching-learning system a 'direct' or 'indirect' one? Or to put this way, is there an intermediary in the learning process?

It is necessary to consider these points in more detail.

The terms 'open' and 'closed' were first used by McIntosh and Bates (1972) to distinguish between the two categories of student group that are discussed below. Do the producers of the course know exactly at whom they are aiming the course? If so, are they able to locate them? The course may be aimed at an 'open' group who may choose to follow the course, but do not have to formally enrol or register in any way, and are therefore not necessarily known. Any course using open network broadcasts, either of radio or television, is likely to have an audience of this kind. Alternatively, the course may be aimed at a 'closed' group who are known, or at least, can be located, since they have to formally register and perhaps pay a fee for the course.

Irrespective of which of these types of groups the course is designed for, the evaluator needs basic information about the characteristics of the students. For 'closed' groups, this and subsequent information is relatively easy to obtain, provided the energy and resources are forthcoming.

For the 'open' category this background information, and indeed any other information, is very difficult to obtain, if only for the reason that there is no infallible means of locating the students or even of knowing how many of them exist. The problem is exacerbated for the 'open' group by the fact that the student may not have the motivation to co-operate that those in a 'closed' group have. By actually joining a 'closed' group the student has committed himself either financially, personally or socially to such a course. This distinction between an 'open' and 'closed' group has implications both for the designer and the evaluator in terms of level and of structure which will be returned to later.

Of course there may also be eavesdropper 'open' audiences for courses designed for 'closed' groups. The desirability and/or difficulty of evaluating these is a separate issue.

The second fundamental distinction between multi-media courses and more conventional courses which needs to be made is one that affects both the designer *and* the evaluator of such courses.

In *conventional* courses, the course designer, lecturer or writer, is usually in *direct* contact with the student, i.e. the user. This direct contact has the strength of adaptability and allows an immediate response to the student. The course can, in effect, be individualised. Design problems are less acute, since mistakes can be remedied individually on the spot. Design is therefore less expensive, and time scales for production are shorter. On the other hand, the course is more expensive to run and less easily transferable to other students and other institutions.

From the point of view of the researcher, however, it is more difficult to evaluate. It is true that 'inputs' and 'outputs' (Astin and Panos, 1971) may be easier to measure, but 'operations' – the means to the achievement of the educational ends – will be more difficult. The course could be viewed as, in effect, a purpose-built product for each individual student. No two products will be the same, since the interaction of the tutor and student will always differ, and attempts to measure the 'operations', even if the same measuring devices are used, will inevitably be affected by the differing nature of the 'operations'.

In a multi-media course, in order to utilise the media to full advantage, one seeks and requires economies of scale. These economies may have to be gained at the expense of flexibility. To this extent, evaluation taken on its own, might be made easier. This will be the case when large numbers of students are studying the course 'directly'.

Frequently, however, it is not as simple as this. The other way to achieve economy of scale is by several institutions adopting the same course, which *may* or *may not* originally have been designed for this purpose. The institution in this way acts as a type of agent or 'intermediary' in the educational process. Yet another 'intermediary' may intervene in the form of a tutor, and more complicated still, the course may be utilised in different ways by different tutors in the same institution. This provides a welcome opportunity to mediate between the, of necessity, undifferentiated educational message and the needs of the individual student in order to individualise the learning system. But although the middle-man or intermediary may introduce flexibility into the educational system, he may alternatively if he is not adequately familiar with the design and objectives of the course actually impede the

Difficulty of evaluating a multi-media course

		Type of audience	
		Closed	Open
	Direct	Easy	Difficult
Teaching system	Via an 'intermediary'	Difficult	Very difficult

learning process. His intervention, and/or the institution's intervention will certainly make the process of evaluation more difficult, since their goals may not be the same as those of the course designers, and in fact they may not be interested in evaluating the course at all.

We can therefore attempt to categorise these multi-media courses in terms of the possible degree of difficulty involved in their evaluation.

Other problems

1 Does the course have an entry requirement, either in terms of ability or attainment, and if so, is this known or not known to the students?

This is important for several reasons. If the course is designed to be 'open' but does, in fact, have an assumed entry requirement, how can the students themselves discover in advance whether or not they match up to this require-ment without a costly commitment either of time, morale or money? Similarly how do the evaluators discover the abilities of the students and whether or not they match up to the entry requirements of the course?

If the course has no entry requirement, then the only measure of success can be an absolute measure of knowledge at the end of the course. Whether this is an adequate measure of success or not will depend on whether the original objective was to bring everyone up to a certain standard irrespective of where they started or if it was simply to produce some (maybe minimal) *gain* in knowledge.

2 The heterogeneity of the student population

The very nature of multi-media courses for mass education is likely to imply a heterogeneous student population. If the course is 'open', this hetero-geneity may not be known. If the course is 'closed', it may be known or partly known, but this is not, on its own, enough. To recognise a problem is not to solve it. The evaluator will at minimum be able to determine some of the more obtrusive characteristics of the student population and may be able to predict with some accuracy which groups of students should be able to benefit from any particular course pitched at any particular level. If courses are likely to be remade, then formative evaluation may be able to make a contribution to this re-making. If the course is not to be re-made, then prior research is even more necessary to attempt to diagnose which students would prove to be unable to benefit. Preferably even before then, the potential student audience should be researched to help determine the level at which the course should be pitched. The more clearly defined the target groups, the easier all these problems are.

3 Possible levels of evaluation

We have already touched on the differing objectives which one course may need to meet for different persons or institutions involved in that course. As an increasing number of stages are involved in the educational process, so the multiplicity of objectives is increased. It is a pre-requisite of educational programmes that they are evaluated at different levels. It is possible to distinguish, at minimum, four different levels:

a) Evaluation of the need and/or the demand for the course
b) Evaluation of the effectiveness of the whole course
  – in the opinion of the student
  – in the opinion of the educator providing the course
  – in the opinion of the buyer, user or employer of the newly trained product
  – in the opinion of outside educationalists
c) Evaluation of individual units or blocks of work on the course, e.g. one week's work
d) Evaluation of the impact or effectiveness of one individual component of the multi-media learning system, e.g. the radio or the written materials

4 Evaluating the course as a whole or individual components

For multi-media courses, it is, in addition particularly necessary to attempt to evaluate the contribution of the individual components of the course. Obviously for the whole course to be optimally effective, it is desirable for each *individual* component of the course to be individually effective. To this end it is possible to invoke a wide variety of research techniques, to pre-test broad-cast programmes for impact and effectiveness, to pilot written materials for clarity and comprehension etc. at minimum; it is possible to argue that each component of the course should be pre-tested individually against its relevant objectives. Romiszowski (1972) suggests that it is preferable to compare media against specific types of learning objectives, and that if one does this; one is automatically forced to evaluate the individual components of the course rather than the course in totality.

It is obviously much easier to accept his view. The problems involved in *pre-testing* the overall effectiveness of the *whole* educational process are formidable.

We do not yet have the perfect formula for evaluating the composite effects of a multi-media course, but we do know enough to consider that to take only an elemental view of evaluation may be dangerous. The model will inevitably be a complex and inter-related one, since

- We cannot assume that all media work [is equal], or communicate in the same way to the same extent to different people.
- We cannot assume that all people are equally able to learn from each of the different media.
- We cannot assume that all messages can be conveyed equally well through each medium.

All of this puts on one side the more practical problems of different production time-scales and widely varying costs for different media. Millions have been spent by commercial researchers in the field of advertising research in their attempts to systematise their choice between the media. They have not yet found the answers. Clearly the resources available in this field are likely to be more limited.

The main problem is that we do not know whether or not the media work in isolation or in co-operation or even antagonism to each other. Is their effect cumulative, and if so, at what sort of rate? Is it an arithmetic or a geometric progression, for example, or does one medium on its own convey say 60% of a message effectively, and the second one add only 20%? The other side of this problem is that individuals may have different learning styles or abilities which cause them to learn differently from each of the media. Some people for example, tend to be visualisers while other are verbalisers.

How do we evaluate in this complex situation? The evaluation of a method of teaching could be done by manipulating the media, the learning situation, or the message. We could experiment with the same message using different media, but it is impossible to ensure that the same message is conveyed equally on different media. Even if we could ensure this, it would be difficult to define what would be the equivalent impact of the same message on different media. In addition, the level of exposure to different media varies from individual to individual. And short-term effects may be different from long-term effects. Marc and Durand (1971) suggest that:

'The principal error in comparative studies is to set, a priori, the media as competitors, when they are most often used in a complementary manner: the source of this error is found in the emphasis put on the concept of "effects" to the detriment of the concept of "communications"'.

In one way, this makes life easier for the course designer, and for the evaluator who no longer needs to seek equivalent standards. On the other hand, it has implications for the course conveyor and the student who may not have all the media *equally* available to them and may, therefore, miss out on some parts of the message.

To evaluate, we need to try to estimate what proportion of each medium has been used by different individuals.

The learning activity, as we have said, is likely to be of a different nature with different media, e.g. print and TV. So if different students have learnt in different ways, can one then use the same measure to estimate the amount of their learning? If, because the learning activities are different, we have to use different measures, how can we ever know if the results are comparable?

The cost and value of evaluative research

Costs involved in the actual setting-up of multi-media courses have three main components.

– The investment in the development of the course itself.
– The basic cost of running the course each time it is put on.
– The variable cost associated with the number of students taking the course. The variable cost will depend not only on the number of students studying each time the course is run, but also on the amount of personal contact with academics that is built into the course. At the one extreme, it may be nil in an 'open' course, or it may include only postage, at the other extreme it may include regular personal contact, and therefore be quite great.

The cost of evaluative research needs to be looked at differently in relation to the three different costs listed.

1. The investment in the development of the course

Inevitably, different media have widely differing costs. The more expensive the medium, the more it is necessary to know how the medium works and how effective it is. Heavy development costs of particular media can only be justified either if the educational gain is overwhelmingly greater than an alternative method, or if the course is likely to reach such a large audience or be repeated so often that the set up cost is spread over such large numbers over time as to be justified. Exceptions to this statement have been argued on the grounds, for example, of the motivation provided by television. This is not yet proven. A more difficult argument is the quasi-prestige one, that a course looks like a poor relation unless it contains television. If a course is to be run once only, then the development cost will be great in relation to its other costs. Theoretically it would make sense to research into it at this stage. On the other hand, if the course is not to be re-run, then *no* action is likely to take place as a result of the evaluation and there is therefore no point in carrying it out.

Additionally, heavy set up costs may not be justified for subject matter which is likely to become out-of-date soon.

2 The cost of running the course

This will be a recurring cost and money spent on researching the operation of the course to reduce this recurring cost may well be cost-effective, particularly if the course is flexible enough to allow amendments to be made before it is re-run.

3. The variable cost associated with the amount of personal support

It is helpful to look at this along a continuum, from the entirely independent learner at one end, to the teacher-supported student at the other. Putting on one side the educational implications, the more an intermediary intervenes, the more expensive the course is likely to be.

The amount that is worth spending on evaluation of this area of cost is likely to depend on the *proportion* of the cost of the course that is 'variable' cost, i.e. the more personal support that is provided, the more this cost is likely to be. At the same time the research will become more difficult and more expensive.

It is possible to look at the continuum in relation to research in the same way.

4 The variable cost associated with the number of students

When one course can meet the needs of large numbers of students without too great a degree of intervention, then the economies of scale are likely to be sufficient to outweigh the increased set-up costs. But as evaluative research does its job better, and more is known about the target audience, so the defined group is likely to become smaller, more specific and less replicable. As this happens, the relative advantage of the media, and of multimedia systems, that of communicating economically to large numbers of students in different places and at different times, becomes less marked in comparison to conventional systems. This is particularly likely to be true as the courses get more advanced and more dependent on previous work. It will be ironic but very useful if our increasing efficiency in evaluative research proves that many multi-media courses are not effective either at a particular educational level, or at the available cost level for the size of the audience. It will, however, be in the best tradition of applied research if we can so specify our objectives and analyse the components of our problem that we are able to decide *in advance* when it is or is not appropriate to devise multi-media courses for specified groups or on specified subjects. Evaluation is conventionally retrospective. Its scope should be extended, since it will ultimately only justify itself if it is able to build up predictors of success or failure and thus avoid investment in poor or not-needed courses.

The 'value' of evaluative research is more difficult to quantify. Since, as we have defined it for the purpose of this paper 'evaluative research' is applied research rather than 'fundamental' or 'basic' research, we are involved in an attempt not to extend the boundaries of knowledge, but more to use our existing knowledge as an aid to the solution of some given set of problems. We are involved in a systematic search for, and analysis of information. Green and Tull (1970) consider research as a 'cost-incurring activity whose output is information of potential value to management decision'.

They state:

'It is apparent that information can never be available to the extent that the decision-maker would desire if no costs were involved. Since obtaining information is a cost-incurring activity, rational decision-making necessarily involves consideration of the *value* of information. The *amount* of information is important only as it affects the value...The *value* of this information can be measured in terms of its use in reducing the costs of uncertainty which are associated with taking action based on an earlier (and less) information state.'

It is interesting that this view of the value of applied research only developed significantly in the sixties, and then mainly in relation to the field of business administration. Hemphill (1969) makes this point, and considers that 'evaluation studies in education can be viewed more appropriately within a context of decision making than within a framework provided by the purposes and conventions of research'. He states:

'Evaluation studies are made to provide a basis for making decisions about alternatives, and, therefore, in undertaking an evaluation study, one at once addresses himself to questions of utility. It may be objected, however, that this is too idealistic a view of the purpose of evaluation studies.'

What is true is that this view is certainly *not* the view widely held by the majority of persons currently involved in evaluation studies. Often it must be said, evaluation is seen as an end in itself, and not a means to an end. It is not unreasonable to suggest that the view stated by Hemphill, and found already to be valid in industry, may be increasingly relevant to evaluative research on multi-media educational systems where the investment of resources is much greater, where the potential audiences are much larger, and the penalties for bad decisions resulting in bad courses and wasted resources are very high.

The analogy with business decision making falls into difficulties however at one critical point, that of the decision-maker. McIntosh (1973) discusses the different characteristics of decision-makers in the public and private sectors, and notes that financial objectives may not be the only ones that need to be met. Other objectives are less easy to quantify. Some objectives may in a sense be irrelevant, for example, motivations of personal prestige. Particularly for educational systems, 'notions of utility' become much more complex and difficult to quantify since social and political concerns may well intrude on educational and economic concerns.

Different judgements may need to be made about formative and summative evaluation. Scriven (1967) describes 'formative' evaluation as conducted in conjunction with the development of new educational programmes, and 'summative' evaluation as that which is used to assess the effectiveness of existing programmes. These two types of evaluation are, of course, complementary to each other and wherever possible if both are to be carried out should be designed as part of one overall programme. However if we accept the purpose of evaluation, as defined by Astin and Panos (1971), given earlier in this paper then there may well be occasions when it is inappropriate to carry out summative evaluation.

This may seem heretical, in the sense that one could argue that it is always important to know what has happened. On the other hand, if a course is not going to be re-run, i.e. if no action is likely to take place as a result of the evaluative study, then clearly the study should not take place. In cases such as this, formative evaluation may be all that is worth doing, using evaluative data collected during the developmental stage of a programme. If as with television, the initial investment cost is very great, then formative evaluation becomes even more important. To gain the most advantage from formative evaluation, it is better not to develop a large number of small programmes, but to try to develop a fairly small number of large programmes each of which can be properly tested and will be widely used and re-used.

Internal or external evaluation?

By internal and external evaluation we mean here whether the evaluation is conducted by the institution that is producing and/or running the course or by some external agency. Since evaluation implies 'the social process of making judgements of worth' (Suchman, 1967) it is often argued that it should be carried out by persons who are external to the programme, thereby presumably guaranteeing objectivity. This argument has become increasingly important as large sums of governmental money have been invested in educational programmes, many of which are multi-media in kind. At the same time the task of the evaluator is made more difficult. If he is charged with formative evaluation, it may be difficult for him to be closely enough involved with the organisation to plan and carry out the formative evaluation effectively, to do it in time, rather than too late, and to ensure that its results are not just fed back, but acted upon. The fact that he is an outsider already creates some problems but he carries the additional burden of being known to be the agent of the funding body, with all that that implies. It could be argued that it is virtually impossible for external evaluators to do formative evaluation well.

Summative evaluation, then, the final judgement of worth, is a different matter. Here it is possibly more important for the evaluator to be objective, particularly if large sums of money are involved. However, without adequate formative evaluation, it is likely that researchers attempting summative evaluation may find themselves without the necessary information on which to work.

How valuable then is external evaluation? To be effective, it must be closely involved with the design and implementation of the system. If it is closely enough involved to be effective, then can it still be objective? One thing that does emerge from this is that the political imposition of external evaluation, for example as a safeguard for tax-payers' money, is likely only to give a spurious air of academic respectability to the project, and not to be of any real benefit to the people involved. Under these circumstances it is increasingly likely to become an end in itself and not a means to an end. This is particularly so if the *funding* is also external. If an institution has committed its own resources, and decided upon evaluation itself then it is more likely to take notice of the results. Of course an institution can use its own funds to commission external evaluation. That is a different matter. It is the role of the external evaluator *externally funded* which is the most difficult.

Problems involved in experimentation for the purposes of evaluation

Experimentation in the social sciences is much less easy than in the natural sciences. This is a major problem for those adopting the agricultural-botany paradigm.

Any 'professional' or scientific evaluation will require controlled conditions that we are rarely able to produce in the social sciences. For example, we would need to know whether the learning we are measuring was the only learning going on at the time, or whether other learning was happening simultaneously. Controlled experimentation would imply a homogeneous group of learners, all of whom we knew could learn in the same way. In fact, of course, we know that people do not learn in the same way. It would be virtually impossible to cause everyone to learn in the same way, even in a one-medium learning situation. With a number of media it would, as we have seen, be similarly impossible to determine what proportion of each of the media had been 'used' by different individuals. The alternative would be to artificially prescribe how the multi-media package should be learnt from. This prior prescription would in itself be dangerous, since it might pre-judge the issue of how the package should be best used and so preclude it from succeeding in its objectives. Problems of this nature are inherent in all experimentation in the social sciences, and evaluators would do well not to pretend to a degree of accuracy and control that they are never likely to achieve. These problems are particularly intractable when one is dealing with an 'open' student population.

Another problem is of a different nature, but no less important. Assuming that we accept that some form of experimentation is possible, then this implies alternative forms of educational treatment and provision. With an 'open' group who are not necessarily studying for qualifications, some form of course experimentation is possible, providing the first pre-requisite of identifying different groups within an 'open' audience can be achieved. With a 'closed' group, although it is administratively easier to experiment and control, if the students are studying for some form of certificate or a degree, it may be morally unacceptable to offer different sets of educational experiences to different students, as one package may turn out to be much less effective than the other and that set of students may be materially disadvantaged through no fault of their own. In a situation like the Open University, for example, this solution would be unacceptable as it might affect students' chances of obtaining a degree.

A further possible alternative would be to seek natural experimental situations, for example where one part of a population has access to TV and another does not. This is again difficult, as it is highly likely that those people without TV are already different for entirely separate and perhaps relevant reasons, from those who have it, i.e. they may be a peculiar section of the intelligentsia, or simply people living in remote areas. In this case, these factors would be likely to obscure the other ones that we were attempting to measure.

It is worth looking in detail, to illustrate the problem, at just one area that would be involved in any experimental design: that of sampling. We would inevitably require matching samples that would have to be selected in some way, either randomly or purposively.

For the purpose of random sampling, we would need a sampling frame or list of the persons involved from which to select our sample. By definition, with an 'open system' such a list is unlikely to be available. If we adopted purposive sampling of some sort, then again with an 'open' group this would assume prior knowledge of the population under study that we might not have. Purposive sampling may well be difficult even for 'closed' groups since to sample effectively in this way requires prior knowledge of the *relevant* characteristics of the subjects to be studied. This assumes two things – firstly that we *have* prior knowledge of the characteristics that we wish to select by, and secondly that we know these characteristics to be *relevant*. If they are not relevant, then we may increase rather than reduce error. Often one of the main objectives of the project itself is to discover just such relevant variables and to presume them in advance may nullify the whole exercise. Alternatively, we may know which variables are relevant in learning terms, but the researcher may not be able to describe them in operational terms of the interviewer to recognise them, e.g. motivation, or different learning abilities. Most samples are matched of necessity on recognisable objective criteria, such as sex, age etc. which may have little relevance for our purpose.

Finally, as we have said earlier, a multi-media course contains different components which may all be used to convey the educational message.

Different courses will use different media, in different combinations. We are here taking a broad definition of media to include not only TV, radio, print and other audio-visual aids, but also personal support by teachers or lecturers.

It is likely that a multi-media course with personal contact will operate differently from a course without any. When an intermediary exists then experimentation becomes even more difficult to control since more uncontrolled variables are introduced. On the one hand the media may come between the teacher and his class. On the other hand, the teacher comes between the media and the student. Which is more important, and how, in particular, can we assess the impact of many different individuals interpreting the message to their students in different ways?

It is perhaps possible to evaluate by *experiment* the conveying of a concept, but not the complex inter-relationship of a whole course.

Unless we know whether the media act separately or whether they act to reinforce each other, or maybe even are counter-productive, attempts to set up instruments of evaluation are of little use. Multi-media systems are inevitably complex. To be effective they must also be flexible and therefore the components will interact. Evaluation must embrace this complexity if it is to have any real value.

A possible framework for evaluation

It may be helpful to characterise multi-media courses in terms of their key features in an attempt to build up a framework for their evaluation. The following set of features, though not exhaustive and not mutually exclusive provide a basis for further discussion:

1. Is the course aimed at an 'open' or 'closed' student, population or both?
2. Is the learning system 'direct' or via an intermediary?
3. Is the course to be repeated, or is it to be run once only?
4. What is the relationship of the cost of the course to the cost of possible evaluation procedures?
5. Does the course have an 'assumed entry behaviour' or not? If yes, then is it known, and if so, by whom?
6. If the course has 'assumed entry behaviour' is it desirable to measure it or not?
7. Is the performance of the student to be assessed or not?
8. What combinations of media are to be used, and in what ways?
9. is the course to be evaluated unit-by-unit; (week by week) or as a whole or both?

Taking the first two sets of features as basic provides a matrix which enables us to characterise the four main types of courses which are likely to confront the evaluator:

		Type of audience	
		Closed	Open
Teaching system	Direct	1. Closed and direct	3. Open and direct
	Via an 'intermediary'	2. Closed and mediated	4. Open and mediated

These categories of courses are not mutually exclusive, and some courses may be designed for both types of audience and/or for both types of teaching system. The Satellite Technology Demonstration in the Rocky Mountain States is an example of a programme which is designed to come into all these categories. Yet again, some courses may be designed for one type of audience, but also be used by chance or as a bonus by the other type. The 'eavesdropper' audience of academic and other interested persons who watch Open University programmes, but are not registered students is an example of this.

It is quite clear that the majority of studies considered by Campeau (1972) fall into categories one and two. Her review emphasises the 'appalling lack of recent objective data on the instructional effectiveness of audio-visual media particularly in the field of adult education'. But her review *excluded by its own definitions and the criteria it adopted* much of the literature on the use of instructional media to teach adults that was published in that period. Campeau (1972) states:

'Most of this non-experimental literature consisted of surveys, testimonials, historical and descriptive assessments, reports of informal evaluations – all of which did not even attempt to deal with or assess the instructional effectiveness of audio-visual media. Instead, assessments were made of user preference for and attitudes toward various media, patterns of media use, characteristics of the post-school audience, problems of educating adults via mass-media and so on. Much of the data offered was in the form of questionnaire responses, enrolment and completion statistics, cost figures and tallies of services provided and extent of user.'

The difficulties of experimentation for the purposes of evaluation have already been discussed. It is quite clear that the only categories in our matrix that are amenable to the imposition of experimental conditions are the two on the left hand side (1 and 2). It is no coincidence therefore that Campeau's screening criterion, 'studies in which adult learners were assigned to experimental and control groups that included, normally, at least 25 subjects each' produced in the main, studies fitting into these categories – a form of self-fulfilling prophecy.

The criterion also made it probable that the studies covered adults learning in relatively conventional learning situations, for example – college students. It is highly likely that the learning situation will be less conventional and therefore more varied and less controllable if multi-media methods are utilised.

What needs to be considered is whether or not it is constructive so to limit the field. It would obviously eliminate any innovatory evaluation of the 'social anthropology' type. Clearly the problems involved in the evaluation of multi-media courses are too complex to be amenable to test and measurement devices under controlled experimental conditions. Some part of their content may and probably must be so measurable, but to assume that all of it is, may be to mistake the wood for the trees.

This is not to put on one side the contribution of the psychologists to testing the actual effectiveness of the educational message, it is to say however, that for multi-media educational systems, other problems may be so important as to change the whole perspective of the evaluator's activities. One example suffices – if an adult worker is not at home at the time of the broadcast, or from experience has decided that TV is a non-assessable part of a course, then the fact that television, after formative evaluation etc, conveys a concept 'perfectly' is totally irrelevant since the student, for entirely different reasons will not have been exposed to the educational message.

Maybe the field is too wide and we are endeavouring to set up some systematic framework for things that are not intrinsically similar. It could be argued that there is no necessary connection between organisations such as the BBC, which use the mass-media for educational courses and individual colleges or institutions who happen to choose some sort of audio-visual aids instead of conventional learning systems for their courses. Any attempt to find similarities may be counterproductive as the dissimilarities are too great.

What they have in common, *and this may not be enough to justify the whole exercise*, is they are trying to construct a situation in which one educational message can be used economically and effectively for large numbers of people, or for people who would otherwise not be able to receive it. And this one message has to meet the differing needs of all these people.

Under these circumstances, no one prescription for evaluation is likely to meet the needs of all kinds of courses.

References

ASTIN, A. W. and PANOS, R. J. (1971) The Evaluation of Educational Programs, in R. L. THORNDIKE (Ed.) *Educational Measurement,* Washington: American Council on Education, pp. 773–751.

CAMPEAU, P. L. (1972) Selective review of the results of research on the use of audio-visual media to teach adults, Council of Cultural Co-operation, Council of Europe, Strasbourg.

ERAUT, M. (1972) Strategies for the evaluation of curriculum materials, in K. AUSTWICK and N. D. C. HARRIS (Eds.) *Aspects of Educational Technology,* London: Pitman.

GREEN, F. and TULL, R. (1970) *Research for marketing decisions,* 2nd edition, Englewood Cliffs, New Jersey: Prentice Hall.

HEMPHILL, J. K. (1969) The relationships between research and evaluation studies, in Tyler, R. W. (Ed.) *Educational Evaluation; New roles, new means,* Chicago: NSSE.

MARC, M. and DURAND, J. (1971) 'Le choix entre les Medias', paper presented at ESOMAR/WAPOR Congress, Helsinki 1971, pp. 349–370.

MCINTOSH, N. E. (1973) The Use of Survey Research in the Planning of Higher Education, Esomar Congress: Budapest 1973.

MCINTOSH, N. E. and BATES, A. W. (1972) *Mass-media courses for adults,* Programmed Learning, July 1972.

PARLETT, M. (1972) Evaluating innovation in teaching, in BUTCHER, H. J. and RUDD, E. *Contemporary Problems in Higher Education,* London: McGraw Hill.

PARLETT, M. and HAMILTON, D. (1972) *Evaluation as Illumination,* Centre for Research in the Educational Sciences, University of Edinburgh.

ROMISZOWSKI, A. J. (1972) Notes on the evaluation of multi-medi teaching systems, Council of Europe, 1972.

SCRIVEN, M. (1967) 'The methodology of evaluation', in *Perspectives of Curriculum Evaluation,* Chicago: Rand McNally, pp. 39–83.

SUCHMAN, E. A. (1967) *Evaluative research,* New York: Russell-Sage Foundation.

VALLEY, John R. (1972) *Increasing the Option,* Educational Testing Service, Princeton, New Jersey.

Two years later, she moved on from setting out the problems of evaluation, to analysing the outcomes and purposes of evaluation. This paper, based on a presentation to an OECD conference on institutional management in higher education in Paris in September 1976, was published by OECD in 1977, a time of retrenchment in educational investment. It includes a summary of the principal themes in the previous paper, but goes much further in policy analysis.

Evaluation and institutional research: aids to decision-making and innovation [21]

Preamble: innovation at a time of zero growth

The time when higher education could count on continued growth and expansion has clearly gone forever. Even if the economic climate in general was not so bleak, it is likely that education would have been getting a decreasing share of national resources particularly in developed countries.

Not only has education not turned out to be an economic panacea promoting economic growth, but it has also not turned out to be the social panacea that many idealists assumed it would. Added to this is a wide-spread pattern of decreasing birth rates in many developed countries, which projected to the 1980s and 1990s, has major implications for the effective demand for education at all levels. The next two decades indicate not just zero-growth, but zero-growth minus for higher education in terms of real resources.

One of the few unknowns is the real strength of the movement towards recurrent education. This is one area which might lead to increased expenditure, but alternatively its implementation might be at the expense of more traditional higher education, or simply become a political totem pole, rather like comprehensive education in the U.K., that many people pay lip service to but few wish to implement for themselves in their own countries. Many countries will, however, continue to face pressures to extend access to higher education to 'more' and maybe 'different' students, even if they do not move rapidly towards a mass higher education system.

---

21. McIntosh, N. E. (1978) 'Evaluation and institutional research: the problems involved in evaluating one course or educational program', *International Journal of Institutional Management in Higher Education*, 2(1), pp. 5–19, and from a longer unpublished manuscript version of the article.

We can safely assume that the same amount of money or less will have to be stretched further, that more priority will have to be given to cheaper kinds of higher education, and to more national planning and co-ordination of systems (Burn, 1976). Increasing numbers of people are demanding higher education as a right, and basing this demand on the democratic notion of equality, or at least equality of opportunity. At the same time democracy requires openness in management structures and in decision making. All levels of staff and students are assumed to have a legitimate interest in the process of decision making. And democracy also demands that institutions should be responsive to the consumer.

How can we reconcile the reasonable demands of the community for more higher education with the maintenance of high academic standards? And how can we combine the cost-effective management of institutions with a reasonable amount of democratic decision making? As Burn (1976) asked, 'Can a university be governed efficiently and democratically?'

These problems are exacerbated because the investment in higher education is relatively inflexible. The bricks and mortar and equipment of university buildings cannot easily be used for alternative purposes. Large student hostels, for example, are no longer seen as desirable living places by many students but cannot easily be lived in by others. Academic staff, in many countries, have tenure and even if they could or would move to another job, would need re-training. The historical reasons for academic tenure were no doubt valid, but it leaves little room for manoeuvre in a time of zero growth.

Innovation is likely to be a particular victim of zero growth. Some institutions have been set up as, and even made a fetish of being innovatory. It is interesting to see for how long an institution can continue to innovate before size and inertia overcome it.

Few, if any, institutions have managed to innovate continuously. Maybe there is, for a new institution, only a limited time period over which it is possible to innovate before the arteries begin to harden.

For existing institutions, innovation is likely to be a marginal activity, responding to new needs, prompted often by the arrival of 'new' staff, and usually implying the availability of 'new' money. Existing staff are often threatened, and may or may not be by-passed as the institution attempts to change course to meet new needs. It is much easier to make new appointments to provoke change, than to cause existing staff to change. Tenure is here again a problem.

New institutions tend to have a higher proportion of younger staff in senior posts, who are inevitably less able or likely to move soon. None of this matters in a growth period, when additional staff can be appointed, or there is reasonable movement of staff between institutions. It does matter in a time of zero growth. Few will be able to move, and few in new institutions will be ready to retire. The Open University, for example, has only three professors over 56 out of a professoriate of 38. The staff most likely to move will be the staff the institution is least likely to wish to lose. Only the best under such circumstances tend to get other jobs. So the natural forces of reaction set in. The less innovatory staff and indeed the bad staff stay, and change is made even more difficult. As a new institution gets larger and its reputation gets safer and better established, so new recruits tend to be safer and more orthodox. They are not the innovators or idealists prepared to put their careers on the line without security. At the same time the initial innovators tend to get 'diluted' by the increasing numbers of later arrivals. And it is likely that the characteristics called for in an innovator will not be the same as those required in the manager of a stable state. The abilities, interests and rewards are all different. Yet universities continue to appoint people on tenure and assume that they are all equally good at different jobs and will continue to be so. Perhaps the greatest challenge is to learn how to manage a stable state creatively and provide a framework for innovation which is not destructive to 'good' existing activities.

Although the purpose of this paper is not to discuss all the possible strategies for the 'institutionalisation of innovation', the starting point for the next section is the proposition that higher education could benefit by being more self conscious, by using institutional research and evaluation as aids to decision making, and that this in itself will be a spur to improvement and innovation.

The need for evaluation and institutional research

In the past the investment in higher education was small, the numbers involved were fewer and the costs were not largely state borne. The possibility of enquiring into how it operated, or measuring its effects was not considered. Higher education has increasingly to accept public scrutiny, to be responsive to public demand and subject to government controls. This requires more information of a variety of kinds than institutions have been in the habit of providing, or even of thinking desirable.

This paper will argue that it is not the availability or the adequacy of information for decision making that is the real problem. A variety of management information and research techniques are available which can be used to obtain appropriate information. The problems relate rather to:

1. the nature of the decision making process
2. the interests and objectives of the decision makers
3. the identification of the decisions to be made
4. the timeliness of the information.

The purpose of collecting information

Information is not collected as an end in itself. We are here concerned with it as an aid to management decision making. Decisions in industry are usually dominated by the necessity to maximise financial pay-offs. The value of information can be directly related to the value of the decision to be made and decision makers have a clear interest in the use of such information. The situation in an educational institution is less clear.

In industry, Green and Tull's (1966) definition of research as 'a cost incurring activity whose input is information of potential value to management decision' is obviously appropriate.

By 1969 the significance of this type of approach was being noted by educational researchers. Hemphill (1969) considered that 'evaluation studies in education can be viewed more appropriately within a context of decision making than within a framework provided by the purposes and conventions of research…evaluation studies are made to provide a basis for making decisions about alternatives…' Hemphill asked what proportion of a project's total resources should be assigned to evaluation activities. This is not necessarily the correct question. It is not adequate to apportion a standard percentage of the total cost of a service to form the budget for evaluation. Expenditure on evaluation should not relate to the total cost of the service but to the marginal cost of alternative decisions. If not, it tends to become an end in itself, and not a means to an end. The main emphasis must be on the amount of information that is used. However, the straight transference from industry of the notion of information as an aid to decision making is too simple. It has, as we noted, been developed in situations where objectives are usually financial, and pay-offs can in some measure be quantified. Attempts to quantify the personal probabilities of pay-offs in the social or educational field (Guttentag, 1973) are more open to question. And there is a built-in reluctance, particularly among academics, to accept the relevance of management techniques developed mainly in the private sector. There is among many an unspoken attitude that they are 'dirty' or in some way not consistent with academic purposes. The tradition of the 'enlightened amateur' as administrator dies hard, particularly in the U.K.

An institution is likely to have a hierarchy of objectives, held by a variety of individuals and groups within the institution. The community funding it may also lay on it objectives which may or may not be in conflict with its own objectives. In addition, there are likely to be several decision makers or groups of decision makers whose interests may not coincide, e.g. academics *and* administrators. Individuals or groups are unlikely to be directly affected by the financial implications of their decisions. Persons commissioning research may have academic, personal or political motives for so doing. These interests may affect not only the commissioning of the research, but also the way in which the results of the research are communicated and used.

Evaluation – the traditional view

Educational evaluation has, until recently, concentrated on the evaluation of curriculum materials, and the dominant tradition within educational evaluation has been the 'semi-scientific' one of 'test and measurement'. It has usually been carried out by outsiders in order to guarantee objectivity. Parlett and Hamilton (1972) comment on the dominance in conventional approaches of the experimental and psychometric traditional in education research. Eraut (1972) similarly commences a discussion of alternative evaluation strategies with a commentary on the operations usually involved in the evaluation of programmed learning. It has assumed a relatively 'tidy' world which can be controlled and tested. The legacy of the experimental scientist is clear and it is no accident that this test and measurement model has now been christened the 'agricultural botany' model. Indeed for some educational researchers there is still no other model!

Parlett (1972) contrasts forcibly the 'tidy' ideal world required by the test and measurement type of evaluation with the 'untidy' reality more usually found, particularly in innovatory educational systems.

'The chief deficiency of a testing-type of evaluation is that the restrictions and pre-structuring required are so formidable…Where are the large-scale innovations, with samples of hundreds of students? The colleges who are willing and able to cooperate in some joint experimental venture? The heads of departments who are prepared to divide students into experiments and controls?'

With larger institutions, more heterogeneous populations, a greater use of the media and new methods of teaching and learning the scope of 'test and measurement' evaluation is even more limited, but the need for research and evaluation is even greater. A more eclectic use of the research strategies available is likely to be more fruitful.

Evaluation – alternative models

Eraut (1972) commented, 'There is no single "process" of curriculum evaluation: there are many different forms of it'.

He classifies them according to the main source of the evidence. This is, in itself, an interesting decision since it implies that the source of the evidence is more important than, say, the purpose of the evaluation. One might argue that any strategy would do well to draw on a variety of sources of evidence. In practice this does not appear to be the case, and most existing paradigms are dominated either by the source of the evidence or the nature of the technique rather than the nature of the programme or the purpose of the evaluation.

Eraut describes eleven models of evaluation, and groups them under five headings according to the source of the evidence.

A. *EVIDENCE FROM STUDENTS*
  i) *the tutorial or classical model.* The intensive study of a few students as they interact with materials.
  ii) *the agricultural botany model.* The study of a large number of students usually through batteries of tests and questionnaires.
B. *EVIDENCE FROM TEACHERS*
  iii) *the anthology model.* A collection of all the best anecdotes and stories. The best 'little Johnny' stories.
  iv) *The teacher opinion model.* The trial of materials in schools and the collection of teachers' opinions on them.
C. *EVIDENCE FROM CLASSES*
  v) *The interaction model.* This model is based on direct observation of interaction in the classroom.
  vi) *The environment model.* This model uses direct evidence from visits about the classroom environment, its layout and the integration of materials with other aspects of the student's curriculum.
D. *EVIDENCE FROM INSTITUTIONS*
  vii) *The cost-benefit model.* The predicted or observed benefits are balanced against expenditure and effort.
  vii) *The political model.* Who adopts the materials and why. Who benefits?
  ix) *The anthropologist's model.* The 'neutral' observer assesses how an innovation changes the structure and value system of the institution as a whole.
E. *EVIDENCE FROM 'EXPERTS' – PEOPLE WHOSE JUDGEMENT IS LIKELY TO BE OF VALUE*
  x) *The desirability model.* Are the outcomes desirable and should they have priority?
  xi) *The feasibility model.* Are the intended outcomes likely to be achieved by the strategy?

Choosing a strategy

It is possible to argue looking at these eleven models, that it is more often the *technique* that has dominated the development of the paradigm, than the nature of the programme or the purpose of the evaluation. The two examples of the agricultural botany and anthropology paradigms show this clearly. Parlett's model was developed particularly for innovatory programmes. But the problem with them is just that. We don't know *how* innovatory programmes work. How can we then *know* which is the one appropriate technique? The main technique of illuminative evaluation is participant observation. This obviously finds little place in a home-based learning system, where the concept of the learning milieu does not apply. To accept as dominant any technique may be to pre-judge the outcome of the evaluation. Similarly, to accept only one source of evidence may be equally misleading. Ideally a researcher should select from a total armoury of techniques those that are suitable for a particular problem within a particular environment and be prepared to seek information from all appropriate sources. It is the purpose of the evaluation and the nature of the programme which must dominate.

Eraut indeed comments that it is probably desirable to use elements from *all* the evaluation models outlines, but it is rarely feasible. He suggests that two main limitations are the total manpower resources available and the nature of the resources. Obviously the question of resource is an important one, but the nature of the educational system is also important and multimedia systems of their own nature impose additional constraints and require greater resource.

The scope of evaluation

How widely does one cast the net in discussing evaluation? Evaluation is in a sense a man-made word – a word designed to up-grade certain sorts of common sense activities which many administrators and businessmen do, as a matter of course in their day to day work, in order to legitimate the activity. In industry, most of what is described in academic life as evaluation is usually called management information or market research.

Kotler (1967), for example, defines marketing research as 'systematic problem analysis, model building and fact finding for the purpose of improved decision-making and control… (In the marketing of goods and services)'. If we replace his final phrase with…'in the production of educational *programmes*' we would not be so far off the stance taken by such commentators as Hemphill, Astin and Panos and Guttentag.

Astin and Panos (1971), for example, take a broad view of evaluation. They note, 'Evaluation involves the collection of information concerning the impact of an educational program. While there are many possible uses for such information, it is assumed that *the fundamental purpose of evaluation is to produce information which can be used in educational decision-making*. These decisions may be concerned with the continuation, termination or modification of an existing program, or with the development and possible adoption of some new program.' This is a much broader net than that traditionally cast by educational evaluation. Their definition of a *programme* is similarly broad. By educational *programme*, they take to be 'any ongoing educational activity which is designed to produce specified changes in the behaviour of the individuals who are exposed to it. Thus, "an educational program" could be:

'a particular method of instruction, a simple classroom lesson, a complete course of study, a programmed text book, the environment of a college, a special remedial program, an apprenticeship or an internship, or an entire school system'.

One of my colleagues, Professor Brian Lewis (1971) in an early internal paper on evaluation at the Open University discussed the possible scope of evaluation at the O.U. At its broadest, he commented,

'No facet of the University's affairs is beyond its reach. In the context of education, we could evaluate students, teachers, the curriculum, the program administrators, the system, the nation. In the case of the Open University, we could evaluate anything – individuals, policies, procedures products ...We could for example, evaluate summer schools, study centres, central and regional full-time staff, part-time staff, consultants, data processing arrangements, marketing policy, the staff canteen, policy on royalties, media production, packaging and mailing, television and radio, correspondence materials, experimental kits, self assessment tests, assignments, examinations, admissions policies and procedures, university committees and so on.'

Educational psychologists have traditionally concentrated on curriculum evaluation. For educationalists within an institution, the system with which they are concerned may be permitted to end at the walls of the institution. It is sociologists, economists and others who are extending its scope. Education after all has social and political arid economic implications.

It is not constructive to try to draw the boundary lines round evaluation too closely, and it is even less helpful to try to distinguish between institutional research and evaluation.

Objectives

The paper has not so far concentrated, as many do, on 'objectives'. This is not to underrate their importance, but to agree with Eraut's view that a too dogmatic use of the 'objectives' approach may be counter-productive. For one thing it assumes that the only outcome likely to be of any value is that specified by the statement of objectives. It may be that unexpected outcomes prove of greater significance. And just to state the objectives does not mean they are worthwhile or that people are agreed on their value.

There are likely to be multiple objectives and probably a hierarchy of them. Different sets of people involved with any course may have differing objectives.

- Society as a whole
- The institution that runs the course
- The designer of the course
- The tutor who runs the local classes
- The student
- The (potential) employer
- Other people, e.g. parents who are funding the student or who are affected by his or her participation in the course

Even if we agree on these objectives, how do we measure their attainment? To do this, implies agreement on the criteria against which they will be measured, and on an appropriate yardstick.

Formative and summative evaluation

Formative and summative evaluation may require different strategies, and involve different decisions. Scriven (1967) describes formative evaluation as conducted in conjunction with the development of new programmes, and summative evaluation as that which is used to assess the effectiveness of existing programmes. These two types of evaluation should of course be complementary to each other. They are not alternatives. There may be occasions when one or the other is not appropriate. For example, if a course, or one similar, is never to be re-run then the expenditure on summative evaluation is unlikely to be justified. In cases such as this it is better to concentrate on formative evaluation, particularly when the initial investment cost, as with T.V., is great. This should include both the pre-testing and piloting of materials before the course, and feedback for remedial purposes while the course is running, so that it can be run better.

Internal and external evaluation

Since evaluation involves a judgement of worth, it is often argued that it should be carried out by external evaluators. This has become very much a political matter in the U.S. where there is now an 'evaluation' industry and government contracts have 'evaluation clauses' built in. This patently leads to some absurdities. The experimental trial of O.U. materials in the U.S. provides just one example. Each campus using the materials was allotted $10,000 to set up the courses, while the external evaluators had a sum of around $? million for the evaluation of the progress of some 400 students. A similar imbalance was to be found in the contract for external evaluation of the Satellite Technology Demonstration.

If a government funded external evaluation team is charged with formative evaluation, their role is very difficult. They are not part of the institution and in some senses they may be thought of as spies or at least not accepted as part of the working team. If they are not accepted as insiders they are unlikely to do formative evaluation *well*, either in time for decisions or so that their recommendations are acted on. Summative evaluation can more easily be done by outsiders, but only if adequate formative and preparatory work has been done. It is no good arriving, as evaluators often do, after the programme is over. It is virtually impossible to try to re-create management information when it has not been collected, and retrospective evaluation is therefore inevitably more limited in scope.

Conclusion

Selecting a strategy should not depend on technique, source of evidence or intellectual fashion, but on an analysis of the problem and the decisions to be made. The objectives are likely to be many, sources of evidence will be varied and endless techniques will be infinitely available. The real problems are three-fold, but the first is easy in comparison to the other two. They are:

1. to determine what information to collect and in what way
2. to integrate all the information from the various sources into a meaningful whole
3. to ensure that the information is *used*.

The second of these papers will attempt to look at these problems in relation to one course or educational programme.

References

ASTIN, A.W. and PANOS, R. J. (1971) The evaluation of educational programs, in R. L. THORNDIKE (Ed.) *Educational Measurement*, Washington: American Council on Education, pp. 773–751.

BURN, B. B. (1976) *Higher education in a changing world*. Reflections on an international seminar, New York: International Council for Educational Development.

ERAUT, M. (1972) Strategies for the evaluation of curriculum materials, in K. AUSTWICK and N. D. C. HARRIS (Ed.) *Aspects of Educational Technology*, London: Pitman.

GREEN, P. and TULL, D. (1966) *Research for marketing decisions*, 1st edition, Englewood Cliffs, New Jersey: Prentice Hall.

GUTTENTAG, M. (1973) 'Subjectivity and its use in evaluation research', *Evaluation*, Vol. 1, No. 2, Minnesota.

HEMPHILL, J. K. (1969) The relationships between research and evaluation studies, in R. W. TYLER, (Ed) *Educational Evaluation; New roles, new means*, Chicago: NSSE.

KOTLER, P. *Marketing Management*, Englewood Cliffs, New Jersey: Prentice Hall.

McINTOSH, N. E. (1973) *The Use of Survey Research in the Planning of Higher Education*, ESOMAR.

McINTOSH, N. E. 'Research for a new institution: The Open University' in *Innovation in Higher Education*, SRHE.

OPEN UNIVERSITY (1972) *Report on the 1971 Admissions Cycle*, April.

OPEN UNIVERSITY committee paper: Clinch, J. *Feedback and Communications with Reference to the Teaching Process*, September 1970.

OPEN UNIVERSITY committee paper: Lewis, B. N. and McIntosh, N. E. *Computerised Assessment Procedures and Feedback*, May 1970.

PARLETT, M. (1972) Evaluating innovation in teaching, in H. J. BUTCHER and E. RUDD *Contemporary Problems in Higher Education*, London: McGraw Hill.

PARLETT, M. and HAMILTON, D. (1972) *Evaluation as illumination,* Centre for Research in the Educational Sciences, University of Edinburgh.

SCRIVEN, M. (1967) The methodology of evaluation, in *Perspectives of Curriculum Evaluation.* AERA monograph series on curriculum evaluation. Chicago: Rand McNally.

After Naomi left the Open University, and indeed after her second (or third) career at Channel 4, her concerns for effective evaluation of public policy, not just in education, grew. She and I wrote this paper in 1993, based on such information as we could extract from UK government bodies about their use of research and evaluation in the formulation and assessment of public policy. Fifteen years later, government should demand that it be repeated.

Evaluation and public policy in the UK: the state of the art[22]

Fifteen years on

In 1978, the authors of this paper presented a paper to the annual conference of the Market Research Society of the United Kingdom, on '*Research for the monitoring and evaluation of public social programmes*' (McIntosh and McIntosh, 1978) which contrasted the primitive state of evaluation in the United Kingdom at that time with the more advanced development in the United States.

We analysed **demand** from government and others, and **supply** from academic institutions and external consultants and researchers; we considered the skills and resources needed for the task; and we proposed ways forward.

In summary, the paper addressed the following themes:

- in the absence of the single measure of success – profitability – which is available to the private sector, government has a responsibility to account to electors and taxpayers for its cost-incurring activities
- such a responsibility may be discharged by evaluation
- however, the British parliament has no tradition of independent evaluation of the activities of the executive branch; insofar as parliament, mainly through the Public Accounts Committee and departmental Select Committees of the House of Commons, does have that role, it has chosen to enact it mainly as a 'relatively trivial' audit function, performed post hoc
- nevertheless, there were some signs of recognition of the defects in the system. The Central Policy Review Staff which served the then Labour government, had published a report in 1975 which stated that:

22. McIntosh, Andrew and Sargant, Naomi: *Evaluation and Public Policy in the UK: the state of the art.* Proceedings of the ESRC/SSRC conference 'Evaluation, Social Science and Public Policy', Ottawa, 10 June 1993.

> 'Government needs better analysed and monitored information about the relative social needs of different groups, about the different distributional effects of social policies and programmes, and about the connections between the two. The links between policy-makers, social statisticians and other professionals could be closer. The part that research plays in policy-making is not always fully understood; existing research could be more fully exploited'

and

> 'Many programmes lack operational yardsticks. Without such information it can be hard to make proper comparisons between programmes and objectives, or to take informed decisions about priorities and phasing'

- we welcomed the recognition in the CPRS report that policy research has a role in the **evaluation** as well as the **formulation** of social policies
- information about evaluation research was hard to come by. Though government departments published annual reports of research expenditure, these were usually restricted to titles, the researchers responsible, costs, timescales, and brief abstracts, inexplicit about objectives or methods
- we analysed two sources of information about policy research:
  The 1976–77 annual research report of the Department of Employment and the (then) Manpower Services Commission: less than 20% of expenditure could be identified as evaluative of actual policies or programmes
  The 1977 annual report of the (then) Social Science Research Council: more than 50% of research funded was on economic policy, and hardly any on social policy
- there was no requirement by parliament, comparable with that by the US Congress, that there should be independent evaluation of public programmes
- there was, in British universities, little of the strong empirical tradition of social science research which exists in the US, with such institutes: as Ann Arbor, NORC, or the Survey Research Center at Berkeley
- as a result, there was no multi-disciplinary evaluation profession in Britain, involving academic, consultants, and researchers, comparable to that which exists in the US
- finally, we argued specifically (to our market research audience) that survey research had a valuable contribution to make to policy formulation and evaluation, which was largely unrecognised, not only by policy-makers and academics, but even by researchers themselves
- this in turn required, we argued, new evaluation organisations, combining
  the skills of the disciplines of social policy – economics, demography, geography, education, etc

  research skills, including survey research, data processing, econometrics

  skills in the analysis of organisations and management.

In 1993, we consider:
- in Section 2, what has changed in public management, and the role government accords to evaluation, and evaluation research
- in Section 3, what is the role of the social science and social research community
- in Section 4, evidence from responses to a questionnaire survey among those who commission and use evaluation of public policy and of research; and practitioners of evaluation research
- in Section 5, the state of evaluation in the UK in 1993.

Public management and evaluation

A recent authoritative, and independent, analysis of public policy and its relation to social science is contained in a lecture at the Royal Society of Arts by Professor Howard Newby, Chairman of the Economic and Social Research Council (Newby, 1993).

Newby identifies three main changes in public policy over the last decade. First, what he calls the 'new public management':

'In essence, the new public management has sought to bring to the public sector a more disciplined approach to the definition of objectives and the efficient use of resources in their pursuit.'

Second, changes in 'the architecture of the state':

'...there have been important changes within the executive over the last decade. The separation of policy and executive functions and the assignment of the latter to Next Steps agencies has been a prominent trend. But this has only been part of a wider differentiation of functions which has also seen the creation of numerous regulatory offices, the strengthening of the audit role, and the establishment of many new quangos to administer services formerly the responsibility of local authorities.'

Third, he notes the emergence of the 'customer paradigm' in public administration:

'Whether as passengers, patients, benefit recipients, tenants or students, we are all being addressed as customers. This culminates in the introduction of the Citizen's Charter. Service providers are everywhere finding their previously unassailable powers tempered by the obligation to increase choice, expand information, introduce appeal procedures, and strengthen regulatory oversight.'

Newby concludes that 'these three kinds of change reinforce strongly the need for public policy to understand and work with the grain of human endeavour'.

Efforts by government to impose systems of management of the public sector are not new. Until the 1920s, there was a Treasury official outposted in each spending department: and even today, anyone who has been involved in negotiation with government departments will be familiar with the silent official in the corner who will make the final decision after the visitors have left.

Over the last 20–30 years, controls have become more formalised

- in the 60s, with PPBS, the UK version of the US Defense Department Planning, Programming and Budgeting
- in the 70s, with PAR, Programme Analysis and Review
- in the 80s and now, with FMI, the Financial Management Initiative.

PAR, which lasted until formally abolished by the Thatcher government on taking office in 1979, was a loose approach, rather than a discipline with its own methodology. Implementation was largely left to individual departments, and was not linked to the public expenditure cycle.

As a result, there were differing views about the objectives of PAR. The Treasury was concerned with saving money; spending departments, with programme safety – ensuring that expenditure did not get out of hand; and the GPRS, with the effectiveness of the policies.

In the early 1980s the Rayner Efficiency Strategy brought in management thinking from the private sector, looking for better value for money, and fewer obstacles to good management and the speedy implementation of change.

FMI was also a development from the private sector, from management information systems. It seeks to ensure that managers at all levels have

- clearly defined objectives and ways of securing them
- responsibility for resources as well as the effectiveness of the operation
- the necessary support in the way of training, information and advice, to achieve their objectives.

Andrew Gray, in a paper to a seminar organised by the Royal Institute for Public Administration (Gray, 1986) has identified problems with FMI which make it an inadequate basis for effective policy or programme evaluation. He points to an excessive emphasis on resources and a lack of techniques:

'...not just a question of building up the numbers of qualified accountants, operational researchers, and other disciplines...it is a matter of systematically developing the capacity of the system as a whole to generate the information (not just data), make the assessment and judgements involved, and effect changes.'

Another paper in the same collection, by Robin Butler, then second Permanent Secretary at the Treasury, and now head of the Civil Service (Butler, 1986), gave some reason to doubt whether the civil service is fully wedded to the ideas of customer-oriented policy evaluation, as Newby sees them.

Butler sees the role of evaluation as attempting to reconcile pressure for improvement to services, with pressure to contain taxation. His concept of programme evaluation is essentially that of a series of management tools – cost/benefit analysis, test discount rates, required rates of return. When he looks to research for evaluation, he looks to 'universities, business schools, and the institutions' – though his view is that 'within a government department there is no sharp line between policy analysis and research'.

However, there were in 1986 some departments and agencies of government who had a more wide-ranging view of the role of evaluation. A third paper in the same collection, by Ian Johnston, (Johnston, 1986) then head of training at the Manpower Services Commission, describes the complex range of evaluative measures applied to the Youth Training Scheme, in a form which could still be a model for such evaluation.

Evaluation of YTS involved monitoring, in the sense of tracking of individuals as well as a management information system: but it also involved coherent programmes of external research:

- the Youth Cohort Survey, placing the subsequent experience of YTS trainees in the context of the rest of their age cohort
- a Providers Survey, of employers and sponsors
- a Wider Labour Market Effects survey, again among employers, looking at experience of YTS 'graduates' in recruitment, turnover, promotion and further training; and dealing with the issues of substitution and displacement
- a Refuseniks/Early Leavers survey, to help to reduce drop-out.

YTS evaluation consciously invited comparisons with alternative policies with related aims – programmes in schools and in further education, subsidies for youth employment, community programmes. Johnston recognises the need to cover the unintended effects of YTS; and the difficulty, inherent with research among human populations, of analysing a control sample to measure 'policy-off' effects.

By 1988 the Treasury itself had recognised the need for wider dissemination of guidance, and published 'Policy Evaluation: a guide for managers' (St Clair, 1988), which sets out in clear, simple, and wittily illustrated terms the issues which a line manager must address in designing and implementing (or commissioning) evaluation. 'Evaluation', says St Clair 'helps policy managers to achieve their objectives.' It is 'to be distinguished from monitoring...routine checking of progress against plan':

'Evaluation requires a critical and detached look both at the objectives and at how they are being met.'

Treasury recognition of the importance of evaluation has not been without its price. The 1970s United States formulation of the 'three Es' – effectiveness, efficiency and equity' (Abt, 1976) as the subject-matter of independent evaluation, has been subtly changed by the Treasury to 'effectiveness, efficiency and economy'. A significant element of social accountability has thus been removed, in favour of further reinforcement of financial control.

By 1992, government recognition of the role of policy evaluation extended to the publication by the Department of the Environment of a valuable analysis of a collection of case studies (Doig and Littlewood, 1992) which provided evidence of work across a wide spectrum of departments and agencies.

In 1993, then, the idea of evaluation is well recognised in the public sector. The need for evaluation has, indeed, substantially increased with the continuing and advancing hiving off of central government activity, by privatisation and by the creation of executive agencies.

We will not be concerned here with privatisation. In many respects privatised undertakings fall within the ambit of a proper view of public policy, to the extent that they are natural monopolies, and that they are regulated according to publicly-determined rules, by regulating officers appointed by government. However, within those constraints they operate on a for-profit basis, and are to that extent comparable to the private sector.

What is much more significant is the move to executive agencies, responsible under their own chief executives for fulfilling annual business plans. Though the concept of 'programmes', in the American sense, is less used in British government, the advent of executive agencies has forced programme evaluation on central government, which has forsworn the previous powers of administrative control, and has to replace them with some other form of control – in practice, evaluation.

In many departments and agencies, every programme, however small, has evaluation (and usually an evaluation budget) built into the operational plan. Such evaluation is usually defined as covering more than monitoring and information systems, to include customer reaction; and independent external evaluation is often specified.

An important issue for government, which has not yet been adequately addressed, is where the responsibility for evaluation should lie. In private business, where the corporate headquarters has overall responsibility to shareholders for the results from the operating companies or units, it is clearly the job of corporate headquarters to see that it has the necessary information for the task; and the ability to correct failure, without necessarily intervening in the business activities of the operating unit.

The same should surely be true for the public sector. Ultimate responsibility for evaluation – which replaces profit reporting in the public sector –

must lie at corporate headquarters, with the Permanent Secretary of the department, who is the department's Accounting Officer to ministers and parliament. Delegation of responsibility for evaluation, which will of course be necessary in practice, must not only pay due regard to the need for independence from the activity being evaluated, but must also honour the needs and responsibilities of the Accounting Officer.

As a result of the changes which have been identified, both in government recognition of the need for greater accountability, and in the move to executive agencies, the evaluation message has spread from central government departments to agencies; to local government; to the national network of 82 Training and Enterprise Councils who are now responsible for the local delivery of government training programmes and for the development of local economies; and in part, to the voluntary sector.

The next questions must be:

- how has the academic and research community responded to the recognition by government of the need for evaluation?

and

- what is the result of these developments – what evaluation is actually being carried out. and what is its impact on public policy?

The role of the social science and social research community

Research in the social sciences usually requires some form of data-collection and rests on an academic base of social science research methodology. Evaluation of research requires knowledge of research methodology as well as of evaluation techniques and strategies.

While evaluation and evaluative research are terms now in more common use among UK policy-makers and funders, most academics still remain wedded to their disciplines, and the content areas of their specialisms. It is symptomatic that the major London University bookstore has no category entitled Evaluation, the classic text 'Evaluation: a systematic approach' by Rossi and Freeman (1989) being displayed under Sociology.

Martin Bulmer, in his first edition of 'Social Science Research' (Bulmer, 1978) offered a five-fold classification of social research, basic social science, strategic social science, specific problem-oriented research, action research and intelligence and monitoring. He then asked how the best use can be made of social research in policy-making, but concluded that policy research 'seems like a jelly' and decided to concentrate only on public opinion polling, action research and social indicators.

He documented the development of social research in the UK, and noted particularly the rise of the professional social survey organisation including those within government, market research organisations and the newer independent research organisations, undertaking social research for academic and central and local government clients, but pointed out the lack of any large university-based survey organisations in Britain such as the Bureau of Applied Social Research at Columbia or the Institute of Social Research (ISR) at Michigan. The result is that survey research has grown separately from universities and has 'not (been) informed by disciplinary perspectives'.

There has continued to be a separation in the UK between the survey research industry and university-based social science research, and it is worth considering this in more depth. Professor Aubrey McKennell, the convenor of an ESRC sponsored seminar in 1985 on 'Social surveys, social science and social policy' is recorded as saying:

'Although a flourishing survey research industry exists, the professional organisations that conduct this work have grown up outside the university system. As a result, the mainstream survey work largely bypasses the academic social science community...In North America, a good flow of survey work goes through university-based institutions. The UK lacks such organisations staffed by career academics who are also survey experts, and who carry out a wide range of policy-oriented surveys while still retaining an allegiance to their discipline.'

McKennell gave three reasons for the difference in experience between the UK and North America. First, that quantitative social science had already been established in US universities before the war, so that after the war social scientists returned to universities and set up academic survey centres. In Britain, key independent companies notably Gallup and Mass-Observation had already been set up before the war, and while their researchers assisted the war-time government, they also carried on work for their companies. The Government Social Survey was set up as a war-time agency, and continued as a separate agency, also developing with hardly any involvement with the academic community, except that of individuals.

The second reason was more fundamental. McKennell notes:

'The cultural lag between the USA and the UK was compounded by short-falls in the development when it did arrive in the UK of both sociology and psychology. ISR and NORC were founded by and are still run by leading figures in these core social science disciplines. In Britain, the neglect of survey research has often and justifiably been laid at the door of those who took charge of the rapid expansion of sociology in the late 1960s. For the most part they espoused arcane methodological positions that ruled out survey research, along with much else that was empirical and quantitative...Similarly, although psychology departments in the 50s provided quantitative training, they failed to provide support for survey research.'

The third factor noted by McKennell was the distancing of these academics from social policy. The sixties saw the arrival of a more theoretical approach to sociology, often Marxist in inspiration and so anti-capitalist in its mission that it even affected students' preparedness to take on industrial year placements in commercial firms.

Added to these was the more prosaic fact that surveys were the most expensive form of social research and therefore 'unless academics were prepared to link with the practical concerns of most funding bodies, they were unlikely to be involved in much survey research'. McKennell concludes that:

'Graduates of such academic departments have been described as receiving negative training for policy research!'

Newby, in his RSA lecture, talks of the emphasis the ESRC is giving to training, not only post-graduate training but also mid-career training. He is more polite than McKennell: he refers to the fact that 'demography and, to some extent, the changing structure of higher education remain obstacles which need to be overcome before we can achieve our goal of modernising social science'. What must be remembered is that the legacy of the sixties is still with us. Some of those academics are still in post, and many will have recruited and instructed cohorts of students in their own image. The prejudices against survey methodology and quantitative research are still strong although attitudes towards qualitative research have softened somewhat.

Bulmer, at the same seminar as McKennell in 1985, is recorded as reckoning that social policy research was 'just about celebrating its coming of age'. He had noted that in the early 60s there were only as many sociologists in the whole of Britain as historians at Oxford. There was little government research, Social & Community Planning Research (SCPR) did not exist and the Market Research Society (MRS) had only 1300 compared with 1985's 4,000 members.

The real social research world in the early 60s was somewhat different, even if invisible to some academics. A significant amount of survey and policy research work was already being carried out by market and opinion research companies for academics and government departments. Examples carried out just by the Gallup Poll were the Marriage Survey for the Population Investigation Commission through LSE, the Education and Training of Mechanical Engineers for the Department of Scientific and Industrial Research and Housing Studies for the Milner-Holland Committee through the Centre for Urban Studies. What was lacking, it is true, was any adequate intellectual interchange between the two sides on the theoretical implications of the work, but the methodological collaboration was demanding and creative.

Developments in research methodology at that point were mainly being made in such organisations. The MRS was building up a serious education programme, controlling entry to full professional membership and setting up a professional journal.

Training was basically on the job, 'by the shoulder of Nellie'. Textbooks in the UK, apart from Moser (1958), were yet to be written. Rossi similarly refers to the training of graduate students:

> 'in the craft lore of social research and in the technical aspects of research practice (which) is better accomplished in the doing of research than in the class-room'.

The late 1960s saw the setting up of the Council for National Academic Awards (CNAA) and the 'binary' system of higher education (now deceased) with polytechnics offering new applied areas of study, including the development of an academic area, Business Studies and Management, which drew on the same social science disciplines, but was organised quite separately, again with virtually no knowledge transfer. New curricula were developed in Marketing Research Methods, which combined with industrial 'sandwich' placements in commercial and public sector research settings transformed the abilities of the graduate output of research methods courses.

At the same time, new American texts, notably Green and Tull's 'Research for Marketing Decisions' (1966) approached research not from the point of view of a parent academic discipline, but from the stance that research produced information to reduce the area of uncertainty around decision-making. This approach focuses attention on the objectives of the decision-maker, the environment of the problem, alternative courses of action and the likely outcomes of those courses of action. Academic disciplines were of no importance per se. What was important was providing information to reduce uncertainty, and this of necessity involved an assessment of the cost and value of that information. Their description of market research as 'a cost-incurring activity whose output is information of potential value to management decisions' became key.

It is worth noting that educational evaluation had until that time been dominated by evaluation paradigms which had developed from academic disciplines, notably the psychometric or agricultural-botany paradigm. Its main successor, illuminative evaluation, was also based on a discipline, social anthropology, and stressed the importance of observing the 'cultural milieu'. It was clear twenty years ago (McIntosh, 1974), that evaluation cannot be dominated by one paradigm and that evaluators must have access to the full armoury of social research techniques, particularly when they are engaged in evaluating innovative programmes. As Rossi notes:

> 'Regardless of the types of social intervention under study, evaluations are systematic to the extent that they employ social research approaches to gathering valid reliable evidence. This commitment to the 'rules' of social research is at the core of our perspective on evaluation. This is not to say,

however, that evaluation studies follow some particular research style or combinations of styles. Indeed, one of the distinguishing characteristics of program evaluation is that its methods cover the gamut of research paradigms.' (Rossi & Freeman, 1989).

The view of market research as an aid to decision-making under uncertainty was soon applied in North America to non-profit and social policy areas of work, and hence to evaluation studies. Newby, in the same lecture, looks at how society is changing in the 1990s and beyond. He also chooses the word 'uncertainty'.

'The recognition that public policy has to operate in a fast-changing, diverse and therefore more uncertain world than at any time in living memory.' (Newby, 1993)

After discussing the nature of change in society, both locally and globally, he comments that it reflects a new kind of relationship between research and policy:

'Typically we find that facts are uncertain, values in dispute, stakes high and decisions urgent, and the framing of the problem involves politics and values as much as science. Frequently there is no rigid demonstration of conclusive proof; rather what is required is a critical assessment of all available information which leads to a dialogue of exploration and decision. Those providing this information are neither gurus nor social engineers. Instead they seek to serve decision-makers faced with multiple choices under conditions of high uncertainty by providing information which can inform options. They do not seek to take decisions, but rather, seek to provide a better stock of knowledge which can inform those decisions'. (Newby, 1993)

Newby's speech could have formed part of those 60s texts, and yet 25 years later, the arguments have not yet been transferred successfully between these two inter-related social science areas.

He concludes that social science does not provide solutions for policy-makers:

'Social scientists can provide better information on which to base policy and can indicate the likely consequences of certain strategic options, but it is not the role of social scientists to make those decisions themselves.'

Why is knowledge transfer in the social sciences so difficult, or more simply, why are academics so unwilling to learn from each other and from outsiders? The structure of academic departments, the power of the academic barons, the 'not invented here' syndrome are all familiar problems. Sadly, it is not likely to improve. Recent changes in the external environment require more competitiveness and less sharing between institutions, and even between departments inside one institution.

Newby, in discussing the claimed inability of social scientists to communicate, especially to non-academics, touches on what he describes as a more fundamental point which still operates:

'Most fundamentally, it is rooted in the reward structures for academic work, which emphasise peer esteem and hard-copy publication in peer-reviewed journals as the pre-eminent measure of that esteem.'

Rossi was concerned about such issues twenty years ago when writing on the problem of the organisational requirements in the social sciences necessary to perform the large-scale evaluative research necessary for social-policy making (Rossi and Williams, 1972). He pointed out that social science research gained from division of labour but that this was not necessarily consistent with academic independence. It also needed participation from different disciplines.

Increasingly these requirements are being met in the UK through the use of management consultants who can bring together a variety of disciplines. Management consultants are paid to work together, academics are not. Management consultants fit in with the ethos of 'public management' referred to earlier. The evaluative process can be deconstructed with contracts being let for separate segments of the study and going to the lowest bidder. Sometimes academics may be partners in a consortium, but increasingly private companies are taking much of the work. Two consequences of this will not improve the quality of evaluative research.

First, there may often be no single person or grouping with an adequate overview of both the policy and methodological implications of the project able to hold the work together and adequately synthesize its findings. Second, knowledge and experience on the field of evaluation is increasingly passing from the public to the private domain, and there is no obligation to make developments in knowledge and experience publicly available. This issue becomes more significant when public funds are being used to pay for the evaluation.

The range of evaluation in 1993

Our analysis in 1978 was restricted to the annual reports of the Employment Department and the ESRC. We had no opportunity to look at the range of individual evaluation projects, and we had no information, other than a very broad indication of policy area, of how, why, for whom, and by whom, evaluation is carried out.

In 1993, we have made an attempt to improve on the quality of the 1978 evidence. Questionnaires have been sent to

A those who commission or use policy or programme evaluation

B those who commission research evaluation

C those who do policy or research evaluation.

Addressees in all three groups were identified from those with appropriate interests and jobs in the membership list of the Social Research Association. The following additional sources were used:

ESRC list of research evaluators: mainly B

Social science research professional heads in government departments: mainly A, but some B

Contributors to the conference on Evaluation, Social science and public policy, Ottawa, June 1993: all categories

Heads of social research in major survey research companies: C

Within the very limited time period available, response was fairly **good** from government departments; patchy from independent evaluators and academics; and non-existent from survey research companies and management consultants.

Some respondents, such as the Employment Service, the Home Office, the Scottish Office and the Joseph Rowntree Trust, were unable to complete questionnaires in the time available, but contributed full documentation on their evaluation activity, which have been taken into account as far as possible in our analysis.

In many ways, the information on evaluation activity which does not fit into our questionnaire format reflects better the way in which some organisations work. For questionnaire purposes, we have been obliged to take a rather narrow view of finite projects, where much evaluation is on a broader scale, of long-continuing programmes. As John Child, head of Research Evaluation Branch at the Employment Service, says (Child, 1993), the broader examples 'give a better flavour of what we do than concentrating more narrowly on more recent or planned evaluations of a given programme'.

However, much evaluation activity does fit into the form of our enquiry, and the pattern of this activity is reported in this section. Twenty-seven completed questionnaires were returned as follows:

	A	B	C
Government departments	9	2	-
Other public agencies	1	-	-
Academic research centres	-	2	9
Independent evaluators	-	1	2
Not-for-profit institutions	-	-	1

Respondents were asked for general information about their evaluation activity, and for more detail about the two most important evaluation projects on which a report or reports had been completed within the past year. Since not all respondents had completed two reports within the year, the detailed project reporting is on

18 projects from commissioners and users of policy evaluation

7 projects from commissioners, users, and doers of research evaluation; and

14 projects from doers of policy evaluation.

Except when there are significant differences between the responses of commissioners and doers of policy evaluation, they have been combined for analysis, as have the responses of all those involved in research evaluation.

The **policy areas** covered by respondents' evaluation activity over the year are inevitably dominated by differential return rates, and should not be taken as representative of evaluation practice:

	Policy	*Research*
Education	11	-
Training	12	1
Employment	3	-
Economic policy	6	1
Social policy:		
Housing, homelessness	2	-
Crime	1	-
Health, social services	1	-
Equal opportunities	2	2
Community relations	10	-
Urban policy	4	-
Arts	1	1
Energy/environment	3	-
Science & technology	3	-
Public sector management,		
performance management, privatisation	3	1
Research organisation, management	-	1
Research quality	-	1
TOTAL	63	7

Clients for the 14 policy evaluation projects which were described in detail by doers were:

Central government	9
Local government	2
European Commission	3
Government agency	1
Private sector	1
ESRC	1

Of the 34 policy evaluation projects reported by commissioners of policy evaluation, 30 involved external specialists, and only 4 were conducted entirely by internal specialist staff.

The **disciplines** used in the evaluation projects reported are:

	Policy	*Research*
Sociology, social policy/administration	12	5
Social anthropology	3	2
Occupational/educational psychology	3	-
Social psychology	4	1
Geography, planning	6	-
Economics, statistics	6	2
Education	3	1
Science, technology	2	-
Survey, market research	13	1
Management, management consultancy	9	3
Audit	1	-
Public administration	2	-
'Professional evaluation'	-	1

Methods used in evaluation projects are:

	Policy	*Research*
Survey methods:		
qualitative	12	1
quantitative	8	1
interviews postal	11	1
telephone	6	-
face-to face	16	2
Observation	8	1
Group discussions	6	-
Case studies	4	-
Sampling, statistics	1	1
Educational testing	1	-
Psychometric testing	2	-
Modelling	1	-
Analysis of secondary data	20	2
Documentary/content analysis	-	4
Literature search	-	2

Allowance must be made for the fact that some of the survey research categories overlap: nevertheless, the amount of 'survey research' done by non-survey researchers is striking.

It has proved much more difficult to identify the **purpose** of evaluation projects. The classic division between formative and summative evaluation simply does not work: almost all projects have both formative and summative aims.

The duration and budget of evaluation projects varies widely:

	Policy	Research
Duration		
Under 6 months	5	3
6 to under 12 months	10	1
12 months and over	12	1
Continuous	4	-
Budget (when known)		
Under £25,000	7	3
£25 - 99,000	13	4
£100.000 +	3	1

Because we restricted detailed questioning to projects reported within the last year, it proved difficult to get conclusive views on problems arising in or from the conduct of the evaluation. In general, commissioners of policy evaluation identify very few problems; doers, not surprisingly, identify rather more, usually relating to the way the project was specified, and the timescale and budget available.

The same problem arises with questions about whether recommendations were made, whether they have been acted upon, whether the evaluation has been used for policy decisions: many recent reports are still under consideration at policy level.

However, negative responses ('it seems to have gone into a black hole', 'sat on a shelf', or 'this was yesterday's project') are in a minority.

There are more frequent reports of the evaluation being used as evidence, being cited by ministers, being published widely. And there are even examples of programmes being altered, or new programmes being designed, reflecting the findings of evaluation:

- a programme on rough sleepers resulted in a consultation paper, which has in turn led to new policy initiatives
- work on a common curriculum has led to new policy guidelines for gender equality
- the results of work on child sexual abuse are now incorporated in training processes
- a project evaluating 'electronic village halls' has resulted in a revised programme, instead of abolition.

Results reported from this small-scale survey are not in any sense conclusive: the sample is somewhat self-selected, and the definition of 'project' inappropriate for many major evaluation programmes. But they do serve to show the diversity, both in demand and in supply, of evaluation work being undertaken in the UK in 1993.

Conclusions

Social science research, of which evaluation research is a part, needs to develop a collective memory of the disciplined sort that is taken for granted in the physical and natural sciences. However, the post-graduate research training paradigm appropriate to the physical sciences does not transfer adequately to the social sciences.

Both evaluation research and research evaluation must be firmly rooted in the 'rules' of social research. This in turn requires an adequate methodological base. Research evaluation is a small part of evaluation research.

Evaluation needs to draw on all available appropriate disciplines and not be dominated by any one discipline: however, the fact that it is a field and not a discipline (Bernstein, 1971, quoted usefully by Elliott Stern, 1993) does not absolve it from the duty to be disciplined:

- social scientists need to work to bridge the gap between academic theory and social research practice
- academics need not to despise quantitative and survey research practitioners
- 'survey-mongers' need to understand what they can learn from academics: e.g. subject matter expertise, reflective secondary analysis, agreement on an overall intellectual framework

If academics and social researchers do not work together in the public domain, evaluation work will be increasingly taken into the private domain both by:

- government, since it has an interest in secrecy; and
- management consultants, who are in competition with each other and have little interest in sharing knowledge.

Since knowledge transfer is not facilitated by the private economy, public policy will then be the poorer, and the quality of evaluation will not improve.

References

ABT, Clark C. (Ed.) (1976) *The Evaluation of Social Programs,* Beverly Hills CA: Sage Publications.

BULMER, M. (Ed.) (1978) *Social Policy Research,* London: Macmillan.

BULMER, M. (1985) 'The contribution of social science to social policy', *Survey Methods Newsletter,* London: Social and Community Planning Research.

BUTLER, R. (1986) London: Royal Institute of Public Administration.

CHILD, J. (1993) *Private Communication Central Policy Review Staff (1975),* London: HMSO.

DOIG, B. and Littlewood, J. (1992) *Policy Evaluation: The Role of Social Research,* Department of the Environment, London: HMSO

GRAY, A. (1986) London: Royal Institute of Public Administration.

GREEN, Paul E. and TULL, Donald S. (1966) *Research for Marketing Decisions,* Englewood Cliff NJ: Prentice-Hall.

JOHNSTON, I. (1986) London: Royal Institute of Public Administration.

McINTOSH, A. and McINTOSH, N.E. (1978) 'Research for the monitoring and evaluation of public social programmes', *Annual Conference Proceedings,* Market Research Society.

McINTOSH, N. E. (1974) 'Evaluation of multi-media educational systems for adults: some problems', *British Journal of Educational Technology.*

McKENNELL, A. (1985) 'Social surveys social science and social policy',
Survey Methods Newsletter, London: Social and Community Planning Research.

MOSER, C. (1958) *Survey Methods in Social Investigation,* London: Heinemann.

NEWBY, H. (1993) *Social science and public policy,* London: Royal Society of Arts Journal Vol. CXLI, No 5439.

ROSSI, P. H. and WILLIAMS, W. (Ed.) (1972) *Evaluating Social Programs,* New York NY: Seminar Press.

ROSSI, P. H. (1989) Observations on the organisation of social research, in *Evaluation: A Systematic Approach.* Rossi and Freeman, Beverly Hills CA: Sage.

ST CLAIR, W. L. (1988) *Policy Evaluation: A Guide for Managers,* HM Treasury, London: HMSO.

STERN, E. (1993) 'Ongoing and participative evaluation', paper presented to conference on Evaluation Social Science and Public Policy, Ottawa, June 1993.

A consumer voice

Naomi's first involvement in consumer issues came about by accident. In 1957 she lived in 18 Victoria Park Square, Bethnal Green, the home of Michael Young and Peter Willmott's Institute of Community Studies. When Michael Young started Which? and the Consumers Association, Naomi helped to paint the garage used for dispatch of the first issue. This, and her lifelong dedication to consumer issues, is described in her contributory chapter to the Michael Young festschrift Young at Eighty *in 1995. Her own involvement was particularly directed to the consumers of broadcasting, but she was also Chairman of the National Gas Consumers' Council from 1977 to 1981, and in 1979 she was prompted by a draft Bill 'to strengthen the consumer voice in relation to the nationalised industries to set out her considered views in a discussion paper for Roy Hattersley, Secretary of State for Prices and Consumer Protection. Much of this analysis still has considerable force in a time of privatised utilities, and of systematic merger of consumer bodies.*

Consumer representation and the nationalised industries: with particular reference to gas[22]

Introduction

Consciousness of the need to protect consumers, and of consumers as needing and having a voice, has increased rapidly over the past decade. Few people will now deny their importance. As Harold Lind commented in a recent article in *Campaign* (6 October 1978): 'Over the past few years the consumer has come to occupy the sort of place in the political pantheon which used to be given to the flag and the Empire'. There is much less general agreement as to how consumers should best be represented and by whom. Nor have the structures for representation been planned and developed in a coherent way. New structures have been added on to existing ones in a relatively ad hoc way without much thought being given to the inter-relation-

---

22. Sargant, N. E. (1979) 'Consumer representation and the nationalised industries, with particular reference to gas; A discussion paper prompted by the "Bill to strengthen the consumer voice in relation to the nationalised industries"', for the National Gas Consumers' Council.

ships between them, the pool of active people available to be concerned in building them and the total resource cost to the country of implementing them.

Some of the important questions are listed here:

1. are the existing structures the most effective way of meeting consumers' needs?
2. how do we know if the country is getting value for money from consumer councils?
3. should there be some structural relationships between the National Consumers' Council and the statutory Nationalised Industry Consumer Councils with responsibilities in the field of the nationalised industries?
4. should there be a common career structure and/or common services between consumer organisations?
5. how can we best select and support consumers to work on consumer bodies when we have no democratic base through which to work.
6. how does accountability through consumers relate to the other sorts of accountability now being discussed for nationalised industries?

Existing structures

Consumers' councils for the nationalised industries represent perhaps the best established models of statutory structures in this field, dating back as they do to the late forties in the energy industries. The gas consumers' councils came into legislative being as a result of the Gas Act of 1972, but their predecessor committees had existed since 1949. The nationalised industries' consumers' councils (NICCs), as they have come to be called, have been set up on the premise that people become homogeneous with respect to their identity as gas consumers, electricity consumers, transport consumers and so on, and that to deal with their problems adequately requires a *specialist* network at local, regional and national levels of both paid professional and paid and unpaid volunteers. Only *specialist* councils it is argued can deal with the range of technical problems, and do this with enough credibility to make an impact on the industries concerned. The White Paper [*White Paper on Nationalised Industries* 1978 (Cmnd. 7131)] has accepted this view in principle and the National Gas Consumers' Council (NGCC) welcomes this.

At the same time over this period, there has been a growth in the number of other agencies such as Citizens Advice Bureaux and Consumer Advice Centres, often provided or funded by local authorities, dealing with enquiries and complaints, often concerning nationalised industries. At the national end, the National Consumer Council was set up in 1975 taking to itself, among other things, an overall interest in consumers and nationalised industries which is spelled out in its memorandum of association.

On the one hand, it could be argued that this profusion of interest, information and support should ensure that nationalised industry consumers are well looked after. On the other hand, such profusion sometimes leads to confusion and overlap. At minimum it is important to ensure that:

1. consumers are not being misadvised or confused
2. bodies are individually and collectively working as effectively as possible
3. public money is being put to its best use.

This last point is made since the cost of the apparatus of consumerism must now be quite high, and growing; it is not possible in this paper to make an estimate for all the nationalised industries, but taking just the example of the gas consumers' councils shows the direct cost to the country as £760,000 (in 1978). This figure excludes any estimate of the time-cost of the hours of labour put in voluntarily by committee members locally and nationally.

Is it possible to measure the effectiveness of a consumer council?

It is difficult to come to a judgement about whether or not £760,000 a year is a reasonable sum to spend on representing consumers of one industry and whether or not it represents value for money. On the one hand, if all fourteen million gas consumers are being protected, both in terms of their existing problems and of their future interest, then it could be argued that five pence per head per year is cheap at the price. It certainly is minute in relation to the total turnover of British Gas. On the other hand, the figure appears a high one if looked at in terms of the number of individual consumers whose problems are dealt with in any one year (43,700 in 1977/78), particularly since the direct cost does not take into account the real cost to the community of the hours of time put in by volunteer members. Of course the actual number of people making complaints or representations to the regional consumer councils represents only one part of the work. There are large numbers of enquiries, over 100,000 in any one year, which are dealt with but not recorded separately.

It is similarly difficult to know whether or not an increase in consumers dealt with means that a consumer council is working more efficiently, because more people have gone to it for help, or a decrease in consumers dealt with means that the consumer council has worked more efficiently on a preventative basis by pressuring the gas region to work more effectively in the first instance!

What would appropriate performance indicators for a consumer council be?

The work of the gas consumers' councils falls into three main areas:

1. the provision of information and advice to all gas consumers, both existing and prospective
2. dealing with consumers' (domestic, commercial and industrial) complaints and representations, both concerning the nationalised industry and the private sector (gas appliance manufacturers and service organisations)
3. endeavouring to influence the policy of the industry in the interests of gas consumers, both existing and prospective.

While the first of these is a function common to both regional *and* national councils, regional councils and their associated district committees are inevitably more engaged in working retrospectively, looking after consumers' complaints, while the NGCC must endeavour to work prospectively, anticipating future needs and adumbrating desirable changes in policy.

Given the problems discussed in the preceding paragraph, it is fair to say that gas consumers' councils do not have any worked out indicators for their own effectiveness. Nor, to my knowledge, do any other consumer councils or committees from the NCC downwards.

A first prerequisite obviously is that consumers know that the councils exist. We pay a lot of attention to this side of the work and have built up a public relations framework which both attempts to educate consumers and make them aware of our existence. Our success in this area has been confirmed by the publication of an NCC survey indicating that the National Gas Consumers' Council had the highest level of unprompted awareness among the population (at 30%) of all the different consumer bodies. In response to a prompted question asking which organisations respondents had heard of, the National Gas Consumers' Council topped the list at 53% followed by Community Health Councils at 49%, the Electricity Consumers' Council at 48% and the National Consumer Council at 46%.

The same survey highlighted one of the consumer movement's perennial problems: that the working classes are much less knowledgeable than the middle class about consumer organisations and about their rights, and these are the people whom we are most concerned to reach. 48% of the upper middle class correctly identified the National Gas Consumers' Council compared with only 15% of the unskilled working class. This is a typical pattern of awareness for such organisations which are marginal to people's lives. The experience of The Open University, for example, has been that it has taken nine years and a large amount of press coverage and advertising to bring the national figure of knowledge up from 31% in 1971 to 69% in 1978. It is unlikely that it will ever be considered reasonable for publicly funded consumer organisations to spend large sums on advertising and this problem will, therefore, continue to be a limiting factor on effectiveness. Even if unlimited advertising budgets were available, there would be a limit to people's knowledge as people tend only to take in this type of information when it is relevant to them.

Are consumer councils seen to be independent?

There exists a degree of scepticism about the independence of the consumer councils. Partly it must stem from the fact that their funding came originally from a government levy on the industries organised through the Department of Energy.

Though funding is now through the Department of Prices and Consumer Protection (DPCP), and the NICCs are titularly independent, there is some evidence that the legacy of the original linkage still remains. The NCC survey, previously quoted, indicates that around one in four of the population still believe that the supplier represents the consumer interest. Such pressure groups as the Child Poverty Action Group and the Right to Fuel Campaign obviously feel that it is virtually impossible for the consumer councils not to be 'in the industry's pocket'. It is a fact that some of the staff of the consumer councils have been recruited from the industries, and it has so far been accepted that their terms and conditions of service could and should be analogous to those of the industries. One implication of this is that consumer council employees may be likely to look for their future career prospects back towards public service industries rather than across into other consumer organisations. It is a matter for debate as to whether the closeness of staff to the industry benefits consumers, as the staff may be able to pressure the industry more effectively because of their detailed knowledge, or whether it harms consumers as the staff may be too easily convinced because of their previous closeness.

In the long run, and I must stress that this is a personal view at this stage, if there is to continue to be an increasing number of permanent structures for the protection of consumers, with increasing security of tenure, then I believe it would assist the independence and integrity of consumer councils for there to be greater movement between consumer councils, including the National Consumer Council, and a structure which allowed for career development.

The proliferation of bodies and people concerned in the nationalised industries, and particularly in the field of energy

The proliferation of interests of consumer representation in this area does pose problems, since there is no planned structural relationship between the bodies and the members sitting on them. The picture looks something like this in the energy area:

> Regional nationalised industry consumer councils
> National nationalised industry consumer councils
> Chairmen of NICCs, sitting on the Energy Commission
> National Consumer Council
> Consumer representatives on ECOSOC, Brussels

While the three consumer Chairmen sit on the Energy Commission by virtue of their individual chairmanships, only two out of three of them (one a recent appointee) sit on the NCC and there are no structural or policy links between the four bodies. Another recent appointee of the NCC is also one of the British representatives on ECOSOC and currently discussing long-term energy policy there. There is similarly no connection between the ECOSOC representative and the three NICC Chairmen sitting on the Energy Commission. At a more local level, while the Electricity Consumers' Council remit covers Northern Ireland, the NGCC's does not and the role of champion for the gas consumers in Northern Ireland has, at the moment, inevitably to be taken by the Northern Ireland Consumer Council.

Working out a policy for all consumers

It might be argued that in an ideal world there should be no problem since everyone is a consumer and the interests of all consumers are identical and one body can, therefore, represent all consumers. However, consumers are not homogeneous in this way. All people are not consumers of everything all of the time. The consumer movement has no democratic base. There is no consumer party and it is, in my view, unlikely that there ever will be since with the exception of 'congenital consumer activists' other consumers are only moved to work together either over a limited time period on a shared problem, or on a limited front which is of continuing concern.

The task of working out, as the NCC has to, how to 'safeguard the interests of (all) consumers' is a formidable one. Apart from specific governmental remits, the NCC chose initially to concentrate on one *class* of consumer, described in its memorandum as 'inarticulate and disadvantaged', rather than on 'consumers of particular goods and services', which of course are the remits of the NICCs. The NCC's valuable work in highlighting the needs of poorer consumers is exemplified in such publications as 'Why the Poor Pay More' and 'Paying for Fuel'.

However it is precisely this work which highlights areas of policy where conflict may well arise between the NCC and the NICCs. A good example is the price of fuel. The White Paper, in paragraph 54, comments,

'When help has to be given to poorer members of the community, it will be given primarily through the social security and taxation systems and not by subsidising nationalised industry prices.'

and again in paragraph 68,

Arbitrary cross-subsidisation between different groups of consumers, which is one result of intervention in the industries' pricing policies, should be avoided.'

While the NGCC, looking after *all* gas consumers, is likely to welcome this, the NCC and other pressure groups concentrating on *poorer* consumers are likely to consider that the most important thing is to keep fuel prices down come what may. Given the finite pool of energy available from fossil fuel, and the need for conservation, it could be better for all consumers to have planned price increases to ensure conservation and longer term availability. Thus a short term policy for one group of consumers may turn out to be in conflict with a longer term policy for all consumers.

Advice about energy

Another difficult area, discussed both in the NCC report [*Consumers and the Nationalised Industries*] and in the White Paper, relates to the proliferation of agencies giving advice and dealing with problems and complaints. While the provision of consumer advice by local authorities and through local authority supported agencies is increasing, it is not a statutory activity. Provision in the country is patchy and subject to political and economic change. It seems obvious that it should be easier for all consumers to go to one centralised source for advice: both less confusing for consumers and more economic for the country. Against this has to be set the vast range of expertise that one such agency requires, and the fear that it would be impossible for them to deal effectively with such a range of problems. The White Paper implicitly recognises this dilemma and says (paragraph 33) 'that it will have further discussion with the ECC, NGCC and those responsible for the local authority and other generalist services with a view to ensuring the most efficient liaison and integration between the various advice agencies'. These discussions are overdue and in the meantime there is little guidance or coordination about new developments. The Office of Fair Trading analysis of consumer complaints appears to indicate that the majority of public utilities and transport complaints do NOT go to Consumer Advice Centres or Citizens Advice Bureaux. The total figure for the last reported quarter (April-June 1978) for this category was 3,777, 1,194 being about gas and 1,260 about electricity. It has been suggested, but not pursued, that a proper integrated experimental scheme should be set up in one or two areas and monitored to see whether an integrated, or simply a better coordinated service would serve the consumer better and cost the country less. The NICCs, I feel sure, would be happy to cooperate in this.

A small but significant opportunity has recently been lost with the Department of Energy's decision not to place the experimental Home Energy Saving Advice Centres either within existing consumer advice centres or within the existing regional energy consumer council apparatus. We would have like to have tried to build on existing structures rather than have totally new ones, as would the NCC. This highlights yet another link in the chain: the relationship between the Department of Energy and the Department of Prices and Consumer Protection in respect to consumer protection.

Membership of consumer bodies: selection, day-to-day work, payment and support

a) *Who members are*

While we know that several thousand people voluntarily give up time to work as consumer representatives, we know very little about who they are, why and how they do it. In one sense the current discussion which automatically denigrates the activity as 'Quango' is not helpful as it devalues an activity which the country has continued to consider important. At the same time the pool of people able and willing to work voluntarily in this capacity is limited and in particular the traditional pool, of women, is reducing. This may in the future be counterbalanced by an increasing pool of people becoming available as the working week gets shorter and there is more early retirement.

b) *The selection of members*

The difficulty is, as noted earlier, that there is no consumer party to select representatives. The widening of the 'trawl' to select potential members this year is obviously to be welcomed but it might also help future selection if there was more systematic knowledge about the motivation and background of volunteers.

The NCC was asked last year to carry out a 'trawl' for new members of the councils. It is by no means clear that the NCC is the right body to carry out the 'trawl' on behalf of all other NICCs. The implication of it carrying some sort of parental role is obviously strengthened by it being asked to undertake such umbrella functions. Obviously at some levels appointments will be political in nature. However, for the health of the structure and for the continued confidence of existing members, it is also necessary for appointers to take account of worthy service by existing members in making re- or new appointments. If, for example, no Deputy Chairman (unpaid) is ever made Chairman (paid) there is little incentive to work as Deputy Chairman.

c) *Support for members*

The degree of support to members obviously varies between organisations. The NCC is currently attempting to strengthen it through its Supports Desk and 'The Clapham Omnibus'. The success of these initiatives is likely to depend in large part on whether or not it is possible to build up enough common consumer identity, and whether there turn out to be enough common needs. There will also be a limit to the amount of paper which people can absorb.

d) *Payment of members*

The vast majority of members work on a voluntary basis, although Chairmen are paid. There is some feeling that the job of being a Chairman is more onerous than the current payment gives credit for. To put it another way – some Chairmen work more than two days a week. On the other hand, if the job became more full-time, many valuable people would be prevented from participating. This is always a difficult one to argue. On the other hand, it is easy to argue that the anomalies in payment between Chairmen and between councils should be ironed out. It seems invidious, for example, for the Chairmen of gas and electricity councils to be paid and for coal not to be. As the tasks laid on the Chairman increase it is more and more diffi-cult to combine it with doing a normal paid job. If this trend continues, it either implies limiting the possible field of recruitment, or of paying the job on a proper basis, including obligations for pension rights. Similarly ordi-nary members of the NCC are paid while members of other councils are not.

The status of consumer council recommendations

Normally one would hope that nationalised industries and their consumer councils would *not* operate on the 'confrontation' model. It has been my experience that one gets a better deal for consumers by setting forth the case and getting policy formulated to take account of it before the decision is finally made, than by complaining and asking for changes, no matter how vociferously, afterwards. It is far more difficult to get people to change their minds post hoc, particularly if the decision is public and they have been involved in it. This argues for consumers being on the boards of industries, but preferably not just one consumer, which would seem mere 'tokenism'. The argument against consumers being on the board is that they would both *lose* their independence and be seen by others as lacking in independence. Undoubtedly it is more politically glamorous and rewarding to be able to complain loudly afterwards about policies which one has not had any chance of affecting, and at the same time be seen to keep one's hands clean. I personally believe that, although it is politically less glamorous, and in practice is a much more difficult job, consumers are more likely to be better protected by the presence of their members on boards than off them.

Experience to date has not thrown up any examples where the additional powers proposed by the NCC would have helped. There are undoubtedly some areas where consumer council pressure is more likely to have effect than others: pressure for better customer service and work on defective new appliances are examples. The important question of price is a clear example where consumer pressure is more difficult to apply and is also unlikely to be the most important factor. The situation in 1977 makes both these points clearly. The December 1976 mini-budget included a requirement for British Gas to repay £100 million of its debt in the next financial year, a requirement which, however necessary in the national interest, caused a gas tariff increase which would otherwise not have been needed. As a result an increase was not needed in 1978, and BGC were able to ask for and obtain an agreement to maintain the status quo. Neither this request, nor the possibility of a possible reduction were discussed with NGCC on the grounds that the Gas Act only required a reference to the NGCC if there was to be a variation in price. In our view this is a breach of the spirit of the Act. However, we accepted that the major factors involved were beyond the control of the industry, and indeed the late announcement of performance targets in December 1978, given for one year only, makes it appear that this year's reference will be similarly artificial with the result of limiting again any genuine role for the consumer council.

If consumers are to be taken seriously in the discussion about tariffs, then performance targets need to be set further in advance and consideration given to the way in which consumer bodies can work more effectively within the Price Commission structure.

Some problems arise from the fact that, like education, British Gas is a national service, locally administered. While some policy is decided nationally, the regions of British Gas have a large amount of autonomy in respect to some areas of work. While BGC may, as in the case of connection charges, promulgate guidelines for a change in policy, individual regions may interpret this in different ways. Regional consumers' councils, if they are prepared to, must then monitor the implementation of this locally, either pursuing it locally and/or feeding information back to national level so that a coordinated picture for the country may be obtained in order to see if the new policy is working: If the regions do not wish to, the NGCC cannot make them. The remit for NGCC to 'guide and coordinate' does sometimes mean exercising responsibility without power. It may be that a more integrated structure such as that proposed for the electricity industry would be more effective in this respect.

The future

Obviously this is only a partial attempt to discuss the issues raised, which will need continuing consideration. In the longer term, if we are moving to working out an overall policy for energy for the country and if consumers are to be advised to make better choices about energy use in an integrated way, then although it may continue to make sense for the industries to be competitive in respect to production and efficient management, it may not make sense to have overlapping industry-based consumer councils. Few people only consume one source of energy. Virtually all gas users also consume electricity. Future gas users may increasingly use gas developed from coal. It seems to me likely that it may well be sensible to plan to bring together not necessarily all advice into general purpose advice centres, but at minimum all energy advice into one centre.

A possible next step after that would be to bring together the three separate fuels into one 'Energy Consumers' Council' providing advice from one source, taking account of the 'consumers' whole energy demand and, perhaps most important, being in a position to encourage conservation.

In conclusion, it would help everyone in the field if we could work out what appropriate performance indicators for consumer councils would be!

Informed consumers of broadcasting, discussed in the previous paper, will eventually look for arenas where their voice can be heard. In the following abridged discussion paper, prepared for the Consumers' Association in 1992, Naomi draws on her experience in broadcasting, social research, and in various consumer organisations, from the National Gas Consumers' Council to the Voice of the Listener and Viewer. She sees no reason why listeners and viewers should be excluded from the general growth of consumer empowerment and proposes a Broadcasting Consumer Council. Certain tenses have been changed because some of the organisations mentioned have ceased to exist. [Derek Jones]

Broadcasting policy: listening to the consumer[23]

'The government places the viewer and listener at the heart of broadcasting policy. Because of technological, international and other developments, change is inevitable. It is also desirable: only through change will the individual be able to exercise the much wider choice that will soon become possible. The government's aim is to open the doors so that individuals can choose for themselves from a much wider range of programmes and types of broadcasting. In this as in other fields consumers will rightly insist on safeguards which will protect them and their families from shoddy wares and exploitation.'

This quotation from the 1988 Broadcasting White Paper, which led to the 1990 Broadcasting Act, provides the text for this discussion paper. Broadcasting is a major informational, social, political, educational and cultural service and force to which every household contributes and also depends on for much of its information and entertainment. This paper argues, by analogy with other models of consumer representation, that not only does broadcasting require regulation but it requires proper consumer representation. Both of these should be transparent in their operation.

There is, however, concern among consumer and viewer bodies about the current lack of consumer representation, about the increasing complexity of the system, how viewers and listeners find their way round it, how much its costs, and to whom the system is itself accountable.

---

23. Sargant, N. E. (1992) Broadcasting policy:listening to the consumer: the case for a Broadcasting Consumer Council; a Consumers'Association Policy Report, London: Consumers' Association.

Nobody would deny that a large part of the function of broadcasting is to provide entertainment. However, other major functions are also what economists would describe as 'merit goods', in which there is a public interest, for example news programmes, weather forecasts, educational and information programmes and programmes for specific disadvantaged groups.

Also significant are the uses of public interest which arise from the fact that, on the one hand, the BBC combines a monopoly of advertising-free programmes with a clear longstanding remit to promote the 'national interest', and, on the other hand, that in the commercial sector, separate regulatory bodies have been set up whose specific purpose is to intervene in the market and prevent broadcasters doing exactly what they otherwise would do on purely commercial grounds. It is these public interest issues which justify the demand by consumers for intervention on their behalf.

The benefits of consumer representation

The 1990 Broadcasting Act has made the structures of delivery of broadcasting more complex and more difficult for viewers and listeners to find their way around. General complaints about ITV programmes, for instance, will now have to be made to individual regional licensees as broadcasters who may not have even made or commissioned the programmes they are transmitting. Programmes may have often been made by independent producers who are not necessarily even trading at the stage the programme is transmitted or repeated. While a central scheduling operation will be responsible for the whole of the ITV network, there are no plans for a new central body to deal directly with the public.

Properly based and focussed consumer representation would not merely safeguard consumers' interests but could contribute to the improvement of the quality of broadcasting and broadcasting regulation by providing an intelligent view of the interests of the community as a whole, and acting as a bulwark against vociferous special interest groups. Providing such representation is broadly based it should provide early and effective warnings of problems that may arise in particular areas and consider whether they may carry important lessons for other areas.

Accountability and responsiveness

The notion of accountability is a slippery one. We know that we want something of this sort, but what is it?

Political accountability, through Parliament, is of course, important, but it is not the only form of accountability which is needed. Colin Shaw (when Director of the BSB) returned to a distinction made by Lady Warnock (a former IBA governor) between accountability and responsibility. She had suggested that what people really wanted was the latter rather than the former:

'In broadcasting the institutions needed to be rather more user-friendly, less aloof, less inaccessible. The public wanted to feel their voice was being heard...They wanted more open acknowledgement that what they thought or felt was being taken seriously by those in a position to take action' (Warnock, *IBA Quarterly*, 1974).

Shaw suggested that what was needed could perhaps be more accurately termed responsiveness.

Another suggested way of looking at the issue is that there is some implicit 'contract' between the broadcasters and the audience (licence payers), which entitles viewers and listeners to have certain expectations of the quality, integrity and array of programming they are being offered. They cannot immediately stop buying tickets for that particular theatre, or walk out of that particular cinema – the market place analogy does not stand up. There is no direct transaction, in that sense, but there is a clear 'interest'. It is reasonable to assume that there is a 'structure of expectation' which people should be entitled, in general, to have satisfied – a reasonable expectation of quality, variety, range, and diversity. People should also be entitled and even be expected to provide feedback, which is taken notice of positively rather than negatively if they are not satisfied.

The original notion of the BBC Governors as the 'trustees of the national interest in broadcasting' (and similar language was used of the Independent Television Authority (ITA), later the IBA, when it was set up in 1954) contained the seeds of this idea, though 'the national interest' nowadays has a rather jingoistic sound. Colin Shaw (in his 1991 Swinton Lecture) suggested that it was now preferable to substitute the term *public* interest. In recent years, such terms as *public, community* and *society* have not found as much favour as *individuals, families, customers,* and *consumers.*, though the basic implications in the context of a service such as broadcasting are much the same. In a previous analysis of the way in which cable technology might meet the needs of the community...the present author referred to the distinction made by the Oxford English Dictionary between two definitions of community:

- the community or people as an organised body; the nation, the state; the commonwealth, the interest or well being of the community
- the community as an aggregate, but not in its organised capacity; hence the members of the community (Sargant, N. *How will IT/Cable serve the Community,* Barbican Papers, 1982).

The argument then was:

'We continue to talk as if the community is an "organised body", and as if we can identify the interest or well-being of the community as a whole.

In fact for most purposes, it is more accurate to regard the community as being an aggregate, not in its organised capacity.

The members of the community are not part of an organised body sharing common assumptions and common needs. It is not necessarily the case that IT/cable will serve the whole community or all members of the community. It will serve some but not others...

While broadcasting in all its plural forms, television or radio, terrestrial, cable, satellite, will meet the needs of different individuals and groups in the community in different ways, and, at minimum, they should be entitled, as an aggregate, to proper consumer representation as individuals, greater benefit is likely to accrue to broadcasting and to our society if consumer representation is broadly based and properly representative of the community as whole.

It is also proper to argue that the BBC, described by Douglas Hurd, when Home Secretary, as the cornerstone of British broadcasting, should continue to meet the needs of 'the community as an organised body; the nation, the state; the commonwealth, the interest or well-being of the community.'

Modern discussions of accountability in broadcasting – a short history

The issue of accountability was considered by the Annan Committee on the Future of Broadcasting, which reported in 1977, and did not believe that relations between broadcasters and the public were satisfactory. Annan noted that 'the most voluminous evidence we received was from those who wanted more public scrutiny of broadcasting' and 'were convinced that there must be some change in the structure of broadcasting so that the public and the interest groups are better able to put their views directly to the broadcasting organisations'.

Annan's cogent summary described the circumstances:

'The BBC and IBA have a duty to discover how the public react to their programmes. They do that partly through audience research...The Authorities cannot, however, have government-appointed consumer councils as the nationalised industries do. A consumer council puts its view direct to the government as well as to the industry; in broadcasting, government does not want to interfere with programme policy, and they might have to do this if they received reports from a consumer council. That is why the BBC and IBA appoint their own advisory bodies as another means of telling them what the public thinks...What do all the advisory councils and committees of the BBC and IBA do? Except for specialist committees, who provide expert advice, the function of the advisory bodies is not to represent consumers, but to tell the broadcasting authorities their own personal reactions to programmes *as people who keep in touch with what others think'* .

The then chairman of the BBC's General Advisory Council is reported as saying, in a revealing aside, that the BBC picked the kind of people with whom it could get on. The IBA's chairwoman, Lady Plowden, claimed that their council provided the authority with a source of valuable, articulate, non-specialist advice, and believed that they could interpret the views of the people in the community.

Annan reported:

'Few of those who gave evidence loved these bodies. Most thought them ineffective as a way of keeping in touch with public opinion. Many thought them unrepresentative; some thought organisations and groups should nominate representatives to them, and the National Council of Women wanted them democratically elected.'

...their seriousness is not in doubt. Nor is their public spirit in giving unselfish service. But many on these bodies...were unclear of their function or whether they had a clear role to play.

Certainly they cannot be regarded as part of the mechanism through which the broadcasters are made accountable to the public; they are appointed by, and operate through, the BBC and the IBA.

Annan proceeds to discuss a variety of ways in which the advisory structures could work better, making their membership more representative and knowledge of their existence more widely available, since 'one of its main weaknesses is that it is remote from most members of the audience'.

Annan also received evidence of widespread public dissatisfaction with the present arrangements for dealing with complaints about programmes from members of the public. In 1972, the BBC had set up a Programmes Complaints Commission, empowered to consider and review complaints against the BBC from individuals or organisations who claimed that they had been treated unfairly in connection with a programme or related series of programmes as broadcast. The three commissioners were independent of the BBC, but the complaints were heard in private and the costs were borne by the BBC. Adjudications were published in *The Listener*.

The IBA's Complaints Review Board had wider terms of reference than the BBC's Commission. It could consider not only complaints from people appearing in programmes about their content or preparation for transmission, but could also consider more general complaints from the public. It considered specific complaints referred to it by the Authority, or when the complainant remained unsatisfied by the reply of the Authority's staff, and, in addition, it reviewed regular reports of the complaints investigated by the staff.

The arrangements did not, in Annan's view, 'command public confidence'. The IBA's Review Board, by its own composition, appeared 'to the public as an example of a body which is both judge and jury'. Both organisations were described as treating people in a cavalier fashion, causing people to conclude that there was little point in complaining. The BBC was described as aggressive and arrogant.

Many organisations considered that a Broadcasting Council should be established on the lines of the Press Council, and able to hear complaints against the broadcasting organisations. Annan did not agree 'that one and the same body should hear complaints from both individuals and organisations who feel that they have been misrepresented or unfairly treated, and complaints from the general public about the taste, content or standard of individual programmes in general'. Complaints about the programmes, the report argued, are matters for the authorities and should be dealt with by them. 'The question of misrepresentation of individuals, however, is quasi-judicial and needs, in our view, to be dealt with by those skilled in the assessment of evidence and knowledgeable about broadcasting. That body should, therefore, be independent of the broadcasters'.

A number of bodies made proposals to Annan which aimed to make broadcasting organisations more responsive to public opinion through some form of Broadcasting Council or Centre. The most detailed proposal for such a body came from two people active in this policy area, Anthony Smith (then Fellow of St Antony's College, Oxford, and later a founding member of the Channel 4 Board) and Dr Jay Blumler (Professor of Public Communication, Leeds University), both eminent academics and media experts. They proposed a National Broadcasting Centre which would conduct audience research, both quantitative and qualitative, develop criteria for monitoring broadcasting performance and keep the system continuously under review in the light of them.

They also proposed that the Authorities should be required to supply the Centre with all the information it needed to fulfil its monitoring and research functions. They should also be required to take account of the Centre's recommendations and findings and to indicate in their annual reports the results of their consideration and what action, if any, had followed.

'They thought that the Centre could keep under review the links between the mass-media organisations in Britain and could study and publish information on developments in broadcasting in other countries. They suggested that the Centre should have a Complaints Division. This should not be a substitute for a Court of Law or a means of securing redress and recompense for infringed rights, but should consider complaints thought to be of general importance to the development of broadcasting and the evolution of policy'.

Though Annan did not agree with their proposal for a Centre, the Committee did agree that there was a gap in the current structure: 'The public have too few ways of making their views known and the broadcasters can retreat too easily into their fortresses'. To meet this concern and to encourage a more informed public debate, Annan proposed what his committee called a Public Enquiry Board for Broadcasting, and suggested a number of duties for it. These included:

- To hold public hearings every seven years on the way each Broadcasting Authority has discharged its responsibility. Their findings of the public's view would be reported to the Home Secretary.
- To discover what the public think about proposals for new services, for example, they mention the fifth television channel or satellite broadcasting services.
- To carry out ad hoc enquiries, as requested by the Home Secretary, or a Broadcasting Authority, for example, into violence on television or educational output.
- To commission appropriate research.
- To appoint members of the Complaints Communication.

The Committee were particularly conscious of the need to be precise about the Board's responsibilities, so that it did not encroach upon the responsibilities of the Home Secretary on the one hand, or duplicate those of the Broadcasting Authorities on the other. While they clearly were concerned to encourage more informed public debate, they did not seem overtly concerned as such about individual viewers and listeners and their rights and interests in the matter.

Annan envisaged a small Board, with a chairman and four part-time members, with a small secretariat which, they emphasised, must not be politically motivated. They were much taken by the Canadian Radio and Television Commission (CRTC), and suggested that the model of its 'public hearings' procedure could be adapted for use in the United Kingdom.

The Broadcasting Complaints Commission

The Broadcasting Complaints Commission (BCC) was the original statutory body set up by parliament, on the recommendation of the Annan Committee, in 1981... (Its) function and authority derived from the Broadcasting Act 1990. Their task (was) to consider and adjudicate upon complaints of unjust and unfair treatment in sound or television programmes actually broadcast, or included in a licensed cable or satellite programme service, or upon complaints of unwarranted infringement of privacy in, or in connection with, the obtaining of material included in such programmes. This function extended to all sound, television and cable programmes, including advertisements and teletext transmission and programmes broadcast by the BBC World Service.

The task of the BCC was referred to as providing a quasi-judicial forum in which organisations and individuals who felt aggrieved by the broadcast programmes could have their complaints considered. The 1991 Annual Report noted that, even after ten years, there was still misunderstanding of the Commission's statutory functions.

'They have no remit to consider complaints from someone who was not directly affected but nevertheless did not like or was offended by a particular programme. They can act only when asked to consider complaints from "persons affected" relating to specific broadcasting programmes, television or radio, BBC or commercial' (Para 7, BCC Annual Report, 1991).

That there was some misunderstanding of the BCC's role is clear from the number of complaints they receive each year and the very small proportion that fall within their jurisdiction:

	1990	*1991*
No of complaints received	550	930
Outside jurisdiction	452 (82%)	803 (86%)
Within jurisdiction	98 (18%)	127 (14%)

A situation in which 80 per cent of broadcasting complaints were misdirected or wrongly conceived ten years after the relevant body was founded implied that something was wrong in the system, either in terms of public knowledge, in terms of raised expectations of possible redress, or, at minimum, in terms of money wasted.

The Broadcasting Standards Council

The Broadcasting Standards Council (BSC) became a statutory body on 1 January 1991. The Broadcasting Act 1990 laid upon it the duty to draw up, and, from time to time, review, a code giving guidance to practices to be followed in connection with the portrayal of violence...(and) sexual conduct in programmes....(and)standards of taste and decency for such programmes generally'. Its other main tasks were to monitor programmes and make reports on the areas within the Council's remit; to commission reports into relevant matters; to consider and make findings on complaints.

The Council clearly viewed itself as an important player, as the chairman's foreword to its first annual report (1990–91) makes clear:

'The Council (is) an institution which, within the specific areas of its remit, can provide a bridge between audiences and broadcaster, dealing with complaints, undertaking research, sustaining a dialogue on such topics as the child-viewer or the limits of violence and monitoring programmes being seen or heard in this country.'

Lord Rees Mogg also noted: 'I have no doubt, from the letters we have received, that there is a real public desire to have complaints considered by a body which is not responsible for the broadcasts complained of, or part of the regulatory system'. He called for a wider-based consumer organisation. 'The complaints reaching the Council reflect a genuine feeling of offence or distress, which call if possible, for a remedy, or at least an explanation. The existence of the Council, as an independent body, to consider these complaints and, when necessary, to require explanations from the broadcasters, marks an advance from the time when, in the first five months of handling complaints, the broadcasting authorities were the only arbiters. With much talk of consumers' rights, it might have seemed anomalous for broadcasting to lack an adequate forum for complaints'.

What was wrong with the BSC was not the actual way in which it was administering its parliamentary charge, but the fact that it was set up as a negative rather than a positive regulator – it had to try to stamp things out and prevent programme makers doing things rather than trying to promote consumer-responsive, high-quality television and radio.

In the first five months of handling complaints the Council received over 700 letters about programmes or advertisements. Of these, 509 were within its remit and 240 (32 per cent) were outside it. Of the complaints within the remit, 402 referred to specific programmes and 107 raised matters of a general nature. The 131 findings which had been confirmed by the Council were in connection with 60 different programmes. Many complaints which were then outside the remit raised matters of balance in political reporting or in current affairs, in particular about different aspects of coverage of the Gulf War. After consideration, there were 117 complaints on which it was considered 'inappropriate to proceed'.

In the 12 months covered by the 1991–92 report, 2662 complaints were received, of which 57 per cent were outside the remit. Two-thirds of these were about the possible transmission of *The Last Temptation of Christ*, which was, in the event, not transmitted! Other complaints outside the remit included political balance, the choice of programme subjects, objections to the advertising of sanitary protection products and criticisms of pronunciation. The majority categories within the remit were taste and decency (48 per cent) and sex (24 per cent). A large group where the BSC felt it was inappropriate to proceed were complaints in respect of bad language; the Council has decided to commission a research study in this area and to use these letters as part of the study.

Colin Shaw, the Director of the BSC, commented on the scope for confusion (between the BCC and BSC) : 'A recurrent theme during the passage of the Broadcasting Bill and after its enactment was the possibility of confusion for the public in its attempts to distinguish between the many agencies which now have some hand in broadcasting'.

The BSC would have relished a larger role for itself. However, its antecedents were against it. It was described by Sebastian Faulks (*Guardian*, 3 February 1992) as 'a toothless consumer body reviled by liberal opinion as an expensive way of backing Mary Whitehouse'. If it was asked to take on a broader and more representative consumer role, a major issue would be to work out how to give it a proper consumer base and a full command of consumer confidence. It would also need to move from its current negative 'censorship' approach to positive promotion of responsive high-quality television.

A more widely based body?

Colin Shaw broached the possibility of combining the functions of the BSC and the BCC (citing) ease of comprehension by the public, some gain in economy of resources, and the greater visibility of a larger body. The evidence provided by the annual reports of both bodies supported these arguments overwhelmingly: the duplication of similar administrative procedures involved in receiving, acknowledging and reviewing complaints, the lack of understanding by the public of the separate functions of the current bodies, and the probability that many complaints fell between the two smaller bodies.

Colin Shaw noted one area of possible danger in a merger: that a larger body could become attractive to some shades of opinion as a centre for all complaints about broadcasting, dragging it into the minefield of impartiality, for example. On the plus side, he suggested, a Broadcasting Forum might undertake the role of a major research centre for broadcasting issues, operating through outside institutions. Such a Forum would also be available to ministers and broadcasters for the study of specific issues affecting broadcasting. The research function, he suggested, could valuably be complemented by the development of a database providing a wide range of information about programme output in Britain. It could also take a continuing interest in the encouragement of media education at all three levels of formal provision.

A central task for any new body being proposed, even if it was merely an expansion of the BSC or a merger of the BSC and BCC, will be to make a major contribution to the definition and monitoring of 'quality'. Fundamental research is needed to discover what viewers and listeners perceive as quality, and whether or not it is being achieved. The views of politicians, committee-persons, broadcasters and programme makers are not a substitute for the audience. An independent consumer body would be better placed to provide this than the BBC and the various other regulators.

The functions of the BCC and the BSC were combined in a new body, the Broadcasting Standards Commission, by the Broadcasting Act 1996. The Commission dealt with standards, fairness, and complaints and undertook research in these areas. It was in turn subsumed in the Office of Communications (OFCOM), established in 2003.

Arrangements for regulation and representation

A major goal of the 1990 Broadcasting Act was to deregulate commercial broadcasting. The ITC was to provide a 'lighter regulatory touch', separating regulation from the function of broadcasting. From 1993, licensees took over responsibility for ensuring that their programme services comply with the Act and the ITC's Codes and Guidelines. The ITC monitored compliance through their headquarters and regional staff and with the assistance of ten regional Viewer Consultative Councils.

Insiders expressed fears about the new regime. George Russell, chairman of the IBA, wrote in his annual report for 1989–90:

'Broadcasting regulation is entering a new era and an early priority will be to resolve areas of potential duplication leading to confusion between the prime industry regulators, the ITC and the Radio Authority, other bodies such as the BSC, the BCC, and other regulators such as the Office of Fair Trading and OFTEL. It is essential that the new bodies and the existing ones have clearly defined roles and procedures to minimise uncertainty and added work for licensees.'

After a decade in which deregulation has been the mission of the government, broadcasters now had more regulators than ever before! There were five bodies and seven programming/advertising codes in operation. There were also increased difficulties for viewers and listeners whose link to the broadcaster, if they wished to make comments or complaints, was made more difficult. For example, if a Yorkshire programme was networked on ITV and the complainant lived in Bristol, the complaint had to go to HTV, the regional ITV company which was transmitting the programme in the region of residence, rather than to the company, who had made the programme.

This line had already been extended by the adoption of the 'commissioning' model, originally by Channel 4, but increasingly within all companies as they move to using their quota of independent producers. Whereas all commissioning editors at Channel 4 saw the Duty Log of phone calls each day, together with summaries of letters, not all producers, whether ITV or independents, were sent extracts of it about their programmes.

While this system may sound inadequate, it has to be remembered that the numbers watching and responding to programmes can be very large, into hundreds of thousands. *No Licence to kill the BBC*, a programme for the Voice of the Listener and Viewer (VLV), stretched the BBC's Open Space Team beyond its capacity with over 800 responses. Some health, consumer and food programmes generate responses of over 50,000. The BBC's 1990–91 Annual Report records a combined total of 216,000 calls and letters received centrally in that year.

There was no direct reference to the audience in the 1990 Broadcasting Act, except in relation to audience research. It is George Russell who referred most clearly to the public:

'And the IBA's success as a broadcasting authority is to be judged, eventually, by the quality, both in technical and programme terms, of the services provided to the public by the companies it regulated. The continued expansion and success of our nation's television and radio services will depend on an equally high level of expertise, flair and responsiveness to the audiences we all serve.'

Under the IBA, there had been, since 1964, a General Advisory Council (GAC), made up of 25 people from many different walks of life and all parts of the UK. As well as providing a flow of useful information and opinions, it had also acted as a 'forum for in-depth discussions of programme issues'. The IBA also had three National Advisory Committees for Northern Ireland, Wales and Scotland, as well as a number of Specialist Advisory Committees. These committees involved over 100 individuals, but not normally in any representative capacity.

The ITC now appointed seven Viewer Consultative Councils (VCCs) in England, and one each for Northern Ireland, Scotland and Wales. Each council had up to 12 members, all are appointed by the ITC. Members were appointed in a personal capacity and therefore contributed primarily as individuals and viewers. Specific organisations or interest groups did not have representatives on the councils. Before being appointed, each member had to demonstrate a definite interest in broadcasting and a commitment to watch television regularly! The leaflet informing the general public about the role of the VCCs, entitled *Listening to the Viewer*, described their function as being advisory rather than executive, and notes that their advice is not mandatory upon the ITC.

This type of structure fell between two stools: it neither provided proper consumer representation on which to frame policy, nor did it provide representative audience research. Structured discussion groups, in-depth interviews, sample-based survey research are all much better ways of finding out what the average person in the street thinks. The optimistic rationale was that these bodies would develop an intelligent and consistent picture of the consumer interest, and not be affected by their own predilections but by a rigorous analysis of what was in the interest of the listening and viewing public as a whole. This was a very difficult task since audience tastes were so varied and required a clear intellectual grasp of the general consumer interest and a clear framework of criteria, based on quality, diversity, variety and range.

There was no requirement on the ITC to monitor the complaints arrangements or any other consumer-related aspects of individual licensees. It would not have been easy for any 'consumer' body to gain an overall view of the effectiveness of these arrangements. There was also concern about the ability and preparedness of the regulators to act in the future when market forces were driving even harder. At that stage, who regulated the regulators and monitored their activities?

Channel 4, hitherto operating under the general advisory structures of the IBA/ITC, was now an independent Corporation, and had no plans to set up any advisory bodies of its own, with the exception of schools television. There was no obligation for it to do so under the 1990 Act, or under its draft licence. It had, of course, always dealt with complaints made to it directly and has been in the forefront of visible response to viewers with the promotion and use of the Video Box, and *Right to Reply*; this programme provision is to continue. Complaints would continue to be dealt with as before.

The ITC ceased to exist with the establishment of OFCOM in 2003. OFCOM is now the body which undertakes research and receives and examines complaints about programmes transmitted by all broadcasting authorities. In making policy, its practice is to issue a consultation document, circulate it widely, allow ten weeks for responses which are published; it may, or may not, take account of these responses.

The powers, responsibilities and obligations laid upon the BBC were vested in the Board of Governors, which was appointed, normally for five-year terms, by the government of the day. The governors were not required to make broadcasting their sole concern; they were drawn 'from a wide variety of backgrounds and experience, so as to represent the wider public interest, as well as being the ultimate authority for everything the BBC does'.

The BBC had been required, since 1947, to appoint advisory councils in its regions in England, and, since the 1952 Charter, a General Advisory Council. National Broadcasting Councils for Scotland, Wales and Northern Ireland were established 'with full regard to the distinctive culture, language and interests of our people in the country for which the Council is established'. The GAC, in fact, went back to 1934, when the BBC established it on its own initiative, in order to 'secure the constructive criticism and advice of representative men and women over the whole field of its activities'. The BBC hoped at the same time that members of the Council 'would use their influence in helping towards a fuller understanding of the BBC's problems and policies on the part of the general public'. The BBC (now) had some 60 advisory bodies involving several hundred people.

The Crawford Committee (1925) recommended that broadcasting should henceforth be conducted by a public corporation 'acting as a trustee for the national interest'. In that sense, the BBC was its own regulator. Colin Shaw, commented that the notion of acting as a trustee for the national interest was a valid one while the BBC's monopoly lasted. However, its credibility as a concept dropped when there were two, three, or four such bodies. The 'national interest' in broadcasting became almost incapable of definition. Broadcasting has become more commercialised and more politicised. He suggests that it is more appropriate to think of the 'protection of the public interest in broadcasting'.

It is the very fact that the Governors were seen as the guardians of the national interest in broadcasting that caused the problem. They were to be the surrogate for the public, 'the man on the Clapham omnibus, the watchdog': 'Dialogue with the licence-payer was seen as superfluous because the Governors were the trustees of the public interest. Thus, they became the means by which the BBC avoided general accountability' (John Dugdale, *The Guardian*, 6 January 1992).

In itself, the system of using 'the great and the good' as surrogates for the community is not impossible. It has been widely used in the UK for many years. Clearly 'the great and the good' are not representative of the people at large, but are asked to take a 'public interest and public service' view of the needs of the community. In practice, the system did not adequately represent different groups in the community, notably women, younger people and ethnic minority groups. It did not even pretend to. Since the power of patronage was held by the government of the day it was also open to political abuse.

On the one hand, the Governors *were* the BBC, ultimately responsible for all its broadcasts and happy to support its executives (or not). On the other hand, they were expected to be the regulators, the preservers of standards, charged with monitoring TV and Radio output, and to act as the guardians of the public interest.

Colin Shaw, an individual with unique experience across the BBC, the IBA and the ITVA suggested that 'the time has come for the BBC Governors to cease to be, in the legal sense, the publishers of the BBC's programmes'. He suggested two possible options for change. First that a fresh body could be created which should apply the Trustee role to the whole of broadcasting, leaving the BBC under the control of an executive board, as were ITV broadcasting companies. The second option would be 'to detach the Governors from a practical responsibility not only for programme matters, but also for the majority of financial and administrative matters. This would allow them to assume a more judicial role and to speak, when they speak on these matters, with their freedom unchecked by direct involvement in the BBC's day-to-day activities. The Governors would have a retrospective role in respect of programmes, considering complaints and reaching conclusions which it would publicise. It would provide broad advice on programming policy, reviewing the output and considering the (programme) balance. It would be a sounding board for the Executive...It would check on the different influences of each of the sources of funding. It should be recruited from a wider circle of people more representative of the public, or ordinary viewers'.

The BBC Trust took over from the BBC Governors in 2007. Now more distanced from the Corporation, it 'works for the public which owns and pays for the BBC, (listens) to a wide variety of voices seeking to understand all opinions and expectations to inform our judgements, (and) vigorously defends the independence of the BBC and equally vigorously holds the BBC management to account' . When other avenues have been exhausted it may also consider and respond to complaints.

Organised consumers

The Voice of the Listener and the Viewer (VLV) describes itself as 'speaking for listeners and viewers on all broadcasting issues' and says that 'it is the only consumer group doing so'. It is a voluntary organisation, founded in 1983, without any political or religious affiliations, funded by its members, and without any financial subsidy. It has a very strong and well-respected chairwoman (Jocelyn Hay; *she retired in 2008 and was succeeded by Richard Lindley*) and approximately 2000 individual members from all over the UK. It has a written constitution, holds an Annual General Meeting and has an Executive Committee.

Its aims are to:

- represent the interests of listeners and viewers
- safeguard the range and quality of broadcast programmes
- promote wider choice of high quality programmes
- encourage multiplicity in ownership so as to guarantee diversity of information and programme sources
- fight undue influence over broadcasting by advertisers, politicians, commercial interests and other institutions
- raise awareness of the vitally important role that broadcasting plays in our national and community life and culture.

It has a number of more detailed current objectives.

The case for one consumer body for broadcasting

While there are a number of bodies with an interest in the field, including some with claims to a seat at the table, there is no existing organisation in a position to take on the nature of the consumer tasks as outlined. There should be a single Consumer Council for the whole of broadcasting, backed up by a Charter for Listeners and Viewers.

It seems realistic to maintain different regulatory structures for the two sides of the system in the short- to medium-term at least, since the imperatives to be served are quite different. ITV companies are competing in the market place. While the BBC has to live in the real world and control its costs carefully, its first priorities are not commercial ones and its regulation must first and foremost look to the public interest in whatever way it is defined at the time.

There are, however, benefits to be obtained from properly based and focused consumer representation, as discussed earlier. At the same time there is a need for a clearer complaints mechanism which would benefit both sides of the system.

It makes good sense, both financially and in terms of access and understanding for consumers, for there to be only one complaints body which deals with all types of complaint, even if internally some of the complaints are dealt with in one way and some in another. (For example, it might be appropriate with certain types of complaint to first have approached the broadcaster direct before taking a case to the Broadcasting Consumer Council – this would closely parallel the position with the existing public utility regulators). With this sort of background the body would be in a strong position to develop knowledge of the whole industry.

More important, one body will combine better knowledge of the industry with the provision of a stronger voice than if there are separate bodies for ITV, the BBC, Radio, Cable and Satellite. The body could build up more expertise and will just simply have more clout. Following on from this, it is easier and provides for more effective advocacy if the same body provides the mechanism for consumer representation.

In summary this proposed new Broadcasting Consumers Council would involve:

- a wide-ranging council of, say, 20 people with a majority of independent representatives
- a wide-ranging definition of 'public interest', including, in particular, the development of a 'positive' view about what makes 'good' broadcasting as well as 'negative' view about what should be excluded.
- a clearly expressed research remit so that views expressed are properly backed up by empirical date and rigorous argument
- an advocacy role
- a responsibility to deal with all types of individual complaints along the lines of the National Gas Consumers' Council.

The research function of such a consumer body would be for policy analysis, understanding of complaints and advocacy. The Council would be appointed on, say, a three-year rolling basis, by the Secretary of State for National Heritage (now the Department of Culture, Media and Sport), with advice from other interested parties.

OFCOM is now responsible for many of the areas which Naomi would have assigned to a Broadcasting Consumer Council. It is reasonable to speculate that she would have argued for a stronger research arm and would have criticised the absence of advocacy and of a charter for listeners and viewers. VLV, which she ardently supported, remains the nearest we have to a body which can have real influence on the broadcasters.

Lifelong learning

For thirty years Naomi Sargant was a major protagonist in the struggle to secure better opportunities for adults to learn. She combined the analytical powers of a public intellectual, the skills of a market researcher, the passion of a polemicist, and a deep and abiding commitment to equality of access to learning as a democratic right – a right denied to too many people. She recognised that evidence and argument are critical to securing that right, and whilst she was impatient with the resistance offered by too many policy makers and politicians, her stamina was formidable. She returned to the argument time and again, to play a key role in all the significant reviews of lifelong learning from the mid 1970s to the end of her life.

This selection of Naomi's writing on adult learners illustrates each of her key qualities. The first is a short extract from her contributions to a debate on 'The challenge of lifelong education', the Eaton Hall lectures, in 1980. Naomi was invited to speak on women's education:

The challenge of lifelong learning[25]

To be asked to be one of three speakers in a series of which the other two are Rhodes Boyson and Neil Kinnock is a somewhat puzzling request. Those of you who are experts in the setting of multiple choice questions – who is the odd one out? To be asked to be the first speaker. Never a good position if you want to win the debate. To be asked to deal with three different topics in the same speech: the Open University, women's education, and the challenge of continuing or lifelong education. I will make here what I hope is my only sexist comment: that it has been my experience, and that of many other women, that you don't just have to be as good as any man to do the same job. You have to be better. (I ask myself – have they been asked to deal with three topics in one speech?) I don't expect on this occasion to match the fiery Welsh rhetoric of Neil Kinnock or the bluff populism of Rhodes Boyson. I will try to bring together some threads from each of the three topics commended to me and point out what appears to me to be a major gap in the education priorities of both the politicians who are to follow in this series.

The occasion of this lecture, the end of teacher training in this institution, is of course in one sense a sad one. It marks the end of an era in this country, an era in which (and I'm showing my prejudices), those marked out to teach were first taught in school, and then were taught in splendid isolation in monotechnic institutions how to teach and then went out to teach – sublimely confident in their ability, trailing clouds of glory and totally uncontaminated often by the real world. Not for them a 9 to 5 job, 49 weeks of the year. No dirty industry for them. Infinitely worthwhile of course, and caring, not very high pay – but long holidays and total security – they'd have a safe job for the rest of their working life.

25. McIntosh, Naomi (1980) Eaton Hall Lectures: *The Challenge of Lifelong Education*, Eaton Hall, pp. 4, 10–12.

But times have changed:

i) education is now no longer the universal panacea it was thought to be
ii) there isn't so much money around
iii)demography – that dread word – has education in its grip.

She moved rapidly on from sorting out her hosts to capturing the ways women were marginalised in public life, and the role of education in reinforcing such inequality with equal brio:

Take London University where I was – Bedford, Royal Holloway and Westfield were originally designed for women, girls and young ladies respectively! All three now have male Principals. Bedford, whose students' union was the training ground for some splendid ladies, Jean Rook and one of our new Euro MPs to name just two, has not had one woman President since the year it went co-ed in the mid-60s. I use the word training ground since the opportunities to administer the union, to chair committees, to speak to large meetings, to manage groups of people and money are important pieces of the apparatus of confidence which men assume they have, and women assume they have not.

What's more, we had magnificent role models. The Principal – she frightened us. Our Professor – Barbara Wootton, an amazing brain – is now in her eighties still fighting major battles in the House of Lords: Gertrude Williams, a formidable economist. Looking back, I now realise that it didn't occur to us that we couldn't do things because we were **women**. On the contrary, they – our Professors – could and they did – we watched them – and so we were encouraged to believe, indeed to assume, that we could too.

We are going through a time period when (with one notable exception) the number of women at the top in this country is decreasing not increasing. It is to be hoped that large numbers of young women are taking better advantage of all the opportunities now opening up for them coming up from the bottom. All I can say is that where I am, somewhere in the middle, it's getting worse. The splendid women at the top of the BBC have now retired, and there is no sign of them being replaced by any women.

There's no woman Permanent Secretary in the Civil Service, nor even a Deputy Secretary. The highest women in the DES are Assistant Secretaries though there are now three of them. There is no woman Vice-Chancellor, no woman Director of a Poly, and so it goes on. In meeting after meeting, on committee after committee there are none or one, or if you are lucky two women. Usually one.

It is difficult to explain without appearing shrill or aggressive quite why it is a problem and how increasingly difficult it is to tolerate it with calm. Can you imagine helping yourself to a cup of coffee from an urn, and having it taken out of your hand by an elderly gentleman saying 'thank you'? Can you imagine being asked what you want as you enter the foyer at BP for a reception to mark Energy Conservation month when all the men are being ushered forward to meet their sponsors? Or when you are invited to a reception on your own to which all the men have had their wives invited? All these have happened to me recently...

Another structural change not in education, but in the social services which has had the same effect is the merging of the Children's Service into Social Service departments. The breed of Children's Officers was an amazing profession of extremely competent women. Now that the Children's Welfare and some of Health functions have been merged into larger aggregates, very few of the top jobs have gone to women. Virtually all the Directors of Social Services departments are men, even though the vast majority of social workers are still women.

It's just not good enough. Why does it happen? Why do we let it happen? In colleges as disparate as the elite Vassar in the States and Bedford and Bulmershe in Britain, immediately the men come in they take over the unions and the clubs. What's more Bulmershe staff tell me that even though men are in a minority and frequently less able than the women, the men immediately dominate the discussion groups.

You who are teaching really have a duty to try to change this.

You who are young women – please find the courage and energy to take up the opportunities which are open to you. They are open to you. The barriers increasingly are in your minds.

You who are married to women – many of you must have wives who are doing jobs which are not good enough for their abilities. Encourage them to do more. Don't let them use you and the family as an excuse for rejecting a challenge that you know they are capable of meeting. Whenever I have challenged senior men in industry or elsewhere about the lack of women, I am told that, and I believe them, that women simply don't apply. More women are now becoming qualified. They also have to **have** the courage to be **encouraged** to put themselves forward and apply.

It does require energy and courage, from both women and perhaps more from men – but it's worth it.

That part of my speech feels to me like the sort of self-indulgence that, as a woman, I have usually forced myself to avoid. I've chosen deliberately to talk in that vein today as I'm becoming increasingly convinced that the problems are getting more difficult to solve and that they are not in the area of legislation, but of individual attitudes, and require courage and commitment from both sides.

The speech went on to consider how continuing education could help address the problem, a theme central to her essay for the Oxford Review of Education, 'To make continuing education a reality' (1980), which was reprinted as a pamphlet by the Advisory Committee on Adult and Continuing Education, Naomi was a leading member of ACACE from 1976 to 1983. In the essay she considers the gap between rhetoric and practice in provision for adult learning, and the instability in the language used to describe the provision:

To make continuing education a reality[26]

There is a remarkable unanimity among a variety of commentators on the value and importance of 'continuing education'.* It commands perhaps even greater acceptance among educationalists than the philosophy of comprehensive education did in the 1960s.

From America, for instance, Cross comments:

> It is quite possible that lifelong learning now outranks motherhood, apple pie and the flag as a universal good. Almost everyone is in favor of lifelong learning, despite mounting confusion over the meaning of the term (Cross, 1978).

As she also implies, there is no unanimity about the meaning of the term, about what it implies for individuals and society, and what strategies and policies need to be adopted if it is to become a reality in our lifetimes. Neither educators nor decision makers are in the forefront of a battle to obtain more education for themselves as adults. Adults as parents are concerned about the quality of education their children receive. It does not occur to many to question the lack of provision for themselves. It is only recently that the Trades Union Congress has included 'continuing education' as a priority in their demands (TUC, 1978). It is also difficult to argue in a time of economic stagnation for education to be given a bigger slice of the national cake, and even more difficult to argue that other parts of the education sector should give up some of their existing resources. Newsam (1979) pointed out recently the 'fallacy that falling rolls would release more and more resources from a fixed

---

26. McIntosh, Naomi (1994) *Occasional Paper Two: To make continuing education a reality*, ACACE: Leicester, pp. 2–5.
* For continuing education, also read 'lifelong learning', 'recurrent education' and '*éducation permanente*'.

total to be redeployed to adult education'. This he said was just not the way the Treasury operated. The financial procedure was to scale down resources to numbers of pupils and then put a bit back for diseconomies of decline. One trouble was that teacher unions were currently demanding disproportionately more of those extras which might otherwise have gone to continuing education.

Adult education has become too accustomed to being the underprivileged sector of education. Its hard-working staff are often part-time and do not have the same organising clout as other professional teachers. While some local authorities do see adult education as desirable, but cannot give it as high priority as the compulsory education sector, others continue to regard it as an unnecessary 'frill'.

This analysis sounds negative set against the assurance of such commentators as Cross. Undoubtedly 'recurrent education' in Sweden and 'lifelong learning' in the US are better known and more widely accepted concepts than 'continuing education' in England and Wales. Both of these countries, however, start off at an advantage in comparison with England and Wales, since education is recognised as a 'good' which people expect and want to have access to.

In both countries substantial numbers of adults are already engaged in some form of educational experience. Cross (1978) put the figure for people in the US engaged in 'organised instruction' as between 12% and 31%, and quotes research estimates to show between 80% and 90% as engaged in some 'form of independent learning project' or as 'making deliberate efforts to learn'. In Sweden, one in three of all adults are estimated to take part in study circles, and that is apart from the more formal structured provision of adult and higher education. Despite this, in neither country is there clarity about the way ahead. In America much was expected of the 1975 Mondale Bill on Lifelong Learning (the 'Lifetime Learning Act'). Staff on the project produced much valuable work, resulting in specific proposals for action. These a nameless commentator recently described as 'now buried six feet down under the Capitol in a lead lined casket'. Similarly even in Sweden although the level of involvement looks very encouraging to us their planners are still concerned at the gap between what they're aiming for and the reality on the ground.

The numbers of adults taking part in any form of adult education in England and Wales although not small, is appreciably smaller than in either Sweden or the US. How do we therefore build on the undoubted belief that the time is now ripe for continuing education while at the same time avoiding the problems that have arisen in other countries, and do this at a time when resources do not seem abundant?

References

CROSS, K. P. (1978) 'The adult learner', in *Current Issues in Higher Education*, Washington DC: American Association for Higher Education.

NEWSAM, P. (1979) 'Providing for a system of continuing education', address to the NIAE Annual Study Conference, University of Nottingham, April.

If the broader field of continuing education for adults struggled for political recognition and adequate resource investment, the field of general education for adults was, Naomi believed more vulnerable. In her 1981 essay, 'Demand and supply in the education of adults', she marshalled the arguments needed to change public opinion and the policy climate to secure recognition of its importance. After a preamble she began by noting some positive features in contemporary policy:

Demand and supply in the education for adults[27]

(T)here has been a welcome commitment by the government to the continuation and some broadening of the Adult Literacy Unit into the work of ALBSU, and encouraging statements of support both by the Secretary of State for Education, Mark Carlisle, and by the Minister of State, Rhodes Boyson, for the middle ground of general adult education – the latter saying, in the House of Commons in January 1980, 'We believe that expenditure on adult education is one of the most purposeful and productive aspects of educational expenditure'. However, these statements of support have not been matched by the commitment of financial resources: on the contrary. The budget reductions for 1979–80 already appeared tough, and few people were prepared for the 1980 Public Expenditure White Paper with its savage cut of £15 million, one third of the total figure for general adult education which has been imposed for 1980–81 on top of these for 1979–80. A major difficulty stems from the fact that global reductions can be and are decided nationally, but the actual flesh has to be cut by other people at local level. This terminology was indeed chosen by Rhodes Boyson who, in the same speech, stated: 'It is essential that local authorities do not cut so near the bone that we cannot get the situation going again once we put more flesh on' (Boyson, 1980.)

General adult education, while only forming a part of the total map of the education of adults, is such a critical part that it is difficult to see how there is any prospect of moving towards continuing education, while this substructure is under such threat. Nor does it look likely that a change of government would mean an immediate shift in policy. *Education* recently reported Neil Kinnock as saying, albeit 'somewhat apologetically', that:

---

27. McIntosh, Naomi (1981) 'Demand and supply in the education of adults', in H. Sockett (ed.) *Educational Analysis*, vol. 3 pp. 25–9, Lewes: Falmer Press.

Adult education would continue to take a back seat in Labour policy-making...Scaling the heights of policy in this area was such an arduous task that it was difficult to imagine anybody would be willing to apply enough resources to achieve it...Until we can secure a stronger understanding and degree of sympathy for adult education and until the people who run it can translate it into a demand and give us a mandate, it will continue to take a back seat.[*]

(Kinnock, 1980)

What is curious about this statement is the assumption that politicians will only put the education of adults on the political agenda if there is a demand and a mandate for it. They have not argued this way about education for children or 'getting rid of hanging' or a variety of other services which they, on our behalf, have taken the lead in suggesting that society needs.

Perhaps the most important task that faces us all over the next few years then, is to change the climate of political opinion from one in which cuts can be made with so little protest, and such statements can be made, into one in which the continuing right of adults to education throughout their lives is accepted just as it is now for children.

There are a number of groups of people who all have to change their attitudes or have their attitudes changed in order to build up this political will. *First*, many individuals who were labelled out of education as failures and think of it as not for themselves, and therefore frequently not for others like them, will need to expect to have access to education as a right and as a good thing. Our research (ACACE, 1981) shows that many more people would have liked access to educational opportunities in the past, but were prevented, and many would like more education now.

Secondly, individuals as tax payers and rate payers need to view the education of adults as a proper burden on rates and taxes as they do the education of children. One problem is the belief that only the individual as a person benefits from education as an adult, that this is a private or personal benefit and therefore should be paid for by the individual. This view emerges very strongly in the DES discussion paper on 'Post-experience vocational provision for those in employment' where it is assumed that employers and employees are the beneficiaries of such education and that therefore they and not the state should pay (DES, 1980). As more people have increased leisure, there are greater needs for retraining rather than up-dating, for coping creatively with unemployment, and the distinction between private and public good will blur.

Thirdly, individuals as employers, many of whom already provide job-related training opportunities, need to extend their view of the type of education and training which is relevant or helpful to adults throughout the life span to include more general education.

Fourthly; individuals as workers need to take advantage of work-related education and training opportunities and, as trade unionists, add educational demands to other sets of demands to be negotiated for. Progress in obtaining many of the entitlements now granted both in Scandinavia and the US has been made due mainly to the demands made by, and the bargaining power of, the unions.

Fifthly, educationalists have to convince their own colleagues that the education of adults is not marginal and a luxury. As Newsam (1980) pointed out, we cannot assume that all educational administrators are informed and well-disposed towards the education of adults. The majority of top education administrators have come from the school sector. It is easier to defend what you have and know. The strongest professional unions are the school level ones. Post-school (in NATFHE, further education staff – mainly full-timers) dominate over adult education – often part-timers. In general it is union policy to protect full-time jobs at the expense of part-time jobs – an unfortunate policy for women. And academics in their own work have concentrated on pedagogy, with little attention being paid to adult learning and the problems of adult learners. This is particularly true within the field of educational research as a recent review of the field makes clear (Derrick, 1980).

Sixthly, and perhaps most important, politicians at local and national level must be convinced of its importance. One reason for urging the desirability of changing the 1944 Act to embody more specific references to adult and continuing education would be to 'concentrate' the minds of the legislators on this issue.

References

ACACE (Advisory Council for Adult and Continuing Education) (1981) *Adults: Their Educational Experience and Needs*, Leicester: ACACE.

Boyson, R. (1980) 'Comment by Minister of State, Rhodes Boyson in House of Commons Debate on Adult Education 16th January', London: Hansard.

DES (Department of Education and Science) (1980) *Continuing Education: Post-experience vocational provision for those in employment*, London: HMSO.

Derrick, T. (1980) 'Some recent trends in British educational research', *Bulletin of the British Psychological Society*, (33).

Kinnock, N. (1980) Reported comment in *Education*, 155(2), 27 June.

Newsam, P. (1980) 'Providing for a system of Continuing Education', paper presented at 1979 NIAE Annual Study Conference, Nottingham.

In 'Lifelong learning – a brave and proper vision' (1994) Naomi looked back some fifteen years later on the ways the policy landscape evolved during and after the years in which the Advisory Council for Adult and Continuing Education did its work. Unlike the Eaton Hall lecture it is possible to tell from the analysis just how large a part Naomi played in elaborating and then re-stating the case for adult learning in the period she analyses. Unlike the earlier extracts this essay is, with minor changes to avoid duplication, reproduced here in full:

Lifelong learning – a brave and proper vision[28]

Lifelong and lifetime learning are two current versions of attempts to find a suitable name for post-compulsory learning. Both have the advantage, from the adult learner's perspective, that they can include both education and training. 'Lifetime' derives particular support through its acceptance and inclusion by the Confederation of British Industry (CBI) and Employment Department (ED) in their agreed Lifetime Learning Targets for Education and Training. 'Lifelong' is preferred within European organisations and is broader in its inclusiveness.

For most people, the term education has been so closely associated with 'schooling' and the classroom, as immediately to invoke negative memories and attitudes. School was compulsory, and was for many people a place to leave as soon as possible. The idea that it is desirable, let alone necessary, to go on learning and being judged as competent or not throughout life is quite threatening. To learn for pleasure or for leisure is one thing, but to be required continually to update oneself or retrain for another career is quite another. Learning is a necessary entry-point to the information society and it must be made available to older people as well as to the young.

---

28. Sargant, Naomi (1990) 'Chapter 4. Lifelong learning – A brave and proper vision', in D. Bradshaw (ed.) *Bringing Learning to Life*, Brighton: Falmer Press, pp. 47–64.

Creating a wider vision: the Advisory Council for Adult and Continuing Education

A practical step forward was taken in 1977, in England and Wales at least, with the setting up of the Advisory Council for Adult and Continuing Education (ACACE). Part of its remit was 'to promote the development of future policies and priorities; with full regard to the concept of education as a process continuing throughout life' (DES, 1977). This was excitingly new and the Notes of Amplification provided by the DES still stand as a brave and proper vision:

> Increasingly we have come to realise that education and training cannot adequately be provided by school and post-school ('front-end') provision; for a variety of personal, social and vocational reasons, adults need to be able to return to education and training throughout life, to explore new avenues or pursue existing interests further...Post-school education and training is increasingly seen as a continuum permitting many different combinations of modes of attendance, subject areas and levels of study intended to meet the almost infinite variety of students' needs and motivation. Adult education and all the other administratively convenient bundles of provision do not therefore have rigid boundaries. Continuing education requires us to think in a student-centred rather than an institution-centred way. (Jones, 1977)

Though ACACE was limited by the fact that its role was advisory, its membership, while not representative as such, covered a very wide spread of involvement from the CBI to the TUC, from the MSC to broadcasting and libraries as well as more conventional providers. This breadth of membership gave it real strength and its Chairman, Richard Hoggart, in urging it not to be afraid to be radical, ensured that its 'reach' should exceed its 'grasp'.

Its paper *Towards Continuing Education* (ACACE, 1979) was designed to provoke discussion, rather than assume agreed solutions, and argued strongly that a shift from the 'front-end' model of education, in which adults are equipped with all the educational baggage they need for their whole lives at the beginning of it, to a model in which opportunities continue to be available throughout life was vital. It proposed the distinction between initial and post-initial education rather than between compulsory and post-compulsory. More important, it preferred not to differentiate between education and training, and criticised the term non-vocational education. It argued from the point of view of the learning adult, not from the point of view of existing provider institutions, funders or embedded vested interests.

There were however structural obstacles and Peter Newsam pointed out that most educational administrators had a background in schools and not in adult work, and would not necessarily be sympathetic to continuing education.

In its six-year life ACACE did much valuable work, made evident through its thirty-four publications, but it did not succeed in its most important task. In its final publication (ACACE, 1983) it criticised itself for failing adequately to raise the level of excitement about the education of adults and for failing to persuade the Government to extend its life and make it an official development body rather than merely an advisory one. No decision as to the future of its work had been made at the point the Council was closed down, and the Government response, when it came, was a 'mouse': they offered the National Institute of Adult Continuing Education (NIACE) £50,000 to set up a 'development unit' later called the Unit for the Development of Adult Continuing Education (UDACE) under the wing of NIACE, and added a similarly small amount for a unit (to be called Replan) to develop education for the unemployed, another of ACACE's pieces of unfinished business. When this sum was offered to NIACE, a number of people who had bridged both organisations considered it derisory and thought it should not be accepted. It is, however, easy to understand why NIACE was interested in accepting it; but it became another clear example of one educational grouping being played off against another: a government strategy which has continued in this area.

ACACE's major report *Continuing Education: From Policies to Practice* (1982a) argued that all adults should be entitled to continued opportunities for education throughout their lives. It did not propose to set up a new 'sector' of such education or develop a new curriculum but to make the 'best' more widely available and give the education of adults an increased priority in the allocation of resources. Issues focused on were:

- the removal of barriers to access;
- the provision of information, advisory and counselling services;
- ways in and through the system, including flexible and modular structures and what would now be termed progression routes;
- the accessibility of institutions, including the need for a network of local centres near people;
- new patterns of learning including open and distance learning and broadcasting;
- issues of financing of provision;
- and financial support for learners, including entitlements.

These issues are all still on the agenda. That report proposed and ACACE's final report ended '...by restating the proposition that the time has come for this country to give the same serious attention to the education of its adults as it gives to the education of its children' (ACACE, 1983).

Richard Hoggart and his colleagues on the Council were genuine in their self-criticism, but they were equally critical of attitudes in the country as a whole. In their final paper, they noted 'the complete absence of any references to continuing education in public speeches about the future of our society...during the election campaign of 1983'. Two of their major reports *Continuing Education: From Policies to Practice* and *Education for Unemployed Adults* (ACACE, 1982a; 1982b) had been sitting on the then Secretary of State's desk for 18 months and a year respectively. Keith Joseph had, 18 months earlier speaking to the NIACE Annual Conference on the Continuing Education Report's publication, described it as 'insidiously seductive' (he was later to explain that from him this was a compliment) but that people had to understand that this was an area for private funding for which people should pay themselves. This proved to be a foretaste of future stronger policies.

The vocational takeover

With the demise of ACACE, and the limited funding offered for continuing work to NIACE, the initiative in the development of opportunities for adults passed from education to training, and from the Department of Education and Science (DES) to the Manpower Services Commission (MSC). The MSC had been created by the Employment and Training Act, 1973 and lasted until its transformation into the Training Commission in 1988. It was one of the small number of quangos which survived the attacks of that time, finding a role which was also acceptable to the incoming Conservative Government. Ainley and Corney (1990) describe the MSC as having set itself three tasks:

> In the widest context...it aimed to abolish completely the dichotomy between education and training that had emerged during the nineteenth century. Within the policy-making context, the MSC's goal was to elevate the importance of education and training and redefine its contribution to productivity and national development. At the institutional level, the MSC attempted the complete overhaul of Britain's education and training system.

It is not surprising that the MSC became seen as a rival to the DES and there was real tension between them. The MSC soon adopted the term 'Vocational Education and Training' (VET) in an attempt to show their interrelationship. An example of a positive, but limited, riposte from the DES in the 'adult' area was their Discussion Paper on *Continuing Education: Post-experience Vocational Provision for Those in Employment* (DES, 1980). This complicated formulation (soon referred to as PEVE) focused on the importance of mid-career courses of vocational education for those at work. It noted: 'This does not deny either initial education, which indeed is likely always to take a large share of education resources; retraining of the unemployed; or general continuing education for adults.' In a footnote, it commented:

> By vocational is meant anything which is broadly relevant to the individual in his development in working life, whether or not it is directly or immediately relevant to his present job. Education should be construed broadly, as embracing activities which might be regarded as training.

ACACE, still working on its long-term plans, was somewhat concerned about this more instrumental direction. The paper, however, made it clear that any such shorter term practical solutions 'need not prejudice any long-term and more general developments across the whole field of continuing education which might be pursued in the light of advice from ACACE'. The use of *continuing* in the narrower and 'post-experience' sense has however tended to become the accepted sense of its use in higher education since that time.

Separately, Jim Prior, as Secretary of State for Employment, had been interested in setting up an analogue to the OU to meet adult training and retraining needs at technician and related levels. The resultant Open Tech Programme was not to be a new institution, but a planned and coordinated range of commissioned projects with two key tasks: to open or widen access to existing training provision and to make new education and training provision which from the beginning can best be met through open learning. Providers were pump-primed to produce open learning materials which would then be widely available, but 'on the assumption that adults retraining through the Open Tech Programme would have to pay for their own self-improvement' (Ainley and Corney, 1990).

It is not possible to review this period in detail. However, the departure of John Cassels for the Cabinet Office in 1981 and his replacement as Director of the MSC by Geoffrey Holland, and the replacement of Richard O'Brien, as Chairman, by David (later Lord) Young, who had been advising Keith Joseph at the Department of Trade and Industry were particularly significant. This is an area where it is not possible to disengage attitudinal issues from the individuals engaged in policy development. According to Ainley and Corney (1990):

> Young's appointment indicated that the future development of the MSC would be in strict accordance with the overall direction of government policy. The MSC might be used to deal with political crises, as and when they arose. Otherwise, its main function was to keep the anti-inflationary strategy on course. Training would be left to the market and would aim to encourage industry to develop and apply the new technologies.

There was as yet no obvious connection with investment in human capital and with the need for an adaptable and flexible trained workforce. The most urgent task for the MSC was to help to deal with mass unemployment, especially mass youth unemployment, which the government was increasingly funding through the Youth Opportunities Programme.

The MSC picks up the adult baton — but drops it

John Cassels had prepared a consultative paper *A New Training Initiative* (NTI) (MSC, 1981a) which aimed to replace the various temporary employment schemes with a permanent, national and comprehensive training programme for all young people. Behind it were all the now well-known arguments about adaptability and flexibility, the unpredictability of the labour market and no single job for life. Arguing that training and re-training for the entire workforce was not only important for the survival of individual firms and for employment prospects but that both were also a cure for unemployment, the NTI argued for the development and improvement of apprenticeships, the chance for all young people under 18 to continue either in full-time education or training and for the *opening up of widespread opportunities for adults* (emphasis added). The last of these was expressed in generous terms: 'We must open up wide opportunities for adults, whether in employment, unemployed or returning to work, to acquire, increase or up-date their skills and knowledge during the course of their working lives' (MSC, 1981b).

This far-seeing statement of adult needs was not to be matched by the allocation of financial resources: youth training remained the priority of the Government. The MSC published their follow-up *A New Training Initiative: An Agenda for Action* (MSC, 1981b) and, on the same day, the Secretary of State for Employment, Norman Tebbit, published *A New Training Initiative: A Programme for Action* (The Department for Employment, 1981) proposing a £1 billion scheme of vocational preparation for people between the ages of 16 and 18. After this age, it said 'the cost of training is basically a matter for the individual employer'. The Youth Training Scheme was to start in 1983, and the valuable Training Opportunities Scheme (TOPS) scheme was to be closed down to help pay for it. Adults, and particularly women returners, would therefore be worse off, as the joint TUC-Labour Party statement *A Plan for Training* pointed out (TUC and the Labour Party, 1984).

Geoffrey Holland, Director of the MSC, found what he described as '...the Government's obsession with the young' unhelpful and was concerned at the major shift away from support for adults. Since the budget that was retained for work with adults was now too small to enable any significant provision of training, he determined that the most fruitful strategy would be to concentrate on changing public and private attitudes towards the desirability of adult training, particularly among employers.

The result was the publication of the MSC's discussing paper *Towards an Adult Training Strategy* (MSC, 1983a) and its subsequent MSC *Proposals for Action* (MSC, 1983b). The Foreword of the Discussion Paper, signed by David Young, then Chairman, was encouraging:

...In the view of the MSC, adult training and retraining will be every bit as important in the 1980s as Youth Training...At the moment adult training and re-training are poor relations. They do not have sufficient priority or attention and they need to find a place on the agenda of employers, unions, the education service and all who are concerned with our training and vocational education system (MSC, 1983a).

The paper argued the economic case for an adult training strategy, suggesting:

more effort should be put into training and re-training those already in employment or about to start a new job, rather than into speculative training or training for stock. Providing the skills base for an economy which is not only viable but flourishing will be the most practical way to open up more opportunities for unemployed individuals.

It identified as particular priorities the management of change, the building of a more flexible and responsive training system to provide access to training for individuals. The language was already one of modules and standards of competence, of continuity and progression. The importance of information and expert advice assisted by the potential of information technology with increased accessibility through open learning systems such as the Open Tech and the OU were discussed. Their follow-up proposals for action included now familiar paragraphs: A National Awareness Campaign, Action at National Level, Achieving and Measuring Competence, Local Level Collaboration and Working with the Market. The Commission saw its role as acting as a focus for the national debate, working with others on achieving adult training objectives, using its resources to form opinion, provide information and act as a broker. It needed also to set an example with its own programmes and resources. The proposals included a number of useful detailed proposals with cross-references to the Open Tech Programme and to the work of ACACE. An earlier proposal that an adult entitlement for training should be considered had not found favour in internal discussions in the MSC. What did emerge was the first reference to a national loans scheme.

In order to raise awareness of and the need for adult training, the MSC commissioned the first significant research into the quality, nature and cost of adult training, management attitudes to training and the relationship between adult training and business performance (IFF Research Ltd, 1985). This indicated that while employers considered that adult training was an essential investment, what they actually invested amounted to only 0.38 per cent of pay roll. High-performing businesses were twice as likely to train, and train twice as many employees, as low-performing businesses. High-performing businesses had increased their training by 25 per cent over the last five years while low-performing businesses had reduced their training by 20 per cent.

It was clear to people reading the fine print that the MSC was from then on to take over and actively pursue many of ACACE's policies but was, not surprisingly, to relate them to only training rather than the broader field of continuing education. While some adult educators were cynical about the MSC's motives, others, more pragmatic, welcomed them as setting precedents which could be built upon in better times. Since then many of the policy developments in this area have indeed come from the Manpower Services Commission and its successor bodies, under the guidance of Geoffrey Holland and his colleagues rather than from the DES.

Education returns to the ring

The fact that many policy developments on continuing education came from the MSC does not mean that there was no movement on the 'education' side, though this tended to be within the institutional groupings rather than through the DES. The University Grants Committee (UGC) established a working party on continuing education in December 1982. The Business and Technician Education Council produced a policy statement titled *Continuing Education for Business and Industry* in April 1983 (BTEC, 1983) and in the same month the National Advisory Body for Local Authority Higher Education (NAB) established a group with wide-ranging membership to consider and advise on the appropriate role and extent of continuing education provision and how it might be fostered. Its first key recommendation was that 'the provision of continuing education should be accepted as a major objective of higher education' (NAB, 1984a). Later in the same year, the NAB and the UGC agreed a joint statement with the recommendation that 'the provision of continuing education in order to facilitate adjustment to technological, economic and social change and to meet individual needs for personal development' be adopted as an explicit national aim for higher education and be added to the 'four purposes of higher education' enshrined in the Robbins report of 1963 (NAB, 1984b).

The mid 1980s saw some hardening of attitudes. Some points stand out. Employers were expected to pay for the costs of training their employees and the divide between providing education and training for the employed and the unemployed widened. For example Lord Young, then Secretary of State for Employment, refused to allow the emergent Open College to serve the unemployed as well as those in work, though the air-time offered by Channel 4 (lunchtime on weekdays) had been offered on that basis. The College's Chairman, Michael Green, said vehemently: 'I did not agree to be the chairman of a college for the jobless...'

The DES lags behind

The DES continued to be mainly preoccupied with the education of the young and with initial rather than post-initial education. The main thrust of the 1987 Education Reform Bill was at school level. However, at the same time as responsibility for higher education was to be removed from local education authorities, their duty to secure the provision of adequate further education to meet the needs of their areas was clarified. Unfortunately the Bill now differentiated between the straightforward provision of full- and part-time education and training for persons over compulsory school age (other than higher education) and the quaintly-worded second category of 'organised leisure-time occupation provided in connection with the provision of such education and training'. This it spelled out as meaning, 'in such organised cultural training and recreative activities as are suited to their requirements ...'

This distinction and the way that it is misused has been damaging. Reappearing in the White Paper *Education and Training for the 21st Century* (DES, 1991), it paved the way for the separation of general adult education from supposedly more worthwhile areas of study. The give-away is, of course, the misuse of 'leisure' as an adjective to describe such courses. The connection with leisure is the simple one that the vast majority of adults who study use their own leisure-time in which to study. Many people who are engaged in work-related study are also using their own time for it, sometimes because their employers will not provide it. And of course, what may appear as a leisure interest now, may become relevant for future employment. Often motivation is known only to the learner and cannot be determined by categorising courses or identifying sources of provision. This is an increasingly sterile argument as working patterns change with people undertaking a larger number of different jobs, living longer and having more leisure throughout life.

The limitation of this distinction is seen most clearly by the success of the employee development schemes being run in an increasing number of companies. The original Ford scheme, the Employee Development and Assistance Programme (EDAP) arose from the 1987 collective agreement between Ford and their Trade Unions. It provided for a company contribution of £40 per head for all 49,000 employees into a jointly managed fund, from which any employee could then draw up to £200 per annum for education, training or health and lifestyle pursuits. The key points are that the choice of what to do is left entirely to the individual, it is not expected to be work-related, neither is the study or activity carried out in work-time, though tuition will usually be offered on work premises. Response to the scheme, and to others like it, has been far higher than anticipated, and many people, once their confidence and interest has been secured have been encouraged to move on to more demanding areas and often vocationally relevant areas of study.

More of a problem arises for smaller companies in implementing such a scheme, but there are projects developing in some TEC areas to provide a framework for a number of local small- and medium-sized enterprises working together, and also where large companies, such as Rover, are opening their study facilities to their suppliers. These schemes provide an imaginative bottom-up complement to Investors in People (IiP). It is possible to see these strands of activity contributing to the idea of a learning organisation.

The emergence, in the 1980s, of the CBI as a major force in shaping policy for education and training lifted the debate nationally. Its report *Towards a Skills Revolution* (CBI, 1989) placed much emphasis on the individual. Working with others, the CBI also helped to establish the National Training and Education Targets (NETTS) required to meet the strategic priorities for action laid down in *A Strategy for Skills* (ED, 1991). The target dates are close. Those for foundation learning seem likely to be met. Achievement of the adult targets seems less certain though IiP UK Ltd, who have the job of getting HP adopted, report a gathering momentum in their area. Moreover some of the value of these targets is that they focus attention on, and legitimate work towards, the achievement of these goals.

Of the strategic priorities of *A Strategy for Skills (op. cit.)*, the third is particularly relevant for this discussion: 'individuals must be persuaded that training pays and that they should take more responsibility for their own development'. It is the setting of this strategic priority which has led to the creation of a new department in the Training Enterprise and Education Directorate (TEED) under the banner of 'individual commitment'. It brings with it echoes of Keith Joseph and David Young, the implication being that while it is clearly a priority, and professional endeavour can be expended on this area of work, the task is to focus on 'hearts and minds' and not on anything that costs money and which would directly support individuals. The positive result of this is active encouragement within the Employment Department and the TECs of the development of coherent individual commitment strategies locally, and the commissioning of much new research which is providing valuable new information for providers.

In addition the TEC National Council set up a Working Group 'to address the web of complex issues that influence the commitment of individuals to lifetime learning in particular, and to the learning market in general'. This Working Group has recently reported to a joint DE/CBI conference on Learning and Individuals with a number of proposals including:

- a major and sustained PR campaign to increase motivation and awareness by individuals and employers of the benefits of lifetime learning;
- incentives for individuals to fund their own learning;
- rapid expansion of information, advice and guidance services at all ages to increase the efficiency of the learning market;

- improved responsiveness of learning suppliers to customer needs (TEC National Council, 1994).

While not new, these are all laudable and the issue of financial incentives breaks some new ground. But essentially the policy returns to exhortation and rhetoric, but little action.

The other major influence on public attitude has been the Royal Society for the encouragement of Arts Manufactures and Commerce (RSA). The reports of Sir Christopher Ball, now the RSA's Director of Learning...*More Means Different* (Ball, 1990); *Learning Pays* (Ball, 1991); *Profitable Learning* (Ball, 1992); *Start Right* (Ball, 1994); and the commitment of the RSA to the development of a learning society have been valuable in changing perceptions and attitudes.

Adult learning: Who should pay?

While many, though not enough, employers have been prepared to train their own employees in work-related skills, they have done this in the knowledge that their workforce has been expected to be basically stable. The decline of manufacturing industry and the increase in part-time low-skilled jobs, often taken by women (as is discussed in Chapter 1), has changed this. Few employers have funded non-work-related training, and by reverse, some employees have paid for their own work-related studies either if their employer would not, or, as often, when they wished to change employer.

A sequence of research studies funded by the ED's Individual Commitment Branch provide valuable new information on underlying attitudes both of employers and learners. The research shows first that the pattern of employer expectation is mirrored by the expectation of adult learners more than half of whom 'agree that employers or government should pay for learning that is to do with jobs or careers' (IFF Research, 1994). Secondly, the study of Individuals' Attitudes notes that:

> Non-learners were more likely than learners to feel that they themselves should *not* be expected to pay for job-related learning (43 per cent and 36 per cent respectively). This group was also more likely to feel that employers or government should fund vocational learning. (SCPR/ED, 1994)

Similarly a recent study of general adult learning carried out for Adult Learners' Week, 1994, shows that while adults consider that individuals themselves should pay two-thirds of the costs of courses which do not lead to qualifications, they reverse the proportions for courses leading to qualifications and consider that two-thirds of these costs should be borne by employers or taxpayers (NIACE, 1994).

Another serious issue is that training is not provided equitably across the workforce. A matching study on Employer's Attitudes (PSI/ED, 1994) records that 95 per cent of employers provided training for some or all of their employees, but as other research has shown, provision was greater for higher occupational groups and amongst larger organisations.

Neither are opportunities for training spread equally between men and women, or between ethnic groups. More training is recorded among the already better trained, and the 1992 Summer Labour Force Survey showed that in every industrial sector except energy and water, women received proportionately less training than men. Since the main growth in the work-force is among women working part-time, the situation is less than encouraging. Research among adult learners show fewer women engaged in current or recent learning in the work place, 12 per cent of women compared with 18 per cent of men (Sargant, 1991). A companion study among the main ethnic minority groups shows only 8 per cent overall learning at work compared with the 15 per cent overall in the national survey (Sargant, 1993). This is not due to their lack of interest in learning, since they show higher rates of learning both formally and informally than the population of Great Britain as a whole.

Entitlements make good sense

The expectation that all post-compulsory training and work-related education can be left to employers has always been mistaken. Proponents of paid educational leave made the same assumption at a time when very many women were not in the workforce and were not therefore eligible for it. That is one reason why ACACE argued for a broader form of entitlement, which was including rather than excluding since people in paid employment are now a minority of the population (ACACE, 1982a). ACACE argued for two forms of entitlement. The first was designed to give to those adults who had left school early the equivalent educational and financial opportunities that are already available to those who take the elite escalator through 'A'-levels to a degree. Along these lines, Sir Christopher Ball had usefully suggested that we learn to recognise 'deferred progression into further and higher education as normal and sensible' (Ball, 1989). The second would be a 'topping-up' continuing educational entitlement which people could choose to use regularly or save up for whatever they most required throughout their adult lives.

Over the past decade there has been continued but fitful discussion of such strategies as entitlements, paid educational leave and sabbaticals. One idea was entitlement for the over-fifties picked up by the Labour Party in a policy review. There are, of course, already a number of schemes which are effectively forms of entitlement: mandatory grants for higher education and training credits, for example. It is clear from such precedents that it is possible to plan an entitlement policy which is not open-ended and can be allocated within agreed priorities.

Turned on its head, the agreement that adults following the Employment Training Programme are supported to the tune of their dole money plus expenses is, in fact, a form of entitlement. It is, of course, limited to those who have been unemployed for over six months and the Learning for Work entitlement is even more limited. The 21-hour rule, the concession to unemployed claimants of benefit which allows them to study part-time whilst looking for work as long as the course does not exceed 21 hours per week, frustrates people because it comes near an imaginative entitlement but fails to achieve it.

The Training Agency and its successor TEED have been serious experimenters with versions of entitlements, the most significant being the piloting of a number of youth training credit schemes through TECs which the Government is now committed to offering to all young school-leavers by 1995 (President of the Board of Trade *et al.*, Cm 2563, 1994). Entitlements for guidance for adults are now built into Skills Choice, experiments with credits for Open Learning are proving very successful and adult training credits are also being tested out. In parallel with these initiatives is the expansion of Career Development Loans and recently the announcement of Small Firm Training Loans. While none of these projects form the basis of an overall policy, there is no question that the existence of these schemes has had a significant effect in changing attitudes.

Little changes without new ideas. Sir Geoffrey Holland recently suggested a framework against which the Labour Party's idea of a satellite University for Industry might develop. It includes many of the planks of recent and current innovation: assessment of prior learning, paid educational leave, modular structures with Credit Accumulation and Transfer Schemes (CATS), complete choice of where and how to study, and the use of new technologies. He also suggested that the unique ingredient which could help drive the project could be individual training accounts rather than entitlements. The idea is that both the employer and the worker could make contributions into such an account which would be tax-relievable and could be called on 'as and when' for people's education and training needs. It is encouraging that the *competitiveness* White Paper suggests that the 'Government will consult TECs, financial institutions and other bodies on how to take such arrangements forward ...' (President of the Board of Trade *et al.*, 1994). However, as usual such ideas raise issues of universality and equity: not everyone has an employer and small employers are less able to engage in such funding. Moreover the structural changes in the labour market outlined in Chapter 1 mean that as far fewer people expect to have tidy careers, working with a single employer or in one career throughout their lives, training accounts will therefore need to be portable.

It is extremely difficult to deal with the lack of opportunities and inequities without any government or taxpayer intervention. And, as the research shows, individual commitment and motivation are extremely diffi-cult to encourage when there are no visible job opportunities. Government policy is to move responsibility for funding education and training from the state to the employer and to the individual. In line with this, the *competitive-ness* White Paper emphasises the need for young people

> to learn how to take responsibility for their own decisions and to appre-ciate the crucial importance of investing in skills. At the same time the providers of education and training should be responsive to their customers. The Government therefore sees attractions in providing all 16–19-year-olds with **learning credits** with a real cash value, *(op. cit.)*

It emphasises that such a far-reaching change in funding would need careful preparation and proposes wide and open consultation. It would certainly impact on 6th forms, on independent schools and on further and higher education. But combined with the notion of individual training accounts, it is possible to see the beginning of an overall entitlement strategy. What we have at the moment are a number of accidental planks of support. The most privileged learners, as Jeff Rooker (1993) in his discussion paper 'Opportunity and achievement' made clear, are the conventional entrants to full-time higher education, even though loans and grant cuts are putting pressure on them. The only other schemes that pay for subsistence/living costs are Employment and Youth Training and the benefits under the 21-hour rule.

Jeff Rooker suggests, as did ACACE, a life-time entitlement to higher education, an educational account to be drawn on after school. He empha-sises five guiding principles: equity, quality, continuity, access and accounta-bility. He focuses on the fact that part-timers get no financial assistance, neither do OU students, and that discretionary grants are being cut with the pressure on local authorities caused by rate-capping. Subsidised loans are made available to full-time degree-level students while tax relief is available only for the costs of study of NVQs. The system is neither rational or equi-table.

Policy for those in employment and the unemployed is determined by the Employment Department, working with the TECs. Policy for those not in employment is, effectively, determined by the Treasury operating with the other side of its brain. The failure is to see that these are two sides of the same brain, that patterns of work, non-work and leisure are changing and that the costs and benefits to society of a well-trained and educated popula-tion are social as well as economic and long-term as well as short-term. Of course resourcing training in a flexible and changing labour market is more difficult but it is vital that we do not plan for a divided workforce and a divided society. Economic necessity and the reality of the arrival of the infor-mation society may persuade the government to change its policy and prior-ities. Otherwise we shall continue paying only lip-service to what really is a 'possible vision' and condemn many to living in an information-poor society.

References

ACACE (ADVISORY COUNCIL FOR ADULT AND CONTINUING EDUCATION) (1979) *Towards Continuing Education,* Leicester: ACACE.

ACACE (ADVISORY COUNCIL FOR ADULT AND CONTINUING EDUCATION) (1982a) *Continuing Education: From Policies to Practice,* Leicester: ACACE.

ACACE (ADVISORY COUNCIL FOR ADULT AND CONTINUING EDUCATION) (1982b) *Education for Unemployed Adults,* Leicester: ACACE.

ACACE (ADVISORY COUNCIL FOR ADULT AND CONTINUING EDUCATION) (1983) *In the Corners of Our Time,* Leicester: ACACE.

AINLEY, P. and CORNEY, M. (1990) *Training for the Future,* London: Cassell.

BALL, C. (1989) *Aim Higher,* London: RSA.

BALL, C. (1990) *More Means Different,* London: RSA.

BALL, C. (1991) *Learning Pays,* London: RSA.

BALL, C. (1992) *Profitable Learning,* London: RSA.

BALL, C. (1994) *Start Right,* London: RSA.

BTEC (Business and Technology Education Council) (1983) *Continuing Education for Business and Industry,* London: BTEC.

CBI (CONFEDERATION OF BRITISH INDUSTRY) (1989) *Towards a Skills Revolution,* London: CBI.

DE (DEPARTMENT OF EDUCATION) (1981) *A New Training Initiative: A Programme for Action* (Cmnd 8455), London: HMSO.

DES (DEPARTMENT OF EDUCATION AND SCIENCE) (1977) *Terms of reference and functions for The Advisory Council for Adult and Continuing Education,* London: HMSO.

DES (DEPARTMENT OF EDUCATION AND SCIENCE) (1980) *Continuing Education: Post-experience Vocational Provision for Those in Employment,* London: HMSO.

DES (DEPARTMENT OF EDUCATION AND SCIENCE) (1991) *Education and Training for the 21st Century* (Cm 1536), London: HMSO.

ED (EDUCATION DEPARTMENT) (1991) *A Strategy for Skills* (Cm 1810), London: HMSO.

JONES, D. E. L. (1977) 'Notes of amplification to ACACE', *The Oxford Review of Education* (1979) 5.

MSC (MANPOWER SERVICES COMMISSION) (1981a) *A New Training Initiative: A Consultative Document,* London: MSC.

MSC (MANPOWER SERVICES COMMISSION) (1981b) *A New Training Initiative: An Agenda for Action,* London: MSC.

MSC (MANPOWER SERVICES COMMISSION) (1983a) *Towards an Adult Training Strategy,* Sheffield: MSC.

MSC (MANPOWER SERVICES COMMISSION) (1983b) *A New Training Initiative: MSC Proposals for Action,* Sheffield: MSC.

NAB (NATIONAL ADVISORY BODY FOR LOCAL AUTHORITY HIGHER EDUCATION) (1984a) *Report of the Continuing Education Group,* London: NAB.

NAB (NATIONAL ADVISORY BODY FOR LOCAL AUTHORITY HIGHER EDUCATION) (1984b) *A Strategy for Higher Education in the Late 1980s and Beyond,* London: NAB.

NIACE (1994) *The Will to Learn*, Leicester: NIACE.

POLICY STUDIES INSTITUTE (for ED) (1994) *Employers' Attitudes to Lifelong Learning*, London: HMSO.

PRESIDENT OF THE BOARD OF TRADE, *et al.* (1994) *Competitiveness: Helping Business to Win* (Cm 2563), London: HMSO.

ROOKER, J. (1993) 'Opportunity and achievement', *The Times Higher Educational Supplement.*

SARGANT, N. (1991) *Learning and 'Leisure'*, Leicester: NIACE.

SARGANT, N. (1993) *Learning for a Purpose*, Leicester: NIACE.

SOCIAL AND COMMUNITY PLANNING RESEARCH (for ED) (1994) *Individuals' Attitudes to Lifelong Learning*, London: HMSO.

TUC AND THE LABOUR PARTY (1984) *A Plan for Training*, London: TUC.

In 1996 the Further Education Funding Council commissioned Helena Kennedy QC to report on measures to widen participation in further education. Naomi prepared a briefing paper for the Kennedy Committee which reviewed the challenges involved in widening access, and the lessons to be drawn from the successive initiatives in seeking to create an institution to complement the success of the Open University in further education and training. Naomi had a clarity about the connections to be made between the forces of technological and social change, and their implications for education policy, forged in her years at the Open University, enriched at Channel 4, and applied in a wide range of policy contexts. In all, the range of her curiosities and competences were quite unusual.

This is a substantial extract from that paper, subsequently published in Pandora's Box*(1997.)*

Access moves up the agenda[29]

'Access' was not a matter of concern to most conventional institutions of higher education in the early 70s. Neither had there been any particular incentive to make more use of the media for degree level or further education/vocational work. The 1990s have seen an increase in participation rates and an increased interest in access particularly in the polytechnics, now 'new' universities. This has led to a significant growth in numbers of students and a concomitant pressure on staff, on teaching resources and space.

At the same time, the tidy vertically integrated single subject degree structures of the past are being changed into modular and more flexible patterns with arrangements for Credit Accumulation and Transfer between subject areas and institutions, a move promoted by the OU in the 70s. If degrees are broken into credit units or smaller modules, these do not need to be studied in linear consecutive form, or in one geographical place. One module may be studied or several, in a time and place of the learner's choice.

Developing Access (UDACE, 1988), a discussion paper on guidance and access, took a positive line and asked what a system *would need to be* in order to be perceived 'as an accessible system' by its users. In a useful analysis, they consider requirements for appropriate entry mechanisms, for the curriculum, for quality of support to individuals, for evaluation and monitoring and so on. At the end of the day what they are requiring is a thoroughly good and effective system. By definition such a system would

29. Sargant, Naomi and Tuckett, Alan (1997) *Pandora's Box: Companion papers on motivation, access and the media*, Leicester: NIACE, pp. 9–34.

have to be accessible! Indeed there are individual examples of such good institutions, but not yet enough of them.

Earlier on, the Leverhulme-funded study on *Access to Higher Education* (Fulton, 1981) made nine recommendations to improve access, several affecting further education, but movement on most of them has been minimal. They included among them six which are still relevant:

4. The sharp administrative and academic distinction between advanced and non-advanced courses should be abandoned.
5. Courses of higher and further education should be available to all those who can benefit from them and wish to do so. All admitting units should admit at least 25% of students using criteria other than A levels.
6. The universities and the CNAA should devise certificates of partial completion of degree courses, to be awarded after appropriate assessment.
7. The present grant system should be replaced with a system of 'educational entitlement' whereby every citizen is entitled to support for his or her education or training, regardless of its level.
8. All institutions, and especially those with highly competitive entry requirements, should undertake significant experiments with positive discrimination...When admitted, such students will need special support...
9. It should be the policy of government and of higher education institutions to encourage the participation of *adults* in courses of further and higher education at all levels, and to make appropriate provision for their special needs.

These recommendations have been quoted at length as a reminder since most of their recommendations and other important work in the area of access has not so far been implemented. It is not necessary to start from scratch and reinvent the policy wheel each decade. It is necessary for there to be enough political will and reallocation of resources towards supporting increased access. While some institutions have made significant advances, many others have not, and the availability of provision is variable and therefore inequitable.

The provision of 'access' courses

Perhaps the most important development has been the increase in the provision of 'access' courses, usually provided through colleges of further education. The development of access courses has become an industry in itself: they have been validated since 1989 and around 40,000 further education students were enrolled on Access to HE courses in 1996–7. The on-line Access courses database contains 1,200 entries. Open College Networks (OCNs), who act as local accreditation/awarding bodies, work together within agreed quality standards through the National Open College

Network (NOCN) and have become the largest awarding body for Schedule 2(d) courses.

Access courses are now included in the remit of the HE Quality Assurance Agency and the issue of Access Course Recognition has recently been reviewed by HEQC who have agreed to fund a modified arrangement focusing on the care and maintenance of the overall scheme through the licensing of the Authorised Validating Agencies (AVAs) which are responsible for the approval of individual Access courses and for the award of Access Certificates to students. It is now proposed that they will work to agreed national quality standards.

The coordinating work of the Access Course Recognition Group (ACRG) was until 1992 of particular importance in championing the importance of Access courses, and been continued under the HEQC. However, their positioning does raise problems of funding, standards and control. What level should they be at? Should there be national standards with an agreed currency? There is concern that they should not merely become an alternative barrier to access. One of their strengths has been the ability to develop in response to the needs of particular groups and localities, and to be matched to particular course and institutional needs. Some educators working locally tend to dismiss the need for a nationally agreed currency for access courses. While OCNS are collaborating in their accreditation within the National Open College Network, they are only beginning to operate through a shared national framework and certainly do not share a common curriculum (Wilson, 1997).

There is a real danger in the success of access courses, which is that their very existence becomes just another barrier to access. The over-organisation and accreditation of Access courses over the country as a whole brings the risk for adults that they simply become another rung on the ladder to be completed by everybody without conventional qualifications instead of A levels. This is a particular problem financially since while Access courses are fundable through the FEFC, they are not eligible for mandatory grants, and discretionary grants in many areas have largely disappeared. Most Access courses are modular and unitised and have been organised to enable part-time study under the 16-hour rule, which is now to be abolished. The original Gateway courses were, of course, also designed for part-time study, as is the Open University, and grants, therefore, although desirable for part-time study are not essential.

Understandably, the curriculum design of Access courses has been varied to meet local needs and interests, particularly for specific disadvantaged groups. However, there are a lot of study elements in common across courses. A major limitation on any broadcaster who might be interested in collaborating with an Access course initiative (as a tele-course or distance learning course) is the lack of any nationally agreed framework of curriculum content for a programme series to work to. If national broadcasters were to provide resources for one or more Access courses they would wish to work to a nationally agreed rubric and offer an open or distance learning study route with national accreditation. The National Extension College or the Open College of the Arts could be franchised to provide such distance learning Access courses.

Indeed, the Open Polytechnic and the NEC tried unsuccessfully to get approval for a nationally available distance learning Access course from the ACRG in 1990, but the approval structures all had to be locally based and to be locally delivered at that point. It is to be hoped that the new arrangements may allow for more flexible and responsive programmes and include distance learning in this.

The need for appropriate adult non-vocational qualifications

Many people have left and still leave school at 16 and wish to return to education later on in life. They need a pattern of relevant qualifications which have currency both for educators and for employers. The widespread provision of Access courses and the development of OCN networks is helpful, but these do not provide a linking or broad enough framework. What is needed is a proper and broad array of qualifications suitable for adults. 'A' levels and other school-level qualifications are not structured nor is the curriculum necessarily appropriate for adults and, for many people, does not offer an appropriate progression route.

It has been a matter of major concern to those engaged in the education of adults that the merger of SCAA and NCVQ has been carried through without any consideration of its implications for the wider educational and accreditation needs of adults. Of course, as Peter Newsam would remind us, the education industry is dominated by those with a background in school-level work. They think about adults only as an afterthought. Adults deserve a forethought as new qualifications structures are developed if lifelong learning is to become a reality. Broadcasters might then have a framework to gear their more systematic offerings to and broadcast resources could be put to increased use. These could genuinely provide a new point of access for many adults and probably help many colleges and sixth forms with resource materials as well.

Open and distance learning

The growth of open and distance learning

Using new technologies of any sort usually involves utilising some form of open and distance learning methods. The place of study is, for many learners, a matter of extreme importance. Most adult learners study part-time. Open and distance learning has proved particularly helpful in reaching part-time learners who are in work, in reaching geographically isolated students, in reaching people, mainly women, who are tied to the home, people working unsocial hours or in unsocial jobs, people in prison etc.

But it is not just a rescue mission: it is important simply because people can choose how they wish to study and fit it in with their other obligations. This flexibility is likely to be of increased importance as more adult learners need to come in and out of education and training opportunities throughout their adult lives.

The OU, for example, continues to attract many people who might otherwise go to conventional universities or colleges mainly because it offers to the learner the choice about how, when and where to learn, even if it is becoming increasingly expensive and a very demanding way to study.

Definitions and descriptions used in open and distance learning

It is sensible to clarify the terminology first. The use and acceptability of different terms has more to do with the sector of education and training using the term, and its habits and prejudices, and less to do with intrinsic differences which matter. A useful general description of open learning is:

> *Open learning describes ways of helping individuals to take advantage of their own learning. Learners may, for example, choose:*
>
> *– what they learn (content)*
> *– how they learn (methods, media, routes)*
> *– where they learn (place)*
> *– when they learn (time)*
> *– how quickly they learn (pace)*
> *– who to turn to for help*
> *– whether, when, where to have their learning assessed.*
>
> (Lewis and McDonald, 1988)

The term 'open learning' is more commonly used in further and higher education and in industry, but it is not necessarily learning 'at a distance'. What differentiates 'distance learning' and its main proponent the Open University as the foremost example of this, is that the learner is 'at a distance' from the designer/provider of the intellectual materials.

The EC memorandum on the subject simply uses the portmanteau term Open Distance Learning (Com 91–388). The EC memorandum is helpful in its extended definition.

Distance learning is defined as any form of study not under the contin-uous or immediate supervision of tutors, but which nevertheless benefits from the planning, guidance and tuition of a tutorial organisation. Distance learning has a large component of independent or autonomous learning and is therefore heavily dependent on the didactic design of mate-rials which must substitute for the interactivity available between student and teacher in ordinary face-to-face instruction. The autonomous compo-nent is invariably supported by tutoring and counselling systems which ideally are provided at regional/local study centres and to an increasing extent by modern communications media. Because open distance learning is meant to be adaptable to the pace of the student, the material is gener-ally structured in units or modules geared to specific learning outcomes
(Com 91: 388 Para 15).

The UK has become the world leader in the development of distance learning, and has similarly taken the lead in Europe in relation to 'open learning', now an EC priority. Distance and open learning techniques, as noted earlier, have proved particularly valuable for busy, mature and moti-vated adults. It is no accident that the Manpower Services Commission and the subsequent training arms of the Employment Department made it delib-erate policy to promote open learning as a valuable and economic means of training adults, funding both the Open Tech initiative and the Open College to develop new resources in order to reach new learners. The MSC/TA/ED support for open learning, coming as it did from outside the educational system, has been successful in legitimating it and embedding it in a number of, mainly large, companies as well as in many education and training insti-tutions. The view is increasingly held that it will not be possible for the UK to reach the National Training and Education Targets without the use of open and distance learning methods.

Developments have included a regularly updated Open Learning direc-tory, regular conferences attracting participants from both industry and education and training, Open Learning Resource Centres in many colleges and public libraries, and the entry into the field of a number of commercial publishers. Indeed, Pearson Professional has recently acquired the commer-cial interest in the Open College and its intellectual property. There is now an active Open Learning Federation with 450 members, 40% of whom are individual members and 60% organisations, mainly FE colleges and compa-nies.

The British Association for Open Learning has also developed rapidly with members mainly representing developers and distributors of learning materials but including FE colleges. TECs and corporate users. It is working on encouraging the use of quality assurance standards for the development and use of open learning. The picture among Training and Enterprise Councils (TECs) is more varied: with their local remits, they have less incen-tive to collaborate in the provision and use of resources. However, several

TECs have developed their own resource centres mainly aimed at small and medium-sized enterprises and other local employers.

Open, distance and flexible learning have more recently been given a boost by the new FEFC funding arrangements which provide the same unit of resource for such learning as for conventionally taught programmes. Many colleges now have open learning centres, providing flexible access to learning support. Increasingly employers are also providing such centres, sometimes staffed by their local FE college. The Employment Department, now merged into the DfEE, has been encouraging the development of open learning centres in public libraries.

A number of colleges have successfully undertaken innovative developments in the delivery of computer-based learning, including Halton College which has developed its own multi-media production facilities. Other examples are Wirral Metropolitan College which has combined network-delivered resources with practical workshop activity, Skelmersdale College which is supporting large numbers of adult students studying at a distance for an IT vocational qualification and Luton Sixth Form College which has established computer-based learning resource centres and electronic self-testing for GNVQ students.

At school level, 'flexible learning' and 'supported self-study' are terms more commonly used and found acceptable by school-teachers. In particular, the Employment Department funded TVEI initiative in schools used the term 'flexible learning'. TVEI money was often used to fund the development of IT in schools which was often associated with the use of flexible learning.

Development and diversification

After reviewing the distinctive experience of the Open University Naomi goes on to consider lessons from other open and distance learning initiatives:

The saving of resources with using the media comes...from delivering one centrally produced message. The message can be personalised in a number of ways, though the more this is done, the more it may cost. Options for personalising messages include face-to-face contact, phone, telex, audio-cassette, post, fax and electronic mail. New technologies have assisted in the development of new and more flexible forms of ODL, involving greater use of these more 'personal media'. They enable individual contact between tutors and students and also between students and other students. At the same time these trends move more of the cost of access away from the providing institution and on to the learner.

Another key variable is the course of study. Switching from 'ways of learning' to 'courses of study' focuses on whether the goal is to make exiting courses available to 'new' students, or to produce new courses for existing students or both. To complete the analysis satisfactorily, it is necessary to develop a multi-dimensional matrix across a number of characteristics of learning systems, noting 'newness' or not of the characteristics, and the objectives to be achieved. 'New' students can, of course, be of different sorts: women returners, employees at work, minority ethnic groups, those with basic skills needs and so on. Some delivery systems are more suitable for some groups than others. This diversification matrix provides a helpful framework against which to consider the rationale for and criteria of success of previous innovative developments in the UK. Apart from the use of new media within existing institutions, there are and have already been a number of 'new' institutions set up aiming to use new technologies or make better use of existing technologies: the main ones reviewed here are the OU, the Open College, the Open Tech, the Open Learning Foundation and the National Extension College.

Learning characteristics	Existing/new	Objective
Types of students Course materials Delivery systems Location of learning Learning of support Qualifications Accreditation		

Figure 4: Characteristics of learning systems

Learning from other initiatives: competition or collaboration

There are lessons to be learnt from the experience of these previous initiatives which are of help in the planning of any major new national initiative or network.

A number of questions may be asked about previous and current projects:

- Who is/was it aimed at?
- What were its original objectives, and how did it expect to fulfil them?
- What qualifications did/does it offer, if any?
- What types of materials and delivery mechanisms did it use?
- How is/was it funded?
- How is its quality rated?
- How does it relate to existing institutions?
- What has hindered its progress?
- What useful lessons can be learnt from its experience?

Using technology, whether for networking or for the delivery of distance learning, is expensive up-front and requires investment in both software and hardware. This usually requires the justification of reaching large numbers, as with the OU, or collaboration between institutions as with the Open Learning Foundation (OLF). The financial burden can also be spread, and the risk shared, through commercial production or through partnerships, both of which enable larger groups to be served cost-effectively, since resources can be bought in small amounts by individual institutions. However, current structures are designed to encourage competition rather than collaboration.

The other relevant trends are towards down-sizing and outsourcing, combined with the principle of individuals purchasing services from providers. The tension between these options is not assisted by the well-known 'not invented here' syndrome which prevents many academics using other institutions' course materials, no matter how good or cheap.

The Open Learning Foundation: a model of collaboration

The Open Learning Foundation (originally the Open Polytechnic) has set itself to work collaboratively. Although some individual polytechnics had involved themselves in open learning over the decade, sometimes as a result of Open Tech projects, many had not, nor was there any network of collaboration between those that did – if anything, there was competition. At the same time an increasing number of polytechnic staff were being commissioned by the OU to write course materials, particularly as the OU started to expand into areas such as Management and Business Studies, areas which had previously been polytechnic territory. Many polytechnics already housed OU Study Centres and also provided many of its part-time tutors. While to some this looked like symbiosis, to others it looked like exploitation, and within this lay some of the seeds of the idea of the Open Polytechnic, set up in 1990. What is surprising is that the ex-Polytechnic sector did not make such a move many years earlier – previous attempts had mainly foundered on competitiveness between institutions. After all, many polytechnics have been in the forefront of innovation in curriculum and access terms and also have available a wide array of audio-visual resources.

The Open Polytechnic was not set up to be a new institution registering its own students but a consortium of 21 members of the sector who had agreed to work together to 'harness existing resources to reach very large numbers of students'. Initial capital was provided by subscriptions from each member entitling them to have access to its services and materials at members' rates. The blueprint emphasised high-quality, mixed-mode opportunities, the opening up of access, opportunities for staff development as well as, more pragmatically, opportunities for cost-cutting and income generation. The strategy was to provide course resources, mainly print, for staff to choose to use in their teaching, rather than for students to choose to use for independent learning (Sargant, 1991).

It now has nearly 30 members giving it the potential of reaching some 400,000 students though its materials are not yet very widely used. Its main content areas include business studies, management, hospitality studies, social work, engineering and health and nursing. But it is a teaching staff- led rather than a learner-led model, and is effectively more like a publishing house. It offers its members access to a wide range of learning materials at preferential rates. It has been sufficiently successful in selling materials and raising additional co-production resources to halve the members' regular subscriptions from the initial £25,000, but the adequacy of the costing mechanisms and pay-back systems is still not clear.

What it does offer to its members is participation in the development of materials, including nominating authors and editors from among the member institutions' own staff. Though this adds to development time, the gain in terms of acceptability and transferability to other members is very significant and overcomes some of the difficulties the Open Tech initiative experienced. It is increasingly assisting its members in the development of their own learning materials, often on a paid consultancy basis.

The OLF is basically a publisher/provider of degree-level independent learning resources, and many of these are likely to be suitable for further education and for work-related learning outside education institutions. Some areas have been developed in collaboration with professional bodies, e.g. Health Services Management and Social Work and there is an increasing overlap in the vocational and professional areas between higher and further education.

It has not made the use of new (or older) technologies a priority, and most of its courses are print-based, though they are mainly distributed on disc under licence rather than in print. An interesting development is the piloting of the distribution of materials on electronic networks and on-demand electronic publishing. It does not register or teach students: this is done through member organisations. However, its aim continues to be to increase access and serve a more diverse learner clientele. Its course materials fit within the HE CATS framework. It is now arranging for independent credit rating of its learning materials where appropriate, so that they can be used by individual learners, e.g. for continuing professional development (CPD).

In conclusion, the proposal which found favour among peers in polytechnics was not to set up a new competitive institution, but to set up a consortium of polytechnics to collaborate to produce new learning resources to assist existing polytechnics and colleges to teach existing students in new, more flexible and economic ways (see Figure 5). The emphasis was less on access than on the efficient and cost-effective management of teaching. However, using new resources to deliver learning is likely to, as a next stage, enable new courses to be developed and should also open up access to new learners.

This could well be a sensible route for the FE system to take. There are a number of areas where high quality learning resources could be developed for use nationally: basic skills materials, ESOL, business studies and accountancy, for example, and there are significant materials already available at this level from other open learning providers such as the Open College or the National Extension College which could be bought in bulk for a network at this level.

Existing students Existing resources	Existing students New resources
New students Existing resources	New students New resources

Figure 5: New resources for increased access

The Open Tech Programme: a funding mechanism

Two other 80s initiatives are particularly relevant for further education, as they were both expected to use media and their goals are still current priorities. The first, The Open Tech Programme, was primarily a funding initiative rather than an institution, and the second, the Open College, was again a free-standing institution aimed at using broadcasting and at being a lower-level vocational analogue to the OU.

Jim Prior, as Secretary of State for Employment, had been interested in setting up an analogue to the OU 'to meet adult training and retraining needs at technician and related levels', and after the publication of a consultation document in May 1981, a Task Group was set up to plan what was to be called *The Open Tech Programme* (MSC, 1981). It was not to be a new institution, but a 'planned and co-ordinated range of commissioned projects'. The programme was described as having two key tasks:

- to open or widen access to existing training provision
- to make new education and training provision which from the beginning can best be met through open learning.

It was to focus primarily on technical and supervisory skills as this was regarded as a key area for economic growth. It was not set up as a new institution but as a **funding mechanism** which aimed to encourage the development of open learning materials to be widely available across the country, building on local expertise in the training and technical field. The programme was to be funded for a limited period of four years, launched in August 1982 and to end in March 1987. The programme had a total government budget of £45 million, which was used to support a wide variety of open/distance learning projects primarily concerned with adult technical training, 80% of the funds being allocated to technical projects, and 20% to supervisory and management training. The programme was designed to build upon existing resources and not establish new competitive institutions. The needs of the learner were to be regarded as central: the system must adapt to the learner rather than vice versa.

Money was provided centrally by the MSC to fund these locally developed open learning initiatives, but they were not controlled within an overall intellectual, curriculum content and quality framework. Yeats, in an assessment of the scheme, describes it in these words:

> OTP *is a decentralised project system. It involves the development of a wide range of materials, delivery, support and practical 'hands on' projects by a large number of contracted bodies.*

It is difficult for any such project to ascertain what are the most relevant current and future training needs. Manpower forecasts available were considered too broad and general. The shortage of information, Yeats notes, led economists in the Training Services division of MSC to advise (in a somewhat defeatist way!):

> *The best way into the problem of determining what needs for supervisory or technician training exist and what their nature may be is probably to follow up and examine more closely the needs signalled in submissions for* OTP (MSC, 1982:16).

Its programme objectives as described are virtually identical to those of the proposed University for Industry and several also relate closely to the role of further education if the national NTETs targets are to be achieved. Yeats records five objectives:

a. Meeting the needs of changing labour market demands
b. Meeting the employment needs and aspirations of individuals
c. Responding to technological change and innovation
d. Applying and demonstrating the role of open learning in vocational education and training
e. Increasing the flexibility of the education and training system

The lack of a defining national framework appears to have been deliberate. Yeats notes that: 'It is difficult to say exactly what has been achieved so far...no agreement exists as to what constitutes a learning unit, or even a learning hour of student time'. Most surprising, and markedly different to the present day, was the virtual lack of any attention paid to the issue of qualifications. Not until April 1985 was a Working Group established to enquire into the current situation regarding vocational qualifications. When it reported in April 1986, its main recommendation was that the Government should establish a National Council for Vocational Qualifications (NCVQ).

The absence of a national framework of standards and accreditation meant that course materials were not readily accepted by others as transferable and usable in other places and situations. Indeed, it appeared to be policy for them NOT to be national in their goals – a policy which caused both their chiefs in turn to refuse the free offer of supporting national broadcasting made to them by the newly set up Channel 4.

As the Open Tech was set up as a 'temporary system', projects were given three-year funding and were then expected to become self-sustaining based 'on the assumption that adults retraining through the Open Tech Programme would have to pay for their own self improvement' (Ainley and Corney, 1990).

As with further education, the Open Tech was also given a social objective, that all OTP projects should be fully available to members of 'special groups' – the unemployed, the disabled, ethnic minorities and women. In the event, only seven projects aimed, for example, at the unemployed. When projects have to survive in a competitive market, Yeats notes, it will be difficult for such 'special groups' to take advantage of the new training opportunities offered without additional financial help.

Projects funded were of three main types: materials development projects, delivery projects, and support projects, e.g. in staff training, marketing, information supply (MARIS) and evaluation and these were considered an important factor in its early success. For example, many people involved in materials production were inexperienced in distance learning techniques and in the operational aspects of open learning projects and the Open Tech Training and Support Unit provided such support. A similar need for such staff training has been experienced by the Open Learning Foundation.

The vast majority, 120 out of the 140 projects funded, were for materials development with much less emphasis on their marketing, delivery and learning support. There was evidence that many projects had little or no idea as to how they would deliver their materials after they had produced them.

Yeats identifies a number of relevant effects. The project suffered from its short programme life. It was more difficult to get projects going in industry and education got in earlier, with 61% of the money going to education and 23% to industry. The degree of collaboration between the two was disappointing. The hoped-for effects of encouraging the industrial sector to take more responsibility for the education and training of workers was only partly achieved.

More specific problems on the industry side noted were possible difficulties with industrial relations in setting up an open learning unit, the issue of the cost effectiveness of open learning, the difficulty of companies collaborating in areas where they would normally compete, and an 'access' issue of how open a company can be to non-employees.

Though technology was regarded as central to the project, this turned out to be observed more in theory than in practice, as with the refusal to use national broadcasting. In the event print continued to be the most important medium, as it has been with the OLE. 'The technology is being emphasised and used more because it is available, rather than for any proven pedagogical superiority' (Yeats). His report also raises the important issue of adequate access to centres for practical skills training and assessment provision.

At the same time, however, the MSC did set up an in-house Learning Technology Unit in parallel to the Open Tech Programme which supported a number of developments of computer-based learning, including Project Author. The unit's work provided training for a new generation of computer-based training designers and authors who contributed to the establishment and growth of many CBT companies in the 1980s. The unit saw itself as encouraging the development of leading edge applications, some of which sadly did not get beyond the blueprint stage, but several did produce significant outcomes which influenced the design and approach taken by later producers of CBT.

A small number of specific Open Tech projects have survived and been the origin of, for example, the Cleveland Open Learning Unit and the Birmingham Open Learning Development Unit, but a lot sank without trace, and many institutions, it is claimed, simply took the money and ran. However, the current network of learning producers and distributors contains many individuals who developed their skills working on Open Tech projects. Some Open Tech projects re-emerged alongside other new initiatives, such as the Open Learning Foundation.

The Open Tech Programme has been considered in some detail since its objectives are still relevant to further education and it offers an alternative strategy for change. It has not generated much in the way of lasting materials, but it has resulted in a larger number of people with skills and experience developing and delivering open learning materials, many of them working in the FE sector. It did not, however, focus adequately on delivery to learners.

It is possible that such an initiative, given the more general acceptance of open learning and the slow, but increasing, coherence of national vocational qualifications might now have a better chance of succeeding. Arguably, it was in advance of its time. Its impetus, presumably, was to allow local ownership of more modestly produced materials than the OU's and to avoid the 'not invented here' syndrome. However, the Catch 22 is that economy in developing such resources only arises from their use with large numbers of learners and requires transferability of credit/accreditation. It did, therefore, have built-in seeds of failure and few materials were used elsewhere.

To set up a model of this sort for further education would require much tighter control of commissioning, of curriculum, assessment, quality and accreditation to ensure transferability of materials and of qualifications and credit. It would also be useful for modest cost initiatives in, say, one TEC or in a group of linked TEC areas, particularly where a cable network or a regional ITV company might be interested in collaborating.

The Open College: a new institution

In 1986 the Training Agency, supported by the Department of Employment, made another serious attempt to use the media to enhance education and training opportunities specifically at further education level. Just as the OU was set up to make alternative provision for higher (degree-level) education, the Open College was originally planned to make the 'curriculum of a good FE college' available to adults who needed to bridge the 16–19 level gap, and thereby to make a contribution to updating and re-skilling the adult population, including, importantly, the unemployed.

Subsidiary goals were to simplify the maze of overlapping vocational qualifications, modernise the apprenticeship system and encourage credit accumulation and transfer systems. Funding was to come from the Employment Department.

Airtime for the main broadcast component had again been offered by Channel 4 – at lunchtime across the weekdays – a time slot which was good for the unemployed and offered an interesting opportunity to work with employers and unions in new workplace-based study opportunities. Colleges would also be able to video-record programmes to add to their bank of learning resources at minimum cost, as well as running some daytime courses.

Government priorities at the time were to over-ride those plans and it determined that the Open College should not try to reach the unemployed, but only deliver vocational education and training to those already in work. This removed at a stroke the rationale for Channel 4's offer of the lunchtime slot, and also removed the numerical justification of large numbers of the unemployed, thus making it impossible to meet the College's original targets, and limiting its potential usefulness. In a similar decision, the government ruled out the provision of GCSE courses, which the OC's own market research had shown was the qualification most recognised and desired by adults and which OC management considered would be a 'comfortable and fruitful' area for investment as it would also attract adults as parents.

Research showed that the Channel 4 broadcasting was initially very effective in raising the level of awareness of the Open College and in stimulating people to seek out Open College learning centres which were located mainly in further education colleges. The timetable had allowed 15 months from start of planning to going on air, but some months were lost getting staff in post. The initial array of courses available was, inevitably, thin and many students who had been stimulated by television to enquire at colleges were seeking courses the OC did not provide. There was also apocryphal evidence of some colleges who simply enrolled the enquiring students on their own courses rather than directing them on to OC courses. Numbers were slow to build up but, two years in, David Grugeon reports that over 30,000 had been recruited through OC Gateway Centres and a further 10,000 through the Open College's (subsequently set up) direct recruitment agency.

The exclusion of the unemployed had not only reduced the numbers available to be reached, but also precluded the use of existing general educational programming material for adults, which Channel 4 had offered the OC as a form of additional subsidy. A further negative factor affecting broadcasting was the tightness of the rules concerning sponsorship of broadcast programmes, and the unexpected unavailability of sponsorship money.

Four years in, after a Government-required review of the College, funding for the broadcast element was withdrawn and the main broadcasting element on Channel 4 ceased, though some other audio-visual support for courses continues. The Government continued to 'capitalise' the college for a further three years during which time it invested heavily in the production of new course materials for onward sales essentially as a publishing house. In 1992, the College made a further, though unsuccessful, bid to the Employment Department for broadcasting time, but to use it for marketing open learning activities and opportunities.

Concentrating on the commissioning and development of high quality open learning materials, the OC succeeded in re-establishing itself as a provider of learning resources and support rather than as a College in the conventional sense and is now a substantial business. It has focused successfully on the corporate market and is a major provider to several blue-chip companies. It delivers a whole range of programmes to public and private organisations in the technical, management and health-care field, and by 1996 was providing open/flexible learning to about 2,000 workplace learners in 152 programmes through 61 different employers. It has 63 part-time, Open College-trained tutors. Almost all of its course materials lead to national accreditation, 20% of which is straight NVQ-based, with the balance leading to traditional qualifications.

It is also now a sizeable publishing house of open and flexible learning material (OFL), probably the second largest after the OU, and probably the largest supplier of OFL to the FE and HE sectors for their own use. 66,757 modules of OC OFL materials had been sold since the start of 1995, and this will increase to 80,000 modules by the end of 1996. Materials have been bought by 560-odd customers, of whom 150 are regular buyers and are providers of OFL training themselves, either HE, FE or 'other providers'. Materials can be bought, used under licence or franchise. TECs and companies make them available through Open Learning Centres, for example. In this way, it is likely that about another 16,000 learners are being tutored and supported by other institutions using Open College materials.

Publishing revenue is now about a quarter of total revenue of £4–5 million. Open learning materials are available for Supervision, Management, Portfolio Development, Training for Trainers and Work Skills and Health and Care and others. Its new nursing materials are to be endorsed by the

Royal College of Nursing (RCN). The latest news of its future is that the College's commercial operation has been bought up by Pearson Professional and been separated from its public sector originated charitable foundation – a version of delayed privatisation!

As with FE colleges, the Open College was not set up with its own accreditation powers, and this was seen earlier on to be a limitation not experienced by the polytechnics or the OU. It now chooses to provide course materials for a wide variety of qualifications and their validating bodies, e.g. EdExcel, City & Guilds and RSA. Its experience has been that different companies/industries are specific in their requirements for, and loyalty to, particular qualifications and the college could better serve people by offering a range of qualifications. As a national body, it could have chosen to be an NVQ Awarding Body, but decided against it for the reason given above. However, it is also now linking to the Oxford University Delegacy for local exams for some accreditation purposes.

Since government subsidy was withdrawn, the College has been able to operate completely independently, building up to a turnover of approaching £4 million a year, some 56,000 learners will have used College developed OFL materials, and over 350,000 modules of materials have been sold. It has run until now as a company limited by guarantee, though it did not make its Annual Report available. Its former Chief Executive commented that it was operating in a very competitive market.

The reputation of the Open College still suffers from its early difficulties; it has been much more successful than most people realise and provides some key lessons for a future structure, as well as being a source of existing materials. Though its work with larger corporate users is encouraging, it has had to target the most efficient means of being self-funding. Whilst it does not have large numbers of SME users or independent learners directly registered with it, these categories have benefited from using its materials through other sources such as FE colleges and TECs, who are both currently considering new ways of reaching SMEs.

A major problem is the confusing plethora of qualifications at FE level which are not as 'desirable' or easily saleable as a degree. Despite good, systematic use of market research to aid its planning, the OC's experience has been that there are few content areas which generate a demand for more than 3,500 copies of a course. These numbers do not bode well for colleges, even in collaboration.

The assessment of competence-based qualifications presents particular difficulties with open and distance learning. With the development of NVQs, the Open College has spent '*considerable resource on the implementation of competence-based programmes and has developed a specific niche in helping organisations to implement standards for staff to obtain associated units and components of NVQs.*' John Trasler, its MD, suggests that its strength lies in helping organisations to implement some of the national training targets by devising non-bureaucratic systems which meet the needs both of business and individuals.

There is much to be learnt from the OC's experience, particularly in its use of open and distance learning and its commissioning and quality control of courses. There should be ways in which further education could make better use of its existing courses and perhaps develop appropriate partnerships to commission and deliver new courses, though the OC's new commercial status may make this more difficult.

Colleges are particularly well-placed to provide learning support for open and distance learners. Initially with the Open College there were real problems of competition with colleges enrolling potential OC students in their own programmes. However, as the NEC has shown with its various schemes with colleges, there are possible methods of collaboration which benefit both sides.

John Trasler, who remains its Managing Director, offers the following OC up-date:

> *The recognition of its success in the corporate training market was shown by its acquisition by Pearson plc in February 1997. The Open College Ltd still focuses on business-driven training and development and now has access to a wider range of intellectual copyright and investment for new material. It has continued to develop open learning, investing in an Internet capability and delivery of learning by such media.*
>
> *The Open College's new commercial status is not in reality any different from the position it has occupied for the last five years and there are many ways in which its material could be used in the further education and SME sectors. In conjunction with Pearson Professional companies, it is also keen to support and promote the University for Industry.*

The National Extension College: a partnership model

NEC is an independent, non-profit-making distance learning college, originally set up by Michael Young (Lord Young of Dartington) in 1963. Michael Young appears to be the first person to have used the term 'open university' in an article in *Where* magazine in 1962 in which he proposed an 'open university' to prepare people for external degrees of London University, many of whom were receiving poor teaching from private correspondence colleges. In referring to such overseas experience as the Soviet Correspondence Colleges and educational television in the US, he proposed the need for a National Extension College to act as the nucleus of an 'open university' with three main functions: to organise new and better correspondence courses for the external degree, to promote lectures and residential schools (working through the extra-mural departments of London and other universities), and to teach by means of television.

NEC is constituted as a Company Limited by Guarantee and, while surviving a number of financial vicissitudes, has managed without any regular grants or subsidy all its life. It was determined to be more ethical than the private correspondence colleges of those years who were renowned for making their money, as Colmans, from the mustard left on the side of the plate, i.e. the learners who paid their fees in advance and then dropped out without completing their course.

Its materials are extremely high quality and are widely used in school and colleges. They are available as courses, as flexible resources or through the purchase of a photocopying licence. It offers a personal tutorial service for its distance learners as part of its package, including assessment arrangements with appropriate examination authorities.

NEC currently provides over 150 courses with personal support through distance learning. Over 15,000 adults enrol each year, either to gain new skills or qualifications or to boost confidence or career opportunities. NEC estimates that nearly 400,000 students have enrolled with it since it was set up in 1963.

In 1995, 80% of students were enrolled on basic or academic and general education courses, 15% on vocational courses, mainly NVQ or equivalent, and 5% on degree, Engineering Council or Institute of Linguist qualifications through directed private study. In addition, it provides a personal tutorial service for London External Degrees.

The majority of its work is for adults, at FE or schools examination level. It has a broad portfolio of courses for adults who want to catch up on previously missed chances from basic skills to GCSE and A levels. It also has an increasing vocational and professional portfolio. As the Open College, much of its business is as a publishing house, selling particularly to FE colleges. It sold over 30,000 packs in 1995, 50% of which were academic and general education, 15% were basic education, 12% were languages, 6% training materials for staff development and 17% NVQ-related materials in Accounting, Administration and Care. In addition, it provides a personal tutorial service for London University External degrees.

It works with other education providers and advisory services to assist progression and accreditation. It also works with major employers such as Ford, Lucas, BT, Mercury, Cable & Wireless, the Post Office and the Stock Exchange. NEC notes that employers are becoming more active in sponsoring learners, either through group schemes or in response to an individual's request to take a course. It has recently set up an exciting new in-company training scheme for Coca-Cola Schweppes to enable school-leavers to obtain a degree in Management while pursuing a full-time career in merchandising. The degree element of the scheme has been set up as an open learning scheme through NEC and Bradford University.

Its array of course materials are clearly of interest to further education, together with its capacity for developing independent learning materials. In 1994, it set up a pilot project with a group of 12 FE colleges to explore the possibilities of a partnership arrangement which would enable the FE colleges to offer NEC's distance learning courses to their students. Called the CoNECt (Colleges and NEC together) scheme, it provides a cost-effective way for colleges to extend their curriculum offer to students and enable them to enrol those individuals who are not able to study on-site. It means they can offer more flexible modes of delivery and offer options for year-round enrolment and self-pacing study. The scheme means that each college does not have to keep its course materials updated for its students, or establish the complex administrative and computer systems necessary to enrol and monitor distance learning students or recruit and train distance learning tutors in all subject areas. Colleges provide pre-entry advice and guidance, access to non-tutorial learner support and study facilities, and assessment and examination processes.

It is starting to produce its materials in multi-media formats as well as print. It provides a competent and conscientious personal tutorial service and research shows a high degree of loyalty and repeat purchase among its learners. It could provide an independent learning tutorial service for a network. It has a strong track record of innovation, providing both courses for independent learners with tutorial support and also a wide variety of open learning resources for institutions. Most important is that, as the Open College does, it works to much lower cost levels and to much faster timescales than the OU.

General lessons of previous relevant initiatives

This brief survey of previous initiatives highlights their similarities and differences and some of their strengths and weaknesses. What is clear is that working at further education and often vocational levels provides a greater challenge for open and distance learning since there is a greater variety of qualifications and a greater need for workplace relevance and delivery to new clienteles and to new milieux.

There are some recurring issues which any new project will also face:

- it is difficult to ascertain/research the most relevant current and future training needs, to discover where the numbers justify using technologies
- using technology requires a longer lead-time and guaranteed funding. 'Short-term' money or money with strings has caused problems with previous projects
- there is a need for a unified national framework of qualifications to ensure quality and transferability of credit
- along with this is the need for proper accreditation systems
- the need for staff development: for materials production and for running open learning operations
- the need for ownership of materials and the 'not invented here' syndrome militate against collaboration

- the appropriateness and availability of new technologies. Despite the apparent promises of new technology, print/post continues to be the most important technology of delivery
- increasing competition between providers.

For learners:

- the provision of independent guidance
- the need for learning support and individualised tutorial support
- the sense of being in a community
- guaranteed quality and coherence of the system.

For companies:

- the cost-effectiveness of open learning
- difficulties of companies collaborating instead of competing
- companies offering access to people outside their company
- companies providing time-off from work for study.

There are some benefits that have been derived from these initiatives:

- increased knowledge in the country of the usefulness of open and distance learning
- a sizeable array of existing materials, though more are needed
- an increasing amount of experience and expertise in the production and delivery of materials.

It is obviously desirable to make use of existing open/distance learning resources, particularly when they have been developed through public investment. Ideally, such materials would require clear 'quality' labelling and their appropriate credit rating. The scale of this task and its cost, for new products let alone existing ones, are high, as BAOL discovered when it considered the quality labelling of open learning materials.

There is increasingly convergence between further and higher education, particularly in professional and updating courses, and the navigation routes through materials must be clearly identifiable for learners together with appropriate guidance mechanisms.

Since a main goal of lifelong learning is to increase the nation's competitiveness and the main area of expansion is likely to be through further education, it is not surprising that the goals of the proposed UFI are very similar both to those of the Open Tech Programme and to the Open College. The Open Tech fell down through lack of an overall framework of control. The Open College is more of a publishing house than a college, and is now clearly following a commercial route. The National Extension College is a modest analogue of the Open University operating mainly at FE and vocational level, but without adequate funding for major expansion or for social subsidy.

Neither the Open College nor the Open Tech were able or allowed to try to reach the unemployed, which the OU with its subsidised undergraduate fees and Student Hardship funds has been able to do in larger numbers. Neither have any of the structures succeeded well in reaching employees of SMEs.

The purpose of this section has been to review experience of national media-based post-school initiatives to inform a discussion about the desirability of having some national framework or organisation, using broadcasting or other appropriate telecommunications, for the delivery and support of media and technology-based open and distance learning in order to encourage access, motivation and flexibility of offering.

Reaching learners through institutions or learners at home

'Closed' and 'open' target groups of learners

A helpful distinction in talking about the use of the media for adult learning is to distinguish between learners in institutions, usually taught in groups or independent learners, often learning at home: either 'closed' target groups or 'open' audiences. Further and higher education and training is usually aiming at 'closed' or known target groups as distinct from broadcasting which is often speaking to an 'open' audience potentially of independent learners. College students will usually use the media offered in a 'closed' or known and controlled learning situation. The material is usually curriculum-led, and often mediated by a tutor, trainer or teacher. This is, of course, also the predominant model in schools, and may be appropriate for sections of youth and adult training. The material may be offered directly to the learner as, for example, multi-media or most broadcast programmes, or it may be designed to be mediated in some way by tutors or teachers. Schools and Open University programmes are examples of this.

Closed and Direct	Closed and Mediated
e.g. Multi-media	e.g. BBC/Channel 4 Schools, Open University
Open and Direct	Open and Mediated
e.g. To learners direct at home	e.g. To learners at home but with access to tutors e.g. literacy and numeracy campaigns

Figure 6: Target groups of learners

Apart from offering the possibility of facilitation face-to-face by a tutor, institutions are also likely to be able to provide access to higher levels of technological equipment and resources than many home learners have.

Given the differing timescales for development of the new technologies and their domestic availability, it is helpful to look at options/scenarios for the short to medium term, say, three years ahead, and for the longer term (say, post-2005). Some of the issues facing institutions in particular are:

- Why is the potential of the electronic media not fully realised?
- Are we making the best use of existing resources? If not, why not?
- How do we train learners and teachers to use the technology?
- How do we help lecturers/teachers and trainers to change to become facilitators and mentors?
- What can be done to improve links between different media?
- Who is going to invest in making the programmes/software?
- How will the money flow? How can we create an efficient market? Will it be a public or private market?
- Who will own the intellectual property?
- What will be the role of public provision, public service broadcasting and libraries, and what will be private?

Horses for courses

Technology is value-free: it is simply a delivery system. One piece of technology is not intrinsically better for education or training than any other piece of technology. The question which must be asked each time is: is this the best piece of technology for the task in hand? The answer will depend on the target group, the nature of the content, the characteristics of the medium and the cost. It is vital to differentiate.

Some of the resistance to new technology has come from disappointed educators using a particular technology which was not suited to the task in view. A continuing problem has been the temptation to allow the availability of new technology to lead the project rather than the educational task. The Internet is at risk of being seen as the latest fashionable example of this tendency.

Pressure for the introduction of new technology has often come from commercial producers, both of hardware and software, or from governmental initiatives rather than from educators. There is a lot of equipment and production capacity sitting in colleges and universities which is not used effectively or enough.

Electronic/media-based learning represents a threat to the educational establishment

Educational establishments are not themselves learning but teaching institutions. Most educators have been taught face-to-face, they have been taught how to teach face-to-face, and now teach face-to-face. Many teachers are threatened by the new media as they have not been trained in its use, it denies the raison d'être of their training and may make them feel professionally inadequate. They also fear it may do them out of jobs.

Institutional structures have been created over many years to control the delivery of education and training and have held a monopoly of it. New media start to break down this monopoly. A similar process has started in broadcasting, with the disaggregation of commissioning from production and transmission, and the arrival of more choice through video, satellite and cable.

Technology does not usually function on its own

Electronically-delivered learning materials usually require some mediation. Much headway has, for example, been made in facilitating the onward educational use of broadcasting. In the educational marketplace this need will become even greater. In the US, for example, there is now a Certificate in TeleTeaching: for people who assist learners in their use of electronically-delivered education. The catch is obvious: the more personal assistance that is provided, the greater the reduction in cost-effectiveness. Using the media should not be seen as a cheap alternative to face-to-face teaching and therefore as a means of axing teachers.

Can we learn from industry?

IT and telecommunications have already had a major impact on industry. Just as the electronic office has reconfigured commerce, so it is (ultimately) likely to reconfigure education. It is this reconfiguration which is at the same time exciting and threatening.

Investment in industry is market-led. Investment in most education and training is not. The user-pays principle does not yet operate. Introducing the user-pays principle into education creates hostility, and not without some reason. We have traditionally treated education as 'free at the point of use'. To charge for it introduces a major barrier to access.

Most public sector education and training is not yet aware of the costs involved in using electronic media for education and training. This ignorance has not been helped by the strategies utilised by the private sector to encourage education into the market. For example, a commercial international database will offer a university six months' free access. After this, the institution has to start paying for the subscription, as well as for ad hoc use. More problems arise if payment is on an institution-wide basis, and the databases are more useful to some departments than others. If individual departments are paying, as they may be, for example, for satellite dishes, they may well not be prepared to let other departments in.

The ownership of intellectual property

Traditionally, academic knowledge has been in the public domain, available in research papers, journals and in books reasonably up-to-date, reasonably accessible and reasonably cheap to produce. Much new 'knowledge' is passing into the private domain, partly because research is to be funded increasingly by sponsorship from private companies and partly because of government-encouraged private investment in the ownership of intellectual property and its storage in privately owned electronic databases. Even when databases remain in public ownership, the additional cost of the electronic storage, the reception equipment and the royalty and telephone line charges becomes too high for some potential users.

Current Government policy in the UK for example, is that the delivery of training should be organised through local Training & Enterprise Councils (TECs), which are run as private companies, with boards mainly composed of local industrialists rather than educators or the public sector. This is a cause for concern as it may mean that intellectual developments in the training area also move out of the public domain into the private domain. Contracting out of training by TECs has also led to competition between private providers and local colleges for training business.

It costs money and takes time and professional expertise to develop a multi-media CD-ROM. This involves production and design expertise and commercial investment and often takes the product out of the public domain and into private ownership and control. However, a number of partnerships have been established between commercial producers and colleges and universities to develop multi-media and other learning materials, which bring together the requisite technical and learning expertise.

Broadcasters are also moving into the multi-media business, since it is often desirable to incorporate existing broadcast/video material in a multi-media project. Reports indicate that while there is a reasonable market for multi-media at school level, where the number of establishments is quite large, the market at FE level is not as developed. Of course, the use of TV material in multi-media raises copyright issues, as does the question of the ability to re-edit materials.

Increasing pressure to distinguish between open education and closed training

Increasingly some people are arguing for the proposition that 'open' education for adults should continue to go out on broadcast channels, and 'closed' education and training, which employers are prepared to pay to deliver and employees are prepared to pay to receive, can go out on subscription channels. Of course, electronic media have been employed in large organisations for much of the last two decades to deliver training. This is largely because training can be closely defined and has clear objectives which makes it suitable for electronic delivery. However, there is also only a limited amount of time on terrestrial broadcast channels which can be used to deliver education free at the point of use. Terrestrial broadcasting has been increasingly deregulated and is, as a result, increasingly competitive. There are no longer any educational obligations placed on ITV as a result of the 1990 Broadcasting Act. 'Open education for adults' is only held in place on Channel 4 and the BBC through the tradition of public-service broadcasting and its regulation.

A major concern about digital terrestrial television is that the attempt to require the 1996 Broadcasting Act to place education and other public service obligations on the new channels failed, so that there are no new educational requirements being made of digital terrestrial television, nor has the successful consortium (BDB) made any commitment to educational programming at all. This is ironic considering the all-party agreement on the importance of lifelong learning, and the additional interactive and data-broadcasting facilities which digital television will provide. There is clear evidence from North America that bespoke satellite channels for education and training are needed and used, and there is no reason why similar provision, delivered through either terrestrial or satellite broadcasting, would not be valued and effective in the UK.

Deregulation and the competition for audience ratings means that there is an increasing tendency to reduce the educational component of broadcasting, particularly difficult areas with little popular appeal. The trouble is that it is the voiceless – the poor, the unemployed, the elderly and undereducated – who are likely to rely more on broadcasting. The other important group for whom cable is not an alternative are people living in rural areas. The responsibility for providing such broadcasting should be made clear by Parliament. The user-pays principle is not appropriate.

Why is the potential of educational broadcasting and other electronic media not realised?

Not enough is known about the effectiveness of educational television. This is ridiculous since many appropriate research techniques are available and are in regular use for measuring that effectiveness of advertising. It has been suggested that 'little attention had ever been paid to its effectiveness because it has no price tag attached to it!' There could and should be high quality research carried out to demonstrate its real effectiveness. However, some cynics have argued such research will only be commissioned when there is a real market in educational provisional and people are paying for it directly.

Industry, in particular, would like to know how the different technologies work, for what purposes, at what costs. Of course, further and higher education also need to know this! Will for example, an electronic campus be cost-effective? Will student residences need to be wired. Do all people learn equally from different media?

What are the forces for change?

The learners of the future will be a great force for change. Children are already growing up it an electronic-rich environment at home. It is children who programme videos, play computer games, have computer smartcards. Forty-five per cent of large families with children now own personal computers. It is parents and teachers who lag behind and lack confidence.

The problem with the education industry is that it has been isolated from telematic changes in industry and from the outside world. It has also been starved by Government of funds for such developments. Many teachers have therefore been cut off from today's technology and reject it because they are fearful of it. Recent research shows many FE teachers without a PC on their desk or easily available to them. The OU did not make a breakthrough with its staff using new technology until it had 'one (i.e. a PC) on every desk'. It is encouraging that The Learning Divide shows computer studies as top of the subjects being studied by adults, among older as well as younger age-groups.

Multi-media PCs are increasingly being bought for home use, especially for large adult households and large households with children. However, while sales are increasing, the trends shown in Figures 7 and 8 indicate that some of it is a replacement market and that the proportions of older people and younger people living alone with PCs are surprisingly low.

It is therefore important to be reminded about the current level of availability of such equipment in people's homes. The assumption that such equipment is already available to most people is not correct. Figure 7 records the increase in ownership of TV sets, videos, phones and PCs over the last decade, showing effective saturation for TV and telephone but not for video and with quite low ownership still for PCs. At the same time, it is likely, given the trends, that ownership among large families has reached 50% by now.

	TV	Phone	Video	PC
1985	98	81	31	13
1989	98	87	60	19
1991	98	88	68	21
1993	98	90	73	24
1994	99	91	77	24
1995	99	93	79	25

Figure 7: Ownership by households (%) of TV set, Video, phone and PC

	TV	Phone	Video	PC
1 person, age 16–59	95	82	70	19
2 people, age 16–59	99	95	92	32
1 person, 60+	98	90	35	2
2 people, 60+	100	98	76	10
Small family	99	93	94	36
Large family	99	88	93	45
Large adult family	99	98	94	43
All households	99	93	79	25

Figure 8: Ownership by household type (%) 1995

Changes in structures of further and higher education

The breakdown of the traditional vertically integrated degree and qualification structure into credits and other smaller modules with Credit Accumulation and Transfer Schemes encourages the use of a variety of flexible learning resources in mixed modes of study. Different electronic media can be selected for specific teaching purposes, as well as providing learners with a choice of methods of study. The move to a unified framework of post-school qualifications will encourage this further. And communications technologies will play a critical role in facilitating these processes in the interests of learners.

Changing learners

More learners will be adults studying part-time, fitting their studies in with their lives and work. Students will vote with their feet, choosing flexibility and openness. It will be essential for further education to be organised in such a way that people can keep their jobs and carry on learning at the same time. Constant retraining will become a fact of life: it will need to be 'hassle-free' and treated as an automatic part of human resource development.

If media-based education can be used to deliver part-time opportunities all over the country, without extra financial barriers, it will also help redress the urban/metropolitan bias in further education.

Changing funding mechanisms

Increasingly funding will not go to institutions as such: it will either be directed at the technologies or at the learners. High tech companies will put money into the technologies which most easily win user support and facilitate learning.

Employers are also likely to support 'open and distance learning' for their employees. Development work by the MSC/Training Agency over the years has increased knowledge and acceptance of open and resource-based learning in industry.

Funding may also go directly to learners in the form of training credits or educational entitlements. Learners will then choose to use their credits on what is convenient for them. User-pays would also become a decisive element in a broadcast system that had to be self-financed, for example, digital satellite.

Who will fund the development of the software?

What counts in electronic education is the software or courseware. This is what the learner sees and interacts with. However, the potential for learning of the hardware has almost always been in advance of the design of the software. The hardware provides new facilities which need to be exploited to aid learning, but there is little point in people buying expensive PCs if there is little appropriate software. CD-ROMs are currently at this critical stage of development, an important point since CD-ROMs look like being particularly useful for educators and trainers since it is possible to store TV and video material as well as sound, stills and text on the same disc, and also provide some interactivity.

There is not, however, enough high-quality educational software or courseware packages on the market to help create a large enough demand for the new hardware, and therefore bring the price of the hardware down to a domestic level. Effort is now concentrating on developing software, but who will invest in it and who will own it? The development of edutainment is expected to help to stimulate the market, and multi-media computers are certainly being bought for the home. This could have a beneficial effect on the development of multi-media products for education and lifelong learning.

The OU has, until recently, worked on the principle that as a distance learning institution delivering to people's homes it cannot be too far ahead of what is happening in the domestic market. It can be slightly ahead, but not well ahead. Conventional institutions can be well ahead because they are dealing with students in an institutional environment. The OU's initial computer scheme in the 70s had to be funded to assist students to acquire computers. At the moment conventional institutions do not (yet) require students to have their own computers, though this option is now being discussed by some. More recently, the OU has decided that for some courses it is reasonable to require high-grade PC ownership, accepting that this may cost £1,000 or more. There is depressing evidence that, as a result of the increased new technology demands, the proportion of women enrolling on the Technology Foundation Course has dropped dramatically.

The desk-top university, the electronic work-station, the wired class-room and the global electronic village

It will not be long before learning is regularly delivered to the desk-top, whether this is at home or at work. The higher up the academic level, the nearer one is to the reality of the global electronic village. Learning can already be delivered at the desk-top, whether at home or at work. Many universities and colleges are finally starting to move away from lecturers reading out from notes as a form of information delivery. A number are already setting up information networks. Heriot-Watt, for example, is linking up student accommodation with an electronic network system. Scotland is doing interesting work with electronic media and open and distance learning partly stimulated by the demands imposed by an isolated and scattered population and a University of the Highlands and Islands is being set up.

One of the most exciting developments in training is that of interactive workstations. Managements are investing in the idea because it saves money. It is cheaper to train people through interactive videos and electronic networks than to bring people together from all over the country, let alone from over Europe. However, while private companies are investing in multi-media and workstations, most colleges will find the costs high.

The Commonwealth of Learning and a European Open University are all moves in this direction. The OU increasingly sees itself as having a world-wide rather than a UK role. Certainly this includes Eastern Europe, where English is acceptable as a language for instruction. At this stage there is a role for trans-frontier satellite provision. Again, who pays?

References

AINLEY, P. and CORNEY, M. (1990) *Training for the Future*, London: Cassell.

FULTON, O. (1981) *Access to Higher Education*, Guildford: Society for Research into Higher Education.

LEWIS, R. and McDONALD, L. (1988) *The Open Learning Pocket Book*, NCET.

MSC (MANPOWER SERVICES COMMISSION) (1981) *An 'Open Tech' Programme*, London: MSC.

MSC (MANPOWER SERVICES COMMISSION) (1982) *'Open Tech' Task Group Report*, Sheffield: MSC.

SARGANT, N. (1991) 'Choosing to use the media', in *The BUFVC Handbook for Film and Television in Education*, London: BUFVC.

UDACE (UNIT FOR THE DEVELOPMENT OF ADULT CONTINUING EDUCATION) (1988) *Developing Access*, Leicester: UDACE.

Naomi's focus on identifying and overcoming barriers to access was developed early, and pursued consistently. Here, in a second extract from 'To make continuing education a reality' she identifies a range of the barriers to adult participation:

To make continuing education a reality[30]

The barrier of educational qualifications

Particularly in England and Wales, with the legacy of a selective educational system, the lack of formal educational qualifications among adults is great. New entry routes will therefore have to be made available which do not depend on the traditional entry through O and A levels or their equivalent. The experience of the Open University has confirmed that of universities and polytechnics who have taken in mature students without qualifications: that ability is not necessarily equated with 'qualifications' and that experience and motivation are likely to prove more significant. Some new routes are already being provided through, for example, specially prepared preparatory courses, NOW courses and pre-TOPS courses, and of course the OU which through its open entry to foundation courses now acts as a substantial feeder to other institutions.

Perhaps it is now timely to consider the introduction of a more comprehensive scheme for educational access such as the 25/4 scheme in Sweden which gives a right of entry to higher education to anyone over twenty-five who has completed four years of employment. This scheme which originally demanded five years of work has now been in operation since 1969 and an evaluation of its effectiveness (Kim, 1979) shows that between 1969 and 1976 a total of 17,500 students had taken advantage of these opportunities. These adults come from a wider age-range and a wider social background than conventional students. They do not, however, any more than the majority of Open University students as *adults*, come from the working class. They did, as OU students did, grow up in a working class environment. She notes '...the 25/5 rule has given many adults who wouldn't otherwise have had the opportunity of higher education, a chance'.

30.McIntosh, Naomi (1994) *Occasional Paper Two: To make continuing education a reality*, Leicester: ACACE, pp. 13–19.

The main point is that a variety of alternative routes into education have to be available at a variety of levels.

The barrier of finance

In this country, provided students are offered a place, achieve the appropriate qualifications and choose to study full-time, the mandatory grant system provides better financial support than in most other countries. In Sweden, for example, although the 25/4 rule confers a right of entry to higher education it does not bring with it the necessary financial support and students are expected to pay for themselves, which they may do by loans. However, in this country, a sizeable number of students still fall through the net of the mandatory system entirely, and that is apart from the large group whose parents do not make up grants to the statutory level. As far as part-time students are concerned, there appears to be an assumption in the DES and elsewhere that adults studying part-time have access to an income and therefore do not need grants in the same way as full-time students. This is simply not the case, and there is no doubt that large numbers of adults, particularly housewives and those from the working class, find even the level of fees charged by the Open University too high (Woodley, 1978). And of course studying as adults has other costs—in travel, in loss of domestic economies or overtime foregone, for example.

Full-time education both at school and post-school level is effectively free to the individual, and paid for by the community through a combination of rates and taxes. If there is to be a major expansion of opportunities for adults, and if many of these opportunities should properly be made available on a part-time basis, or in a combination of full- and part-time, then it is difficult to see the justification for marking out some areas of post-school education as not free to the individual. Some more equitable method of providing financial support will need to be found, which allows for retraining, credit transfer, a mixture of full and part-time study and so on. Some possibilities are looked at in more detail in a later section of this article.

Structural barriers

Included under this heading are barriers which arise from the way in which provision is made: timetabling, requirements to attend a given number of classes at a given location, the requirement to study a given course in its entirety within a given timescale, the requirement of some universities that a given time period must elapse between matriculation and graduation. While for some, the simple provision of more part-time courses would meet their needs, for others even the part-time attendance requirements would render them inaccessible. More part-time provision during the day would help some kinds of people, for example mothers with children at school and shift-workers. Evidence of this is the experiment at Bulmershe College of Higher Education where the agreement between the OU and Bulmershe goes further than simple transferability. OU students are also allowed to take Bulmershe courses as part of their OU degree where these provide academic opportunities not available through the OU. Since Bulmershe operates on a modular basis and organises the timetable accordingly, quite a few OU students find they can attend one full day a week more easily than several evenings, and are studying such subjects as languages, Art and Design, and Sport and Leisure, often at the same time as OU courses. They obviously value the opportunity since sizeable groups of students have joined the scheme for three years running, often travelling long distances to attend.

What is obviously difficult is for an institution which is predominantly staffed, funded and geared up to deal with full-time students, to do equal justice to part-time students. Part-time students are not accorded the same priority, they do not count the same in the funding ratios and with some notable exceptions the majority of full-time staff are not interested in teaching them, since many simply do not wish to work unsocial hours. Part-time staff have to be engaged to teach part-time courses: they do not enjoy the same security of tenure, or the same status, and neither can they be asked to accept the same level of responsibility. Some creative way through these dilemmas will need to be sought and it will need the active help and commitment of the professional teaching unions. Many of these structural barriers could be removed quite cheaply and easily if the will were there, as a few institutions have already shown.

A related barrier, and one which comes within the category of Newsam's request for immediate proposals, is the lack of adequate range of provision for children under school age. For many women, this is the single largest barrier. While a small number of colleges are now providing crèches, this is probably not the optimum solution in the long run; nor is it satisfactory to rely on employers to make provision. Mothers may go in and out of education and in and out of work. The promised expansion of nursery schools has not happened on the hoped-for scale.

This gap has to some extent been filled by the expansion of pre-school play groups, but dangerously so, because they do not provide the type of opportunity needed or wished for by many mothers, particularly those who wish to work or study. Neither is the provision of part-time nursery classes, typically from 9.00 to 11.30 am or 1.30 to 3.30 pm, though undoubtedly good for children, of much use to such mothers. With declining primary school rolls, space is becoming available which could be used to provide more comprehensive provision for under fives. What are needed are nursery centres where children can receive the quality of care over the hours of the day (at least 8.30 am to 5.30 pm) and weeks of the year (49-50) that day nurseries expect to provide, with the educational input that nursery schools expect to provide. To plan for this is difficult but should not be impossible.

It means bringing together different departments within local authorities with different financial arrangements—sometimes even different local authorities, as, for instance, in the ILEA area—and more difficult still, different professional groupings with their different vested interests and terms and conditions of service. It is to be hoped that teachers would see this as a welcome area of expansion for a declining profession. Given that some space is likely to become available, the opportunity for this expansion should not be let slip.

Geographical barriers

Geographical barriers are more difficult to remove in the short term than structural or financial barriers. The physical location of existing institutions is a limiting factor on their accessibility. Some adults are able to move to another location, although often only when some other change has already happened in their lives, e.g. redundancy or a marriage breakdown. The majority, however, are tied by families and jobs. As increasing numbers of women work, there are frequently two jobs to be taken into account. The strength of the Open University provision has been that it has not *demanded* physical attendance, and it has enabled people to study in their own geographical location and also not to have to give up their studies if they did have to move somewhere else. However, the negative side of the OU is that distance learning, relying heavily as it must on the printed word, is a lonely and hard way to learn. It is not the best option to offer to those who may be educationally disadvantaged and whose confidence and therefore motivation is likely to be low. If we are right in our assumption that many people would prefer to study nearer home, often part-time, then this argues for a different pattern of provision on the ground, with a larger number of smaller centres nearer to people rather than a limited number of larger centres. It may be that the nature of their provision will change from the traditional classroom based taught course to the provision of educational diagnosis, brokerage and facilitation of a range of learning opportunities. The new media are likely to be of assistance in helping this new role, as will be the increased use of cooperatively or centrally produced learning materials, which can be used very effectively for adults *within* institutions as the National Extension College Flexistudy programmes and the use of OU materials in American colleges and elsewhere has shown.

We should therefore take a long hard look at the physical provision of buildings in terms of their geographical location, and try to ensure that as many adults as possible are within reasonable access to a college or adult education institution of one sort or another. Some buildings can be saved from the guillotine over the next few years and redesignated as adult learning centres or community colleges. It will be important to ensure that the traditional barriers between educational providers do not prevent the flexible and open use of buildings for adults.

There will however continue to be large numbers who are debarred by distance or circumstance from attendance at such colleges. Distance learning systems providing a range of courses at all levels, both vocational and general, will still be needed to complement the provision described here.

References

KIM, L. (1979) 'Widened admission to higher education in Sweden (the 25/5 scheme)', *European Journal of Education*, 14(2), 2.

WOODLEY, A. (1978) 'The impact of increasing costs of study at the Open University', paper prepared for the Open University Council for submission to the Department of Education and Science, April.

One major barrier to adult participation identified by Naomi in the 1970s was the poverty of data to identify 'who isn't there?' For ACACE in 1980 Naomi designed an instrument for a major representative sample population survey to inform the Council's work. From 1989 she led the work of the National Institute of Adult Continuing Education in collecting data from a sample of 5,000 firstly every three years, and since 1998 annually. By 1999 the impact of this work, complemented by a government National Adult Learning Survey was the adoption of a national participation target which survived until the Learning and Skills Council abandoned it, despite a clear demand that it be supported in the Secretary of State's remit to that body. In her chapter, 'Learning and "leisure"' (1995), for the Open University's M.A. reader Boundaries of Learning, *Naomi compares the findings from the 1980 ACACE survey and the first NIACE survey, which was published in 1990:*

Learning and 'leisure'[31]

Much more is understood now than twenty-five years ago about what adults are interested in learning, how and where they choose to learn and for what reasons. We are indebted to the work of a number of key researchers for these understandings, which make it clear that adult learning is not confined within conventional institutions or conveyed only by qualified teachers. Much adult learning is self-planned and quite deliberate. It may be, as Tough noted in 1971 'initiated for highly practical reasons' and be motivated by 'curiosity, interest and enjoyment'. The learning that goes on in public places, whether it is described as education, training or community development, is only the tip of the iceberg.

To attempt to map all such learning is, by definition, a daunting if not impossible task. Some obvious and orthodox research techniques are not available – observation, for example. Neither is it possible to rely on information collected through institutions since many non-conventional or disadvantaged learners will not have had access to them. The main option that remains, though an expensive one, is to survey a sample of the adult population as a whole, and ask them directly to provide details of their own experience. The first such national population study covered England and Wales and took place in the winter of 1980. The report, funded by the Department of Education and Science (DES) and carried out by the Advisory Council for

---

31. Sargant, Naomi (1995) 'Learning and "leisure"', in *Boundaries of Learning*, Milton Keynes: Open University.

Adult and Continuing Education (ACACE), appeared as *Adults: Their Educational Experience and Needs* (ACACE, 1982).

The mischance of the demise of the Inner London Education Authority (ILEA) in 1990 was to provide the first opportunity, happily exactly a decade later, to use the report of 1980 survey (ACACE, 1982) as a benchmark against which to measure future change. The ILEA commissioned the National Institute for Adult Continuing Education (NIACE) to carry out a study to document the ILEA's contribution to adult learning and it was possible to ensure that comparisons could be made in *Learning and 'Leisure'*[1] (Sargant, 1991) with key sections of the 1980 survey, and extend the sample to cover Scotland. Even a sample of 2500 people was not large enough to produce useful numbers of minority ethnic groups and the Employment Department, as a contribution to Adult Learners' Week 1992, commissioned a further study of the education and training experience of six selected minority ethnic groups resident in Great Britain, published as *Learning for a Purpose* (Sargant, 1993).

Drawing on these two surveys, this chapter looks at participation in education and training by adults, their interest in current study and in future learning. Patterns of participation in adult learning are strongly related to educational advantage and to age, but also vary significantly across regions of Great Britain. Some types of provision are more accessible to particular groups and individuals than others. It is clear that the ability to take up educational opportunities is affected not just by people's own motivation and circumstances, but by their knowledge of and the availability of learning opportunities. Informal learning also plays a significant role, particularly among minority ethnic groups, and whether this is from choice or necessity is an important question. There are interesting variations in cultural and educational activities in different parts of Great Britain. And there are greater differences in participation between the different minority ethnic groups than there are between those groups as a whole and the general British population.

The use of leisure time

Children learn automatically and have already been learning for many years before we put a label round part of their lives and call it 'schooling'. Our habit of placing learning within schools is a relatively recent one in historical terms, and is being challenged not just by some educators but also by newer technologies and many of the young themselves. The custodial function that schools provide for parents and the community is, however, a useful one, and as a society we are unlikely to decide that we wish schools to stop providing it. The formal framework within which children learn is therefore not a voluntary one: attendance at school is compulsory between the ages of five and sixteen. The phrase 'post-compulsory' is an ugly but correct one to cover all the education that goes on after sixteen. The important point is that most learning after the age of sixteen is voluntary. It is also true that for young people following the tidy academic track through A levels to college or university it may well not feel voluntary.

Workplace-determined education and training is another grey area which may or may not feel voluntary. When it takes place at work and is organised by the employer, it is effectively compulsory. However, much vocational learning is determined by individuals rather than employers and is often aimed at job change rather than current work.

Most adults interweave their learning with the rest of their lives, their work and their family and use some of their leisure time for their studies. The *Oxford English Dictionary* definition of leisure makes the point neatly: 'Freedom or opportunity to do something specific or implied' and in the narrower sense: 'opportunity afforded by freedom from occupation'. For some people the boundaries between leisure and learning are virtually invisible. Frequently, leisure activities provide a bridge into active learning. On the other hand, many people learn from their leisure activities without realising the knowledge or skills they are gaining.

Gardening is a classic example of this, involving soil chemistry, the climate, botany, plant genetics and issues of chemical pollution. The continued active membership of local horticultural and allotment societies, with their programmes of lectures and competitive flower and vegetable shows, involves a high level of learned theoretical and practical knowledge and organisation, which for some people also turns into profitable employment. Alternatively, there are people who choose actively to construct their learning as leisure, often providing a different perspective to the rest of their lives.

It is not, as the Government has increasingly suggested, that there are subjects which are vocational and work-related and other topics which are 'leisure' subjects. The same subjects may be vocational for some people and of general interest to others. Such distinctions rest on the motivations of the learners, not on the subject of the course or the form of its provision.

Demands on people's leisure and their leisure activities change over their life-time, often in relation to family position and ownership of property. The varying activities of the age-groups are interesting (Table 11.1). Not surprisingly, social activities and sport figure high on the list for the young, whereas interest in gardening and handicrafts (including DIY) increases only as people get older. Voluntary service and committee work also become increasingly important as people get older: they seem to replace some of the time previously spent on social activities. Languages appeal across the age-range though at a low level as a 'leisure' activity. They emerge more strongly as a 'learning' activity.

Comparisons between main leisure interests in 1980 and 1990 show remarkable stability. Despite general fears that reading would diminish as television viewing became more dominant, reading has maintained and slightly increased its position at the top of the list: from 48 per cent in 1980 to 51 per cent in 1990. This increase is, however, among women, who read much more than men, and may well be partly accounted for by the increase in the proportion of older women in the population as a whole. Both sexes record an increase in physical sports, a category which includes non-competitive sports such as walking and fishing. One-half of all men list physical sports as a main activity compared with one-third of women. It is interesting that sport, which featured strongly as a 'learning' activity in the 1980 survey, now shows an increase as a leisure activity and a major drop as a learning activity. The trend over the last decade for sports provision to be made through leisure centres rather than through adult education appears to have affected people's definition of it as leisure rather than learning.

Table 11.1 Main leisure interests and activities, by age

Age (%)	17–19	20–24	25–34	35–44	45–54	55–64	65+	Total (%)
Reading	38	45	43	56	49	55	60	51
Social activity	69	70	55	50	40	30	26	46
Sports	47	50	49	44	36	37	25	40
Garden	3	9	23	35	44	53	49	34
Handicrafts	12	23	32	38	38	42	36	34
Indoor games	11	13	12	12	9	11	11	11
Voluntary service	4	4	5	10	9	13	12	9
Committee work	1	2	4	10	7	11	9	7
Play	5	8	5	4	4	5	3	5
Music collecting	2	5	4	6	6	5	4	5
Listen music	3	2	3	3	4	5	5	4
Foreign languages	2	2	3	4	3	3	3	3

The only area to have shown a marked drop as a leisure activity, somewhat surprisingly, is the general area of handicrafts and DIY, including activities such as sewing and woodwork. This has always been a stronger area of interest among women, where the proportion is still high, though it has dropped from 51 per cent in 1980 to 43 per cent in 1990. The figure for men is down to 24 per cent and a possible inference, for men at least, is that doing up the house is no longer seen as 'leisure', but as a necessity about which they have little choice. This is confirmed by the very small numbers who now include such subjects in their current study.

Current participation in study

The ACACE survey (ACACE, 1982) adopted a wide-ranging definition of education and used a question designed to include study in its broadest sense, whether full- or part-time, at work or elsewhere since the completion of full-time education. The 1990 survey used effectively the same question: 'Are you studying currently, or have you done any kind of study, learning or practising, part-time or full-time, at work or elsewhere since you completed your full-time education?' In addition, everyone was asked a question designed to elicit information about informal learning along the lines of the theories implicit in the work of Tough (1971): 'Are you trying to learn about anything (else) at the moment, or trying to teach yourself anything, at work, at home, with friends or in a club – for example, cooking, how to use a computer, photography, etc.?'

The 1990 survey shows one in ten adults as engaged in some form of current study. A further 16 per cent have been studying within the past three years. Therefore one-quarter of all adults describe themselves as current or recent students. At the same time 17 per cent of adults indicate that they are learning something informally, the most of whom (10 per cent out of the 17 per cent) are not also studying formally. So over one-third (36 per cent) of the adult population is or has been studying or learning informally in the past three years. Three per cent of the sample interviewed, (who were all 17 or over) were still at school or in some form of full-time education.

Whereas the overall proportion studying now or recently has increased by 7 per cent since 1980, the proportion of men studying has increased more than that of women (by 9 per cent compared with 4 per cent). The sex differences in participation are similar to those quoted in *Training in Britain* (Rigg, 1989) which also shows a higher proportion of men receiving vocational education and training in the last three years.

Though the participation of women in post-school education has increased over the last decade, in particular in degree courses in higher education, they are still in a significant minority in much of the lower level education and training provision. More detailed research (Woodley *et al.*, 1987) shows that men predominated on courses leading to qualifications in polytechnics (now new universities), specialist colleges and in university postgraduate courses. Women formed the majority in art colleges and in colleges of further and higher education. On courses not leading to qualifications, the proportion of women was very high: almost eight out of ten in LEA classes and in the sector as a whole. Even in the non-LEA classes there were virtually two women to every one man. LEA classes have always been particularly important for younger women who are at home caring for children and have few other options.

It is for this reason that the proposals in the 1991 White Paper *Education and Training for the 21st Century* (HMSO, 1991) to separate further education from local authority provision and to provide national funding only for specified areas of mainly vocational and qualifying provision were seen as likely to do serious damage to opportunities for women, many of whom use such opportunities to keep in touch and return to learning and thence to paid employment as their children get older. The lack of protection for general adult education funding since the 1992 *Act* has indeed led either to a reduction in LEA provision or an increase in costs in many areas.

An increasing number of women are now working part-time, and indeed the main increase in new jobs is in part-time service industry jobs, usually taken by women. In addition, training opportunities are more widely available to full-time rather than part-time workers, and to higher rungs of the employment ladder, i.e. to men rather than to women. Women, often coping with a double agenda of paid work and family management, are doubly disadvantaged. They are particularly dependent on local part-time learning opportunities and have been traditionally the greatest users of adult education, often as a means of re-entry to vocational opportunities. Neither are many of them well-placed to pay additional fees.

Regional differences in participation

There are marked differences between Scotland, Wales and English regions in leisure habits, cultural activities, religious attendance, and awareness of and participation in learning and study. There is no obvious pattern to these differences, and there is a paucity of information nationally about provision and expenditure which would enable proper regional comparisons to be made.

However, the range of variation between the regions is much less in relation to cultural and leisure activities than it is in relation to educational activities. Some areas emerge positively, recording high proportions of the different indicators. For example, East Anglia has the highest awareness of use of local adult education centres, the highest regular use of libraries, and the highest number learning at work, while the southwest has a high level of reading, the highest proportion of informal learners and the highest expressed desire to learn in the future. Other areas emerge negatively, although not usually in all respects. Some clearly do present a mixed profile, or indeed no clear profile at all.

What is curious about Scotland, a country which is proud of its educational tradition, is that whilst it shows the highest level of knowledge of providers, it also records the lowest level of current/recent participation and the lowest proportion wanting to learn something new in the future. Wales records low proportions of awareness of provision and of attendance at local centres, but expresses a high desire to learn.

Although differences in provision and participation will to some extent have developed in relation to local circumstances and local needs, the degrees of difference do raise the question as to whether access to continuing opportunities for education and training for adults are being made available on an equitable and accessible basis over the country, particularly since much provision is nationally funded and controlled, and relates to national and not just local and personal needs. Recent changes in legislation and funding structures are affecting provision locally. The major decision under the 1992 *Further and Higher Education Act* to move the funding of further education away from local authorities, to give independence to further education and sixth form colleges, encourage competition between individual colleges, and to place the funding of a large part of post-sixteen education under a Further Education Funding Council (FEFC) has both positive and negative effects on provision.

What is at risk in many areas is the provision of general (mainly uncertificated) adult education in its traditional sense. Although local education authorities have an obligation to 'secure adequate provision' for 'further education', there is no laid-down definition of adequacy, the definition is quaint, being spelled out as meaning 'in such organised cultural, training and recreative activities as are suited to their requirements' and the calculation of the amount that the government has allowed for the provision of adult education in the Standard Spending Assessment for an individual local authority is not published and its expenditure can, therefore, not be monitored. In some areas, notably those which have had their expenditure capped, adult education has been cut back or is no longer provided.

On the encouraging side, there has over recent years been a marked increase in mature students entering higher education – they are indeed now in a majority – often studying part-time, and mainly through the new universities. There is also an increase in the number of adults entering further education. Of more concern is the pressure on provision, usually not accredited, that relates to personal and social needs. Parent and health education, English for speakers of other languages, training for school governors, and computer studies are all examples. Also under pressure are courses for women to return to learning, or to take up science and engineering and courses for older people to prolong their active citizenship. More flexible working arrangements, early retirement and longer life, as well as increased unemployment and the reduction of public transport, all argue for an increase in a wide variety of locally available part-time provision.

Demographic differences in participation

Another major discriminating factor is, of course, age. The educational system has been designed to provide front-end education rather than continuing education or lifelong learning and young adults clearly dominate the formal system. One half of adults aged 20–24 were studying or had studied in the past three years compared with one-third of 25–34 year olds and 35–44-year-olds. Over forty-five, the proportion dropped to one-quarter.

The 1991 White Paper (HMSO, 1991) focused its discussion on the young even though there had been general debate and agreement about the impact of the decline in the birth rate and the likely requirement that more older people, particularly women, would be required to rejoin or stay longer in the work-force over the coming decades. The recent White Paper *Competitiveness: Helping Business to Win* (DTI, 1994) again focuses far more attention on the young than on adults, arguably a limited view since the young form a very small proportion of the total workforce.

The major factor affecting participation continues to be social class. The upper and middle classes stay at school longer, go on to post-school education at a higher rate and are then much more likely to return to continue their education as adults than the working classes. The proportions of people studying recently in the 1990 survey were 42 per cent of ABs (upper and upper-middle classes), 37 per cent of C1s (lower middle-class, 29 per cent of C2s (skilled working-class) and 17 per cent of DEs (unskilled working class). Two-and-a-half times as many ABs are or have been studying in the past three years as DEs and twice as many C1s as DEs.

Subjects of study

People study an incredible variety of subjects, many of them clearly vocational and others of general interest. The desire to differentiate between vocational and non-vocational subjects has its roots in the philosophy and politics of adult education as well as in the ideology and economics of government policy rather than in learning needs. The judgement as to whether a subject is vocational is ultimately made by the learners who know what they want to learn and why they want to learn it. Examples of this are two of the currently most popular subjects: foreign languages and computer studies.

Vocationally related subjects do, in fact, dominate the 1990 list: vocational qualifications (9 per cent), foreign languages (9 per cent) computer studies (8 per cent), engineering and electronics (7 per cent), shorthand/typing/office skills (6 per cent), business administration and management (6 per cent). Engineering, though had halved its numbers since 1980, as had science. Subjects which have increased in popularity since 1980 tend to be in the harder, more vocational, areas, which are also traditionally male ones and the ones that government policies have mainly supported in the last few years. Subject areas which have decreased include the arts and social sciences, academic and domestic subjects, and some vocational areas which were traditionally occupied by women.

Sports and physical activities have also dropped dramatically, but only, as noted earlier, in the sense of being thought of as subjects of study. As leisure activities, they are more popular, reflecting both the increase in interest and, probably, the increase in provision through leisure centres rather than through adult education.

Subjects of study chosen by learners of different backgrounds

There are clear differences in subjects of study between working women and non-working women. Working women are studying shorthand/typing/office skills (16 per cent), computer studies (9 per cent), other vocational qualifications (9 per cent), business administration/management (8 per cent), and social work (6 per cent). Women not working or working part-time are studying languages (18 per cent), shorthand/typing/office skills, English language/literature (7 per cent) social work (6 per cent), handicrafts (6 per cent), cookery (6 per cent), and arts and cultural subjects (6 per cent). The current emphasis on vocational training is likely to disadvantage women who are not working, whether they are young mothers or older or retired women.

Men who are not working or are retired study across the conventional subject divide – 14 per cent are studying foreign languages, 12 per cent engineering, 12 per cent computer studies and 12 per cent the arts and cultural subjects.

In terms of social class, the lower middle class (C1s) are particularly motivated to pursue vocational studies/qualifications, as is the group (some of whom are the same people) who left school at 16 or 17. Languages are more attractive to the upper and middle classes, as are arts and cultural subjects. The caring areas show a flat class profile, whereas home skills, both male and female, are of more appeal to the working class.

Minority ethnic groups surveyed in 1992 (Sargant, 1993) are far more vocational in their choice of subjects studied than the GB sample: overall summary comparisons for main subjects studied are shown in Table 11.2.

Table 11.2 Main subjects studied – the surveys compared

	Minority ethnic sample (%)	*Learning and 'leisure' (%)*
English language/skills	18	3
Business/management	11	6
Computer studies	8	8
Social work/sciences	8	6
Other professional quals	7	5
Science/maths/statistics	6	3
Foreign languages	6	9

Subjects of informal study

As noted earlier, we do not know whether informal learning is a preferred choice for many learners or whether they choose it for some subject areas rather than others. The fact that most informal learners in the 1990 survey are *not* also learning formally would seem to indicate a conscious preference, but may also indicate the inaccessibility of conventional provision. More people from the minority ethnic groups overall were studying informally (23 per cent) than from the 1990 sample (17 per cent), and this figure rises to 31 per cent among the African group, with the Chinese next (27 per cent).

Many of the subjects of informal learning are instrumental in their use and may well relate to vocational purposes, as well as assisting in personal development and life enhancement. Learning about or how to use a computer is a clear example of this and ranks as the subject most often mentioned by one in five (19 per cent) of all informal learners in the 1990 sample. Ten years ago, although many people had bought home computers, few people were actively using them. Over the decade the situation has clearly changed. Among the minority ethnic sample, the proportion of people learning about computers informally is even higher (27 per cent). Learning foreign languages is also mentioned by a higher proportion of informal learners in the 1990 survey (12 per cent) than formal students (9 per cent).

The minority ethnic sample is again more vocational in its choice of subjects of informal learning and it is interesting to compare some of the main subjects in both modes (Table 11.3).

The main subjects which appear in only one list are for *informal learning*: photography, handicrafts and childcare/parenting; and not *formal study*: other professional and vocational qualifications of all sorts as well as a range of academic subjects. There is obviously scope, particularly with English, computer studies and business studies to offer more provision or support to those now learning these subjects informally. There may also be scope for engaging people in informally, for example, photography.

Table 11.3 Comparison between main subjects both being studied and learned informally

Ethnic minority weighted sample	All studying now/recently (%)	All learning informally (%)
English	18	11
Business management	11	6
Computer studies	8	27
Foreign languages	6	5
Cookery	2	11
Religion/theology	2	4
Typing/word-processing	5	2

Where current or recent study or learning took place

Where people are actually studying, as opposed to at what type of institution, becomes a more significant question with increase in open and distance learning and of informal learning. In the 1990 survey, more than one half of learners were not studying at an educational institution. While formal educational institutions were the dominant provider (39 per cent) in the 1990 survey, just over one-quarter said they were learning at home from a book and 11 per cent at home from a prepared course. An even higher proportion of minority ethnic groups were learning at educational institutions (48 per cent). This choice of place appears to be confirmed by their answers to a question about preferred styles of learning: by far the largest group of others learners, the most familiar method of education for most people.

In terms of work-related location, 7 per cent of both surveys say they are learning at a training centre, but double the number in the GB sample are learning at work (15 per cent) than in the minority ethnic sample (8 per cent). More men (18 per cent) than women (12 per cent) are learning at work in the GB sample. In the minority ethnic sample, similarly, more men than women from the Indian sub-continent are studying at work (11 per cent of men compared with 6 per cent of women). With the Afro-Caribbean group, however the position is reversed with 11 per cent of women studying at work compared with 5 per cent of men.

These figures raise two important issues. First, that although most of the subjects minority ethnic groups are studying are vocational in nature and their reason for studying are work- or qualification-related, only a small proportion of them are Enterprise Companies and for employers. Second, that minority ethnic groups are more reliant on conventional provision than the GB population. It is, therefore, particularly important, as the new FEFC funding arrangements begin to affect the nature of local provision, for colleges to ensure that they really are accessible to learners from ethnic minorities, since in many areas local authority provided community and adult education is being cut back.

Subjects people would like to learn about

Nearly one-half (47 per cent) of the adult population in Great Britain said they would like to learn about something they had not previously studied. This figure is substantially lower than ten years earlier. In the country as a whole, interest in learning about new subject areas increases as terminal age of education increases. In terms of age, it peaks at 25–34 and decreases thereafter (Table 11.4).

Table 11.4 Main groupings of 'new' subjects people would like to learn about, by age-group

	17–19	20–24	25–34	35–44	45–54	55–64	65+	Total
Foreign languages	17	21	23	24	21	24	21	22
Arts/culture	14	13	19	21	24	30	26	22
Home skills	10	16	19	23	22	21	19	19
Science/maths	14	12	12	11	7	9	7	10
Business/professional	7	12	17	14	8	2	4	10
Sports	7	6	4	5	4	6	6	6
Computers	4	5	7	4	6	3	1	5
Social sciences	4	3	5	5	3	1	3	4
Want to learn	50	52	55	51	45	46	35	47

The subjects that have remained stable or increased are mainly vocational, for example, computer studies and work-related subjects. The decreases are much more marked in leisure and other non-vocational subjects. It is possible that some people are re-defining 'leisure' to include some activities they would previously have thought of as 'learning' as indeed the Government suggested in the White Paper, *Education and Training for the 21st century* (HMSO, 1991). It is also possible that they are excluding some domestic functions which are now thought of as necessary activities rather than pleasurable leisure.

People as learners do not easily differentiate between what is vocational and what is non-vocational. These are terms used by politicians, funders and some providers. The breadth of people's interests and motivations cuts across such boundaries.

The desire to learn something new tends to take on a broader form as people get older and to be less narrowly confined to short-term vocational concerns. There is a clear need for a generous range and variety of provision to be maintained, without unreasonable financial barriers, as the social and demographic trends of increased early retirement, unemployment and active old age are likely to increase need and demand. The most recent national survey shows even fewer people of age sixty-five and over to be engaged in current or recent study (6 per cent) compared with the 1990 survey (9 per cent). There is concern that the changes in funding arrangements which leave the provision of most general adult education to be funded under already straitened local authority budgets has already diminished the very provision which is most accessible to older people; in particular older women.

The proportion of people wanting to learn something new among minority ethnic groups is higher than among the British population (58 per cent compared with 47 per cent), though it is not surprising that many of the subjects are the same. There is, of course, the obvious difference that English (for speakers of other languages) ranks as the highest subject, mentioned by one in five (21 per cent) who wish to learn. Additionally, nearly as many from these groups (17 per cent) wish to study other foreign languages. Groupings of subjects which are clearly vocationally-related are nearly all ranked higher by the minority ethnic sample than the 1990 sample: professional/work-related subjects (12 per cent compared with 5 per cent) computer studies (9 per cent compared with 5 per cent), social studies (8 per cent compared with 4 per cent).

Non-participants: identity and learning needs

Educators continue to be concerned and challenged by those people who do not participate or do not appear to wish to participate in adult learning. Those with minimum initial education, manual workers and the elderly are consistently under-represented in education as adults. The general pattern of participation recorded over the last twenty years, including the *Adequacy of Provision Study* (NIAE, 1970) and the ACACE study (1982) has, as McGivney (1990) notes in her valuable review of the literature of non-participation, shown little change. It is important, however, to note that in order to keep the project to manageable proportions, her review did not include any private providers, employers or distance education schemes, but was confined to the main statutory and some voluntary providers of organised educational activities for adults. This means that her review omits any reference to the significant body of research into the large body of adult students at the Open University (OU), the National Extension College and other correspondence colleges, as well as much work-oriented learning.

In particular, using, as both ACACE (1982) and McGivney (1990) did, the useful terminology of Cross (1978), it means that the two major 'situational' barriers to access – time and place – may tend to be underestimated in comparison with 'dispositional and 'attitudinal' barriers. There are clearly good reasons why thousands of adults apply every year to study with the OU rather than through their local university or college. It is highly likely that the same inflexible barriers of time and place which prevent them studying locally also prevent many from participation in *any* form of education as adults. The reasons given for not studying by the minority ethnic groups confirm time pressures as just such a reason, both due to work (28 per cent) and due to family pressures (28 per cent). Relatively few people from these groups mention lack of money (3 per cent) or other typical barriers to access.

Nearly two-thirds of people interviewed in 1990 were 'not studying now, or recently', or 'not learning now' 62 per cent of men and 62 per cent of women. More than half of them did not want to learn about anything new, ranging from 47 per cent of 17–24 year olds to 85 per cent of people aged 65 and over. One-quarter of the minority ethnic sample says 'there is nothing I want to study'. Evidence from recent studies on individual commitment to adult learning provides clear evidence that many people's motivation to study is directly related to its relevance to their current or future work.

A major difficulty has been the success of the Government over the last fifteen years in focusing attention and funding only on those learning activities which contribute to enhancing narrowly defined vocational skills. For many people who have no job in view, and limited financial means for study, study options which appear relevant are genuinely more limited. It must be remembered that the education of adults is a goal of social policy as well as of economic policy. It is therefore necessary to return to a more generous notion of the relevance and scope of adult learning if we are to provide for the needs of adults throughout their lives, let alone if we are to meet the national training and education targets!

Note

1 The survey published under the title *Learning and 'Leisure'* is referred to, for convenience, as the 1990 or GB survey, since it covered England, Wales and Scotland.

References

ACACE (ADVISORY COUNCIL FOR ADULT AND CONTINUING EDUCATION) (1982) *Adults: Their Educational Experience and Needs*, Leicester: ACACE.

CROSS, K P. (1978) 'A critical review of state and national studies of the needs and interests of adult learners', in C. B. Stalford (ed.) *Adults' Learning Needs and the Demand for Life-long Learning*, Washington: National Institute for Education.

DTI (DEPARTMENT OF TRADE AND INDUSTRY) (1994) *Competitiveness: Helping Business to Win*, White paper, London: HMSO.

HMSO (1991) *Education and Training for the 21st Century*, Cm 1536, London: HMSO.

McGIVNEY, V. (1990) *Education's for Other People*, Leicester: NIACE.

NIAE (NATIONAL INSTITUTE OF ADULT EDUCATION) (1970) *Adequacy of Provision*, Leicester: NIAE.

RIGG, M. (1989) *Training in Britain: Individuals' Perspectives*, London: Training Agency/HMSO.

SARGANT, N. (1991) *Learning and 'Leisure'*, Leicester: NIACE.

SARGANT, N. (1993) *Learning for a Purpose*, Leicester: NIACE.

TOUGH, A. (1971) *The Adult's Learning Projects*, Toronto: Ontario Institute for Studies in Education.

WOODLEY, A., WAGNER, L., SLOWEY, M., HAMILTON, M. and FULTON, O. (1987) *Choosing to Learn*, Milton Keynes: SRHE/Open University Press.

The Learning Divide identified through Naomi's quantitative research was paralleled, she recognised, by a digital divide which excluded the same groups from participation. In a passage from 'Technology and adult learners : the medium is not the message' , her keynote address to NIACE's Annual Study Conference in 1997 she argued:

Technology and adult learners: the medium is not the message[32]

What matters, as we approach the great 'telecommunications highway' is that we determine how to use and manage these developments rather than allowing the technology or the market to dictate how they are used. The education story is littered with projects where the latest piece of technology is hailed as the wonder-solution which solves all learning problems. We need to be clear about what business we are in: what are we trying to offer to learners, what sort of people are we trying to reach, with what sort of content and what sort of resources are available to help in this task?

New technologies have brought new choices, but they also impose some new limitations. We have tended to regard some structural changes in society as political when their cause is primarily technological. In the UK, for example, the BBC and ITV together held, until 1982, a monopoly of television broadcasting. Its breakdown was hastened by the arrival of Channel 4 and the beginning of the disaggregation of the component parts of what had previously been a 'vertically integrated' broadcasting production and distribution system. However, the main cause of its breakdown has been the arrival of the new technologies of cable, satellite and video.

An eminent UK social scientist, Michael Young, used a series of evocative images to describe a set of related changes which had already taken place. He noted that there had already been a shift of scale of people's lives outside work.

The small (and private) has increasingly replaced the large (and public). The watch has replaced the public clock. The fridge has replaced the ice factory, the washing machine, the public laundry. The private bathroom, the municipal baths and the washing machine the public laundry. The car, the bus or train and TV the cinema.

---

32. Sargant, Naomi (1997) 'Technology and adult learners: the medium is not the message', Keynote address NIACE Annual Conference, pp. 4–6.

And even so, he suggested that the new home computer and teletext might replace the newspaper. What all these changes have to do with is accessibility, freedom and choice. It is obvious that the small (and private) are more accessible to the individuals and families that possess them than the large (and public). However, those who do not possess them are placed at an increasing disadvantage.

The provision of these services had developed into monopolies or near-monopolies of supply more because of their technological scale and nature than for any political or ideological reason. The 'community' as a whole paid for their provision, which was then available free to the citizen/user at the point of use. A benefit was that the provision was universally available, but the negative was that the structures did not allow much flexibility and individuality in use, particularly in relation to geographical location. An important characteristic has been that such institutions have tended to be production-led rather than user or market-led.

Schools and universities have historically had just such a monopoly of supply and have been able to continue to be producer and production-led rather than being led by the needs of the learners.

The same has been true of broadcasting. But with both of these we have taken for granted the good principle of universality of access. What changes, in the new technological and market-led scenario is that those who can afford the small and private maintain their access while those that cannot are increasingly denied it or may only be provided with a lower standard of service: the increase in car ownership has, for example, led to a reduction in public transport, whose users are now the ones with less money and less choice, the old, the young and the poor.

Behind this change lies the key question of who pays and at what point in the process. As with schooling, the UK has traditionally provided the further and higher levels of full-time initial education free at the point of use to the majority of learners and it has been paid for by the community. This assumption is not carried over to part-time study, and is increasingly under pressure for full-time higher education with the means testing of maintenance grants and the introduction of student loans.

Government has also increasingly been differentiating between education and training and between vocational and non-vocational education – a peculiar view to many in higher education who expect to 'train' teachers and doctors as well 'educate' scholars, writers, researchers etc.

For most learners, the difference between education and training is not a relevant or helpful one. However, it is evident that the UK Government and, indeed the European Union, continue to wish to differentiate between them and this affects policy developments and funding which in turn affects the provision of education and training and the ways in which these are funded and provided.

It is possible to identify a number of characteristics which differentiate education and training and also relate to the structures of broadcasting and the newer media and to the distinctions made earlier. We tend to look at education and training differently in a number of ways, and these interrelate with broadcasting and new technologies, as Figure 1 shows.

The point, and it is a threatening one, is that just as new technologies have broken down the monopoly power of broadcasting, so the application of new media for open and distance learning is in a position to break down the monopoly of power of conventional educational institutions. On the good side, for learners it removes the barriers to access of time as well as of place. Open/distance learning can be delivered to or bought by people for use anywhere they wish. The danger is that finance becomes a new barrier to access.

Figure 1

Education

As an investment in the community
As feeding into public
(i.e. society's) capital
Working on longer timescales

Free at the point of use/paid for by
the community
Universality of provision

Training

As a personal or private good
As feeding into private or personal
capital
Shorter time-scales/requires quicker
pay-off
Paid for by individual/employer

Selective provision

Public service

Provision through 'large and public'
Large educational institutions with
conventional (face-to-face) teaching
Available in limited places
Broadcasting – limited choice of
channels

but free at point of use

Private market

Provision through 'small and private'
Open/distance learning available in
flexible ways, in small units
Available anywhere
Narrowcasting and other media
- video
- cable/satellite
- interactive video
- CD-ROM, CD-I (compact disk
interactive) etc
but NOT free to the user

Broadcasting continues to be of vital importance as it is able to deliver educational programming without financial and geographical barriers whether it is at the level of the Open University, for basic skills, for family literacy or for the proposed University for Industry. It is vital for the unemployed, for older people, for illiterate or handicapped groups who need to continue to be served by broadcasting free at the point of use, and whose needs must be protected with the arrival of digital terrestrial broadcasting.

The function of opening people's eyes to new areas and stimulating the 'wantless' to want and to pursue something new, certainly requires broadcasting, preferably on 'mass' channels, whether publicly or privately run. It is for this reason that adult educators argued, sadly unsuccessfully, for the 1996 Broadcasting Act to require some guarantee of educational provision on the new digital channels.

However, we must not and cannot be Luddite about new technological opportunities. Providing proper 'public service' functions are protected and maintained, it will be equally important to add to the array of provision and to people's choice by using new technologies and new narrowcast options as effectively as possible.

Naomi returned to the theme in the work of the technology sub-group of the National Advisory Group for Continuing Education and Lifelong Learning, established following the election of a Labour government in 1997, during the period of intense policy focus on lifelong learning, which culminated in the publication of the Green Paper, The Learning Age. Naomi summarised the work of the group, exploring in more detail measures the government could constructively take to secure public access to new technologies to overcome the barrier of cost:

Discussion Paper: Changing access to technologies[33]

While communications technology in all its forms is developing fast, it has not yet reached most homes, learning centres or even colleges at affordable prices. The challenge for the next time period is two-fold: first, to ensure that best use is made in the shorter term of the existing technologies, particularly those such as TV and videos, which most people already have in their own homes and which they can use free at the point of use; and second, at the same time to plan systematically for the medium to longer term, when the new and more demanding technologies will be more widely available.

Issues of access to the information superhighway cannot only be left to the private market. While the proportion of people owning personal computers and other technological equipment is increasing, there are large differences in ownership between employment categories, between large and small families, between regions of the country, and by age and gender.

After reviewing the reach of different technologies across the UK, she continued:

while many people will have the resources to provide such technologies for themselves, many others will need to obtain access both to the necessary skills and to the telecommunications themselves through user-friendly public spaces. (See section 6.) A network of such user-friendly centres for adult learning is not a new idea, but the understanding of its urgency is new. It is not an accident that several areas of government are considering versions of such centres. The UfI project assumes the necessity of a national network of

---

33. Sargant, Naomi (1998) *Changing Learners, Changing Technologies: Report of a subgroup of the National Advisory Group for Continuing Education and Lifelong Learning*, Leicester: NIACE, pp. 2–4.

kite-marked learning centres in a wide variety of locations from libraries to workplaces, schools to supermarkets. The DTI's programme 'IT for All' aims to offer people the opportunity to find out through accessible hands-on experience how new technologies can benefit them in their everyday lives. It already has more than 200 partners providing more than 700 activities at over 500 locations. Their stated aim is to create 2000 new access opportunities by March 1998, building up to 4000 sites by the end of 1998. Also under the wing of the DTI is the network of 89 Business Links with 240 outlets, providing information, counselling and business skills training for small businesses (SMEs). Of course, people's needs for and interest in information technology differ and their needs may change over time. While the DTI's attitudinal research still shows sizeable groups of people who are 'unconvinced' or 'alienated' by information technology, it records, overall, 'some positive changes in attitude since 1996, particularly amongst women, older age-groups and the C2, D and E economic groups' (DTI, 1998).

For the community at large, the library network is an obvious source of information and an entry-point for lifelong learning. Many libraries are already equipping themselves for these new roles and, along with school-teachers, librarians are to be funded for IT training through new Lottery arrangements. *New Library: the people's network* makes a powerful case for the changing role of libraries in the information society, 'complementing formal education provision by providing a resource base and a platform for people of all ages to participate in lifelong learning'. 'There are 4,759 libraries in the UK, of which 693 are mobile libraries, plus 19, 136 service points in hospitals, prisons, old people's homes etc.' The report proposes among new networked public library services, education and lifelong learning, business and the economy, training and employment, information for citizenship as well as the National Digital Library. The BBC expects to repeat and extend its very successful campaign 'Computers Don't Bite' this year and has found libraries an especially effective partner.

Alongside these developments lies the Government's plan to connect every school and every library free to the National Grid for Learning. While the proposals for the establishment of the grid are obviously to be welcomed, there is clear concern in the consultation evidence that the recommendation that the project should start only with structures and content designed for schools and their teachers will be too limiting. It is almost inevitable that a model which is primarily designed for schools will not be the most appropriate one to also serve the greater variety of lifelong learning needs, and may, if the two models are not developed in parallel, prejudice the flexible development of later stages of the scheme for lifelong learning.

It is evident that there is a large amount of activity already in train nationally, and that this is taking place under the aegis of a number of different government departments. Clearly coordination between the major players interested in these networks of centres is an early priority. The information society is too important and entails too great a cost to the country for its development to be thought of in a piecemeal way. There needs to be an over-arching plan, but this needs to be developed swiftly before individual pieces are put into place which inhibit the best grand design.

In parallel to these plans, a National Working party on Social Inclusion in the Information Society (INSINC) set up by IBM in collaboration with the Community Development Foundation has been looking at these issues from the perspective of communities and community organisations, 'a spectrum which extends from very informal networks and activities based around households, to more formalised community groups and community-based organisations'. Their report *The Net Result* is a searching document whose implications go far beyond community needs. Its relevance is the wish to move from discussion of 'information have-nots' to 'recognition that some groups of people might become disadvantaged by being denied *access to the communications opportunities* which the technology is beginning to provide'. They argue for a network of Community Resource Centres, providing opportunities for raising awareness, and access to multi-media and online technologies at local level. They suggest that it should use 'appropriate bases such as schools, libraries and community centres, and that the centres should be publicly funded and based on sustainable business plans'.

At local level, the evidence is of great interest in and demand for such opportunities, but that many projects have had to work on short-term funding, with no security or confidence that the work can continue unless there is a local champion to underwrite development. The cost of the technology combined with the necessity to serve local populations dictates collaboration rather than competition (see section 14). It is vital to share good practice in running such centres and the new DFEE-funded report on IT awareness provides valuable advice in this regard. Section 6 suggests guidelines and criteria for running such centres.

The scale of the task of offering access to technologies for lifelong learning to the population at large is enormous. It will not be achieved through any one type of provider or level of provision, or even through the aegis of one government department. It will require the use of public and private spaces, particularly at the workplace, and putting together of public/private alliances. A UfI network of learning centres, for example, will be extremely necessary and desirable but not 'sufficient' for the large lifelong learning task. If the UfI is asked to be a lead player in setting up local learning centres, those centres will have to offer a wider gateway to lifelong learning as well.

Technological equipment is too expensive and necessary skills too valuable for resources not to be shared and opened up to as many learners as possible. Schools, colleges, universities and adult centres all have a role to play and a duty to play it as flexibly and imaginatively as possible. What is necessary is to replace competition between different providers with coordination and collaboration in offering accessible provision for learners. This requires assessment of local education and training needs and audits of telematics resources in order to develop local plans.

Naomi's important work on adult participation was grounded in the recognition that policy affecting adult learning had, too often in the past, been short of reliable data. She was also frustrated that policy memory in government departments was often in short supply. As a result this essay on future research priorities contributed to a volume examining the continuing challenges posed by the learning divide, began, characteristically, with a review of the lessons to be drawn from surveys as far back as the 1930s:

Research agendas: present and future[34]

Participation as a continuing research issue

The sequence of national surveys described in these volumes has established the importance of participation as a key element of research in the field of adult learning, and ensured that such research is recognised as important by government. The 1997 *National Adult Learning Survey* (Beinart and Smith, 1998) was a development from the SCPR (Park, 1994) survey discussed earlier and sought particularly to understand informal learning, workplace based learning and non-participation. Information from these early studies was instrumental in the formulation of the idea of a learning participation target, and while the nature of the targets is developing, the government is committed to continuing research in order to measure their attainment. The setting up of the Learning and Skills Council (LSC) and its local arms has added impetus to this work and the extension of the English Force Survey (ELLFS) to cover local LSC areas using the same questionnaire is much to be welcomed.

With devolution and the growth of regional government, it will continue to be necessary to look in detail at regional and local differences, since these may raise issues, among others, of access and equity. However, the ELLFS is just that, and only covers England. Larger sample sizes are also needed regularly in the other nations and it will be important for national surveys to include some common core of comparable information in order to make useful comparisons across the UK. Similarly if local LSCs want to commis-

34. Sargant, Naomi (2003) 'Chapter One: Research Agendas: present and future', in F. Aldridge (ed.) *Adult Learning and Social Division: A persistent pattern*, vol. 2, Leicester: NIACE.

sion more detailed local studies, it will be desirable to include a common core of comparable information in order to enable useful comparisons to be made across the UK at local level. This was an important lesson made clear in the numerous attempts to monitor, compare and transfer good practice through the TEC national network. It is to be hoped, that the LSC, which is one organisation, will make more coherent the desire for new knowledge about participation across the country.

It is also necessary to understand more about the participation and learning needs of ethnic minority groups. A start on this was made in *Learning for a Purpose* (Sargant, 1993) a NIACE-led study of participation in education and training by adults from different ethnic minority groups. Issues of particular interest in that survey related to the amount and nature of informal learning, ESOL needs and recognition of overseas qualifications. The 2001 census should provide an up-to-date picture of the size and scatter of these groups in the UK and indicate whether or not the ELLFS will provide an adequate framework to cover England and if so what is an appropriate strategy for the other nations. A similar need either for a large sample or for more purposive sampling also arises with special groups such as older people or those with learning or other disabilities.

Field (1999), in an article on participation, comments on the current tide of debate over lifelong learning and also confirms the importance of participation as a topic for research. He draws attention to the wider community of policy-makers, managers, teachers and learners both in Britain and overseas who are now concerned with the issues of lifelong learning. He goes on to comment:

'Within this wider shift, one topic stands out from the others: participation. As lifelong learning has moved up the policy agenda, the question of who participates and who does not (and why) is posed ever more sharply. Research will also want to examine why this is such an important issue for policy-makers.'

He argues that Britain is now relatively well-served in the volume and quality of research about participation but goes on to suggest that this raises policy issues implicit in the suggestion that '*everyone* must constantly acquire new skills and knowledge in order to adapt and innovate in their present job or to enhance their employability should they need a new job...the more this argument is accepted by government and others, the wider the gulf between the "knowledge-rich" and "knowledge-poor" so that considerable efforts have to be devoted to social inclusion strategies'. This proposition parallels many of the arguments put forward in the NAGCELL (National Advisory Group for Continuing Education and Lifelong Learning) reports [NAGCELL, 1997 and 1999] and in the research evidence that focuses on social inclusion and the information divide.

Field (1999) in the same article comments usefully on other needs and omissions: firstly the omission from research of what he calls 'coerced' learning: the learning which is required by employers or professions, whether the learners want to do it or not such as health and safety; secondly, the need to understand better why some people define themselves firmly as non-learners: thirdly the effect of focusing on the accumulation of individual educational capital rather than the larger returns to social capital. The 2002 survey has been able to make a modest contribution to the first of these, identifying 6% of people who did not choose their learning. It is encouraging that an analysis of benefits of learning found that this group of learners are most likely to have been helped or expect to be helped in their current job (29%). However the findings also suggest that they may be less likely to experience some of the wider benefits of learning that are so valued by other learners, such as increased self-confidence, meeting new people and enjoying learning more. The survey report and Field's own chapter on social capital demonstrate the interrelationship between individual educational capital and access to social and cultural capital: the challenge is how to widen the virtuous circle.

The current national research scene as it relates to life-long learning

Though lifelong learning is still high on the national agenda, its priorities are not now as clearly and broadly articulated as they were at the time of *The Learning Age* Green Paper. There have been five different Ministers in charge of lifelong learning since the 1977 election. While the Learning and Skills Council has an Adult Committee its policies have received little media coverage and perhaps inevitably most attention is focused on the young, up-skilling and, increasingly, work-force development.

Some benefit has accrued from the increased focus by government on social science research. David Blunkett both castigated and encouraged social researchers, including educational researchers, in a key speech on the relationship between social science and government.

> 'I believe passionately that having access to the lessons from high quality research can and must vastly improve the quality and sensitivity of the complex and often constrained decisions we, as politicians, have to make.'
> David Blunkett, ESRC Lecture: *Influence or irrelevance: can social science improve government?* 2 February 2000

Attention has increasingly been focused on the need for more quantitative capacity in UK social science and this has been linked with the adoption of an evidence-based approach to research for policy-making, similar to that utilised in clinical research. It is encouraging that the ESRC is taking a number of steps to improve research methods capacity, notably by setting up a new five-year £4 million Research Methods Programme and producing new Postgraduate Training guidelines requiring training in the use of both qualitative and quantitative data.

While educational research shares some of the difficulties of social science research in general, it faces some specific difficulties, particularly in relation to research into adult learning. A somewhat political issue is that for most people, teachers, parents, politicians and administrators, education is still synonymous with schooling. Adult learning is an afterthought. The field of educational research is similarly dominated by the interests of schools, schooling and its providers and with the exception of higher education has rarely been extended to the education of adults. This dominance has carried through to funding research, assessment panels and other decision-making structures. It has led and still leads to the omission of proper consideration of the needs of adult and lifelong learning.

A significant example is the National Educational Research Forum established in September 1999 with the remit of providing strategic direction for education research and developing a national framework within which a coherent research programme relevant to policy and practice can be developed. Its follow-up papers *A Research and Development Strategy for Education: developing quality and diversity* (NERF, 2001) also identifies the need to expand research capacity.

Written at a macro level, it identifies five characteristics of an effective strategy all of which are generally relevant to any educational research, but none of which have anything particular to say about adult learning:

- a coherent set of objectives;
- a plan that will focus simultaneously on theoretical issues and those of practical relevance;
- enhanced coordination and sustained resourcing to underpin the plan;
- ways of understanding and assessing the impact of research;
- methods for monitoring, evaluating and reviewing progress.

It suggests a Foresight Exercise specifically about education and a Standing Group to establish criteria for setting priorities. It recommends a regular national survey of practitioners and institutions' priorities and a forum of funders. Initial membership of the forum and its working groups included only one person specifically from the field of adult and lifelong learning. In its discussion of capacity, while it does include NIACE and the British Educational Research Association (BERA), it does not include the post-school research groupings SCUTREA, UCACE or SRHE and mentions lifelong learning only once.

More positively the document does recognise that educational research is located within, and draws on, many other disciplines requiring a broad range of methodologies, and may need to be multidisciplinary and move beyond 'the polarised debate between quantitative and qualitative approaches'.

All these recommendations are unexceptionable. What is unacceptable and a matter of great concern is that despite specific requests from NIACE and other professionals engaged in lifelong learning, the paper is still silent on the research needs of adult learning at a time when adults now form a larger population group than those in schooling and pose a number of quite different methodological problems. It is especially ironic that the closing sentence of the Strategy Paper looks forward to the OECD visit 'which will be conducting a review of education research' as an 'opportunity to review progress and identify future priorities'. In the event, the DfES Background Report (DfES, 2002) concentrated on 'pre-collegiate' education and therefore their interview schedule arranged did likewise. While some of its general conclusions are of general interest, the inspectors note:

> 'Our interviews and the DfES Background Report concentrated on pre-collegiate education. Our focus has thus been almost exclusively on pre-collegiate practice and policy. As a result the review provides very limited analysis of higher and adult education' (OECD, 2002).

Each time an opportunity such as this is missed, the needs of adult learning become more invisible. It would be interesting to know whether the decision to focus the background report for the OECD inspection only on schooling was a matter of omission or commission.

Issues in common across educational research

Educational research has, indeed, faced a number of difficulties over the years. First, most academic research in higher education is funded through and driven by academic disciplines, psychology, sociology, economics etc. and education is not a discipline as such, but rather an applied research area which needs to draw on each of these and some others. Second, disciplines tend to fight for territory and compete for resources rather than collaborate. Most disciplines favour or utilise particular research methodologies and are not generous about recognising other methods. 'My data are hard, your data are soft' is a typical criticism. For example, psychology uses experimental design, test and measurement and attitude scaling, among others and anthropology uses participant observation. Neither of these paradigms, nor that of illuminative evaluation, were of particular use to the Open University who had to develop sophisticated self-administered questionnaires to samples of learners studying on their own at home.

The large-scale sample surveys used in social and market research have been out of favour with academics partly for socio-political reasons and partly because they are too expensive and technical for most academics to mount. Individual academics researching on their own, whether psychologists or sociologists, can handle smaller sample sizes, focus groups, in-depth interviews with content analysis and ethnographic approaches more easily. Qualitative approaches have been particularly favoured for classroom and observational studies. The choice between qualitative and quantitative research needs to be taken rationally: the academic battleground over recent decades has been unhelpful and has played its part in reducing capacity and academic effectiveness.

Professor Bruce in the September 2002 ESRC newsletter (ESRC, 2002) writes eloquently on this issue about his own field of religion. He comments that when writing in 1989, he and a colleague had 'praised particularly the British tradition of detailed ethnographic studies of sects, cults and new religious movements. In the years since, my admiration for detailed case studies of religious groups has not faded, but I have become increasingly aware of a major weakness in...the sociology of religion generally: an unwillingness or inability to engage in the statistical analysis of large-scale quantitative data...Numbers are not everything, but they are something...I do not want to assert that quantitative studies of religion are better than ethnographic case studies, only that they are essential in two ways. First, without reliable large-scale data we may easily mistake the meaning of our case-studies...Second, large-scale data is necessary to test the plausibility of explanations based on case-studies.'

Education as an applied research area, needs to be able to employ a range of research techniques: to analyse a problem and choose the most appropriate technique to research that problem. Different research techniques should not be seen as in competition with each other. The move to evidence-based policy is helpful as it focuses on evidence which addresses the policy decision to be made, though its experimental origin stemming from clinical and medical research as well as the test-and-measurement 'agriculture-botany paradigm' is that of 'randomised control trials' and is not particularly suitable for uncontrollable adult learners or, with equity, for disadvantaged school children.

This matters in terms of research strategy and capacity since the key research issues in adult learning and the methodologies used are likely to be significantly different from those appropriate in closed classroom situations. While there is more potential linkage between techniques used in closed classrooms, whether it be in school or in further/higher education, increasing numbers of adults are studying in the workplace, at home, or through open/distance learning and have to be reached through sample surveys of learners by post or individual interview and not in controlled and observable environments. Informal learning is also likely to require new approaches. It may also not be ethical to offer some people opportunities and not others, whether chosen at random or not. Issues of curriculum and assessment are likely to require different approaches for adults than for the young.

In terms of capacity, the tradition of applied social research and its training, including most educational research, is weaker methodologically in the UK than it is in North America. Few academics have a strong research methods background. We lack the number of major non-profit applied social research agencies there are in the US. There is little interchange of professional staff between market and opinion research agencies and academic departments. Academics tend to underestimate the professional skills involved in questionnaire design, for example, and work on longer timetables. Social and academic researchers tend to look down on market researchers. Without external funding, few academics can afford the large data sets that are necessary for much applied educational and social research. The case for large-scale sample surveys has been weakened further by the fashion for focus groups which are increasingly used as a substitute for rather than a complement to quantitative research.

The dominant post-graduate research training paradigm, the three-year individual supervised research project has developed from the physical sciences, where the notion of working with the professor as part of a research team in a lab, or as a research apprentice is still the norm in medicine and the sciences. It is much less useful in the social sciences, where the analogy would be that of a consultant only learning about one illness, rather than a GP dealing with a variety of problems.

A vital issue in the social sciences is that there is no pressure to have a collective memory or agreement about what constitutes an advance in knowledge in the way that science and technology must. In science, a new finding or discovery is seen, evidenced, published and disseminated and then, typically built on by the next wave of researchers. This does not necessarily happen in the social sciences. As noted earlier, in social science there continue to be battles between disciplines, there are fashions in methods and theories, grounded theory, epistemology, *etc.* References over ten years old are old-hat even if they were seminal and have not been disproved. An example currently of the lack of connection is Gorard's work described in Chapter 5 (Gorard, 2003), which echoes the classic work on education and social mobility in the 1950s and 1960s carried out with- in by sociology (Glass, 1954) at LSE and then at Nuffield College, Oxford, and also pursued in relation to social mobility among Open University students (McIntosh *et al.*, 1976).

The impact of the Research Assessment Exercise is not without guilt in this game-playing and is feeding the growth of social science journals covering even more specialist disciplines. And peer review tends to reinforce discipline-based boundaries!

What of the future?

More effort is now going into research into post-school education and it will be important to monitor its impact. The ESRC's Learning Society Research Programme directed by Frank Coffield has produced much valuable work, including Coffield's (2000) own text on Informal Learning. Field and

Schuller (1999) in a helpful paper entitled 'Investigating the learning society' reviewed the programme, commenting, inter alia, that adult practitioners were in a minority among those involved in the programme. They identified a number of future research priorities that had emerged from the work so far, under seven headings:

- Definitions of the field
- Participation, distribution and change
- Learners' environments
- Learners' careers
- Time and money
- Complementarity and competition
- The knowledge base

It would be important to identify how far conclusions from this major programme have already fed into policy and into academic thinking, and in which areas research is continuing. The Learning Society and Teaching and Learning Research Programme (ESRC) series contains research from a variety of disciplines and it will be interesting to see how far the knowledge base developed is capable of being synthesised, or if academics are interested in such a challenge.

Looking ahead, there are three promising developments, the new set of Research Centres set up under DfES auspices, the next round of the ESRC Teaching and Learning Programme (TLTP2) and the Research Strategy (2002–2005) of the Learning and Skills Research Centre (LSRC) under the Learning and Skills Development Agency with funding from the DfES and the LSC. The new set of DfES research centres are described elsewhere and Chapter 3 focuses on one of them. The LSRC sets out ambitious goals:

'It aims to be an authoritative source of knowledge and ideas, informing and influencing the future development of a successful and sustainable system of post-16 learning. The LSRC will create a strong body of evidence from rigorous research, focused on creative, critical and innovative thinking, and models for the long-term development of post-16 learning. The Centre will work to ensure that research has a strong and positive impact on the development of policy and practice.'

They note that the LSRC is the first centre sponsored by the DfES to focus solely on post-16 learning and that four main factors have driven the Centre's initial strategy. These are:

- deep-seated problems that are relevant to policy development and practice in post-compulsory learning, e.g. social exclusion, disengagement from the democratic process;
- far-reaching trends that will need to be addressed to provide learning for the 21st century: e.g. globalisation, the communications revolution, demographic change, the implications of free trade and mobility of labour;

- government policies in moving towards a knowledge-based/learning society;
- research needs identified by existing users or practitioners.

The distinctive features, principles and values are unexceptionable, but written at a very general level and with all the right words. But, as with most good research, there will be few quick answers.

The Research Strategy identifies five programmes: 1) participation in post-compulsory learning; 2) vocational learning, skills and work; 3) developing learning and teaching; 4) the organisation of learning; 5) developing the work force for post-compulsory learning. Underpinning these programmes, they note, is a focused strategy designed to increase the impact of research, develop research methods, build research capacity and develop knowledge management systems. Described as the Building Effective Research strategy, it will focus on developing capacity and innovation. 'It will investigate how to enable impact and ensure that research evidence is clear, timely and used effectively for policy and practice.' To achieve this, as an applied researcher, is, of course, to find the Holy Grail!

This is not the place to examine the five programmes in detail and the texts make convincing arguments for each of the programmes, identifying for each topic, the first year's priority. Programme 1 will focus on the role brokers and intermediaries can play as enablers of participation. Programme 2 will focus on an effective VET system for the 21st century, enabling access and coherent routes to successful learning for individuals, employers and the economy. Programme 3 will focus on non-formal learning and its relationship to formal and work-based learning, including the impact of assessment regimes, and the challenges of assessing informal and e-learning. Programme 4 will focus on funding learning in the future, to include identifying what different groups of people think and do about financing their own and their families' learning; and what we can learn from other countries about the financing of learning. Programme 5 will focus on the leadership behaviours needed to create tomorrow's successful learners. Finally in respect of the overarching Building Effective Research strategy, the first year's work will focus on effective models of research impact.

Managing a programme of applied research on this scale with a tight timetable is a daunting project. It is not clear whether all the work is likely to be done in-house or whether some areas will be contracted out and some academic departments tend to work on longer time-scales. There are clearly likely to be issues of overlap with Phase III of the TLRP which has also been through a major consultation exercise with some of the same players. The next round of TLRP has £8 million plus to spend on post-compulsory education and training as a whole including higher and further education, community education, work-based learning (including continuing professional development) and lifelong/adult learning. 'Developing research capacity is a key objective of this phase!' Projects are due to start in June 2003 and the three themes identified are:

- Learners and learning
- Teachers, trainers and learning environments
- Learning communities

It is clear that there will be plenty of work in sight for anyone with a half-way decent CV in education or social science research methods. The challenge will be to ensure that these major programmes do not overlap unnecessarily and that appropriate linkages, networks and partnerships are set up at an early stage. The review commissioned in preparation for TLRP III from the Tavistock Institute should be helpful in this regard.

Paying lip-service to lifelong learning

The Learning Age: a renaissance for a new Britain (DfEE, 1998) gave encouragement that there would be a real move to an overall vision for lifelong learning which would ensure that people would be able to move in and out of appropriate educational opportunities at any age as they needed or as they wanted. The traditional barriers and battles between sectors and levels were to be removed. Five years later it is evident that this is not the case. Already the ESRC's prestigious TLRP programme (*sic*) 'will focus on teaching and learning in post-compulsory education and training *including higher and further education, community education, work-based learning (including continuing professional development) and lifelong/adult learning*'. While the breadth of educational activity to be included in their £8 million research programme is to be welcomed, lifelong learning no longer provides the overarching vision, but is on the margin as just another category grouped with traditional adult education.

It could be argued that terminology should not matter but the evidence is that it does. There have been continued attempts to find an acceptable term to distinguish between schooling or education for children and young people at the start of their lives and what might follow on from that initial education whether it finished at school, college or university. In the 1970s, while OECD favoured 'recurrent education', UNESCO preferred 'éducation permanente' and the US adopted 'lifelong learning', utilised particularly in relation to Mondale's ill-fated plans for Lifelong Learning. Debate in the UK was given impetus by the Open University's Report of its Committee on Continuing Education (1976) chaired by Sir Peter Venables, and the setting up in 1977 by the then Labour Government of the Advisory Council for Adult and Continuing Education, chaired by Richard Hoggart.

This interest did not translate itself into government policy or financial commitment in the 1980s, though there were advances on the training and vocational education front (VET) which helped adults, mainly led by the MSC and its successor agencies under the leadership of Geoffrey Holland. Continuing education in the 1980s became coterminous with continuing professional development and the government's focus was on work-related education rather than on a more generous view of adult learning, with funding streams continuing to favour the young. The setting up of the ESRC's Learning Society programme in 1994 came as a significant break-through.

Field and Schuller (1999) commented on the explosion of public interest in lifelong learning in the second half of the 1990s, both among policy-makers and practitioners, and suggested that the language used in a number of countries 'was more or less distant from the older, more established discourses of adult and/or continuing education: notably the use of the term 'lifelong learning' and the phrase 'the learning society'. They went on to ask what the new language signalled for research: was it just a modish trend, a re-branding, or did it denote a more substantial change? Some people hoped for the latter.

However, looking across Europe, an increasingly important player in the field of adult learning, it is evident the different ways in which adult education, continuing education and lifelong learning are used and translated has more to do with language, culture and fashion than with deep educational or philosophical differences. What is still needed is a generic term which has general recognition and can be used to gain general support from the wide variety of stake-holders in adult learning, preventing individual interests being picked off in a way which weakens the overall cause.

Lifelong learning does not yet appear to be a strong enough term to achieve this, even apart from the fact that for some it is taken to mean 'from cradle to grave'. Adult learning continues to be a helpful halfway term as it has shifted the focus on to the learner and away from the provider, and made it clear that it is the learner's motivation that determines whether learning is work-related and vocational or not, rather than the decision of the provider or the funder. It is too early to assess the impact of the Learning and Skills Councils on general adult and community provision locally. However, current policy priorities are not encouraging for general adult learning. Young people are back up the agenda, there is a renewed focus on skills with the Skills Strategy in planning, and the latest favoured term is workforce development, seen to be a key to employers involvement and running along-side the work of the new Sector Skills Councils.

It will be increasingly important to have cogent evidence of the wider importance of adult learning for an inclusive society and for active democracy.

References

BEINART, S. and SMITH, P. (1998) *National Adult Learning Survey 1997*, Sheffield: DfES.

BLUNKETT, D. (2000) ESRC Lecture: *Influence or Irrelevance? Can social science improve government?* 2 February, London: DfEE.

COFFIELD, F. (ed.) (2000) *The Necessity of Informal Learning*, Bristol: Policy Press.

DfEE (DEPARTMENT FOR EDUCATION AND ENTERPRISE) (1998) *The Learning Age: A Renaissance for a New Britain*, London: HMSO.

DfES (DEPARTMENT FOR EDUCATION AND SKILLS) (2002) *Research and Development in England: Background report prepared for the OECD review*, Sheffield: DfES.

ESRC (ECONOMIC and SOCIAL RESEARCH COUNCIL) (2002) 'The Book of Numbers', *Social Sciences*, Issue 52, London: ESRC.

FIELD, J. (1999) 'Schooling, Networks and the Labour Market: explaining participation in lifelong learning in Northern Ireland', *British Educational Research Journal*, 24(4), 501–15.

FIELD, J. and SCHULLER, T. (1999) 'Investigating the learning society', *Studies in the Education of Adults*, 31(1).

GLASS, D. (ed.) (1954) *Social Mobility in Britain*, London: Routledge.

GORARD, S. (2003) 'Lifelong learning trajectories in Wales: results of the NIACE Adult Learners' Survey 2002', in *Adult Learning and Social Division: A persistent pattern*, vol. 2, Leicester: NIACE.

McINTOSH, N. *et al.* (1976) *A Degree of Difference*, Guildford: SRHE.

NAGCELL (NATIONAL ADVISORY GROUP FOR CONTINUING EDUCATION AND LIFELONG LEARNING) (1997) *Learning for the Twenty-First Century* available at: http://www.lifelonglearning.co.uk/nagcell/index.htm.

NAGCELL (NATIONAL ADVISORY GROUP FOR CONTINUING EDUCATION AND LIFELONG LEARNING) (1999) *Creating Learning Cultures: Next Steps in Achieving the Learning Age* available at: http://www.lifelonglearning.co.uk/nagcell2/index.htm.

NERF (NATIONAL EDUCATIONAL RESEARCH FORUM) (2001) *A Research and Development Strategy for Education: developing quality and diversity*, NERF.

OECD (2002) *Educational Research and Development in England: Examiners' Report*, Paris: OECD.

OPEN UNIVERSITY (1976) *Report of the Committee on Continuing Education*, Milton Keynes: Open University.

PARK, A. (1994) *Individual Commitment to Learning: individuals' attitudes*, Sheffield: Department of Employment.

SARGANT, N. (1993) *Learning for a Purpose*, Leicester: NIACE.

Finally, I cannot resist adding Naomi's conclusion to the Executive summary of Learning and 'Leisure' the NIACE 1989 survey. It would not do badly as an aide memoire to current policy makers.

Learning and Leisure: Conclusion[35]

It will be a step backwards if the current need to assess and measure economic benefit imposes artificial definitions of what is educationally, socially and culturally valuable, even if it is more difficult to define these qualities.

If these artificial definitions laid down centrally control what should be provided locally and within which particular structures, it is likely that the broad-based and open-ended needs of adults for learning will go on not being met.

---

35. Sargant, Naomi (1991) *Learning and Leisure: A study of adult participation in learning and its policy implications*, Leicester: NIACE.

Appendix

Obituary, *The Times*, August 11, 2006

Naomi Sargant

Social reformer who championed lifelong learning at the Open University and pioneered educational broadcasting at Channel 4.

Andrew McIntosh

NAOMI SARGANT, a pioneer of lifelong learning, spent much of her life battering at traditional barriers to education for adults.

She had the qualities and good fortune to be in at the beginning of two powerful and innovative institutions which had a profound impact on opportunities for adults to learn throughout their lives: the Open University from 1970 to 1981, where she became pro-vice-chancellor (Britain's first woman pro-vice-chancellor) for student affairs and professor of applied social research; and Channel 4 from 1981 to 1989. There, as senior commissioning editor for educational programming, she was responsible for meeting the statutory requirement that 15 per cent of output be of educational value.

It was her skills that helped to make the OU and Channel 4 exemplars of lifelong learning, a step change from the old-fashioned notion of adult education as filling leisure.

At the OU she was the voice of the students, who were mature, studying part-time, at home, away from a campus. Her work on students' hopes and needs, how they could cope with course material, even what time they got home from work to watch the programmes, provided invaluable feedback to the more open-minded OU course teams and BBC production staff about what was working well or less well. She fronted the Open Forum radio and TV feedback for students. Her research and advocacy brought her a world reputation, and many invitations to visit and lecture in higher-education institutions in four continents, as an applied social researcher in education, worthily recognised by a personal OU chair.

At Channel 4 her deep understanding of the new opportunities offered to adult learners by broadcasting was put to the test and not found wanting. She commissioned programmes which were instantly recognisable as being educational, but which fell into no existing category or syllabus: science and arts, yes; but also consumer programmes, gardening (a lifelong passion), food and wine, adult literacy and numeracy, the environment and health, and programmes for women, children, people with disabilities, the unemployed and older people (as she put it, those with more time than money).

In the field of broadcasting commissioning and production, it was clear to those around her that she had excellent natural judgment of people, front of camera and behind it, of themes which would be effective and popular, of scheduling opportunities, and especially of programme titles. She was particularly good at picking women producers and presenters, including many themselves new to television. Her work was recognised when in 1996 she was admitted to the Royal Television Society Hall of Fame.

Leaving Channel 4 at the age of 55, she returned to the main theme of her life: how to make lifelong learning opportunities available to all, especially those previously denied them. Distance learning, including broadcasting, was a part of it. Breaking down barriers between adult learning for its own sake, and vocational training, was another — and particularly important because governments tend, for economic reasons, to favour skills training.

Her thinking will surely leave a mark with her seminal report — *Continuing Education: from Policies to Practice* (1982) — for Richard Hoggart's Advisory Council on Adult and Continuing Education. A particularly important recommendation was to set up local learning centres to provide collegiality for adult learners; only now is this happening.

In 1975–77, with Edwin Kerr, of the Council for National Academic Awards, she pioneered credit transfer between the OU and the polytechnics. She continued to work with the National Extension College, with the Basic Skills Unit, contributing to Helena Kennedy's report on widening participation in further education and Bob Fryer's on lifelong learning, as a member of the Ofcom group on media literacy, as chairman and then president of the Open College of the Arts, and as first pro-chancellor of the University of East London. She spent 20 years with the National Institute for Adult Continuing Education, as researcher, speaker, trustee and inspirer of good research, advocacy and policymaking.

Sargant commanded respect and affection in the world of lifelong learning because of her academic authority; because she had herself pioneered distance learning and educational broadcasting; because she understood the technology and knew how to keep it in its place; and above all because she saw education, especially education for adults, as the foundation stone of democracy, and fought tirelessly in powerful writing, speeches and debate against all who would try to restrict it.

Naomi Ellen Sargant was born in London in 1933, into a campaigning family, the daughter of Tom Sargant (later first secretary of Justice, campaigning for the rule of law and against miscarriages of justice) and Marie Hlouskova, a philologist who was active in the wartime Czech government-in- exile. Her political sense was developed in the Quaker environment of the Friends' School, Saffron Walden, and at Bedford College, London, where she was active in national student politics.

After spending 12 years in market and social research, she became a senior lecturer at Enfield College of Technology, where she was an early enthusiast for the Robbins agenda of expansion of higher education from the traditional universities to polytechnics, providing access to students from all parts of society, all parts of the world, and above all those who had missed the classic school-to-college-at-18 route.

She was always a strong advocate for consumers, as well as for students. Living in 18 Victoria Park Square, the home of the Institute of Community Studies, in 1957, she helped to bundle up the first mailing of *Which?*, and this was the beginning of a long and fruitful, though often tense, relationship with Michael Young, who had founded the Consumers Association that year. As chairman of the National Gas Consumers' Council (1977-80), she was never afraid to clash with ministers; and she went on to serve on the National Consumer Council, the Energy Commission, the Commission on Energy and the Environment, and as vice-chair of the National Council of Voluntary Organisations.

A lifelong socialist, she served on Haringey Borough Council, 1964-68. As chair of the children's committee, she abolished caning, and put in heating in bedrooms in children's homes. As chair of the Great Ormond Street Hospital for Children NHS Trust, 1997-99, she worked to involve child patients and their families in developing the hospital's services.

At home in Highgate, North London, and in her beloved house in Bonnieux in Provence, her love of gardening found an outlet in her garden and allotment, in her presidency of the Highgate Horticultural Society, and as chair of the Harington Scheme, a horticultural training scheme for young people with learning difficulties.

She died of cancer, conscious and lucid, knowing that this was the end: no miracle recovery, no consolations of religion. In her last week, she set about seeing her family, friends and colleagues, to gossip, to remember the good times, and to have her final say on the issues of lifelong learning and educational broadcasting.

Her first marriage to Professor Peter Kelly ended in divorce. She is survived by her husband, Andrew McIntosh, Lord McIntosh of Haringey, a son from her first marriage and two sons from her second.

Naomi Sargant, educationist, was born on December 10, 1933. She died on July 23, 2006, aged 72

Obituary, *The Guardian*, July 28 2006

Naomi Sargant

Social researcher adept at taking education to new television audiences

Jeremy Isaacs

Naomi Sargant, who has died of cancer at 72, devoted much of her career to extending the reach and range of education through television. At the Open University, whose purpose she embodied, she was professor of applied social research. As Channel 4's senior commissioning editor for education, she inspired and delivered programmes that informed and delighted a wide spectrum of viewers. As much as any figure in the field of continuing education, she made a bold and lasting mark; added to which her lifetime of public service was one of solid achievement.

Naomi was the daughter of Tom Sargant, a businessman and politician who became the first secretary of the campaigning organisation Justice. She was educated at Friends' school, Saffron Walden, Essex, and Bedford College, London. With a BA in sociology, she trained as a market researcher, joining Social Surveys Ltd in 1955 and remaining there until 1967, when she became senior lecturer in market research at Enfield College of Technology.

Her move in 1970 to the Open University began with her appointment as senior lecturer in research methods, and after successive promotions she was made pro vice-chancellor for student affairs from 1974 to 1978, then professor of applied social research until 1981, when she left to move into broadcasting. Naomi had always seen consulting the public as a vital democratic tool and, aware of their needs, she never underestimated their eagerness to learn. So catering for television audiences was to prove meat and drink to her.

However, it did not seem so at the time; her appointment to the infant Channel 4 (C4) as senior commissioning editor for educational programming was controversial, and the risk she took in giving up tenure at the OU considerable. In the beginning, it was a one-woman operation. With no premises arranged, no systems yet in place, Naomi found she had just two years to get a department up and running that would deliver seven hours of programmes a week to meet the Independent Broadcasting Authority's requirements.

She transcended the challenge, urging that distance education should be defined as broadly as possible and targeting viewers of all ages and backgrounds. As the first chief executive of C4, I hired her knowing that her experience was just what we wanted, and that she had the strength of character to make good our intentions. Naomi's political skills enabled her to deal confidently with like-minded spirits at the IBA and in education. The programmes she commissioned did not have to be part of curricular structures; she was free to add to what other broadcasters offered, catering to the viewers who might be unemployed, disabled or retired.

Topics she listed for action included arts, history, science, the environment and such basic skills as literacy and numeracy, health and the family. She catered for leisure interests, including wine, and signed up Jancis Robinson for her TV debut. Out of her own interest in gardening grew Gardener's Calendar and Plants for Free - she was good at titles - which attracted 4 million viewers, a massive success. Naomi recognised and promoted the educational value of a documentary series, brought to her by her commissioning editor, Carol Haslam, on China, Africa and the environment, which was titled Fragile Earth. Another series, Years Ahead, reached out to older viewers; Chips Comic was for children with disabilities; Everybody Here celebrated cultural diversity. Quilts in Women's Lives - an archetypal C4 title - controversially brought down the wrath on C4 of those who could not follow where imagination led. Naomi saw to it that all of these projects were backed up with pamphlets and books to encourage further interest by viewers. The educational world applauded; a listing paper, See 4, went out to 200,000 recipients.

Naomi's many other public service appointments included chairman of the National Gas Consumer Council (1977-80); president of the National Society for Clean Air (1981-83); pro chancellor of the University of East London (1992-94); chairman of the Great Ormond Street hospital for children NHS trust (GOSH, 1997-2000). She served on the Labour-controlled Haringey council, and was chairman of the children's committee (1964-68).

After she left C4 in 1989, she continued to devote herself to distance learning as an executive member of the National Institute for Adult Continuing Education and many other organisations; indeed, she never stopped. Naomi was made an honorary fellow of the Royal College of Art (1988) and a fellow of the Royal Society of Arts (1991). In 1996, she was inducted into the Royal Television Society's Hall of Fame. Apart from work, duty and her family, her greatest passion was her allotment, where she slaved happily away, taking out on the soil frustrations that she experienced elsewhere. Even in her last days, she was discussing the crop of tomatoes and potatoes.

Naomi was a socialist in the fine line of RH Tawney, Michael Young and Peter Townsend. Serving others, she bent her mind to doing good. Her colleagues were disconcerted that sometimes when pressured she would burst into tears, but all knew that behind that lay strength, courage and commitment.

Naomi was married twice; first in 1954 to Peter Kelly, by whom she had a son, David; then in 1962 to Andrew McIntosh (Lord McIntosh of Haringey), by whom she had two sons. All survive her.

Jane Collins, chief executive, Great Ormond Street hospital for children NHS trust, writes: Naomi Sargant made many important contributions to GOSH in her three years as chair of the trust board. Ahead of the times, she was particularly concerned about involving our patients and their families in developing our services so they can best meet their needs, and her perspective as chair was particularly helpful when the interim report of Sir Ian Kennedy's inquiry into children's heart surgery at the Bristol Royal infirmary was published in May 2000. We had been somewhat complacent in thinking we already worked in partnership with families. Naomi and this report reminded us that the perceptions of children and families might be very different, and we needed to really listen to what they were saying.

Her other major contribution was to increase awareness and ensure action was taken to address equality and diversity issues. She was particularly concerned that our workforce did not reflect the ethnic make-up of our patients. This was most marked in nursing: it reflected in no way on the quality of the staff, but as a result we actively worked with the nursing school at South Bank University to encourage recruitment from ethnic minorities into children's nursing, with demonstrable success. Naomi will be remembered with affection by many of the staff at GOSH.

Naomi Ellen Sargant McIntosh, television executive, educator, consultant and writer, born December 10 1933; died July 23 2006

Tribute, *Times Educational Supplement,* July28, 2006

Naomi Sargant, one of the great post-war figures in FE, died this week. Alan Tuckett pays tribute

Naomi Sargant numbers among the most distinguished adult educators of the post-war era. She pursued her passion for learning to the very last moments of her life.

Naomi learned last week that her cancer was inoperable - that she was dying. Characteristically she set about making the best possible use of her time. She drew up a list of visitors to see and issues to sort out.

Hours before she passed away last weekend, she told one visitor, fresh in from New York: "The challenge is to bring the worlds of adult learning and vocational education much closer together, and to make them sexy." Not a bad agenda for FE Focus and not a bad description of an important theme in her life's work.

Naomi was an exceptional authority in so many arenas. First, as an academic, her groundbreaking work shaped much of the debate about adult participation for three decades. Second, as a broadcaster, she had an outstanding track record of innovative educational programming. Third - as someone who recognised very early how technology would break the boundaries between computing, broadcasting and telephony - she saw the potential for an electronic revolution in adult learning. And, fourth, as a public citizen, Naomi shaped the evolution of policy to challenge inequality of opportunity wherever she found it.

Born of a Czech mother and English father in 1933, she fled the Nazis as a child in 1938, travelling in a locked railway carriage across Europe. It had a profound influence, making her a passionate advocate for the rights of refugees, which she pursued to the end as vice-chair of the campaign group MediaWise Trust.

Educated at Friends School, Saffron Walden, Essex, and Bedford College, London university, where she took a BA (Hons) Sociology, Naomi soon moved to adult education.

Her early career was influenced by working closely with the great social entrepreneur, Michael Young. His eye for unmet need and her skills in market research led to her leading role in the National Consumer Council.

She then took that experience to the Open University, and championed the educational aspirations of the working class, women and other under-represented groups.

I met her first when she was pro vice-chancellor at the OU, at a Ruskin history workshop conference on women's history, just as the women's movement was flowering. She was passionate, brilliant, argumentative, engaging, and infuriating in turns - but always memorable.

In 1976, she was appointed to the Advisory Council for Adult and Continuing Education, established by the then education secretary Shirley

Williams to address exactly the question Naomi highlighted in her final hours. How do you bring together strategies to strengthen learning throughout working life with liberal adult education's concerns with active citizenship, second-chance education, and cultural enrichment?

Naomi led the council's work on future trends, with the first major national detailed studies on adults' experiences of learning. With Richard Hoggart, she played a central role in shaping the council's final report, Continuing Education - from policies to practice.

Naomi went on lead the new Channel 4's educational work as one of its first senior commissioning editors. Her groundbreaking work led to education being included in the full range of the channel's programming - complementing broadcast programmes of great flair with off-air back up materials, helplines and networks.

Her success can be seen from the way these techniques have shaped the whole industry. We have memorable series on history, adult numeracy and consumer rights, programmes for people with more time than money, and programming for people with disabilities.

Her work in broadcasting led naturally to her concern with the potential of the new technologies. She advised successive national policy initiatives on e-learning, notably Dame Helena Kennedy's seminal work on widening participation in FE and Professor Bob Fryer's advisory group on continuing education and lifelong learning. Naomi's interventions changed the detail of successive broadcasting bills in adult learners' favour, most notably by securing a media literacy remit for Ofcom just two years ago.

While enjoying a close family life - married to the current broadcasting minister Lord McIntosh - she was active in local government, held office with the National Gas Consumer Council and played a leading role in the National Extension College.

She was also deputy chair of the University of East London and of the National Council for Voluntary Organisations, and chaired Great Ormond Street's hospital trust, and the Open College of the Arts.

Naomi has also been a towering influence on the development of the National Institute of Adult Continuing Education for the past two decades, leading its quantitative research, helping to create Adult Learners' Week and prodding, challenging, encouraging, in her writing, speaking and forensic committee skills. She led a life rich in ideas and relationships, dedicated to the public interest.

No one did more for adult learners in her time. She was exceptional, a polymath, and a dear friend.

Acknowledgements

The publishers are very grateful for the financial support of the Robert Gavron Charitable Trust.

Much of the material included in this book was published by NIACE, the Open University or Channel 4. The editors are grateful for the support of these institutions in allowing the material to be reproduced here.

The following items are included by permission of the publishers:

Blackwell-Wiley journals: McIntosh, N. E. (1975) 'Open Admission – an open or revolving door?' *Universities Quarterly*, Spring 1975, pp. 171–81; Sargant, Naomi (1974) 'Some problems involved in the evaluation of multimedia educational systems', *British Journal of Educational Technology*, 3(5), 43–59.

Society for Research into Higher Education: 'Establishing a baseline', from *A degree of difference: A study of the first year's intake of students to the Open University of the United Kingdom*, N E McIntosh, J A Calder and B Swift, 1982.

Taylor and Francis Group: McIntosh, N. E., Alan Woodley and Val Morrison (1980) 'Student demand and progress at the Open University – the first eight years', *Distance Education*, 1(1) pp. 37–60; Moss, G (1991) 'Interview with Naomi Sargant: Women at the top in Television' *Women: A Cultural Review*, 2(1), pp. 29–39; McIntosh, N. E. (1975) Open Admission – an open or revolving door? *Universities Quarterly*, Spring 1975, pp. 171–81; Woodley, A and McIntosh, N. E. (1980) *The door stood open*, Lewes: Falmer Press, pp 246–248; Catterall, P. (1999) *The Making of Channel 4*, London: Routledge, pp. 134–61; Sargant, Naomi (1990) 'Chapter 4. Lifelong learning – A brave and proper vision', in D. Bradshaw (ed.) *Bringing Learning to Life*, Brighton: Falmer Press, pp. 47–64; McIntosh, Naomi (1981) 'Demand and supply in the education of adults', in H. Sockett (ed.) *Educational Analysis*, Brighton: Falmer Press, vol. 3 pp. 25–9.

The Guardian: Obituary of Naomi Sargant, 28 July 2006.
The Times: Obituary of Naomi Sargant, 11 August 2006.
Times Educational Supplement: cartoon on page 38; 'Tribute to Naomi Sargant', July28, 2006.
Times Higher Education Supplement: 'Don's Diary, by Naomi Sargant, July 1987.

Index

Notes: Abbreviations used in this index are: C4 (Channel 4, OU (Open University), NM (Naomi McIntosh), NS (Naomi Sargant)
Page numbers in **bold** are for figures and tables in the text, e.g. applications, for OU courses 1970–75 **27**
Organisations are indexed by their acronyms, followed by the full form in brackets, e.g. ACRG (Access Course Recognition Group)